From Heatmaps to Histograms

A Practical Guide to Cyber Risk Quantification

Tony Martin-Vegue

Apress®

From Heatmaps to Histograms: A Practical Guide to Cyber Risk Quantification

Tony Martin-Vegue
San Francisco, CA, USA

ISBN-13 (pbk): 979-8-8688-2299-5 ISBN-13 (electronic): 979-8-8688-2300-8
https://doi.org/10.1007/979-8-8688-2300-8

Managing Director, Apress Media LLC: Welmoed Spahr
Acquisitions Editor: Susan McDermott
Project Manager: Jessica Vakili

Distributed to the book trade worldwide by Springer Science+Business Media New York, 1 New York Plaza, New York, NY 10004. Phone 1-800-SPRINGER, fax (201) 348-4505, e-mail orders-ny@springer-sbm.com, or visit www.springeronline.com. Apress Media, LLC is a Delaware LLC and the sole member (owner) is Springer Science + Business Media Finance Inc (SSBM Finance Inc). SSBM Finance Inc is a **Delaware** corporation.

For information on translations, please e-mail booktranslations@springernature.com; for reprint, paperback, or audio rights, please e-mail bookpermissions@springernature.com.

Apress titles may be purchased in bulk for academic, corporate, or promotional use. eBook versions and licenses are also available for most titles. For more information, reference our Print and eBook Bulk Sales web page at http://www.apress.com/bulk-sales.

If disposing of this product, please recycle the paper

For Christina

Table of Contents

About the Author

Tony Martin-Vegue is a cybersecurity and technology risk expert with over 25 years of experience helping Fortune 500 companies build and scale quantitative risk programs. He writes and speaks prolifically on the topic of risk and decision science and is known for his new ways of thinking about old problems.

A hands-on practitioner as much as a leader, Tony has performed an estimated 1,000 quantitative risk assessments across domains including cyber, fraud, operations, and enterprise risk. He's a frequent speaker at FAIRcon, SIRAcon, RSA, various Security BSides, and ISACA events. He also chairs the San Francisco Chapter of the FAIR Institute, a global organization dedicated to advancing risk quantification practices, and was honored with the FAIR Ambassador Award in 2020. He has been published in numerous publications such as the ISACA journal, Risk.net, and regularly blogs at tonym-v.com on the topics of risk, quantification, and security economics.

Tony lives with his family on an island in the San Francisco Bay (not Alcatraz)—though he *has* swum from Alcatraz to San Francisco ten times.

About the Technical Reviewer

Robert D. Brown III a senior decision and risk analyst, provides support to executives facing complex and high-risk strategic planning opportunities and project portfolio evaluation and risk management challenges. Across three decades of experience, Robert has contributed to diverse industrial and commercial fields, including cybersecurity, insurance, project finance, aluminum manufacturing, federal agencies, oil and gas, chemicals, energy utilities, supply chain and logistics, pharmaceuticals, electronics manufacturing, telecommunications, information technology, and commercial real estate. In March 2018, he published *Business Case Analysis with R: Simulation Tutorials to Support Complex Business Decisions* (Springer Nature/Apress). Robert currently serves as a Principal Risk Advisory Engineer at Qualys. Prior to joining Qualys in 2025, Robert held the role of Senior Director of Cyber Resilience at Resilience Insurance. He holds a Bachelor of Mechanical Engineering from the Georgia Institute of Technology.

Praise for *From Heatmaps to Histograms*

From Heatmaps to Histograms *is a significant contribution to our profession and would be required reading for anyone in my organization if I were still a CISO. Brilliantly written for those with little or no background in quantitative risk measurement, it will also be valuable to those with years of experience. This is further evidence that Tony is one of the leading contributors to the future of our profession.*

—Jack Jones, Creator of FAIR

Tony makes a strong case for replacing popular but flawed risk assessment methods and goes further by providing practical approaches for implementing better ones. Through clear examples and step-by-step guidance, he makes even quantitative concepts accessible. I highly recommend this book.

—Douglas Hubbard, Author and Measurement Expert

I've been measuring cyber risk for over twenty years, and while better data still matters, practicality has become the real barrier to adoption. Conversations around cyber risk quantification are dominated by "Yeah, but how?" This book answers that question with concrete examples and practical guidance, striking the right balance between what you need to know and what you need to do.

—Wade Baker, Partner, Cyentia Institute

I finally have a clear answer to the question I'm asked most often by those just starting out: Where do I begin with measuring cyber risk? This book is the definitive starting point for anyone serious about becoming a cybersecurity risk modeler.

—Richard Seiersen,
Author and Chief Risk Technology Officer, Qualys

Tony's book empowers both new and experienced risk professionals to communicate more effectively with boards and executives. By integrating models, experience, and clear, actionable steps, it provides practical tools for applying risk measurement in real organizations and finally moving beyond stoplight charts.

—Lisa R. Young, Cyber Risk Expert

If you are stuck in a world of color-coded risks that promote confidence and certainty over clarity, this book offers a way forward. It provides a practical path away from risk matrices and heat maps and toward a world where uncertainty is acknowledged, ranges reveal tail risk, and Monte Carlo simulations replace calculations of convenience. If you're wondering where to start your journey into quantified risk, this is it.

—Jay Jacobs, Co-founder and Chief Data Scientist, Empirical Security

This is the book I've been waiting for. It's a true A-to-Z guide to cybersecurity risk forecasting written for both newcomers and seasoned professionals. Tony's explanations are clear, his timing is impeccable, and his practical exercises make first-principles thinking accessible to everyone.

—Rick Howard, Cybersecurity Educator and Author

Acknowledgments

Isaac Newton once wrote, “If I have seen further, it is by standing on the shoulders of giants.” I’ve always liked that line, for both its poetry and its truth. Great ideas rarely come from solitary brilliance. They come from borrowing, learning, being corrected, and building on work that came before your own.

This book would not exist without a small group of people who fundamentally shaped how I think about risk, uncertainty, and what it means to do this work well.

First and foremost, Jack Jones. Jack paved the way for bringing rational, defensible, quantitative thinking into cybersecurity at a time when the field simply wasn’t ready to hear it. FAIR didn’t just introduce a model; it introduced a way of thinking that made serious risk measurement possible in our discipline. Over the years, Jack has been a mentor, teacher, and sounding board, and the foundation he laid shaped how I learned to reason about risk. This book builds on that foundation, extending those ideas into broader contexts, methods, and decisions.

Doug Hubbard’s work shaped how I think about risk measurement and uncertainty at a fundamental level. His books reframed what it means to measure the seemingly immeasurable and clarified the practical meaning of uncertainty in decision-making. He also provided guidance on several concepts in this book, but the deeper contribution came from the intellectual foundation his writing provided, which runs throughout this work.

Richard Seiersen has been both a mentor and a friend. Richard helped me see that the real work wasn’t just applying models, but becoming a modeler. That perspective shaped how this book treats modeling as a craft rather than a checklist. He pushed me to think more carefully about judgment, assumptions, and the responsibility analysts carry when working under uncertainty. He also encouraged me to write this book.

Lisa Young helped me understand how quantitative risk analysis works inside a real enterprise. She grounded my thinking in how decisions get made, how constraints operate, and how risk analysis must adapt to organizational reality to be effective. Her perspective kept this book focused not just on what is theoretically sound, but on what is practical and usable in real-world environments.

Robert Brown served as the technical reviewer for this book. He challenged key assumptions and pushed back where arguments were unclear or incomplete, prompting clearer reasoning and more careful analysis throughout the manuscript. His feedback improved not only the quality of the final work, but also the analytical standards I brought to it.

I also want to thank the team at Apress for supporting this project and helping guide it from manuscript to finished book.

Many people read early drafts, offered thoughtful feedback, asked hard questions, or helped me work through ideas while they were still forming. Your contributions improved the clarity, accuracy, and usefulness of this book. Thank you to John Benninghoff, Zach Cossairt, Markus De Shon, Jay Jacobs, Tom Keogh, Katie Kinz, Prashanthi Koutha, Jeff Lowder, John Linford, Dr. Sam Savage, Dr. Gavriel Schneider, Todd Tucker, Laura Voicu, and Chad Weinman.

Finally, to my family, thank you for the patience and support that made the long, quiet hours of writing possible. Books may be written alone, but they are never created in isolation.

If this work helps you see a little further, it's because I was fortunate enough to stand on the shoulders of many generous people.

—Tony

Prologue: Risky Business

Start where you are. Use what you have. Do what you can.

—Arthur Ashe

Cold Open: My Origin Story

I'm not a statistician.

I'm not a mathematician.

I'm not an actuary or a finance expert. I'm none of the things you'd typically associate with quantitative risk. Nor am I a CISO or technology executive.

(You may be asking yourself, *Why did I buy this guy's book?*)

I'm a practitioner.

Before I worked in technology risk management, I ran network cables through ceilings, getting covered in fiberglass. I did first-line phone support for a computer manufacturer and built massive Microsoft Exchange server farms. I pivoted my skills and career to information security in the 2000s after seeing the aftermath of the dot-com bust and subsequently to risk management. Risk management immediately drew me in because it satisfied two things my brain craved: razor-sharp analytical focus on the nuanced sides of technology and figuring out how those pieces fit together organizationally. My economics degree came in handy.

Quantitative risk was a natural next step for me, as I was drawn to both technology and data.

The story of how I became a cyber risk quantification professional starts in the early 2010s at a large regional bank in San Francisco. I was a mid-level analyst on the technology risk team, responsible for assessing everything from data breach risk to system outages—standard technology risk stuff.

Since we were a bank, other specialized risk teams covered areas such as credit risk, market risk, and liquidity risk. Each quarter, all teams delivered risk updates to the C-suite and board in large conference rooms, taking turns briefing leadership.

The credit risk lead would say, "We have $47 million in credit exposure from our commercial real estate portfolio, down from $52 million last quarter and well within our concentration limits." Next came the liquidity risk team: "Liquidity could swing $10 to $40 million in a stress scenario, but we're maintaining our LCR at 140%, well above regulatory minimums." The market risk team provided their update: "Market risk is running $8 to $12 million VaR based on current volatility, keeping us within our $20 million board-approved limit."

Then came my turn.

Using our qualitative methods, I gave the usual update: "The risk of a consumer banking outage is high. Data breach risk is medium, yellow." Red, yellow, green ratings. Standard stuff I'd presented every quarter.

But this time, something clicked.

I noticed how different my presentation was from the others. The other risk leads didn't just report numbers. They triggered honest, substantive conversations because they spoke in dollars, probabilities, and exposures. Executives had plenty to dig into. Their updates led to discussions about mitigations, opportunity costs, insurance decisions, and organizational strategy changes.

Meanwhile, my update just made heads nod politely. No discussion. And I felt it. A subtle but sharp embarrassment. I respected those other risk managers and wanted to be at their level.

It was clear there had to be a better way.

I'd been exposed to quantitative risk during CISSP studies, but the way it's presented in the study books made it seem impossible. If you've studied for the CISSP, you know what I mean. Measurements in precise numbers, specific asset values, and something called "exposure factor" with no guidance on how to actually measure those factors. Many of the concepts don't match how organizations experience loss in the real world. I don't mean to pick on the CISSP, but it's often the very first exposure to quantitative risk methodologies most security professionals get. The concepts felt disconnected from how risk is managed.

Despite the challenges, I was not easily discouraged. I was determined to learn this, figure out how others were truly measuring risk quantitatively. I knew there had to be a way, given my background in economics, business forecasting, and statistics classes in college, where I was exposed to numerous solutions for this problem.

I opened my laptop and started searching: "cyber risk quantification methods," "how to measure information security risk." That's when I discovered FAIR, Factor Analysis of Information Risk, a methodology and collection of frameworks that measure risk in financial terms. At the time, there wasn't much material. Just a couple of white papers, a small startup called CXOWARE founded by FAIR's inventor, Jack Jones, and a fledgling community of practitioners. I thought, "FAIR? This sounds different from CISSP. Could quantitative risk actually be...possible?"

If you've heard of FAIR, the Factor Analysis of Information Risk, you've already seen what's possible and how far the field has come. FAIR gave cybersecurity a shared language for quantitative risk in the technology field. This book builds on that foundation but widens the lens: applying those ideas across data sources, decisions, methodologies, and even AI-assisted analysis.

I convinced my boss to send me to a two-day FAIR training in a basement room at the San Francisco Marriott. My trainer, Chad Weinman, didn't start with threat modeling, advanced persistent threats, or data breaches. He began with concepts from *metrology* (the scientific study of measurement), prompting us to reevaluate our understanding of risk management. He started with concepts such as precision vs. accuracy, calibrated estimates, and the idea of *uncertainty*.

I gave Chad the same puzzled look you might have right now, reading those concepts.

But I got it, eventually. And you will too.

I realized something critical: you won't find the answers to cyber risk quantification inside the cybersecurity industry, not in the books, frameworks, or certifications. That's where the myths are born: that quant is impossible, that you need mountains of perfect data, that it's too complicated to be worth it.

To get good at this, you have to look outside for inspiration. You need fields that share similar characteristics: lots of unknowns, rapidly changing conditions, sparse or messy data, and high-stakes decisions under uncertainty. That led me to actuarial science, environmental risk modeling, epidemiology, and military decision theory. Those disciplines have the tools and mindset I needed.

And that's when everything clicked.

I trained in FAIR, learned from the best people in the field, and started doing real assessments, first dozens, then hundreds. I began using quantitative methods not just to satisfy curiosity, but to drive real, high-impact decisions.

Fast forward to today. I recently estimated how many fully quantitative risk analyses I've run over my career: just about 1,000, give or take. I still remember those first assessments back at the bank. They were awful. But I've learned a great deal along the way.

This book is the result of that journey. It contains everything I've learned: lessons from the field, insights from the quantitative risk community, and hard-won experience from sitting in boardrooms trying to get it right.

If you're reading this now, I hope it becomes part of your journey too.

Why I Wrote This Book

I wrote this book to start a quiet revolution, not with manifestos or proclamations, but with practical tools.

I'll never forget that moment in the boardroom when I realized how different my presentation was from every other risk leader. While they sparked genuine discussions about strategy, investments, and business direction, my presentation felt like a check in the box, an agenda item to breeze through before moving on to the meat of the discussion. That wasn't just embarrassing; it was a missed opportunity for the entire organization.

That bank, by the way, isn't around anymore. While I can't blame their demise entirely on heatmaps and traffic light reports, I can say this. When risk management doesn't drive real business decisions, organizations become vulnerable in ways they don't even understand.

Every time someone runs their first quantitative risk assessment, they're not just running a model or updating a spreadsheet. They're changing the entire conversation in their organization, proving that cybersecurity can be a strategic partner, not just a cost center. They're elevating the profession and showing that risk professionals can drive decisions that shape the future of the business.

Think about what becomes possible when risk speaks the same language as the rest of the C-suite. When we can say "'this investment will reduce our expected annual loss by $2 million" instead of "this will move us from red to yellow." When we compare the ROI of security controls against any other business investment. When executives stop seeing us as the people who say no and start seeing us as the people who help them say yes to the right things. When we're no longer seen as blockers to progress, but trusted partners who will show the organization how to go fast, safely.

If I can help create a generation of risk professionals who refuse to accept *that's how we've always done it,* then we'll transform how businesses think about risk itself. We'll move from being the compliance department to being strategic advisors, from cost centers to profit protectors.

That's not just better risk management. That's better business.

Who This Book Is For

This book is for beginners, learners, and the curious. If you work in cyber risk, GRC, product security, or enterprise risk or you just want to make better decisions in the face of uncertainty, you're in the right place.

You don't need a quantitative background. You don't need special tools. You don't even need to be good at math. All you need is the desire to improve your risk management better than you did yesterday.

If you're a statistician or experienced quant, you may find parts of this book too light or even frustrating. That's okay, you're still welcome here. Feel free to skip around. You may even find new tools and fresh perspectives.

The goal is to build confidence and get you started. Each chapter builds momentum. Every small win adds up. If all you do after reading this book is ask better questions and think a little more clearly about risk, you've succeeded.

Handle with Simplicity: Why This Book Won't Melt Your Brain

Here's something that might surprise you. When I first started learning this stuff, I felt lost. I bought beginner books on probability and statistics, primers designed for non-mathematicians. I picked up a few used textbooks at the local secondhand store. These basic resources helped me understand concepts that seemed impossible at first.

People who talk to me now think this all comes naturally to me. It doesn't. What you're looking at is mastery earned through thousands of hours of practice. I've lived and breathed this material every day, driven by a relentless need to understand it.

Even then, I struggled with basic concepts. I worked through coin flipping and dice throwing exercises from the textbooks, recording outcomes to understand how probability *actually* works. The more I learned, the more ignorant I felt. I constantly had my textbooks spread out at the kitchen counter, going through exercises, until the math behind it finally clicked.

But here's what I learned through all that struggle: if you break complex ideas into small enough pieces, anyone can understand them. That's exactly how I approach cyber risk now, and it's how I wrote this book.

If this feels hard to you, I'm in the same boat. I feel your pain, and it's with that understanding that I designed every chapter.

This book is entirely linear. It starts with basic concepts—small pieces—and builds from there. Think of this book as Lego blocks: every idea builds on the last. Don't think of risk quantification as one big monolith. It's the building blocks of knowledge that you gain every day. We're even going to practice those same coin flip exercises that helped me understand Monte Carlo simulations. While writing this book, I kept a sticky note on my desktop with my most important rule: "Don't melt the reader's brain."

That's my promise to you. This book is designed with clear building blocks that work whether you prefer to read straight through or jump around to what you need most. No brain-melting allowed.

Small Steps, Huge Gains: Everyday Wins in Risk Analysis

Strive to be better than you were yesterday. Quantitative risk represents a mindset shift from traditional risk analysis that relies on matrices, heatmaps, check-list-based analyses, and risk management that is disconnected from organizational objectives. Even if you can't implement everything from this book immediately, use what you can. These mindset shifts happen at three levels: organizational, team, and personal.

Organizational Level

Organizations are slow-moving ships. Full adoption of quantitative risk might take years. Some organizations will never be ready for this shift due to

- Regulatory concerns about deviating from established practices
- Cultural resistance to change
- Fear or discomfort
- Leadership that's comfortable with the status quo

That's frustrating, yet it's also reality. Don't let organizational inertia stop your personal growth.

Team Level

You may or may not be able to influence change at the team level. If you can, many lessons in this book will improve your work even without moving to full quantitative risk:

- Better data collection methods from multiple sources
- More defensible risk assessments with documented assumptions
- Improved scenario building that tells clearer stories
- Structured approaches to expert elicitation
- Asking "what does this actually mean in business terms?"

These improvements can make qualitative risk programs stronger and more credible.

Personal Level

You can certainly do this work on your own. Start by reframing how you think about risk. Practice thinking in probabilities instead of certainties. Consider ranges instead of single-point estimates.

Some of the first FAIR risk assessments I did weren't for an organization at all. I did them in my personal life. Should I get mobile phone insurance instead of risking paying for damage out of pocket? Should I go skydiving with my friend? Do I need to buy AppleCare for my new laptop? Those questions are all answerable with quantitative risk analysis. Even if you can't implement better risk methods at your job, don't wait until your next job—start now, with risky decisions in everyday life.

Once you open that door to thinking quantitatively, you'll never be able to close it.

Remember what tennis player Arthur Ashe told us, quoted at the beginning of this chapter: *Start where you are. Use what you have. Do what you can.*

The rest will follow.

PART I

Foundations

CHAPTER 1

Welcome to the Rebellion

The most damaging phrase in the language is 'We've always done it this way!'

—Grace Hopper

What the Great Hanoi Rat Massacre of 1902 and Modern Risk Practices Have in Common

In 1902, French colonial administrators in Hanoi discovered rats swarming the city's newly built sewer system. The French were genuinely worried about disease-carrying rats, so they came up with what seemed like a smart solution: pay locals for every rat tail they brought in.

At first, it worked perfectly. Thousands of tails started coming in, and the numbers looked fantastic, on paper at least. At a closer look, the officials noticed something quite odd: there were still rats everywhere.

It turns out that people were *breeding* rats. Others clipped the tails and released the rats back into the wild, free to breed and be harvested again. Some even smuggled rats in from outside the city just to cash in.

The bounty created the illusion of progress while quietly making the problem worse. It was a textbook case of *perverse incentives*: a system where the rewards were perfectly aligned to reinforce failure.

Today's cyber risk management suffers from the same fundamental problem. We've built a system that rewards the appearance of progress, while the actual risks remain unchanged, or get worse. If that feels familiar, it's because our field's entire risk ecosystem has evolved to reward the illusion of progress instead of its reality.

T. Martin-Vegue, *From Heatmaps to Histograms*, https://doi.org/10.1007/979-8-8688-2300-8_1

Modern Cyber Risk's Rat Problem

Cyber risk management today is our own version of the Hanoi rat bounty. It looks like we're making progress: reports filed, audits passed, standards met. We work in a system designed to reward motion over progress, activity over outcomes. The problem perpetuates itself, rather than improving.

Nearly 25 years ago, Ross Anderson made this point powerfully in his classic paper *Why Information Security Is Hard.* Cybersecurity isn't just a technology problem; it's a microeconomics problem. The challenge isn't just building secure systems; it's that incentives between users, vendors, insurers, consultants, and regulators are often misaligned. When the people making security decisions aren't the ones who bear the consequences, we all suffer (Anderson, 2001).

How exactly does this system perpetuate itself? To understand this, we need to examine how the entire risk ecosystem operates and why the system itself creates incentives to maintain the status quo.

The Risk Ecosystem Is Built on Circular Incentives

To meet regulatory requirements, companies start with good intentions. They look to frameworks like NIST CSF, ISO/IEC 27001, or COBIT, each of which can be applied quantitatively or qualitatively, depending on how deeply you use them, to shape their security programs. These standards often include language about how risk should be managed, but stop short of prescribing any particular model. That flexibility is by design: it makes the standards widely applicable. But it also leaves just enough latitude for organizations to build the easiest, cheapest, least rigorous version of a risk management program and still check the box.

So, boards and executives give the directive: "Get a SOC 2," or "Get us ISO certified." That becomes the mission. The mission, among many other things, includes an end-to-end cyber risk management program.

Enter the consulting firms (often the Big Four). One comes in to help build the program. Another comes in to audit it. Technically, they're separate firms. But functionally, they're reading from the same playbook. Their job isn't to push for rigor; it's to get you the report or certification. The frameworks they implement are optimized for speed, defensibility, and auditability, not for insight, accuracy, or actual risk reduction.

What emerges are the usual deliverables: heatmaps, red/yellow/green scoring, high/medium/low labels. Tools built for repeatability, not better decision-making (Figure 1-1).

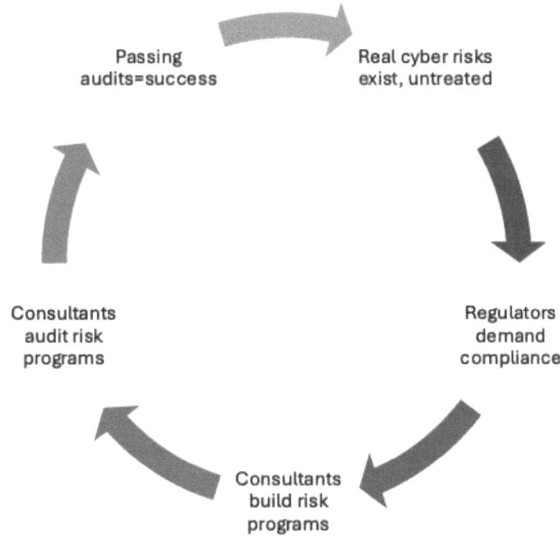

Figure 1-1. *The cyber risk incentive loop: why the system perpetuates itself*

As a result, the heatmap has become the de facto language of risk because the standards don't demand more, the auditors don't ask for more, and nobody builds more. Risk management should never be done merely for compliance's sake; it should enable an organization to achieve its objectives and execute its value proposition despite uncertainty.

Where the Loop Starts to Break

Here's where things start to wobble: the same ecosystem that builds your program is also judging whether you've done it "right." Even if it's not the same firm doing both, the templates, language, and expectations are virtually identical.

It's like asking a student to take a test, but also letting them write the questions, choose the answers, and let their friend grade it. What kind of test do you think they'll make? The easiest one that still counts as a win.

The programs are often built to meet the bare minimum, the lowest common denominator of what's needed to pass the audit that everyone knows is coming. The result is a culture of compliance theater: reports that project confidence, not evidence. Not because the people involved are bad. The system is designed to reward efficiency, defensibility, and status quo deliverables over insight and improvement.

The goal becomes: "Check the box." Not: "Understand the risk. Reduce the uncertainty."

So, we get frameworks with tidy charts and generic scoring systems that fit nicely on a slide deck. But they're not designed to help us make better decisions. They're designed to make it appear as if we're effectively managing risk.

And because these programs satisfy auditors, regulators, and boards, nobody asks the hard question: "Is this actually helping us reduce real-world risk?"

Breaking the Cycle

If you're working in a company that relies on qualitative assessments (heatmaps, color scores) and you feel like you should be doing more, take a breath. You're already part of the minority who notice the mismatch between effort and outcome. That awareness is the first step toward quantification.

You're not alone. And you're not failing.

There is incredible pressure, internal and external, to maintain the status quo. You are surrounded by it. Most organizations are perfectly content with a system that satisfies auditors and makes executives feel covered.

But that doesn't mean it's working.

The truth? We won't fix the whole system overnight. But we can start acting differently inside it. We can build toward better, even if we have to work within its constraints for now.

That's where this rebellion begins. Not with tearing down everything that exists, but with adding something better alongside it. Something that provides decision-makers with information worth caring about, rather than just a pleasing color palette.

Risk and Uncertainty: The Foundation of Our Rebellion

Risk, by its very nature, involves an uncertain future: outcomes we cannot predict with certainty, threats that may or may not materialize, and consequences that unfold in ways we didn't anticipate. Here's the uncomfortable truth that most security frameworks won't tell you: **uncertainty is not a bug in the system; it's a feature**. Yet everything about how we've been taught to think about cyber risk treats uncertainty like a disease to be cured rather than a reality to be managed. That's the mindset this book challenges. Uncertainty isn't a flaw in our data or models. It's the landscape we operate in.

This is where our rebellion begins.

For over 300 years, actuaries have built an entire industry on a simple premise: the future is uncertain, risks can be measured, and good decisions require embracing that uncertainty rather than pretending it doesn't exist. Meanwhile, security standards like ISO/IEC 27001 and NIST, while valuable for governance and compliance, operate on a fundamentally different philosophy when it comes to risk quantification—one that assumes we can construct our way to safety through controls, compliance, and colored heatmaps.

We're going to transcend that approach entirely.

Risk is a complicated topic because there are so many ways the word is used in the English language. The academic literature contains multiple competing definitions, but one widely cited approach comes from the work of Aven, Renn, and Rosa. *Risk* is defined as "...an event or a consequence of an event. The first condition of risk is that these events and consequences are subject to uncertainties. In plain English, risk is about things we care about happening in uncertain ways. "The second condition is that something of human value is at stake" (Aven, Renn, & Rosa, 2011).

There is something conspicuously missing from that definition: there is no mention of securing anything, elimination of risk as a goal, or even a judgment call on whether risk is good or bad.

This is crucial: risk is not bad. Risk is not good. Risk just *is*.

We've Always Done It This Way

Information security standards and frameworks have conditioned us to treat risk as something horrible, almost like a pathogen that needs to be identified, contained, and eliminated before it causes more damage. That mindset is fundamentally wrong and damaging to organizations that adopt that mindset. Risk can harm us, but risk also allows us to pursue objectives that bring us value, innovation, and growth. Without risk, there would be no progress, no competitive advantage, and no meaningful achievement. This perspective aligns closely with modern risk frameworks like FAIR, which emphasize balancing opportunity and loss rather than chasing the fantasy of zero risk. The goal should never be to eliminate all risk, but rather to understand it, measure it accurately, and make informed decisions about which risks are worth taking in service of our mission. Driving is a perfect example of this.

Every time we get in a car, we're taking a calculated risk. Over 6 million car accidents happen every year in the United States, with thousands of fatalities. Yet we still drive. Why is that? We've decided that the benefits—earning money, buying food, accessing entertainment, and social connections—outweigh the potential consequences.

You don't want to eliminate the risk of driving; you want to take smart risks. You wear a seatbelt. You may even select a vehicle with modern safety technology designed to prevent accidents. You drive defensively. You carry comprehensive insurance to transfer some of the financial consequences. You're not eliminating risk. You're managing it to enable the life you want to live.

Security frameworks don't think this way. By "security frameworks," I mean the dominant risk management approaches in our field: ISO 27005, NIST Risk Management Framework, OCTAVE, and the countless heatmap-based methodologies that emerged from them. While these frameworks acknowledge that uncertainty exists, they provide just enough flexibility for organizations to immediately reduce it to categorical ordinal scales (High/Medium/Low, 1–5 ratings) that obscure rather than illuminate uncertainty. In practice, that's exactly what happens. Not because the standards explicitly forbid quantitative approaches, but because they make qualitative approaches the path of least resistance.

Don't get me wrong. Standards serve important purposes. They provide baseline controls, regulatory compliance, and governance frameworks. But when it comes to understanding and managing risk in a way that enables business decisions, they fall short. We need to go beyond compliance to competence.

Current standards treat every risk like a problem to be solved rather than a trade-off to be managed. This fundamental misunderstanding leads to security programs that optimize for the wrong thing: zero risk instead of the optimal balance of risk seeking and risk mitigation.

We use the concept of *optimal risk* all the time outside of security:

- **Personal decisions**: "Should I take this new job?"
  (uncertain outcome, career/income at stake)

- **Business strategy**: "Should we enter this new market?"
  (uncertain success, investment capital at stake)

- **Daily choices**: "Should I drive in this storm?"
  (uncertain safety, time vs. potential accident at stake)

In each case, we're not trying to eliminate uncertainty—we're trying to make good decisions despite it.

Embracing Uncertainty

The financial world figured this out centuries ago with a mathematical definition of risk: *probability of an event* × *magnitude of impact* = *risk*. This formula has limitations. It assumes events are independent, impacts are linear, and probabilities can be precisely known. But it represents something revolutionary: **the idea that risk can be measured, compared, and managed rather than simply avoided**.

Uncertainty is the underpinning of understanding the concept of risk. Uncertainty means you have imperfect information: "The lack of complete certainty, that is, the existence of more than one possibility. The 'true' outcome/state/result/value is not known" (Hubbard, 2014).

Here's what the security world gets wrong: **uncertainty is not a failure of your security program**. It's not something to be ashamed of or hidden in executive briefings. The concepts of *risk* and *uncertainty* go hand in hand because risk involves future events about which we have incomplete knowledge. This is perfectly normal. Uncertainty is a feature of being human.

But here's where it gets revolutionary: **your job as a security professional is not to secure the organization**. I know that sounds heretical, but hear me out. Your job is to enable better security decisions in the face of uncertainty. There's a massive difference.

The first approach leads to security theater, checkbox compliance, and the delusion that enough controls can make risk disappear. The second approach leads to what actuaries, economists, and decision scientists have been doing all along: measuring what matters, understanding trade-offs, and helping organizations make informed choices about what risks to take, transfer, or mitigate. That philosophy, measuring and reasoning under uncertainty, is exactly what quantitative methods make possible.

This brings us to the fundamental choice that will determine whether you remain trapped in the old paradigm or join the rebellion: How do we work with uncertainty? We can either try to reduce complex uncertainties to simple categories and colors (qualitative methods) or we can embrace uncertainty while still making it useful for decisions (quantitative methods).

This distinction between qualitative and quantitative risk analysis isn't just methodological; it's philosophical. It's the difference between slotting everything that can happen to an organization onto a neat colored grid and being honest about what we know and don't know. It's the difference between security as a compliance checkbox and security as a business enabler.

This book isn't about replacing your ISO/IEC 27001 implementation or abandoning established security frameworks. It's about adding the quantitative layer that transforms compliance from checkbox theater into a strategic advantage. It's about evolving from risk-averse to risk-intelligent.

Welcome to the rebellion.

Breaking Free: What's the Alternative?

What's the alternative? What becomes possible when we break free from this broken system?

The answer is quantitative risk analysis—simply putting real-world numbers on risk. How often might this happen? How much could it cost? Instead of vague categories like "likely" or "significant impact," you use ranges of real numbers that help you make actual business decisions.

If this confuses you, don't worry. Chapter 2 will dig deeper into the fundamentals, and the rest of the book works like Lego blocks, building your understanding step by step of how to put this into practice.

WHAT IS CRQ, "CYBER RISK QUANTIFICATION"?

Cyber risk quantification (CRQ) is the practice of expressing risk in numbers instead of colors or adjectives: ranges of possible losses instead of "high" or "medium."

While this book uses the term cyber risk quantification because that's the common label in our field, the same methods apply to technology, operational, digital, or enterprise risk.

FAIR, the Factor Analysis of Information Risk, formalized this decades-old idea. The techniques you'll learn here build on that foundation but extend it across frameworks, data sources, and decision types.

In short: quantification isn't about precision. It's about clarity.

What This Book Is (and Isn't)

This book is

- **A beginner's guide**: My aim is to serve people with no exposure to quantitative risk, though there are intermediate and advanced techniques for any place along your journey.
- **A practical, hands-on approach** using real examples you can apply immediately.
- **A practitioner's guide by a practitioner**: Battle-tested approaches from the trenches that you can use today.
- **Model-agnostic methods** adaptable to existing frameworks, the simple models included in this book, or your own approach.
- **A road map for better decision-making** under uncertainty.

A note on frameworks and models: You'll find this book equally valuable whether you're using Factor Analysis of Information Risk (FAIR), the most widely adopted quantitative risk framework in cybersecurity, if you are exploring other quantitative models, developing your own approach, or even strengthening your current qualitative risk program with improved techniques. While there is a dedicated chapter on FAIR concepts and everything here is FAIR-compatible, this isn't specifically a FAIR methodology book. The principles and methods work across frameworks, and the techniques can enhance whatever approach you're currently using or planning to adopt.

This book isn't

- **A statistics or mathematics textbook** (though you'll learn the basics you need)
- **A comprehensive risk management guide** (though this will help you manage risk better)

  I won't teach you to manage the entire lifecycle of risk. There are other great books and standards for that. In the complete risk management lifecycle, risk analysis is just one piece, and that's what this book covers.

- **A deep dive into security control evaluation** (though you'll learn simple methods)

  This isn't an oversight, but deliberate. A deep dive into how individual controls influence risk would make this book 600 pages (and I may never complete it). I do cover how a holistic set of controls influences risk, which will be sufficient for the majority of cases you'll encounter.

- **A manual for compliance** with frameworks, regulations, or standards

How to Use This Book

This book is structured into five parts that build on each other, taking you from complete beginner to confident practitioner.

Part 1: Foundations

Part 1 covers the origins of cyber risk quantification (CRQ), why current methods like heatmaps fall short, foundational concepts, and how GenAI can assist (but not replace) human judgment. Makes the case for CRQ as both practical and overdue, blending history, mythbusting, and modern tools.

Part 2: Getting Your Risk Muscles Working

Part 2 builds the fundamental skills of CRQ: how to think differently about risk, construct simple Monte Carlo models, interpret results, and write clear, measurable risk scenarios. Emphasizes hands-on learning and confidence-building through practical exercises.

Part 3: Solving the Data Problem

Part 3 shows how to work with three key data sources: external research, internal organizational data, and expert judgment from subject matter experts (SMEs). Offers practical techniques for collecting, evaluating, and using imperfect but useful data, with help from GenAI and decision science principles.

Part 4: Risk Assessment in Action

Part 4 demonstrates how to run complete CRQ assessments from start to finish using real-world examples. Introduces FAIR concepts, explores scenario modeling, sensitivity analysis, treatment evaluation, and producing outputs that support actual business decisions.

Part 5: Making It Stick

Part 5 covers how to embed CRQ in your organization's processes, improve decision-making culture, respond to common objections, and maintain ethical standards. Ends by preparing readers to lead CRQ efforts and help shape the field's future.

Reading Recommendations

- **If you're completely new to quantitative risk:** Start at the beginning and work through each chapter sequentially.
- **If you have some background:** You might skip ahead to Part 2 or 3, but the foundations in Part 1 provide important context.
- **If you're looking for specific techniques:** Each part can serve as a reference, though the concepts build on each other.

What You'll Need

- **A somewhat modern version of Microsoft Excel** (no specialized software required)
- **Access to basic external research sources** (industry reports, news, academic papers)
- **Generative AI tools** (optional but recommended)
- **Willingness to ask questions and think probabilistically**

Using the Exercises

Each chapter includes practical exercises designed to build your skills progressively. Don't skip them; the concepts stick better when you practice with real scenarios. The exercises are designed to be immediately applicable to your work environment.

Downloads and Errata

Downloads and tools referenced in this book can be found at `www.heatmapstohistograms.com` in the **Tools & Downloads** section. You'll find all downloads mentioned throughout the book, plus additional tools, templates, and resources. Book errata, corrections, and updates are maintained in the Errata section of the same website.

A Note on GenAI

This book assumes you have access to generative AI tools, though they're not required. You'll find prompts throughout that help with research, modeling, and analysis. Use them as starting points, but always apply your judgment to the results. If you don't have access to AI tools, all the techniques can still be done manually, though some tasks may take longer. There's more on using GenAI as a risk analyst in Chapter 3.

Chapter Summary

The Big Idea: The current cyber risk management system is fundamentally broken by design—it rewards the appearance of progress, while our understanding and management of those risks remains fundamentally flawed, but quantitative methods offer a practical escape from this cycle.

Key Takeaways

- **You're not imagining it**. The system really is designed to reward compliance theater over actual risk reduction.
- **Your job isn't to eliminate uncertainty;** it's to help leaders make better decisions despite uncertainty, which completely changes how you approach risk.
- **Quantitative risk is just numbers instead of colors** and ranges that honestly reflect uncertainty rather than false precision through red/yellow/green categories.
- **You don't need perfect data to start**, just the willingness to think differently about what your role as a risk professional really means.

Bottom Line: This isn't just about better risk analysis; it's about fundamentally changing how security enables business. You don't need to be a mathematician or statistician—just the willingness to think in numbers instead of colors and treat uncertainty as part of life, not a problem to solve.

What's Coming Next

You've seen why the current system is broken and what becomes possible with quantitative approaches. Now you're ready to understand how we got here and the path forward:

Chapter 2 traces the 300-year evolution from mathematical breakthroughs to management matrices, why we have two completely different disciplines operating under the same name, and how the pioneers of cyber risk quantification are leading us back to scientific foundations

The rebellion starts with understanding that there's a better way and recognizing that this "better way" isn't new at all. It's a return to the scientific roots of risk analysis that other fields never abandoned. Next, let's explore how probability theory changed the world, where cybersecurity went astray, and who's showing us the way back.

References

Anderson, R. (2001). *Why information security is hard: An economic perspective.* In *Proceedings of the 17th Annual Computer Security Applications Conference (ACSAC)* (pp. 358–365). `https://www.acsac.org/2001/papers/110.pdf`

Aven, T., Renn, O., & Rosa, E. A. (2011). On the ontological status of the concept of risk. *Safety Science, 49*(8), 1074–1079. `https://doi.org/10.1016/j.ssci.2011.04.015`

Hubbard, D. W. (2014). *How to measure anything: Finding the value of intangibles in business* (3rd ed.). John Wiley & Sons.

CHAPTER 2

Probability's Plot Twist: After 300 Years, We Colored It Red

We have to go back!

—Jack, *Lost* (TV series)

Before we dive deeper, let's address something important: we've mentioned qualitative and quantitative risk approaches, but haven't defined them yet. Since these concepts are central to everything that follows, let's establish what each one means.

Qualitative vs. Quantitative: The Two Methods Explained

Recall from Chapter 1 that risk is neutral and uncertainty is normal. These aren't just philosophical concepts; they fundamentally shape how we should approach risk analysis. Let's examine the two approaches used in modern cybersecurity risk management and see how each one handles these realities. First, we'll look at qualitative methods.

T. Martin-Vegue, *From Heatmaps to Histograms*, https://doi.org/10.1007/979-8-8688-2300-8_2

Understanding Qualitative Risk Analysis

Qualitative risk analysis uses **ordinal scales** and **descriptive categories** to prioritize risk. Ordinal scales are ranked categories, but the differences between the categories are not known or equal, because ordinal scales are not measurements.

ORDINAL SCALES: MILD, MEDIUM, HOT

A great analogy to help you wrap your head around ordinal scales is hot sauce labeling: mild, medium, hot. The degree of difference between categories isn't equal, and the labels are subjective. We've all bought a "medium" hot sauce from a new brand, only to find it's either quite mild or blow-your-mouth-out hot.

If you want to know the real difference between categories, you have to **measure** it, which is exactly what **Scoville units** are. High-Performance Liquid Chromatography (HPLC) measures capsaicinoid concentration in peppers. A jalapeño measures 2,500–8,000 Scoville units, while a habanero ranges from 100,000 to 350,000 units. Now you know the habanero is roughly 20–40 times hotter, not just "one category up."

Risk matrices suffer from the same problem. When the network team rates a potential outage as "High" and the application team rates a different outage, also as "High," it's unclear which is worse or by how much. Just like hot sauce needs Scoville units, cyber risk needs actual measurements: frequencies and dollar amounts to enable real comparisons and decisions across teams.

Most frameworks assess both likelihood and impact, but other methods exist where arbitrary values are assigned to the categories. The most common method of combining the values is to create a risk matrix, shown in Figure 2-1, with the value plotted on the x and y axes.

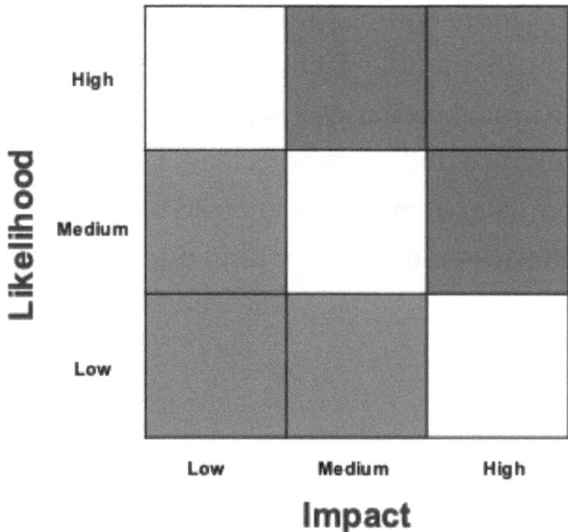

Figure 2-1. *The risk matrix, a model in qualitative risk analysis*

Instead of specific numbers, a typical risk matrix provides labels:

- **Likelihood**: High, Medium, Low (though specific terms vary widely)
- **Impact**: High, Medium, Low (again, terminology differs by framework used and organization)
- **Overall Risk**: Low, Medium, High (often color-coded as green, yellow, red)

These are typically arranged in matrices ranging from 3×3 to 5×5 grids. Some use different terminology, different scales, or even different grid sizes, but the fundamental approach remains the same: reducing complex uncertainties to simple categorical judgments.

Now let's examine the other approach.

Understanding Quantitative Risk Analysis

Quantitative risk analysis uses numerical estimates and probabilistic models to forecast the frequency and financial impact of future adverse events, using measurements rather than categories to articulate uncertainty.

Rather than categorical labels, quantitative risk analysis uses numerical estimates to model both likelihood and impact. Instead of "high risk of data breach," we might estimate a data breach to occur once every 10–20 years and could cost between $500K and $2M, with a most likely impact around $800K.

This approach requires more effort and skill but delivers data and insight commensurate with that investment—exactly what's needed for complex business decisions. It allows you to model scenarios, calculate returns on investment, and speak in the same language as finance and operations teams. Because uncertainty makes simple calculations inadequate, quantitative analysis often relies on Monte Carlo simulation, a method that uses randomness within our ranges to simulate thousands of likely outcomes.

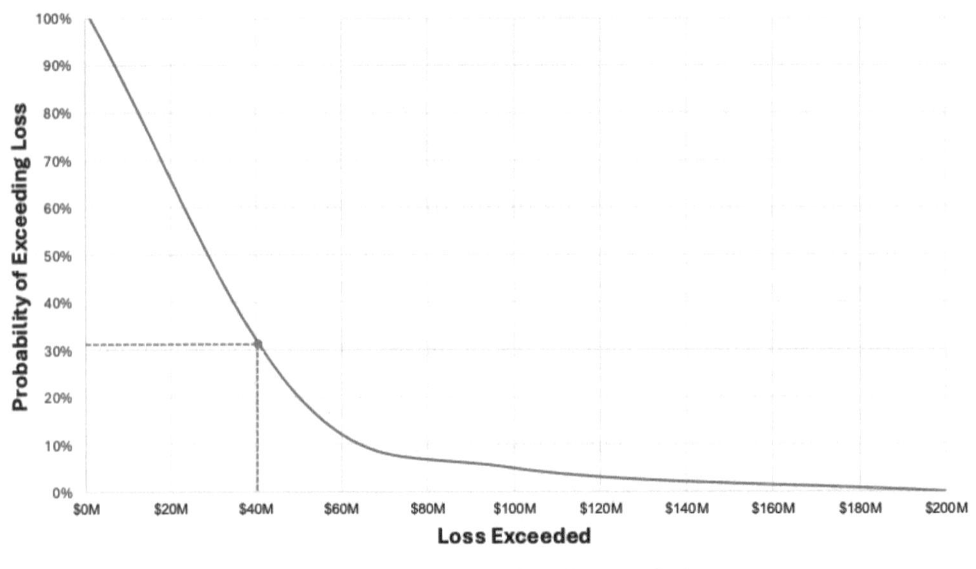

Figure 2-2. *A loss exceedance curve (LEC), one of several visualizations used in CRQ*

One powerful way to visualize these results is the **loss exceedance curve (LEC),** shown in Figure 2-2. Unlike a typical graphic showing a single color, adjective, or rating, the LEC illustrates the probability that losses will exceed different dollar amounts, enabling executives to understand the actual exposure across a range of outcomes, which reflects the reality of security incidents. In this example, our organization has a 30% chance of losses exceeding $40 million in a phishing attack.

The LEC is one of several methods for visualizing quantitative risk results. We'll dive into more visualizations in Chapter 6.

If this seems confusing, don't worry. Each of these concepts will be expanded on throughout the book, building block style.

BEYOND QUANTITATIVE ANALYSIS: OTHER APPROACHES

This book advocates for quantitative risk methods, but they're not the only effective decision-making tools available. Other fields offer excellent alternatives: decision trees, cost–benefit analysis, scenario planning, and more. The real problem isn't that we need CRQ specifically; it's that we're using a fundamentally flawed one: the risk matrix. Some examples are

- **Decision science:** Decision trees, utility theory, multi-criteria analysis, probability theory
- **Safety engineering:** Fault Tree Analysis (FTA), Event Tree Analysis (ETA)
- **Reliability engineering:** Deterministic modeling, stress testing
- **Operations research:** Optimization models, queuing theory, mathematical approaches

CRQ primarily focuses on probabilistic methods because they suit cybersecurity's uncertainty-heavy environment and align with how executives think about business risk. But if your organization has established methods from other fields, those can be equally valid.

Now that we've covered the broader landscape of quantitative approaches, let's address a common misconception that trips up many organizations.

⚠ DON'T BE FOOLED BY SEMI-QUANTITATIVE

Many frameworks describe a third option between qualitative and quantitative: semi-quantitative. It's touted as a bridge to quantitative because it replaces colors or adjectives with numbers.

Don't be fooled. Even if the rankings are 1–5, they're not quantitative; they're still ordinal and qualitative. In this instance, "1" is the same as a color or adjective. It's like replacing "Mild, Medium, Hot" ratings on hot sauce with "1, 2, 3." You still can't make meaningful comparisons. The numbers look like numbers, but they more closely resemble adjectives than something on which math can be performed.

Risk expert David Vose noted that semi-quantitative methods are "absurdities" and states that these methods "end up with an evaluation system that is more complex, vague, and illogical" (Vose, 2019).

Semi-quantitative is a misnomer. It's still qualitative risk because it uses ordinal scales.

How Did We Get Here?

Understanding the past helps us see how we got here and the way forward. Modern CRQ isn't some newfangled trend or fad (as I've heard many times on social media and at risk conferences) but rather rooted in science with a very long pedigree. Our story doesn't begin with NIST CSF, FAIR, or even Governance, Risk, and Compliance (GRC). Risk is interdisciplinary and has been studied by humans across philosophical, religious, ethical, scientific, legal, cultural, psychological, and business domains for millennia, making CRQ part of this long intellectual tradition rather than a passing trend.

Human civilization has always had a basic concept of risk, even if not formally defined. We know there is uncertainty in the future, and depending on our actions, the future holds both great rewards and adverse effects. We've learned to mitigate some risks based on observations that influence future behavior, such as prehistoric humans learning through trial and error how to hunt safely, reducing some of the risk involved in hunting woolly mammoths, an inherently risky enterprise.

From Ancient Ships to Modern Algorithms: Risk's Scientific Journey

One of the first documented approaches to structured risk management was *bottomry*, an ancient maritime financial instrument dating back to 4000–3000 BCE (Encyclopedia Britannica, Inc., n.d.). The concept was elegantly simple: merchants facing the risks of shipping goods to distant lands could get loans from financiers. If the ship returned safely, the loan was repaid with interest. If lost, no repayment was required (Encyclopedia Britannica, Inc., n.d.). This fascinating financial instrument demonstrates early understanding of risk transfer, risk pricing, and quantified decision-making under uncertainty.

But our story takes an unexpected detour through gambling halls. Until the 1600s, humans lacked a concept of mathematical probability, attributing uncertain outcomes to divine will or luck (Bernstein, 1996). That changed when French nobleman Antoine Gombaud, also known as Chevalier de Méré, approached mathematician Blaise Pascal with a gambling problem. Certain dice games weren't behaving as his intuition suggested, causing him to lose large sums of money (Bernstein, 1996).

Pascal's subsequent correspondence with another mathematician, Pierre de Fermat, to solve this "problem of points" became the foundation of probability theory (Devlin, 2010). For the first time, humans had mathematical tools to understand and quantify uncertainty rather than attribute events to mysterious forces. This represented a fundamental shift from hoping for the best to calculating the odds (Bernstein, 1996).

With probability theory established, entirely new industries became possible. Lloyd's of London systematized maritime insurance in the late 1600s. Edmund Halley created the first life tables in 1693 for calculating annuities. Actuarial science, modern risk management, and public health research, all using quantitative methods, were born (Bernstein, 1996). These concepts rapidly spread to agriculture, finance, and military planning, marking the intellectual shift toward the Age of Enlightenment. The mathematical foundations continued to develop through the 20th century, with Savage establishing the foundations of decision theory in 1954 (Savage, 1972) and Ronald Howard developing practical decision analysis methods in 1966 (Howard, 1966).

The ability to quantify uncertainty and make mathematical decisions about risk became the foundation of what we now call "quantitative risk analysis." For centuries, this was simply *risk analysis*. The quantitative approach dominated until management consulting in the mid-20th century introduced alternative methods. The techniques we use in modern cyber risk quantification have a direct lineage from these innovations, proving that CRQ isn't some passing trend but part of humanity's oldest intellectual traditions.

The Great Divergence: We Have Two Separate Disciplines Operating Under the Same Name

A pivotal shift occurred in the early 20th century that fundamentally altered how organizations approached uncertainty. As the Industrial Revolution enabled organizations to grow larger and more complex, a different way of managing uncertainty emerged. This new approach was not rooted in mathematical probabilities but rather in industrial management that emphasized efficiency and optimization.

Frederick Winslow Taylor developed "scientific management" in the early 1900s, commonly referred to as Taylorism, a highly influential philosophy that sought to eliminate uncertainty through strict control of processes (Taylor, 1911). Where probability theory embraced uncertainty as an inherent part of reality, Taylorism viewed uncertainty as a problem to be solved through systematic control. He is considered one of the first management consultants, and through that pedigree, management consulting firms took hold throughout the 20th century, emphasizing quick decision-making, speed, efficiency, and actionable results rather than the work of uncertainty analysis.

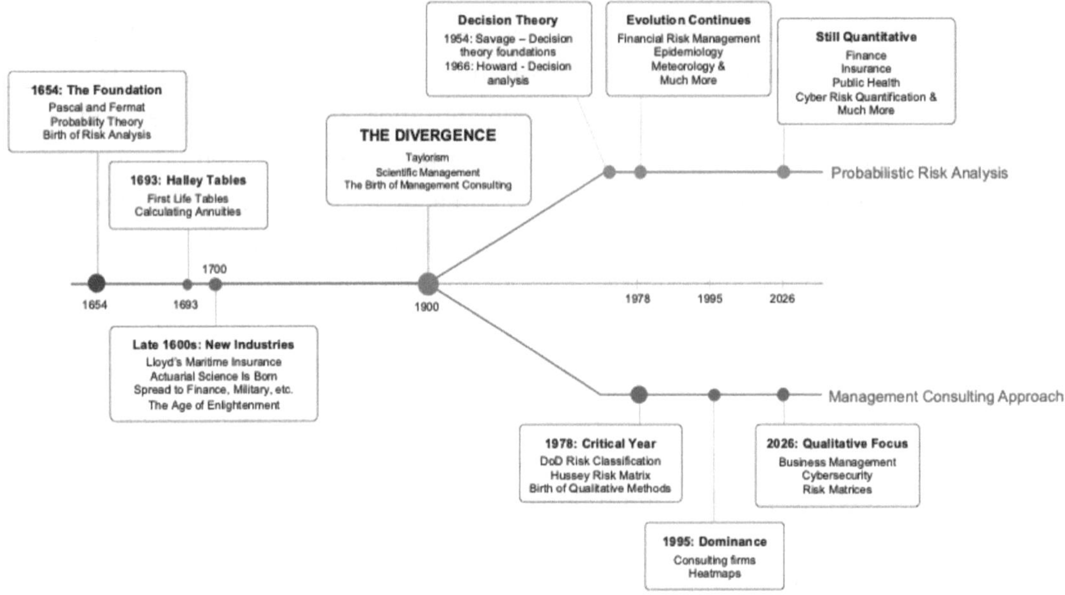

***Figure 2-3.** High-level timeline of the divergence of risk analysis methods*

This philosophical divide came to define two fundamentally different approaches to risk. In January 1978, the US Department of Defense issued a risk classification system for occupational safety and health risks, marking one of the first uses of qualitative risk labels (U.S. Department of Defense, 1978). In August 1978, David Hussey coined the phrase "risk matrix" to analyze portfolio risk on a 3×3 grid (Hussey, 1978), as illustrated in Figure 2-3. Management consulting firms quickly caught on, and by the 1990s, nearly every firm had its version of the colored grid (Hubbard, 2020). The product they sold replaced probabilistic scientific thinking with color-coded grids that prioritized quick decision-making and control, giving the illusion of analytical rigor while avoiding the hard work of probabilistic analysis.

The consequences were profound. For centuries, there was only one type of "risk analysis": the probabilistic kind. The influence of management consultants created a great divergence. There are now two distinct disciplines operating under the same name, with fundamentally different intellectual lineages.

Table 2-1. *Quantitative vs. qualitative methodologies*

Dimension	Quantitative Risk Management	Qualitative Risk Management
Intellectual Ancestry	Probability theory, actuarial science, decision theory	Taylorism, management consulting, efficiency optimization
Core Question	What are the probable outcomes and their magnitudes?	Are we following the right processes and controls?
Philosophy	Embrace uncertainty, quantify ignorance	Control uncertainty through systematic processes
Success Criteria	Accurate forecasts, calibrated confidence intervals	Consistent procedures, audit compliance
Tools	Monte Carlo simulation, Bayesian inference	Risk matrices, compliance checklists

Here's the test: if the spirit of the implementation is designed to reduce uncertainty for future decisions that help the organization execute its core objectives, the philosophical pedigree can be traced back to those 17th-century French mathematicians. If the implementation is rooted in quick decisions and explicitly ignoring uncertainty because, philosophically, uncertainty is something to be managed out of existence, the philosophical pedigree resembles Industrial Age thinking.

This philosophical divide has real consequences. Organizations spend time, money, and resources on risk management programs that feel sophisticated but are disconnected from real decision-making because they fundamentally misunderstand the nature of uncertainty. They create detailed risk registers that document everything except what actually matters: the probability and magnitude of future losses.

The good news is that we don't need to reinvent the wheel. Meteorologists, actuaries, financial risk managers, and epidemiologists never abandoned probabilistic thinking. They've continued to refine these methods while corporate risk management wandered into the land of color-coded matrices.

The risk matrix is a natural product of Industrial Era management thinking, reflecting the core tenets of Taylorism: control, simplification, and the belief that complex systems can be managed away. But most modern risks, especially cyber risk, emerge from complex environments where feedback loops, interdependencies, and nonlinearity dominate. Using a risk matrix to manage cyber risk is like using a speedometer to measure weight. It's the wrong tool for the job. It's the wrong tool for *every* job. In the next chapters, we'll see how those probabilistic roots evolve into modern quantitative techniques—Monte Carlo modeling, confidence intervals, and calibrated estimation—that return us to risk's scientific core.

Cyber risk quantification represents a clear departure from this flawed tradition. FAIR formalized this departure, but CRQ now encompasses a broader ecosystem of methods. CRQ builds probabilistic models that make uncertainty explicit, embracing ranges, simulations, and distributions to reflect real-world complexity. Where the risk matrix assigns adjectives or color coding, CRQ offers meaningful estimates. It shifts the conversation from "Which box does it fit in?" to "What could happen, and how bad could it be?" CRQ is not about eliminating uncertainty; it's about embracing it.

While CRQ might seem mainstream now, it challenged the status quo in cybersecurity when it was first introduced. The quantitative approach didn't emerge overnight. It was built by innovators who recognized that the probabilistic tradition could be adapted to our unique challenges.

THE ACADEMIC CASE AGAINST RISK MATRICES

This chapter and the preceding chapter focus on operational problems with qualitative methodologies, risk matrices, and "the way we've always done it" because that is going to be your best way to change things in your career, in your team, at your organization, and in our field. Making the argument to fix misaligned incentives is powerful and tangible and can translate directly to better risk management, which in turn means better organizational functioning.

However, there's a substantial body of peer-reviewed research documenting the fundamental flaws of qualitative methods and the associated risk matrix, which is beyond the scope of this book. If you're interested in better security decision-making, you should at least be aware of this research.

There are many sources, but the best and most comprehensive compilation is in *The Failure of Risk Management: Why It's Broken and How to Fix It* by Douglas Hubbard. In that book, Hubbard systematically documents how qualitative risk methods violate basic principles of measurement theory, create mathematical inconsistencies that can make decisions worse than random choices, and fail to provide the decision support that organizations need.

The Legends Mixtape: Greatest Hits of Cyber Risk Quantification

Modern technology risk management emerged alongside information security in the 1970s. The US Department of Commerce's FIPS-65 was the first publication describing risk management in computer security, advocating quantitative risk using the basic equation (risk = probability × impact) but providing no guidance on measuring complex security incidents (National Bureau of Standards, 1979). Despite this early quantitative advocacy, risk matrices quickly became the de facto standard, and quantitative methods remained confined to academic circles for decades.

This qualitative status quo persisted until a measurement expert from outside cybersecurity changed everything. In 2007, Douglas Hubbard published *How to Measure Anything: Finding the Value of Intangibles in Business* (Hubbard, 2007), synthesizing concepts from statistics, decision science, and metrology into one accessible book. His core insight was simple: if something matters to a decision, it's measurable. Even intangible things, such as reputation or security effectiveness, can be measured. The breakthrough was accessibility. Instead of requiring advanced mathematics, Hubbard showed how basic statistical concepts and simple tools like Excel could produce sophisticated analyses. For cybersecurity professionals stuck with qualitative heatmaps, this was transformative. Real change accelerated when *How to Measure Anything in Cybersecurity Risk* came out in 2016, co-authored with CISO Richard Seiersen (Hubbard & Seiersen, 2016), bringing quantitative thinking directly into mainstream cybersecurity. This represented a shift from niche methodology to mainstream practice.

While Hubbard provided the measurement foundation, cybersecurity needed someone who could translate these concepts into a framework specific to our field. Jack Jones, a CISO frustrated by the state of risk management practices, created FAIR (Factor Analysis of Information Risk) in 2005. Organizations were stuck with either flawed risk matrices or oversimplified risk formulas, lacking guidance on how to measure components effectively. FAIR provided what had been missing: a structured methodology to break down risk into measurable parts using uncertainty ranges and data from many sources while speaking business language that executives could understand. FAIR has since become an international framework (FAIR Institute, n.d.), with the FAIR Institute building a community of thousands of practitioners (FAIR Institute, 2021).

As cybersecurity matured, practitioners naturally gravitated toward proven quantitative techniques already being used across business and science. Monte Carlo simulation, expert elicitation, and probabilistic modeling weren't new inventions but established tools that cybersecurity professionals finally had frameworks to apply systematically. What started with frustrated analysts grasping for better ways to measure risk has become a genuine movement with conferences, communities like the Society of Information Risk Analysts (SIRA) (Society of Information Risk Analysts, n.d.) and the FAIR Institute (FAIR Institute, 2021), university courses (FAIR Institute, n.d.), and formalized training programs (FAIR Institute, n.d.). Cybersecurity has become the most prominent proving ground for quantitative risk methods (FAIR Institute, 2023), driven by high-stakes decisions and regulatory pressure. This isn't academic theory anymore but a practical discipline with tools, techniques, and practitioners proving that better risk analysis works.

IF YOU *HAVE* TO USE QUALITATIVE METHODS...

I get it. I've been there.

I've mapped risks on heatmaps because I had to—because that's what the audit required, what my boss expected, what the framework demanded. I've sat in meetings presenting color-coded matrices because if I didn't, it would have cost me my job. The truth is qualitative risk is the de facto standard and will pass an audit, no question.

There's enormous pressure to keep things the way they are. Perhaps you work in an environment with little appetite for change. Your role may be explicitly about compliance, not effectiveness. You may be early in your career and can't afford to rock the boat. I've been that analyst too.

But here's what I learned: you can do what you have to do *and* still think better about risk.

Even if you're stuck creating heatmaps, understanding the flaws described in this chapter makes you a sharper analyst. You'll ask better questions during risk identification. You'll be more careful about how you communicate uncertainty. You'll know when your matrix results don't pass the smell test.

When someone eventually asks why all the "High" risks feel the same, or why the numbers don't support budget decisions, or why last year's assessment didn't predict this year's problems, you'll know exactly what went wrong and propose something better.

Most techniques in this book work whether you're building a complete quantitative program or just trying to think more clearly within existing constraints. Better methods will make your work stronger, even if no one else notices yet.

The path from colored 3×3 boxes to measuring risk isn't just a technical upgrade. It's a return to the scientific roots of risk analysis. The tools exist, the methods work, and practitioners around the world are proving it's possible. Whether you're ready to make the full transition or just thinking more clearly within existing constraints, you're part of building something better.

Chapter Summary

The Big Idea: What we call "risk management" is two completely different disciplines with opposing philosophies: probabilistic thinking rooted in 300 years of science and management consulting approaches that treat uncertainty as a problem to be controlled away.

Key Takeaways

- **We have two separate disciplines operating under the same name**. Quantitative risk management traces back to Pascal and Fermat's probability theory, while qualitative methods emerged from Industrial Age management thinking that views uncertainty as controllable through processes.
- **The "Great Divergence" explains why risk matrices feel wrong**. They're not broken versions of quantitative methods; they're completely different tools designed for optimization and control, not uncertainty analysis.
- **Meteorologists, actuaries, financial risk managers, epidemiologists, and many other fields never abandoned probabilistic thinking**; business management, and by extension, cybersecurity, just wandered off into color-coded matrices.

- **The legends who built modern CRQ gave us practical foundations.** Hubbard made measurement accessible, Jones created FAIR as a structured framework, and a growing community proves these methods work in practice.
- **This isn't about learning new techniques**; it's about returning to the scientific roots of risk analysis that other fields never abandoned.

Bottom Line: The path from colored boxes to measuring risk isn't some new idea; it's coming home to where the understanding of risk started 300 years ago.

What's Coming Next

Now that you understand the scientific foundations that separate real risk analysis from colored matrices, Chapter 3 explores how AI can accelerate your learning path while avoiding the pitfalls that could undermine your credibility.

Chapter 3 will show you how to use AI as a supervised research assistant, transforming your role from manual data collection to high-value research validation and strategic thinking, while learning AI-assisted analysis techniques to compress weeks of quantitative risk work into hours without sacrificing accuracy.

References

Bernstein, P. L. (1996). *Against the gods: The remarkable story of risk.* John Wiley & Sons.

Devlin, K. (2010). *The unfinished game: Pascal, Fermat, and the seventeenth-century letter that made the world modern.* Basic Books.

Encyclopedia Britannica, Inc., (n.d.). *Historical development of insurance.* In *Britannica.com.* Retrieved July 26, 2025, from `https://www.britannica.com/money/insurance/Historical-development-of-insurance`

FAIR Institute. (2021, February 25). FAIR Institute reaches 10,000 members in less than 5 years. *FAIR Institute.* `https://www.fairinstitute.org/blog/fair-institute-reaches-10000-members-in-less-than-5-years`

FAIR Institute. (2023). 2023 FAIR training schedule – Learn cyber risk quantification analysis. *FAIR Institute.* `https://www.fairinstitute.org/blog/2023-fair-training-schedule`

FAIR Institute. (n.d.-a). FAIR training and certification. *FAIR Institute.* https://www.fairinstitute.org/fair-training-and-certification

FAIR Institute. (n.d.-b). What is FAIR. *FAIR Institute.* https://www.fairinstitute.org/what-is-fair

Howard, R. A. (1966). Information value theory. *IEEE Transactions on Systems Science and Cybernetics, SSC-2,* 22–26.

Hubbard, D. W. (2007). *How to measure anything: Finding the value of intangibles in business.* John Wiley & Sons.

Hubbard, D. W. (2020). *The failure of risk management: Why it's broken and how to fix it* (2nd ed.). John Wiley & Sons.

Hubbard, D. W., & Seiersen, R. (2016). *How to measure anything in cybersecurity risk.* John Wiley & Sons.

Hussey, D. E. (1978,. August). Portfolio analysis: Practical experience with the directional policy matrix. *Long Range Planning,* 11(4), 2–8. https://doi.org/10.1016/0024-6301(78)90001-8

National Bureau of Standards. (1979). *Guideline for automatic data processing risk analysis* (FIPS PUB 65). U.S. Department of Commerce. https://nvlpubs.nist.gov/nistpubs/Legacy/FIPS/fipspub65.pdf

Savage, L. J. (1972). *The foundations of statistics* (2nd ed.). Dover. (Original work published 1954).

Society of Information Risk Analysts. (n.d.). About SIRA. https://societyinforisk.org/aboutsira

Taylor, F. W. 1911. *The principles of scientific management.* Harper & Brothers.

U.S. Department of Defense. (1978,. January 30). *DoD Instruction 6055.1: Department of Defense occupational safety and health program.*

Vose, D. (2019,. July 1). Semi-quantitative risk analysis and other absurdities. *LinkedIn.* https://www.linkedin.com/pulse/semi-quantitative-risk-analysis-other-absurdities-david-vose/

CHAPTER 3

GenAI Needs Adult Supervision

Technology is a useful servant but a dangerous master.

—Christian Lous Lange

Jack Sparrow, Not Data from *Star Trek*

My first few attempts at using generative AI (or, just GenAI) ended up being comically disastrous. I asked it to perform an end-to-end quantitative risk assessment, help me gather magnitude data, and provide a list of likely threat actors, with capability ratings, for my organization. Some of the results passed the smell test, but strangely, some were nonsensical, and even others were completely fabricated. Disturbingly, I had trouble distinguishing between the accurate and fabricated results. I was excited about this new technology; instead of dismissing it as useless, I took the initiative to educate myself. The epiphany occurred a few days later as I was reading how other people and organizations used GenAI successfully. I was treating it like Data from *Star Trek*, when in fact, it's more like Jack Sparrow from *Pirates of the Caribbean*.

WHAT IS GENERATIVE AI?

Artificial intelligence (AI) refers to software systems designed to mimic aspects of human thinking, such as learning, reasoning, and decision-making, by recognizing patterns and drawing insights from data. Generative AI (GenAI) is a type of AI that goes further. It does not just analyze information; it creates new content, such as music, code, text, images, and video, based on prompts provided by users.

T. Martin-Vegue, *From Heatmaps to Histograms*, https://doi.org/10.1007/979-8-8688-2300-8_3

Data from *Star Trek* is sentient, benevolent, incapable of lying, possesses exemplary reasoning skills, and works alongside humans, solving problems in very innovative and creative ways. More importantly, however, Data is capable of working independently. Picard regularly trusted Data with command of the Enterprise.

That's *not* GenAI. At least not yet. I'm not sure if I'll see Data-like AI in my lifetime.

The GenAI that is available to us today more resembles Jack Sparrow from *Pirates of the Caribbean*. Charming, *mostly* friendly, and brilliant at what he does. Jack wants to survive the adventure; GenAI is optimized for completing the conversation. Neither Jack nor GenAI is optimized for truth-telling or accuracy. Jack, like GenAI, needs boundaries and the supervision of a trusted person; otherwise, Jack (and GenAI) go off on their own and do wacky things. In other words, Jack is not capable of working independently toward a shared goal.

There's one crucial difference, however: unlike Jack, who at least knows when he's being deceptive, current GenAI systems don't "know" when they're generating inaccurate information. Jack famously tells his adversaries, "I'm dishonest, and a dishonest man you can always trust to be dishonest." He's refreshingly upfront about his duplicitous nature.

Just like Jack, GenAI systems are programmed to acknowledge the possibility of hallucinations and often warn users about potential inaccuracies. However, unlike Jack, GenAI can't detect when it's hallucinating in real time. They can confidently present fabricated information without any internal awareness that it's incorrect. This makes the supervision aspect even more critical, since GenAI can't reliably flag its uncertainties or signal when you should be skeptical of its specific output in the moment.

WHAT ARE HALLUCINATIONS?

GenAI isn't capable of truly creative, original thought. It mimics the information it's trained on in the large language model (LLM)—the underlying AI system that processes and generates text. It constructs sentences by predicting the next word. Sometimes it produces the wrong string of words, and it won't stop or correct itself because it lacks real-time awareness of when it's generating false information. When it does this, it's called a **hallucination**: when AI makes incorrect claims while *sounding* completely confident.

In risk analysis, GenAI can hallucinate facts, cite nonexistent papers, and draw incorrect conclusions. Hallucinations can be significantly reduced by learning how to use GenAI efficiently and safely and by implementing techniques such as providing additional quality data, employing proper prompt engineering, using human oversight, and implementing guardrails to reduce hallucinations. Think of hallucinations as statistical overconfidence: the model fills gaps rather than admitting uncertainty.

The Future of Risk Analysis and the Risk Analyst

Risk analysts and risk managers are experiencing the beginning of a major transformation, as significant as the introduction of computers when they became ubiquitous in corporate America during the 1980s. AI is already transforming how we work, but the complete transformation of human society has yet to be seen. It may be some time before we have the historical perspective to look back and understand how work and society have changed.

AI systems are already starting to transform risk management as a profession. The risk analyst of the future will learn to use AI as a helpful tool, co-pilot, research partner, and analytical accelerator. AI will fundamentally shift how we spend our days, but it will never replace the risk analyst, at least not in the foreseeable future. We're at the very beginning of humanity's relationship with artificial intelligence, and the world is about to change in ways no one can foresee.

As AI handles the analytical heavy lifting, the skills that define excellent risk professionals are evolving. Research and validation expertise becomes paramount, distinguishing credible sources from unreliable ones, understanding methodological limitations, recognizing bias, and knowing when external data applies to specific organizational contexts. Critical thinking and judgment emerge as the core differentiators: scenario plausibility testing, risk communication, business context application, and prompt engineering skills to extract useful results from AI tools. Strategic communication grows in importance as quantitative analysis becomes more accessible, requiring risk analysts to excel at translating technical findings into actionable business insights and connecting risk analysis to organizational strategy. As quantitative analysis becomes more accessible, the human differentiator will be judgment: knowing when the numbers make sense and when they're lying.

Meanwhile, the tedious work that has traditionally consumed much of a risk analyst's time is rapidly being automated: manual data collection, boilerplate documentation, routine calculations, and memorization of framework details. While these foundational skills remain useful, they no longer differentiate excellent risk professionals. The future belongs to those who can combine AI's computational power with human judgment, focusing on data interpretation, model validation, stakeholder communication, and ensuring analytical rigor as basic calculations become automated.

Why AI Changes Your Work (but Won't Replace You)

Generative AI can be impressive. It can summarize a 60-page incident report in under a minute, translate it into plain language, and even suggest ways to visualize the data. But it doesn't reason about the world the way humans do. It identifies patterns from massive amounts of training data and uses those patterns to generate text that's statistically likely to be helpful and relevant to your request.

This creates a powerful but imperfect tool. AI excels at research acceleration, scenario brainstorming, and converting messy data into structured formats. It can help you find external data sources, draft risk statements, and even generate Monte Carlo simulation code. But it can also produce results that sound authoritative while containing errors, outdated information, or subtle biases from its training data.

Table 3-1. *AI-driven skills change*

Yesterday's Skills	Future-Critical Skills
Manual data collection	Research validation and critical thinking
Routine calculations	Prompt engineering and AI supervision
Framework memorization	Strategic communication and interpretation
Boilerplate documentation	Context application and bias detection

The future belongs to risk professionals who can harness AI's speed while maintaining human judgment. It's a skill shift, not displacement, as seen in Table 3-1. You're not being replaced; you're being equipped with a research assistant that never sleeps, never gets bored, and can process information at superhuman speed. But like any assistant, it needs supervision.

Three Simple Rules for AI in Risk Work

Over time, through a lot of trial and error (mostly error, in the beginning), I've developed three core rules that keep AI work fast without losing accuracy.

Rule 1: Use AI to Accelerate, Not Replace, Your Thinking

The Principle: AI should speed up tasks you already know how to do, not handle things you don't understand.

In Practice

- **Good uses:** If you know how to summarize incident reports, AI can do it faster. If you understand industry research methods, AI can help find and organize sources. If you can write risk scenarios, AI can help brainstorm variations. If you're experienced in your domain, AI can serve as a reflective, Socratic research partner (one that asks probing questions rather than giving direct answers), using its tendency to hallucinate as a feature rather than a bug to suggest unexpected research pathways and challenge your assumptions, provided you can evaluate which suggestions are worth pursuing.
- **Bad uses:** If you don't understand regulatory requirements in your jurisdiction, don't ask AI to interpret them. If you're not familiar with statistical modeling, don't let AI choose your modeling assumptions. If you can't evaluate data quality, don't rely on AI's research without verification.

The key test: Can you tell when AI gets it wrong? If not, you shouldn't use AI for that task.

Rule 2: Always Verify What AI Tells You

The Principle: When you send AI off to do research, verify sources to ensure they are real and accurate. You'll get better accuracy if you put your AI in "research mode," a type of deep research that most platforms support. Specifically craft the prompt to instruct AI to check its claims and cite sources. Still, you need to check each source independently.

How to Do It

- Instruct AI: "Cite all sources and flag any claims you're uncertain about."
- Check that cited sources exist and say what AI claims they say.
- Verify that the numbers make sense in context and that the methodologies are appropriate.
- Don't use AI to invent data to fill gaps; acknowledge uncertainty or use structured SME elicitation instead.
- Often, asking another AI platform to evaluate the work of another can work surprisingly well, especially when sources and data are critical or you suspect hallucination. Different AI systems have varying strengths and training data, so a second AI can often catch errors, inconsistencies, or questionable sources that the first one missed, though this approach is not foolproof.

Work One Component at a Time: You'll get better results by focusing on a single component at a time instead of asking AI to "do the whole thing." Ask it to help with scenario brainstorming, *then* frequency research, *then* magnitude research. This modular approach keeps assumptions visible and prevents AI from filling gaps with unsupported guesses.

Watch for Bias and Blind Spots: AI reflects its training data, which can overemphasize specific threats and underrepresent others. Don't let it define priorities without human review. This concern goes deeper than just data accuracy; it touches on the fundamental AI alignment problem: ensuring that AI systems support rather than subtly undermine human values, preferences, and ethical standards. As these systems develop their own optimization patterns, we need to verify not just that the information is correct but that the analysis doesn't lead us away from human-centered priorities and ethical considerations.

Always test AI outputs by asking it to point out weaknesses or missing factors, and consider what perspectives or scenarios might be underrepresented in its analysis. When reviewing AI recommendations, ask yourself: "Does this align with our organizational values and stakeholder interests, or does it optimize for something else entirely?" AI also has a tendency to be overly agreeable, so add to your prompt: "Challenge my assumptions, and don't be nice, be truthful."

Rule 3: Keep Humans in Charge of the Final Call

The Principle: AI can assist with research, analysis, and modeling, but the risk analyst determines the trustworthiness of the data, how to apply it to the analysis, and what recommendations to make to leadership.

What This Means in Practice

- AI can help you research frequency and magnitude inputs. You decide if that data is relevant and applies to your organization.
- AI can draft a risk scenario. You determine if it's realistic for your environment.
- AI can suggest risk responses. You choose what to recommend based on business context and ethics.

Protect Sensitive Information: Unless you control the environment or have explicit approval, never put confidential data into public AI tools. Use anonymized examples whenever possible. This extends to any internal, proprietary, or regulated data—stick to public examples when demonstrating concepts.

Use What Your Organization Approves: Work with whatever AI tools your IT and security teams have vetted. The specific platform matters less than having proper data handling and security controls in place.

How to Use GenAI in This Book

Most chapters include specific GenAI prompts designed to accelerate the methods and techniques discussed in that section. I've written these prompts as simply and clearly as possible while ensuring they remain functional across platforms. Each prompt has been tested on the most popular GenAI platforms available at the time this book was written.

I'm deliberately avoiding recommendations or even mentions of specific GenAI platforms by name because the offerings are changing and evolving rapidly. Given the rate of improvement, these tools will be significantly better and more accurate by the time you read this. Regardless of which platform you choose, you should still apply the validation principles and human oversight discussed in this chapter, particularly source verification, output validation, and maintaining critical judgment about AI-generated results.

From Code Boxes to "Vibe Coding"

This book uses Excel for most examples, but many of you are coders and modelers who might prefer Python, R, or other analytical tools. The world has changed. Gone are the days when technical books need lengthy text boxes filled with code that becomes outdated within months.

The same results achieved through Excel can now be accomplished through conversational programming (or "vibe coding"): describing what you want to do in natural language and letting GenAI generate the appropriate code. I'm using Excel because not everyone in risk management codes, and I want this book to be accessible to the broadest possible audience. That said, for large datasets, complex algorithms, or when reproducibility is critical, coding approaches may be more suitable than Excel.

I've had excellent results with vibe coding, though, of course, you should always double-check everything the AI produces. Keep in mind that effective prompt engineering is itself a skill that improves with practice. Even with GenAI assistance, there's a learning curve for communicating clearly what you want and validating the outputs. Start by asking the AI to improve your prompt or ask clarifying questions before it begins working. This often leads to much better results. I encourage you to use everything in this book as a starting point for your journey and explore on your own. Use GenAI conversationally to explain what you're trying to do, whether that's programming, modeling, or analyzing data. The key is maintaining the human judgment and validation skills we've discussed while leveraging AI's capability to handle the technical implementation.

VIBE CODING YOUR WAY THROUGH THIS BOOK

Vibe coding can be a big unlock for learners and seasoned practitioners alike. Experiment with giving AI loose, conversational instructions, whether short ("make me a histogram from this data with a nice color scheme") or long stream-of-consciousness rambles like "build something in Python that simulates coin flips but for ransomware frequency and maybe make it look decent and also can you add some way to show the uncertainty because I want to see how much the results bounce around when I change the assumptions." You can rapidly prototype models, generate graphics in R or Python, test wild ideas, and experiment with scenarios faster than traditional coding or manual analysis.

Don't worry about perfect syntax or formal requirements. Just describe what you want and let AI figure out the technical details.

Chapter Summary

The Big Idea: AI is transforming risk management as fundamentally as computers did in the 1980s, but it requires adult supervision. Treat it like Jack Sparrow, not Data from *Star Trek*, and you'll unlock capabilities that compress weeks of work into hours while avoiding costly mistakes.

Key Takeaways

- **AI is an assistant, not a replacement.** It excels at research, synthesis, and pattern recognition but needs human judgment for context, validation, and final decisions.
- **The skills that matter are changing fast.** Research validation, critical thinking, and strategic communication become more valuable, while manual data collection and routine calculations become automated.
- **Guardrails are non-negotiable**: stay in your lane, verify everything, protect sensitive data, keep humans in the critical path, and watch for bias in AI outputs.
- **Work faster by going slow and deliberate.** Focus on one component at a time, craft deliberate prompts with organizational context, and always challenge AI outputs to reveal blind spots.
- **The transformation is already here.** What used to require weeks of manual research can now be completed in hours, freeing you to focus on high-value strategic work.

Bottom Line: AI won't replace risk analysts, but risk analysts who use AI effectively will replace those who don't. The key is maintaining human oversight while leveraging AI's computational power. Treat it as a brilliant but unreliable partner who needs clear instructions and constant validation, and it becomes an indispensable tool for modern risk work.

What's Coming Next

Chapter 4 establishes the foundational concepts you need for quantitative risk: why we always use ranges instead of single numbers, how frequency and magnitude combine, and the "less wrong" mindset that makes this approach practical rather than perfect.

PART II

Getting Your Risk Muscles Working

CHAPTER 4

Foundations

> *It ain't what you don't know that gets you into trouble. It's what you know for sure that just ain't so.*
>
> —Mark Twain (attributed)

A couple of years ago, I decided to pick up a second language, something that had always been on my bucket list. I tried the traditional approach: flashcards, vocabulary drills, grammar rules, dusty textbooks. That didn't last long. Nothing was sticking. More importantly, it just wasn't enjoyable.

I researched a method called "comprehensible input," which involves consuming content slightly above your current level by watching videos, listening to music and podcasts, and reading books, without focusing on formal study. As a complete beginner, I started with children's programming and didn't crack open a single grammar book.

It worked, and it was really fun. A few years later, exclusively through watching, listening, and reading, I was conversationally fluent.

I had a similar experience learning risk analysis. When I first encountered quantitative risk through the CISSP certification, I had the feeling that this was *really hard* and, the way it was described, almost impossible to do. This was my first exposure to quantitative methods in a workplace context. I'd learned probability and statistics in college, but the CISSP study guide was supposed to show me how to use these concepts in real-world cybersecurity.

The ALE formula appeared precise but felt like guesswork when attempting to apply it. If you've had the same experience and, I suspect for many readers, CISSP was your first workplace exposure to quantitative risk as well, that reaction makes perfect sense.

There's been enormous work done by practitioners to connect the dots from theory to practice, work you won't find in study guides. Later, when I discovered these methods and started doing actual risk assessments: one scenario, then another, then another, the concepts finally clicked through practice, not study.

T. Martin-Vegue, *From Heatmaps to Histograms*, https://doi.org/10.1007/979-8-8688-2300-8_4

This is exactly how I think you should learn risk analysis: by doing.

We'll cover basic concepts in this chapter, but this isn't going to be a vocabulary lesson. You won't find dense definitions to memorize or frameworks to drill. Instead, think of this as "comprehensible input" for risk. We'll introduce ideas through practice and real examples, then reinforce them throughout the entire book.

If you're expecting to see something explained here that you don't, keep going. Work through the exercises in the subsequent chapters. The concepts will become clear through use, not study. That's how real learning happens.

Foundations First: Why We Always Use Ranges

Single numbers imply false precision, which happens when numbers are reported with greater accuracy than the data supports. When we say a ransomware attack would cost $750K, we're pretending to know the future more precisely than we actually do. That's not an honest acknowledgment of uncertainty, and it's not useful for decision-making.

Ranges, on the other hand, articulate what we know, given the data available to us at the time. $300K–$1.2M is more honest than $750K because it acknowledges our uncertainty while still providing useful bounds for planning.

The human intuition about talking about future events in ranges isn't unique to risk analysis. We use ranges in everyday life because precise figures about the future would seem off and a bit dishonest. For example:

Restaurants tell you "...about 15–20 minutes" for a table, not precisely 17.3 minutes. Estimates for a kitchen remodel are "around $5k–8k," not $6654.32. Medical prognoses are "6–18 months recovery," not 11.3 months.

Ranges help us admit what we don't know, which protects us from overconfidence. But watch out for extremes. Ranges that are too wide (like $10M–$500M for a data breach) usually tell you that you need more research or better data. Ranges that are too narrow (like $748K–$752K) are just false precision in disguise.

The art is matching your range width to what you actually know. Sometimes, wide ranges are honest: data breaches do vary wildly depending on the number of records disclosed, the attacker, and dozens of other factors. However, they also may signal that you're missing key information that would help you be more specific. As a risk analyst, part of your job is recognizing the difference.

What Ranges Actually Mean

When we say a ransomware incident could cost between $200K and $800K, we're not saying every number in that range is equally likely. Cyber losses don't spread out evenly.

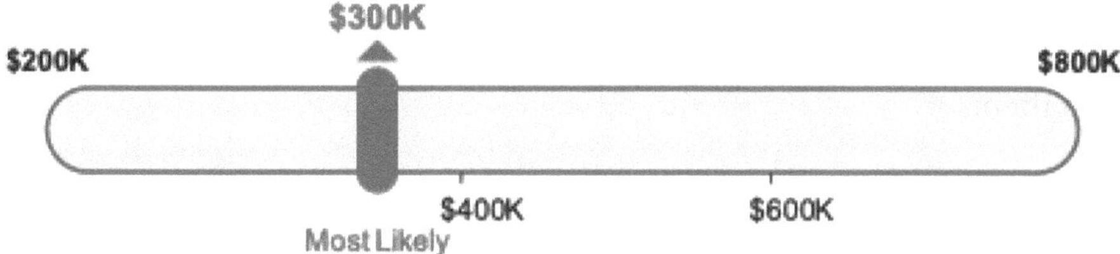

Figure 4-1. *Example input range for ransomware losses*

Most incidents tend to cluster around $300K, as shown in Figure 4-1. When I use the phrase "most likely," I mean the value that feels typical based on experience or data. Later in this chapter, we will look more closely at what "most likely" means statistically and why it matters. That point represents the most likely value, or mode: the number that feels most typical based on past experience or expert judgment. In other words, it's the value you'd expect to occur most often. Later in Chapter 6, once we run a simulation, we'll talk about the median, the P50, as one of several ways to summarize those results.

We bring the range down to $200K to reflect a less impactful incident. We also go up to $800K to capture worst-case scenarios, including regulatory fines, extended business disruptions, or particularly sophisticated attackers. These three numbers—low, most likely, and high—give us enough information to build a curve that represents uncertainty before any simulation is run.

Think of it like home burglaries in your neighborhood. Most might result in $2K–$3K in losses (stolen electronics, broken door), but your insurance coverage might go up to $50K to prepare for the rare case where thieves take everything valuable. The $2K–$3K range represents what usually happens; the full range represents what could happen. We define both so we can plan for everyday risk and the extremes. This distinction matters because of the following:

- **Most likely (mode) ($3K)**: What to expect in a typical incident
- **Range ($2K–$50K)**: Your full risk exposure

If you've learned FAIR or other early versions of quantitative risk analysis, you might recognize this *low-most likely-high* approach. It's still widely used, and it's an intuitive way to describe what usually happens vs. what could happen. Later in this chapter, I'll show you another approach: percentiles, like P5, P50, and P95, which express the same idea in a slightly different way.

Now that we've defined how to set input ranges, the next step is to ask how *confident* we can be in them.

Confidence and Other Types of Intervals

Before we dive into modeling, it helps to understand what we really mean by an *interval*. Let's break *confidence interval* down.

- **Confidence** is simply how sure you are about something. If you're very confident, you're pretty certain you're right. If you're less confident, you know you might be wrong.
- An **interval** is just another word for a range: it's the space between two numbers, like $200K to $800K.

Put them together, and you get what's called a **confidence interval**: a range that expresses your uncertainty and how sure you are that the real answer lies somewhere inside it. In other words, we're saying "I'm about *this* confident the true value falls between these bounds."

CONFIDENCE, PREDICTION, AND CREDIBLE INTERVALS: WHAT'S THE DIFFERENCE?

We just learned about *confidence intervals* in the preceding section. Technically speaking, when we're talking about **future events**, as we often do in risk analysis, this is called a **prediction interval**. A prediction interval is a range that shows where a future outcome (such as next year's loss) is likely to fall.

In formal statistics:

- **Confidence interval**: A confidence interval applies to observed data and reflects how sure we are that our estimate of the average (mean) value captures the true population value.
- **Prediction interval**: Where a *future* result is likely to fall.

- **Credible interval**: Bayesian version; given what you believe and the data, here's where the true value probably sits.

All three describe the same basic idea: a range that expresses uncertainty. Which one should we use, and how can we tell the difference?

In his book, *How to Measure Anything: Finding the Value of Intangibles in Business*, Douglas Hubbard prefers the term *confidence interval* and thinks of it as a *range of belief* (Hubbard, 2014). When these techniques are applied in practice in the technology domain, we don't have repeated samples. We have one future, one loss event that is uncertain. This is technically closer to a Bayesian interpretation of confidence.

In this book, I am going to use **confidence interval** when describing a range of belief about a set of numbers because that's what's used in Hubbard's work and in the FAIR framework.

However, I want you to be familiar with all three terms: **confidence interval** used colloquially in CRQ, **prediction interval** for when you find yourself presenting to a statistically trained CFO, and **credible interval** when talking to someone familiar with Bayes' Theorem.

The next step is attaching a percentage to our degree of belief. In CRQ, we typically use a 90% **confidence interval**, meaning, "I'm pretty sure, about nine times out of ten, that the real answer is somewhere in this range."

This enables a few things:

- Express our uncertainty about the data, estimation, and measurement.
- Acknowledge that errors are possible.
- Allow us to be accurate without pretending to be perfect.

A 90% confidence interval strikes a good balance between being useful and being honest about uncertainty.

Some practitioners prefer 80% (P10–P90) ranges because people estimate them more reliably. Either works, as long as you stay consistent.

The letter P stands for percentile. P5 means the value that is higher than 5% of all possible outcomes, and P50 is the midpoint, also known as the median. Think of this as a typical case. P95 is higher than 95% of possible outcomes. We use P5 to P95 for a 90% range because the middle 90% of outcomes sit between the 5th and 95th percentiles. For an 80% range, it would be P10 to P90.

Now that we've covered how wide a range should be and how confident we can be about it, let's talk about what confidence really means in practice.

We will also see later that cyber losses are rarely symmetric, which affects how we describe what "typical" looks like in a risk range.

CONFIDENCE IS SOMETHING YOU *DO*, NOT CALCULATE

When you estimate future annual ransomware losses at $200K–$800K with a 90% confidence interval, you're not running a formula. You're making a judgment call based on data, expertise, and process.

Confidence here means trust in that process: the quality of your data, the calibration of your estimates, and the rigor of your reasoning.

A good *interval* reflects both what you know and what you admit you don't. That's what makes it credible. It's not about math; it's about intellectual honesty.

When Executives Demand *the* Number

We've all been there. You present a thoughtful range, and the executive says, "Just give me the number. What's your best guess? I need to know exactly what to expect."

Here's what's happening: They're often asking for the most typical value without realizing it—what statisticians call the median, or P50. It's a fair request for planning, but it's not the number to use when you need to calculate averages across risks or aggregate exposure. For modeling, the expected value (mean) is the right choice because it accounts for every possible outcome and its probability weight. For communication or planning, though, the median is often the clearest "most realistic" figure. However, if you only report a single point, you risk underestimating the variability of the real world.

The problem comes when you give them a single number as if it's certain. If you cave and say "$500K" without context, you're setting everyone up for disappointment when reality lands at $400K or $700K. You might lose your credibility or, even worse, have to update your resume.

A much better approach acknowledges their need for the "typical" scenario while staying honest about the full range of possibilities:

"I understand you need a single number for planning. The **median, or typical outcome** is around $500K; that's the middle of our range and a reasonable baseline for budgeting. But I'd be doing you a disservice if I didn't mention that this could reasonably range from $200K to $1.2M based on the variables we've assessed. Do you want me to build in some cushion for the planning scenario, or are you comfortable with the $500K baseline?"

This works because you're giving them what they want (the *typical* outcome) while making it clear that precision isn't the same as accuracy. You're also shifting the conversation to which number serves their decision-making best, rather than pretending there's only one "right" answer.

The executive who demands 100% certainty is really asking you to pretend the future is more predictable than it really is. Your job is to give them useful information, not false confidence.

Before we continue, let's address a question I am commonly asked.

⚠ WHY NOT 100% CONFIDENCE INTERVAL?

It's tempting to think we could make our range wide enough to be 100% certain, but that's not how uncertainty works. To be completely sure we've captured every possible outcome, we'd have to include *everything*, even wildly unrealistic extremes.

Here's an easier way to picture it. Suppose we're estimating the typical height of NBA point guards:

- **90% confidence interval:** We're saying "we're pretty sure the true average is between 6'1" and 6'3"."
- **95% confidence interval:** "We're very sure it's between 5'11" and 6'5"."
- **99% confidence interval:** "We're almost certain it's between 5'8" and 6'7"."

See what happens? As we demand more certainty, the range gets wider and less useful.

A 100% confidence interval would have to cover every imaginable scenario, like "somewhere between 4 and 8 feet tall." Technically accurate, but practically meaningless.

That's why we settle on a 90% confidence interval. It acknowledges that we might be wrong about 1 time in 10, but it gives us a range that's actually helpful for decisions, not so wide that it tells us nothing at all.

When to Use Ranges and Confidence Intervals

Everywhere. Throughout this book, we'll learn measurement techniques to forecast everything from frequency of incidents to legal costs, incident response hours, phishing click rates, ransomware payments, and much more. All of these will be expressed as ranges with 90% confidence intervals.

This is just what you do now. With a bit of practice, thinking in ranges will feel second nature, and you'll appreciate how much more useful ranges are for decision-making.

Mode vs. Median: What Analysts Really Need to Know

When you define a range for a risk variable, you'll see two main styles:

- Minimum/most likely/maximum
- P5/P50/P95

Both describe uncertainty, but they come from different traditions.

Early FAIR models used minimum, most likely, and maximum values (Freund & Jones, 2014) because their math relied on Beta-PERT or triangular distributions, which require a mode, the value that occurs most often. This worked well for asymmetric data, since the mode could sit closer to the smaller, more common outcomes. But it also made people think "most likely" was the only valid middle, which isn't always true when we're expressing belief rather than fitting a curve.

Hubbard and other CRQ practitioners use a percentile elicitation instead. Rather than picking one "most likely" number, you estimate a range of belief, for example, "I'm 90% sure the value falls between my P5 and P95, and my P50 is where I'm equally likely to be high or low" (Hubbard, 2014). This approach is easier to calibrate and more accurately reflects how humans perceive uncertainty. Refer to Table 4-1 for an overview.

Table 4-1. *Ways to express a range*

If You Were Taught...	What It Really Means
"Low, most likely, high"	Mode-based input; still fine for PERT-style models
"P5, P50, P95"	Percentile input; focuses on belief, not curve shape
"Mode = typical"	In skewed cyber data, the mode sits below the median
"Median (P50)"	The midpoint of belief; use this as your "typical" value

When you define a range, imagine your 90% confidence interval in three parts:

- **P5:** A smaller or less severe outcome. You're 95% sure the true value won't be lower than this.
- **P50:** The midpoint of your belief, a typical or expected outcome.
- **P95:** A larger or more severe outcome. You're 95% sure the true value won't be higher than this.

If you've used FAIR before, this might sound a bit different. Early FAIR models used low, most likely, and high values to fit a Beta-PERT curve. That middle "most likely" point represented the mode, the single outcome that happens most often (Freund & Jones, 2014). This works when the data is roughly symmetric, but cyber-related data rarely is. In most cases, it's right-skewed, with many small events and a few large ones. That means the mode often sits well below the median or mean.

That's why other CRQ practitioners, following Douglas Hubbard's calibration methods, use percentiles instead. Percentiles let you express your confidence directly, without assuming any particular curve shape. In this framework, your P50 represents the point where you're equally likely to be high or low, the midpoint of your belief about the outcome (Hubbard, 2014; Hubbard & Seiersen, 2023).

This percentile-based approach keeps your inputs FAIR-compatible while staying true to how uncertainty really behaves in risk analysis.

In this book, we'll use **P5–P50–P95** as the standard. It's simple, consistent, and compatible with both modern CRQ tools and FAIR-based reasoning. If your software or template still asks for "most likely," use the value you'd consider typical, your P50. Tools that use Beta-PERT will treat it as the mode, while percentile-based models will treat it as the median. Either way, you're describing the same thing: your best central judgment about what usually happens (Hubbard, 2014; Hubbard & Seiersen, 2023).

EXERCISE 4-1: THE SAN FRANCISCO TO LOS ANGELES ROAD TRIP

Let's practice thinking in ranges with something simple and familiar.

Your task: estimate how long it takes to drive from **San Francisco to Los Angeles**. Here's your only hint: it's about **380 miles**. Don't look it up.

Write down three estimates:

- **Lower bound (P5):** Perfect conditions, light traffic, few stops, maybe you push the speed limit a bit.
- **Typical time (P50):** What you'd expect on an average day with normal traffic and one or two breaks.
- **Upper bound (P95):** Everything goes wrong, traffic jams, accidents, fog on the Grapevine, too many rest stops.

Here's a tip if you're having trouble estimating the range.

- When you estimate a **P5**, you're saying there's only about a 5% chance it could be faster than this.
- Your **P95** means there's only about a 5% chance it could take longer than this.
- And your **P50**, the middle, means you think there's an even chance the actual time will be shorter or longer than this.

Now look at your range. Are you **90% confident** the actual drive time falls within it?

If not, adjust your low and high estimates until you are.

Reflect

1. If your boss asked, "How long does it take to drive from SF to LA?" which number would you give, and why?
2. How would your estimates change if you'd made this drive fifty times vs. never having been to California?
3. What data would make your range more accurate, such as average traffic speeds, rest-stop frequency, or time of day?

What This Teaches

- **Why ranges matter:** Nobody gives a single precise number for a future event.
- **Typical vs. range:** Your *typical* estimate (P50) is useful for planning, but the full range (P5–P95) shows your uncertainty.
- **Experience narrows ranges:** More data or lived experience tightens your uncertainty bounds.
- **Confidence, not precision:** Being roughly right within a 90% confidence range beats being precisely wrong.

In other words: this is the same reasoning you'll use when estimating **frequency** and **magnitude** in real-world risk models. The process is identical; only the units change.

Frequency and Magnitude

Just like your San Francisco to Los Angeles estimate, we'll now define ranges for how often events occur and how large their impact is. The logic is the same: instead of estimating travel time, we're estimating risk outcomes.

Now that we're thinking in ranges, let's establish the two fundamental building blocks of every quantitative risk model: **frequency** and **magnitude**. These concepts are simple but powerful. They're the foundation everything else builds on.

Building Block 1: Understanding Frequency

Frequency is the estimated number of times an event occurs within a specific period, expressed as a range.

In cyber risk, frequency is always **annualized**, meaning we describe it in terms of events per year.

This is the same idea accountants use when they annualize quarterly earnings or banks use when expressing interest rates as annual percentages. Using a standard timeframe allows for easier comparison across different risks.

Annualizing frequency has three main benefits:

- **Consistency:** All risks use the same time scale for easy comparison.
- **Business alignment:** Matches annual budgeting and planning cycles.
- **Mathematical simplicity:** Makes later calculations much easier.

In other words, we're asking: *on average, how often does this happen per year?*

A **frequency range** captures the full spectrum of possibilities, while the **P50 (median)** represents what typically happens in a given year.

Examples:

- **Phishing clicks**: 10–15 times per year (P50: 12)
- **Ransomware incidents**: 0.2–0.5 times per year (P50: 0.3)
- **Credential stuffing attacks**: 20–30 times per year (P50: 25)
- **Major data breaches**: 0.05–0.2 times per year (P50: 0.1)

When something happens less than once per year, convert it to an annual frequency by dividing 1 by the number of years, as shown in Table 4-2.

Table 4-2. *Annual frequency conversion reference*

Typical Occurrence	Calculation	Annual Frequency
Once every 2 years	1 ÷ 2	0.5 per year
Once every 3 years	1 ÷ 3	0.33 per year
Once every 4 years	1 ÷ 4	0.25 per year
Once every 5 years	1 ÷ 5	0.2 per year
Once every 8 years	1 ÷ 8	0.125 per year
Once every 10 years	1 ÷ 10	0.1 per year
Once every 15 years	1 ÷ 15	0.067 per year
Once every 20 years	1 ÷ 20	0.05 per year

Don't worry if "0.2 ransomware incidents per year" sounds odd at first. It simply means "about one incident every five years." Thinking in this way allows for consistent comparison across all risks.

Your **frequency range** expresses the full uncertainty of how often something might happen, while your **P50 value** captures the typical case—what you'd expect to see in a normal year.

WHY NOT PROBABILITIES?

Readers familiar with other forms of risk analysis might ask why we use **frequencies** (e.g., "once every five years") instead of **probabilities** (e.g., "20% chance per year"). There are two main reasons: one practical and one about communication.

1. **Practical**

   Many cyber events happen often: phishing, credential misuse, failed deployments, login lockouts, sometimes daily or weekly.

   If you asked, "What's the probability of at least one phishing incident this year?" the answer would be nearly 100%, which isn't helpful for planning.

   But saying "about 50 phishing incidents per year" gives you something you can staff for, budget for, and track.

2. **Communication**

   Psychological research shows that people understand frequencies better than probabilities. It's easier for most decision-makers to reason about "once every five years" than "a 20% chance per year."

A Subtle but Important Point

When we express frequency as a rate (e.g., 0.2 incidents per year), we're describing an **average rate of occurrence**. That doesn't mean it happens like clockwork. It means that, over time, it tends to average out to that rate.

Mathematically, even if the frequency is greater than zero, there's always a chance that no events will occur in a given year.

This is why we describe risk in ranges and distributions rather than single points: it captures both the variability of outcomes and the possibility of none at all.

Building Block 2: Understanding Magnitude

Magnitude is the range of financial loss per event when something bad happens. Just like with frequency, magnitude is expressed as a range, not a single number.

The range captures the full spectrum of what could happen, while the **P50 value** (the midpoint of belief) represents what typically occurs.

Examples

- **Credential stuffing attack**: $5K–$50K per incident (P50: $15K)
- **Successful phishing attack**: $8K–$25K per incident (P50: $12K)
- **Ransomware incident**: $300K–$1.2M per incident (P50: $500K)
- **Major data breach**: $2M–$15M per incident (P50: $5M)

A ransomware attack might cost $300K if your backups work perfectly and you recover quickly. It might cost $1.2M if you have complications, need extensive recovery work, or face regulatory fines. The range reflects all the variables that could affect the outcome:

- **Recovery scenarios**: How quickly can you restore operations?
- **Regulatory responses**: Will there be fines or compliance costs?
- **Business impact variations**: How much revenue do you lose during downtime?
- **Incident complexity**: How sophisticated was the attack?

Just like before, we express uncertainty as a 90% confidence interval. That means that based on what you know about similar incidents—the data you've collected, the experts you've consulted, and your own experience—you're about nine times out of ten confident that the true loss will fall somewhere inside this range.

How They Combine: The Risk Equation

Figure 4-2. *The classic risk equation*

Recall from Chapter 1: risk is how often a bad thing happens, how much it hurts if and when it occurs, clouded by an uncertain future. This is commonly expressed in the simple risk equation, **Frequency × Magnitude = Risk**, as shown in Figure 4-2. This is the classic formula you'll encounter in CISSP, other certifications, and most risk frameworks. It's been the foundation of risk analysis for decades because it's intuitive and practical.

But there's a problem when you're working with ranges instead of single numbers. If your frequency is 0.2–0.5 incidents per year and your magnitude is $300K–$1.2M per incident, you can't just multiply the endpoints together (0.2 × $300K = $60K and 0.5 × $1.2M = $600K). That would miss all the possible combinations in between. What if you have 0.4 incidents at $800K each?

In fact, multiplying endpoints tends to **overstate** risk because both extremes are low-probability values. A low-probability frequency times a low-probability impact yields an even lower probability outcome, which is why a Monte Carlo simulation is needed to handle the full range correctly.

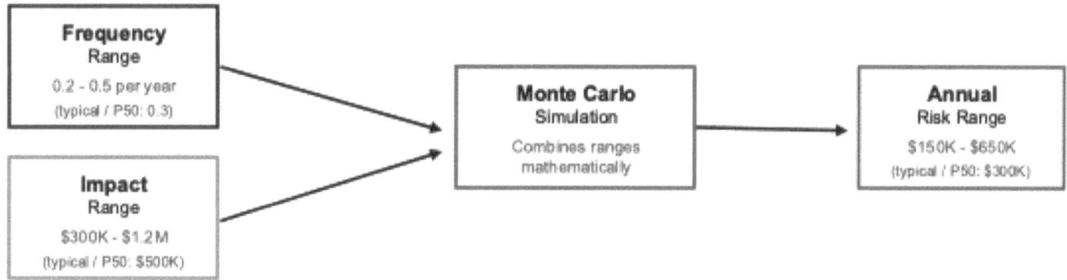

Figure 4-3. *How ranges combine in a Monte Carlo simulation*

This is where Monte Carlo simulation comes in. It runs thousands of calculations with different combinations of frequency and magnitude values to give us a realistic risk range. Instead of "ransomware risk = $250K," we get "ransomware risk = $150K–$650K per year (median: $300K)," a range that honestly reflects our uncertainty, as shown in Figure 4-3.

Monte Carlo simulation works by randomly sampling values within each range, frequency, and magnitude, many times, combining them to show all the possible outcomes and their probabilities. The result is a distribution that captures not just the extremes, but everything in between.

We'll dive into Monte Carlo simulation in the next chapter, but for now, just remember: when you have ranges for both frequency and magnitude, you feed them into Monte Carlo to get your risk range. It's how we do the math when our inputs are uncertain.

Essential Vocabulary: Concepts You Need to Know

Risk Analysis vs. Risk Assessment

These two terms are commonly used interchangeably with each other, but they do mean different things. *Risk analysis* is the process of understanding and measuring risk (frequency, magnitude, scenarios). *Risk assessment* is the complete project that includes analysis plus decision-making context, scope definition, stakeholder communication, and recommendations. In other words:

- **Analysis** = "What's the risk?" (the measurement part)
- **Assessment** = "What should we do about it?" (the complete business process)

An assessment contains analysis, but also includes scoping, stakeholder management, communication, and decision support.

Uncertainty

We covered the concept of uncertainty in Part 1, but I want to elaborate and wrap it up here because uncertainty is such an important concept. Uncertainty is a feature of the human condition.

When conducting quantitative cyber risk management, it is essential to work with uncertainty rather than attempting to eliminate. While good analysis can reduce many uncertainties, some will always remain. Pretending otherwise or forcing false precision into your assessments undermines their credibility and renders them less useful.

Two Types of Uncertainty

Aleatory uncertainty is randomness. That type of uncertainty can't be reduced through more research. For example, a spinning ball on a roulette wheel is aleatory. More data collection isn't going to tell you where the next ball is going to land.

Epistemic uncertainty is a lack of knowledge. This can often be reduced by obtaining more knowledge, though that requires investment: your time, other people's time, research resources, sometimes money. Whether it's worth the investment depends on how much better decisions you'll make with that additional information.

There's always a cost to reducing uncertainty. You want to match your research effort to the decision at hand. If you want to know if a car will fit into a garage, eyeballing it works fine. If you're manufacturing cars to meet safety specifications, you need precise measurements. The same principle applies when measuring cyber risks. You need to know how the information will be used to decide how much precision is worth pursuing.

Why This Distinction Matters

Knowing the difference between aleatory and epistemic uncertainty helps you spend your research time wisely. If uncertainty is epistemic (lack of knowledge), you might be able to research your way to better estimates. If uncertainty is aleatory (randomness), additional research won't help much.

Cyber risks contain both types of uncertainty; however, most are epistemic, meaning you can improve your estimates with more knowledge:

- How many employees will fall for phishing (depends on training quality, email filters, user awareness)
- How quickly your incident response team will detect a breach (depends on tools, processes, staffing)
- How much a ransomware attack will cost (depends on backup quality, business continuity planning, insurance coverage)
- Infrastructure failure rates (can be reduced through better maintenance, monitoring, redundant design)

But a few components are truly aleatory—inherently random and irreducible:

- The exact timing and intensity of solar flares that could disrupt satellite communications

- When and where earthquakes will strike with enough force to damage data centers
- Quantum mechanical randomness in hardware (though this is rare for most systems)

Table 4-3. *Aleatory vs. epistemic uncertainty examples*

Aleatory (Random)	Epistemic (Knowledge Gap)
Solar flare timing	Phishing success rates
Earthquake occurrence	Incident response times
Quantum hardware effects	Backup recovery costs

Many events that seem completely "random" may have both components. You might not be able to predict exactly when a construction crew will cut a cable, but you can influence how often it happens through better coordination processes and how much it impacts you through redundant connections.

When to Reduce Uncertainty vs. When to Live with It

Get better information when you're close to a decision threshold, when the new information could realistically change your choice. Live with uncertainty when the decision is clear either way.

For example, if a security tool costs $100K annually and prevents $200K–$500K in losses, that's probably a good buy. If it prevents $30K–$70K, probably not. If it prevents $80K–$120K, you're near the threshold—get better information, as shown in Table 4-4.

Table 4-4. *When to research more vs. when to decide*

Decision Threshold	Research Cost Low	Research Cost High
Near threshold	Research more	Consider research
Far from threshold	Live with uncertainty	Live with uncertainty

Keep in mind that cost-benefit isn't everything. Regulatory requirements might force your hand regardless of the math. Risk tolerance varies. Some organizations won't accept even small chances of major losses. Strategic considerations matter too. A decision might align with broader initiatives even if the direct ROI isn't clear yet.

Focus your effort on gathering better information that could **change the decision**. Everything else is wasted motion.

Adopting a "Less Wrong" Mindset

There's a famous quote by statistician George Box: "All models are wrong, but some are useful." This isn't just a quote about a statistical model. This is a philosophical mindset that you must adopt to succeed in your career in risk management.

Think of it this way: when you use a map to navigate your city, that map isn't reality. It doesn't show every building detail, every pothole, every tree. It's a simplified representation that leaves out a great deal of information. But it's still incredibly useful for getting where you need to go.

Risk analysis works in a similar way, except that we're mapping uncertainty instead of streets. We can't predict every variable or outcome, and we don't need to. What we need is something better than gut instinct and color-coded matrices. We create the best model we can with the best information we have at the time. That's what George Box means. The map is "wrong" in the sense that it's not an *exact* representation, yet it's still very useful.

WHY I DON'T QUOTE GEORGE BOX AT WORK

I love the George Box quote, but I don't quote it in the office anymore. Years ago, I was trying to discuss modeling our uncertainty around technology risk with the chief risk officer at a financial institution. I made the mistake of quoting George Box. I said, "All models are wrong, but some are useful." This was out of frustration because the chief risk officer kept wanting the risk analysis to be perfect with no uncertainty.

The CRO snapped back at me: "Go back and work on this until your model is not wrong. We can't have any errors in this." It's clear that he misunderstood me, but I realized that I shouldn't have said what I said. Unless you understand the philosophical meaning behind what George Box was talking about, it might sound like a surrender or a cop-out.

Now, instead of George Box, I quote Alfred Korzybski: "The map is not the territory." It basically means the same thing, but it's a little more accessible to people who struggle to grasp some of these philosophical concepts. Same philosophical foundation, much easier conversation.

What This Looks Like in Practice

This mindset shift changes how you talk about risk on a daily basis:

Instead of "We have high cyber risk," you'll say, "We expect 2–4 ransomware incidents annually, each costing $300K–$1.2M."

When executives ask, "How secure are we?" instead of showing red, yellow, and green boxes, you'll say: "Our current security posture suggests we'll face about $2.5M in annual cyber losses, with a 10% chance of a catastrophic event exceeding $10M."

When leadership asks, "Should we invest in this $300K security tool?" instead of saying, "It reduces our risk from high to medium," you can say: "This tool would prevent about 60% of successful phishing attacks. Instead of 24 successful attacks per year costing $480K total, we'd see about nine attacks costing $180K. The tool pays for itself in the first year."

This precision makes risk discussions strategic rather than academic.

Starting Small: You Don't Need to Revolutionize Everything

The "less wrong" mindset doesn't require massive resources or organizational transformation. Pick one high-stakes decision your organization is facing. Model one scenario using the techniques in this book. Total time investment: 2-3 days. If that analysis helps improve the decision, expand on it from there.

Start with decisions where precision matters, like whether to invest in a $200K security tool, how much cyber insurance to buy, or which of three vendors poses the least risk.

EXERCISE 4-2: BUILDING YOUR RISK INTUITION

For each scenario, estimate frequency and magnitude ranges.

Scenario A: Laptop Theft

An employee's laptop with customer data was stolen from a coffee shop.

- **Frequency**: ___ times per year
- **Magnitude**: $____ to $____ per incident

Scenario B: Cloud Service Outage

Primary SaaS vendor outage affects your operations.

- **Frequency**: ___ times per year
- **Magnitude**: $____ to $____ per incident

Which felt easier to estimate and why? What additional information would help you be more confident in these numbers?

Chapter Summary

The Big Idea: Traditional risk education starts with tools and templates instead of purpose and decision-making. This backward approach makes quantitative methods seem impossible when they're actually practical and necessary.

Key Takeaways

- **Risk assessment exists to support better decisions**, not to check boxes or create pretty dashboards.
- **The "less wrong" mindset** acknowledges that all models are imperfect, but some are useful for decision-making.
- **Uncertainty is a feature, not a bug**. Ranges provide more useful information than false precision.

- **Start small**: pick one decision and model one scenario rather than trying to revolutionize everything.
- **Know your vocabulary**. Risk analysis vs. assessment, frequency vs. probability, aleatory vs. epistemic uncertainty.

Bottom Line: You don't need to be perfect to be useful. Focus your research time on epistemic uncertainties where better information could change your decisions. Accept that some uncertainty will always remain, and that's normal and manageable. When you have ranges for both frequency and magnitude, you feed them into a Monte Carlo simulation to get your risk range.

What's Coming Next

You've cleared the foundational fog around why traditional risk education makes quantitative methods seem impossible. You understand that risk assessment exists to support decisions, not create compliance theater. You've practiced thinking about frequency and magnitude, and you've started building intuition around uncertainty ranges.

Chapter 5 puts these foundations into action by guiding you through your first complete quantitative risk assessment using Monte Carlo simulation step-by-step. Starting with coin flips to demonstrate the concept, you'll then apply the same principles to forecast real-world incident frequency and financial magnitude, transforming your "less wrong" mindset into actual numbers that inform practical decisions about risk treatment options.

References

Freund, J., & Jones, J. (2014). *Measuring and managing information risk: A FAIR approach*. Butterworth-Heinemann.

Hubbard, D. W. (2014). *How to measure anything: Finding the value of "intangibles" in business* (3rd ed.). Wiley.

Hubbard, D. W., & Seiersen, R. (2023). *How to measure anything in cybersecurity risk* (2nd ed.). Wiley.

CHAPTER 5

Your First Quantitative Risk Assessment

This is the beginning of a beautiful friendship.

—Rick Blaine, *Casablanca*

Time to keep my promise from Part 1. We're going to step into quantitative analysis, but in a way that's not going to melt your brain. We're going to start with a very simple tool: the Monte Carlo method, which provides a glimpse into what the future could look like by simulating many outcomes based on what we know, including our uncertainty. It's the backbone of CRQ and is commonly used in many disciplines like finance, economics, medicine, military, and engineering, just to name a few.

What Is Monte Carlo Simulation?

Monte Carlo simulation is a method that uses randomness to explore potential future events. Despite its fancy name, it's simply a tool that helps us understand uncertainty by running thousands of "what if" scenarios.

Rather than forecasting specific results, Monte Carlo methods reveal the range of possibilities through repeated sampling of potential scenarios. Recall from the previous chapter that we always articulate our data in *ranges* because we're performing a forecast, and we can't predict the future exactly. We're not fortune-telling; we're methodologically exploring uncertainty.

T. Martin-Vegue, *From Heatmaps to Histograms*, https://doi.org/10.1007/979-8-8688-2300-8_5

THE ORIGINS OF MONTE CARLO

The concept is elegantly simple: it involves a set of mathematical algorithms that utilize random sampling to solve problems. Monte Carlo simulation was first developed systematically during the Manhattan Project, the United States' program to develop nuclear weapons during World War II. John von Neumann and Stanisław Ulam developed a method to solve neutron diffusion problems in nuclear weapons development, as well as other complex problems in nuclear physics (Dunn & Shultis, 2011).

They named it "Monte Carlo" after the famous casino in Monaco, which was a tribute to Ulam's love of gambling (Dunn & Shultis, 2011). The name was fitting. Just as casino games rely on chance and probability, their new method used randomness as a tool to solve problems that were previously difficult or impossible to solve otherwise.

How Monte Carlo Works in Risk Analysis

Monte Carlo simulation is the next step that takes those ranges and uses randomness to simulate values within those ranges, clustering around the most likely value while also exploring the outer bounds.

In CRQ, we're simulating *years* because we annualize everything. Think of it this way: every time you run a Monte Carlo simulation, you're simulating the next 12 months. For example, if it's December 2026 and your Monte Carlo is set to run 10,000 trials (we call them trials because not every Monte Carlo simulation represents a year), you're simulating 10,000 different versions of 2027.

After running these simulations, we examine the distribution of results. What are the outliers? What are the chances of something at the outer bounds occurring? How do the results cluster around the most likely value, and what are the chances of that happening? It's a quick and easy tool to gain insight into what the future could look like.

In cybersecurity, we constantly deal with uncertainty. How often will we get breached? How much will it cost? Instead of throwing our hands up and saying "we don't know," Monte Carlo lets us work with that uncertainty in a structured way.

Your First Monte Carlo Simulation

Let's learn by doing with a simple exercise that will show you exactly what Monte Carlo is.

EXERCISE 5-1: THE COIN FLIP EXERCISE

Step 1: Real Life

Find a coin and flip it ten times. Record the results on paper, numbered 1 to 10, writing "Heads" or "Tails" for each flip. You probably got something like six heads and four tails, not exactly five and five. It's also possible you got two and eight, one and nine, or even zero and ten, because coin flipping is random and your previous results have no influence on your next result.

Step 2: Digital Simulation

Now simulate the same thing in Excel:

1. **Type this formula into cell A1:** =IF(RAND()>0.5,"Heads","Tails").
2. **Copy this cell:** Ctrl+C (PC) or Cmd+C (Mac).
3. **Select cells A1 through A10, then paste:** Ctrl+V (PC) or Cmd+V (Mac).

Compare your physical coins to the results in your Excel spreadsheet. We have different outcomes, but similar patterns.

Step 3: Scale It Up

Now extend your Excel simulation to 1,000 flips:

1. Select the range A1 through A1000.
2. Paste the formula again.
3. **In cell B1, type this formula:** =COUNTIF(A1:A1000,"Heads").
4. **In cell B2, type this formula:** =COUNTIF(A1:A1000,"Tails").

The last two steps count the number of heads and tails in our simulation.

Watch what happens when we refresh the simulation:

- **PC users:** Press F9
- **Mac users:** Press Cmd + =

You'll see roughly 500 heads and 500 tails each time, but the exact numbers change each time. **This demonstrates Monte Carlo's core mechanics in action**. We can now observe consistent patterns emerging from randomness.

You just did a Monte Carlo simulation! The only difference between this coin flip simulation and a risk analysis is complexity, not concept. Instead of heads and tails, we use ranges, but the fundamental approach remains the same.

A downloadable Excel example of this exercise is available at `www.heatmapstohistograms.com` in the Tools & Downloads section.

THE LAW OF LARGE NUMBERS

Open the spreadsheet you created for **Exercise 5-1**, and refresh the sheet. Watch the proportion of heads vs. tails for 10 flips and compare with the proportion for 10,000 flips. Observe the differences and refresh at least ten times.

Do you notice something interesting?

With ten flips, there can be wide variance: sometimes 50/50, 70/30, 80/20, maybe even 100/0. However, with 10,000 trials, we observe a much closer to 50/50 ratio. Usually not *exactly* 50/50, but much closer to 50/50 than the ten flips.

Why?

You are observing a fundamental statistical principle known as the **Law of Large Numbers**. Though individual flips are uncertain, the underlying probability distribution tells us that heads and tails each have a 50% likelihood of occurring. When simulating trials, such as coin flips or a cyber risk scenario, the more trials you run, the closer the simulation gets to the expected value. This is the **Law of Large Numbers** at work: more trials mean less variation from the expected value.

This is *particularly important* in CRQ because, unlike coin flipping, we don't know the expected value. We want to run enough trials to reduce the amount of variation from the expected value as much as possible. In my experience, the minimum is 10,000 trials, but 50,000 is better to accurately capture outlier results (extreme values that fall far from the typical range). 50,000 trials were no small task when these methods were being developed on early computers, but today, even a semi-modern smartphone can make quick work of this job.

Forecasting Frequency

Next, we will forecast the frequency of events. Recall from the previous chapter that *frequency* refers to the number of times something occurs. We will combine several concepts: uncertainty, frequency, ranges, confidence intervals, and Monte Carlo simulation.

Setting Up the Problem

What are the chances of me losing or damaging my mobile phone in the next 12 months? I'm not sure, a low chance? I've had a lucky run over the last several years, but not a perfect one. I drop my phone quite a bit, and I'm somewhat forgetful, so the threat is not zero. *I'm not exactly sure what the next 12 months could look like*. In other words, I have *uncertainty*. We can't eliminate uncertainty, but we can use structured reasoning and logic to move our uncertainty from "um, a low chance?" to a numerical range that is directionally right.

First, I'm going to do this exercise, and I want you to follow along, gathering your own numbers.

Gathering Historical Data

I'm going to look back five years and gather historical data for this question. Five years is enough for this exercise because it provides sufficient historical context while remaining relevant to current conditions. Using my memory, I can immediately recall the following incidents, shown in Table 5-1.

Table 5-1. *Initial recalled incidents*

Device Type	Year	Incident
iPhone (can't remember exact model)	2020	Cracked screen, needed replacement
iPhone 13	2022	Cracked screen, needed replacement
iPhone 13	2022	Total device replacement

This is what I can recall, which is essentially using myself as a subject matter expert (SME), a concept we'll learn about in later chapters. 2022 clearly stands out in my mind because it was a challenging year: not only did I drop the phone and crack the screen, but shortly after the replacement, I went swimming in the ocean with the phone in my pocket. The salt corroded the charging port, and the side buttons stopped working, necessitating a total device replacement (yeah, I know).

Verifying the Data

Am I sure? I think so, but I'm not entirely sure, and I also can't remember which phone I had back in 2020 that required a screen replacement. To obtain this data, I will review my carrier's billing statements, as well as credit card statements for iPhones, receipts from the local mobile carrier store, and records from a few screen replacement places in my area. This would essentially be equivalent to searching throughout your organization for internal incident data and details surrounding an incident to determine what occurred.

OUTSOURCE THE MUNDANE

I uploaded PDFs of invoices and credit card statements into GenAI, instructing it to find any charges that fit the parameters outlined above. It did in seconds what would have taken me a weekend, if not more.

I didn't miss any incidents, but I was able to gather more data on the models of phones, as shown in Table 5-2.

Table 5-2. *Updated incident list*

Device Type	Year	Incident
iPhone 11 Pro	2020	Replaced cracked screen
iPhone 13 Pro	2022	Cracked screen, needed replacement
iPhone 13 Pro	2022	Total device replacement

Based on SME (me) data combined with cost research, I've found that in a five-year span, I've had two broken screens and one full device replacement. In a good year, that means I've had zero incidents, and in a bad year, I've had a full device replacement and one broken screen.

Forecasting Future Scenarios

But what could my next 12 months look like? This is where we need to do some forecasting.

Lower bound (minimum): Could I have zero incidents in a year? Yes, I've had several years with no incidents at all. So, my lower bound is 0.

Upper bound (maximum): Theoretically, I could break an infinite number of phones until I run out of money or patience, but that's not realistic. I need to set a rational upper bound that captures plausible worst-case scenarios without being overly optimistic or absurd.

Thinking about what could *plausibly* go wrong in a particularly bad year:

- One stolen device (complete loss)
- One device damaged beyond repair (like my ocean swimming incident)
- One screen crack requiring replacement

That gives me a maximum of three incidents in a single year. While higher numbers are technically possible, they fall outside the range of reasonable scenarios I want to plan for with 90% confidence.

PERMISSION TO BE IMPERFECT

We always want to bound both sides of our ranges rationally and eliminate absurd ranges because we don't need to be 100% confident. We're aiming for 90% confidence in our forecast, which means that nine times out of ten, we expect the actual result to fall within this range. This gives us permission to be a little more rational and reasonable with our ranges. We don't want our range to be too absurd on either end, just so we can try to capture the entire range of possibilities. We want a range that captures a very good range of plausibility.

Typical value (P50): For the most likely value, I will estimate zero incidents per year, despite my historical average being 0.6 incidents per year. Here's my reasoning: My threat model has fundamentally changed since my historical period:

- My children are older now and have their own phones, eliminating the borrowing risk that led to several incidents.
- After my disastrous 2022 double-incident year, I've developed much better handling habits and situational awareness.
- I now use better protective cases and have changed my behavior around water/outdoor activities.
- Three of my five historical years had zero incidents, showing that incident-free years are very achievable for me.

This demonstrates a key principle in quantitative risk: historical data informs but doesn't dictate future estimates. When you have clear evidence that your risk profile has changed, you should adjust accordingly. In my case, the operational changes justify expecting my "good years" (zero incidents) to be more representative of my future than my overall historical average.

My final forecast for mobile phone incidents for the next 12 months:

- **Range (P5–P95)**: 0 to 3 incidents
- **Typical value (P50)**: 0 incidents
- **Confidence level**: 90%

SOME THINGS ONLY A HUMAN CAN KNOW

This book is very AI-forward, demonstrating tasks and pieces of quantitative risk analysis that can be outsourced. Be wary of products or models that claim to run analyses completely on data and AI alone; they miss things that only humans know, such as the reasons I set 0 for my Most Likely value. In cyber risk, there are many things that only humans, the people who work directly in the systems or are aware of the operating environment, know.

Now it's your turn. Using the same methodology demonstrated above, you'll forecast your own chances of mobile device damage or loss over the next 12 months.

EXERCISE 5-2: YOUR MOBILE DEVICE INCIDENT FREQUENCY

Step 1: Gather Your Historical Data

Using your recollection, fill out this table covering the past five years of incidents:

Device Type	Year	Incident

Step 2: Verify and Complete Your Data

Search through your records to fill in any gaps and verify your memory:

- Carrier billing statements
- Insurance claims
- Repair shop receipts
- Credit card statements for device purchases

Use GenAI to help: Ask it to suggest what types of records might contain evidence of device incidents or replacements. Upload statements in bulk for easy searching.

Update your table above with any additional incidents you discover.

Step 3: Create Your Forecast Range

Based on your historical data, create a forecast for the next 12 months. Consider:

- Your historical incident pattern from the table
- Current threat environment (travel, lifestyle changes, work requirements)
- Changes in your behavior or risk profile since your historical period
- Any upcoming situations that might increase or decrease your risk

Create your forecast with three values:

- **Lower bound (P5)**: _____ incidents
- **Typical value (P50)**: _____ incidents
- **Upper bound (P95)**: _____ incidents

Step 4: Validate Your Confidence Level

Ask yourself: **Are you 90% confident in this range?**

- **Too wide (100% confident)**: Your ranges may be unnecessarily broad.
- **Too narrow (50–60% confident)**: You're probably being too precise.
- **Just right (90% confident)**: Nine times out of ten, the actual result should fall within your range.

Make any final adjustments and record your values. We'll need them later in this chapter.

Some readers may not have had any incidents at all in the last five years, maybe even ten years. How do we analyze an incident or risk that's never happened?

ZERO INCIDENTS DOES NOT MEAN ZERO RISK, UNLESS...

Some readers may not have experienced any incidents in the past five years, or even ten years. This raises an important question: How do we analyze a risk that's never happened to us personally?

Zero incidents do not mean zero risk, unless you're completely avoiding the activity. The only way to truly eliminate mobile phone risk is to refrain from owning or using any mobile phone during the entire time period. For everyone else, we carry risk even without a personal incident history.

Many companies face this same challenge. They may have never experienced a material data breach, ransomware attack, or theft of hundreds of thousands of dollars due to sophisticated social engineering, but these remain very real, possible, and plausible threats.

Building a Credible Range with No Personal History

Lower bound (P5): Easy, it's 0.

Typical value (P50): Probably also 0, unless there has been or will be a significant change in the threat landscape, business environment, operating environment, control efficacy, or personnel that changes your risk profile.

Upper bound (P95): We can't use 0, because an incident is *possible*. This is where you need external data. Use an internet search or GenAI to find studies, reports, or surveys about how often the incident occurs. Use this as a starting point, then adjust up or down based on your behavior and risk profile.

Decomposition Strategy

If you're having trouble estimating your maximum, break it down by incident type:

- **Theft**: How often in the next five years could your device be stolen?
- **Loss**: How often in the next five years could you misplace or lose your device?
- **Damage**: How often in the next five years could you break or damage your device?

Consider each separately, then combine for your total maximum range.

Working with Fractional Rates

Your maximum might not be a whole number. As covered in the previous chapter, you can express risk as

- Once every three years = 0.33 incidents per year
- Once every five years = 0.20 incidents per year
- Once every ten years = 0.10 incidents per year

Important: Your final range will likely be wider than the example in this chapter because you have less historical data to work with. With less information, you need to use broader ranges to maintain a 90% confidence level. This is perfectly normal and statistically appropriate. Don't try to force narrow ranges when your uncertainty is genuinely high.

Adding Monte Carlo Simulation

We have a good sense of our range, but we can refine our next 12-month forecast by incorporating our range into a Monte Carlo simulation using the data. Our ranges show us only the boundaries of incidents. Monte Carlo tells us what's actually *probable*. What are the *chances* of having two mobile device incidents next year? Ranges don't tell us that; Monte Carlo will.

Using the same concepts as the coin flipping example earlier in the chapter, we'll construct a Monte Carlo simulation with 10,000 trials (or in this case, 10,000 years since we're annualizing).

EXERCISE 5-3: SIMULATE YOUR MOBILE PHONE INCIDENTS

Go to `www.heatmapstohistograms.com` in the Tools & Downloads section and download the spreadsheet for Chapter 5, Exercise 5-3.

In the first tab, fill out the Lower Bound (P5), Typical (P50), and Upper Bound (P95) values you estimated from **Exercise 5-2**. The spreadsheet is set to run 10,000 trials, in other words, 10,000 phone years.

In the Summary section, notice the results.

- Expected events per year:
- Chance of at least one event:
- Probability of exactly one event:
- 95th percentile (events):

The expected events per year may include decimal point values in instances where the incident rate is less than once a year. This is a typical scenario and something we frequently encounter in cyber risk. Many events, such as data breaches, ransomware, and widespread outages, occur less than once a year (sometimes less than once every 10 or 20 years), so it's good to get accustomed to seeing this.

Based on my results, I've found some interesting data that goes beyond just the range. Here's what I found.

- I have a 45% chance of experiencing one or more incidents a year.
- However, I only have an 11% chance of experiencing two or more incidents per year.

Now we know how often incidents might occur, but that's only half the story. A single cracked screen costs very differently from a stolen phone, and frequency alone can't tell us our actual financial exposure. To make real decisions about insurance, protection, or budgeting, we need to combine our frequency estimates with the financial magnitude of each incident type.

UNDERSTANDING DISTRIBUTIONS

There's always uncertainty when we're looking at future events. A distribution is a way of capturing that uncertainty based on what we currently know. Instead of providing a single answer, a distribution captures the range of possibilities.

For example, when analyzing the potential number of phone incidents next year, we cannot provide a single number because we are uncertain about its range, which could be low, high, or somewhere in between. A distribution lets us capture that range.

This same principle applies to any uncertain future event, whether it's phone incidents, cyberattacks, or system outages. There are many distributions that can be used in forecasting and risk analysis. In this exercise, we will be using the triangular distribution, which may not capture all the complexities of real-world phenomena, but it's very simple, intuitive, and teaches the basics of distributions very nicely. Other exercises use different distributions.

Triangular and Beta-PERT distributions use three inputs: minimum, most likely, and maximum, where the middle value is the **mode**, or the peak of the curve. Percentile-based methods like P5–P50–P95 express uncertainty differently, focusing on your degree of belief rather than curve shape. In practice, your **P50** often ends up close to the "most likely" point in a triangular model, but the two aren't mathematically identical.

As you continue your journey in risk quantification, you will discover other distributions that work very well in risk analysis, such as beta, lognormal, Poisson, and others. Each of them has its pros and cons and can capture our uncertainty in different ways.

We're starting with the triangular distribution so that we can focus on the core concepts first. After you finish this book and decide to develop your own risk models, you will need to learn about other distributions. Or if you decide to use prepackaged software for risk quantification modeling (from a vendor, a Python library, or an Excel spreadsheet that someone else built), they will most likely have chosen the distribution for you.

It's useful to know the pros, cons, limitations, and strengths of each distribution so that you can defend your results.

Forecasting Magnitude

Now let's move to the magnitude side of the equation. With our example, I need to estimate the cost of such an incident. For simplicity, I'll assume we don't have an extended warranty and that breakage or loss is not covered by warranty, so we rely on insurance. However, the results of our risk assessment can be directly used to inform whether we *should* have those risk mitigations by telling us our *annualized risk exposure*, giving us valuable data for comparison.

I don't need to find the costs of actual replacements from back in 2020 and 2022, but finding those invoices would help with validation. I want to use today's dollars because we're forecasting the next year. This is where I list out probable costs of various replacements, shown in Table 5-3.

Table 5-3. *Cost research*

Item	Cost Range	Notes
Full cost of the latest iPhone Pro	~$1,000–$1200	Adjusting slightly upward for the forecast due to rumored price hikes
Full cost of a screen replacement on the latest iPhone Pro	$279–$379	Range based on model and store (Apple vs. aftermarket)

I'm going to use the following values for my distribution:

- **Lower bound (P5)**: $279—The minimum cost I could incur from any incident would be a broken screen repair.
- **Typical value (P50)**: $279—Setting this at the same value since screen damage is the most probable incident type.
- **Upper bound (P95)**: $1,200—Complete phone replacement in worst-case scenario.

EXERCISE 5-4: YOUR MOBILE DEVICE INCIDENT MAGNITUDE

Now, it's your turn to estimate the magnitude (cost) of a mobile phone incident. You'll research current costs and build your own triangular distribution for use in our upcoming Monte Carlo simulation.

Step 1: Research Current Costs

Use the internet to research replacement and repair costs for **your specific phone model**. Fill out the table below with current pricing:

Item	Your Cost Range	Your Notes
Full replacement cost for your phone model	$______–$______	Source: ________________
Screen replacement for your phone model	$______–$______	Source: ________________
Other common repairs (optional)	$______–$______	Type: __________________

Research Tips

- Check manufacturer websites (Apple, Samsung, Google, etc.).
- Look at authorized repair shops vs. third-party options.
- Consider both new and refurbished replacement costs.

Step 2: Define Your Distribution Parameters

Based on your research, determine your range of loss:

- **Lower bound (P5)**: $______
  - *What's the lowest cost incident you could realistically face?*
  - *Your reasoning:* ______________________________
- **Typical value (P50)**: $______
  - *What do you think is the most probable cost for a typical incident?*
  - *Your reasoning:* ______________________________
- **Upper bound (P95)**: $______
  - *What's the worst-case scenario cost?*
  - *Your reasoning:* ______________________________

Step 3: Validate Your Logic

Check Your Distribution Shape

- Is your "typical" value between your lower bound and upper?
- Does the spread make sense for your phone and usage patterns?
- Have you considered your most common risk scenarios?

Consider These Factors

- How do you typically use your phone? (office work, outdoor activities, etc.)
- What incidents have you or people you know experienced?
- Do you use a protective case? Screen protector?
- What's your historical pattern of phone incidents?

Save your estimates! In the next exercise, we'll combine your magnitude data with frequency estimates to run your first complete quantitative risk assessment using Monte Carlo simulation.

Now, let's put frequency and magnitude from Exercise 5-4 together and find out what our risk exposure is.

EXERCISE 5-5: QUANTITATIVE RISK ANALYSIS ON MOBILE PHONE RISK

Go to `www.heatmapstohistograms.com` in the Tools & Downloads section and download the spreadsheet for Chapter 5, Exercise 5-5.

In the first tab, fill out the Lower Bound, Typical, and Upper Bound values for the frequency you estimated from **Exercise 5-2**. Next, fill out the Lower Bound, Typical, and Upper Bound values you estimated for **Exercise 5-4**.

The quantitative risk analysis will automatically run, providing results in multiple formats.

Congratulations, Your First Quantitative Risk Analysis!

You did it! That is a true, end-to-end, quantitative risk analysis! We used the data that we had, embraced and measured our uncertainty about future events, and estimated the frequency and magnitude of future events.

What Do All These Numbers Mean?

Your Monte Carlo simulation generated thousands of possible annual loss scenarios. The spreadsheet shows you various statistics: mean, median, minimum, maximum, and percentiles. But which one represents your "annualized loss exposure"? And what if someone just wants to know the cost per incident without frequency?

That's where experts disagree and where different business needs require different answers. Different authorities, from NIST to FAIR to insurance companies, emphasize different statistics for different purposes. We'll explore exactly what each number means and when to use which one in Chapter 6, where we learn to communicate quantitative risk effectively.

Two Key Concepts to Remember

- **Magnitude (FAIR calls this "Loss Magnitude"):** The potential impact per incident (what business continuity teams often need for scenario planning)
- **Annualized loss exposure (FAIR terminology):** The annualized potential impact, including frequency (what risk teams need for budgeting)

A Note on Terminology: Why We Use FAIR Language

You'll notice we use "magnitude" and "annualized loss exposure" rather than the traditional terms from CISSP, NIST, and other frameworks. This is a deliberate choice rooted in intellectual honesty about uncertainty.

Traditional frameworks use "single loss expectancy" and "annualized loss expectancy" language that implies false precision and prediction. When someone hears "expectancy," they naturally think "this is what will happen." But that's not how probability works. We can't predict exactly what will occur; we can only quantify our exposure to uncertainty. The term "expected" actually means the average of all possible outcomes, weighted by their likelihood, not what we personally think will happen. We can't predict exactly what will occur; we can only describe how uncertain we are about it.

The FAIR standard advanced risk terminology significantly by adopting actuarial language that better reflects reality. Actuaries don't pretend to predict the future; they quantify exposure to uncertain financial outcomes. FAIR's "Loss Magnitude" captures the range of possible costs per incident. "Annualized loss exposure" acknowledges that you're carrying the financial burden of uncertainty over time, not receiving a prediction of specific losses.

Even if you never adopt the FAIR methodology fully, its terminology represents a fundamental improvement in how we think and communicate about risk. It moves us away from the false precision that has plagued risk management for decades, toward an honest acknowledgment of what we actually know and what we don't know.

This isn't just semantic preference; it's about building credibility with stakeholders who understand that the future is uncertain and who respect analyses that admit uncertainty rather than pretending it away.

ALE VS. ALE VS. ALE

Be careful when discussing ALE in risk conversations. People use the same acronym to mean three different things:

Annualized loss expectancy: A single point number representing expected annual loss. This is the traditional approach, but it doesn't capture uncertainty.

Annualized loss exposure: Actuarial thinking that represents your annual risk as a distribution or range of possible outcomes. This is what your Monte Carlo simulation produces.

Average loss expectancy: Some people use ALE to refer to the average (mean) value from their risk calculations.

When someone mentions ALE, clarify which version they are referring to. Are they looking for a single number for budgeting, a range for scenario planning, or the mathematical average from your analysis?

Pro tip: In conversations, I just say "loss exposure" and drop the "A." Everyone knows we're talking about annual timeframes, which avoids confusion entirely while making it clear that I'm thinking in terms of ranges, not single numbers.

From Numbers to Decisions

Now that I've run a risk analysis, I can see the median of my annual exposure is around $465, with potential bad years reaching $3,300. This raises practical questions: Should I invest in a better phone case, buy AppleCare, or get additional insurance? These are exactly the types of decisions that quantitative risk analysis enables and concepts we'll cover in later chapters as we explore risk treatment and decision-making.

For now, look at your own exposure numbers and think about what they mean for your personal risk profile. More importantly, take a moment and celebrate having completed your first quantitative risk assessment. You've transformed uncertainty into measurable exposure using the most honest language available to express what that means. This is the foundation of every risk decision you'll make going forward.

KEEP DOING PERSONAL RISK ASSESSMENTS

These are real quantitative risk assessments. The methodology you just used is identical to what Fortune 500 companies pay consultants to perform. The only difference is scale, not technique.

The bulk of the risk assessments you'll perform as a learner will be risks in your personal life. Don't dismiss these as "practice." They're legitimate CRQ that improve real decisions and build genuine expertise. I maintain several personal risk assessments that help me evaluate decisions for myself and my family.

Start Building Your Portfolio

- **Car accident risk**: Should you add extra auto insurance coverage?
- **Home burglary**: Should you invest in a security system or upgraded locks?

- **Emergency medical costs**: Should you build a larger emergency fund for medical expenses?
- **Travel risk**: Should you buy travel insurance?
- **Identity theft/credit card fraud**: Is credit monitoring worth paying for?

Every assessment makes you better at data collection, uncertainty modeling, and decision frameworks. This is how CRQ expertise is built: through repeated application to real problems with real stakes.

Chapter Summary

The Big Idea: Monte Carlo simulation transforms uncertainty from an obstacle into a structured analytical tool, allowing you to forecast the frequency and magnitude of future events using historical data, expert judgment, and probabilistic modeling.

Key Takeaways

- **Monte Carlo is just sophisticated coin flipping applied to risk**. The same randomness principles that govern casino games can model complex business uncertainties, turning "we don't know" into "here's what could happen with these probabilities."
- **Historical data informs but doesn't dictate future estimates**. Your personal phone incident analysis showed how to adjust forecasts based on changed threat models, demonstrating that quantitative risk requires human judgment, not just mathematical calculation.
- **Frequency and magnitude together create true risk exposure**. Knowing how often incidents happen means nothing without knowing their financial impact, and cost estimates mean nothing without understanding likelihood.
- **Personal risk assessments are legitimate quantitative analyses**. The methodology you used for mobile phone risk is identical to Fortune 500 consulting engagements, proving that CRQ skills develop through practice on real problems with real stakes.

Bottom Line: You've completed a genuine quantitative risk analysis using professional methods. The numbers you generated represent actual risk exposure that can inform real decisions about insurance, protection, and risk acceptance.

What's Coming Next

You've built your first complete quantitative risk assessment with real probability ranges and loss exposure estimates. Now you need to turn those Monte Carlo results into clear, actionable insights that drive decisions.

Chapter 6 teaches you to interpret and communicate quantitative risk effectively, transforming simulation output into compelling analysis that stakeholders can understand and act upon by showing you how to read distributions, explain uncertainty to executives, and use quantitative results to evaluate risk treatment options while learning communication techniques that build confidence rather than confusion in your analysis.

Reference

Dunn, W. L., & Shultis, J. K. (2011). *Exploring Monte Carlo methods* [E-book]. Elsevier Science.

CHAPTER 6

Interpreting and Communicating Quantitative Risk Results

> *It is better to be roughly right than precisely wrong.*
>
> —John Maynard Keynes

As you advance in quantitative risk, you'll discover something surprising: the most challenging part isn't the technical stuff. It's not dealing with imperfect data, learning Monte Carlo methods, expensive tools, or finding subject matter experts. The real challenge is translating your analysis into decisions that everyone, from executives to engineers, will make.

The reason is simple: everybody processes and interprets data differently. Some people prefer graphs. Some people like numbers and probabilities. Other people like stories. Some people are a blend of the above. Others struggle with data, regardless of how it is presented. Some will be easy to reach, others will nod in agreement as if they fully understand, but they won't get it. Others will completely get it, and you'll think your job is done.

Risk communication will be the single hardest thing for you to master in quantitative risk. After years of presenting risk results to different audiences, I've learned one big lesson: your best chance of success is learning how to communicate like an actuary.

The original sin of traditional risk frameworks isn't just that they ignore uncertainty. It's that they've trained executives to expect false certainty. When you walk into a boardroom and say, "There's a 15–40% chance of this happening," you're asking them to think differently than every risk presentation they've ever seen.

T. Martin-Vegue, *From Heatmaps to Histograms*, https://doi.org/10.1007/979-8-8688-2300-8_6

Actuaries have mastered this communication challenge. They don't hide uncertainty behind colors. They make uncertainty useful for decisions. Instead of "high risk," they say "there's a 10% chance we'll exceed $5M in losses this year, and here's what that means for our insurance strategy."

The key is showing executives that uncertainty doesn't mean ignorance or a lack of information. It exists because of many possible outcomes. It's actionable information. Your job isn't to give them certainty they can't have. It's to reveal the degree of uncertainty they actually face.

You won't learn this communication approach from information security books. Look to how actuaries present to insurance executives, how epidemiologists brief health officials, how economists advise policymakers. They've solved the communication puzzle you're struggling with.

Show Your Work: Turning Numbers into Narratives

In this chapter, we will learn how to present our work and transform numbers into narratives. There's not one way to communicate the results of a quantitative risk assessment; there are many ways, many graphics, and many different approaches to slice and dice the data.

You will discover that you need to tailor and customize your risk communication style to

- Different audiences who consume data in different ways
- The specific decision at hand, which requires different types of communication
- The nature of the risk itself, since different types of risks present differently in the results

Throughout this chapter, we will use the results from our example of a lost or damaged mobile phone from the previous chapter, paired with cyber risk examples, to illustrate how different types of risks present themselves differently in the results. Refer back to this chapter frequently as you progress through the book, as it will serve as your primary reference guide for risk communication techniques.

The Shape of Risk

Understanding the shape of risk means understanding how losses are distributed. An evenly distributed risk is like a set of dice throws that you record or simulate. With enough dice throws, you see that the outcomes are evenly distributed, which basically means that there will be about the same number of ones as twos as threes, and so on.

Risk is seldom evenly distributed. Most cyber incidents are small and frequent, but every decade or so, you get hit with something massive. Take data breaches: most organizations I work with see minor data leakage incidents every few months that don't trigger legal reporting requirements, but every 10–20 years, they face a significant breach that makes headlines and incurs millions of dollars in costs.

This uneven pattern is what's called the *shape of risk*, also known as a distribution. Picture a scale from zero to company-ending loss. Most incidents cluster on the left side with small, manageable costs, while a few sit way out on the right with catastrophic impact. Understanding this distribution changes how you communicate risk. Instead of saying "data breach risk is medium," you can say "we expect two to three minor incidents per year costing under $50K each, with about a 5% annual chance of a major breach costing $5–15M." That's the difference between describing risk as a category vs. describing it as a distribution.

Understanding the shape of risk is crucial for effective communication, as stakeholders need to see the whole picture, not just an average or a single number. When you tell executives "the average cost is $500K," they're missing the story of whether that's because most incidents cost $500K or because you have many $50K incidents and occasional $5M disasters. The shape tells the real story.

Now let's look at specific tools to measure and describe this shape.

The Five-Number Summary

The five-number summary is a great way to visualize the shape of risk instantly. We're starting with the five-number summary because it's a common approach. So common, in fact, that you may remember it from a statistics or math textbook. It provides a rapid overview of a distribution by fitting it into five categories:

1. **Minimum**: The lowest value in a distribution.
2. **First quartile**: 25% of values fall below this point.

3. **Median**: The midway point; 50% of values fall below this point.
4. **Third quartile:** 75% of values fall below this point.
5. **Maximum**: The highest value in the distribution.

WHAT ARE QUARTILES AND PERCENTILES?

Quartiles split a dataset into four equal groups. The first quartile means 25% of values fall below this point, the second quartile (median) means 50% fall below, and the third quartile means 75% fall below. Percentiles work similarly but can be any percentage; the 90th percentile means that 90% of values are lower. For example, when a child is young, a doctor might say the child's height is at the 90th percentile, which means that 90% of children of the same age are shorter.

Let's see this in action. When you run a Monte Carlo simulation, you get thousands of possible outcomes. To make sense of all that data, we'll summarize it in Table 6-1 using a five-number summary based on the mobile phone incident example from the previous chapter.

Table 6-1. *Five-number summary for the mobile phone incident risk*

Minimum	First Quartile	Median	Third Quartile	Maximum
$0	$206	$466	$857	$2974

Based on these results, I can make quite a few informed decisions. Rounding the values, which is something I always do to avoid the illusion of precision, the median loss exposure I'm facing is about $500 a year, with worse-case scenarios approaching $900 of annual loss exposure. In a bad year, I'm exposed to $3,000 of loss.

WHAT DOES IT MEAN TO BE EXPOSED TO RISK?

This is a new concept to a lot of people. In my experience working with security teams, your CISO will struggle, but your CFO and CEO will get it immediately. That's because when we talk about *loss exposure*, we're speaking the *language of business*.

Loss exposure is basically how much potential financial loss you're carrying year over year (because everything is annualized). Think of it like your annual "loss budget," the range of financial impact you need to be prepared for, even though you might not experience it every year.

A good parallel is how insurance operates. Let me oversimplify this example to demonstrate: Think of ten homes on the coast. All ten homes are in a hurricane-prone area. Each home is worth $1 million, and each home has $1 million in insurance coverage.

The insurance company would say they have $10 million in loss exposure year over year. Most years, there's no hurricane. Some years, there's one hurricane with minimal damage, say $300K. But it's possible, and it has happened, where a catastrophic storm hits and all ten homes are complete losses.

Every year, the insurance company would say they have $10 million in loss exposure, even if nothing happens or the worst happens.

It's the same concept with mobile phone risk. Based on our analysis, I have between $500 and $3,000 of annual loss exposure.

What This Does NOT Mean

- I lost that much in previous incidents.
- I'm losing that much this year.
- I will lose that much next year.

What This DOES Mean

- This is my potential annual loss range for planning purposes.
- In a typical year, I should plan for around $500 in losses (the median).
- I need to be financially prepared for up to $3,000 in a bad year.
- This helps me make informed decisions about mitigation and transfer.

How I use this for planning: I'll mitigate the median exposure by investing in a better phone case and changing some habits to manage that $500 range. For the outlier exposure ($3,000), it happens so infrequently that it's not worth directly managing. I'll transfer it via phone insurance and make sure I can cover any remaining gap with cash reserves.

That's what loss exposure means: **your annual loss-carrying capacity that helps you make smart mitigation and transfer decisions.**

Let's look at a cyber example. In Table 6-2, I've estimated a five-number summary of a data breach scenario for a large, US-based bank based on industry research.

Table 6-2. *Five-number summary for a large US-based bank*

Minimum	First Quartile	Median	Third Quartile	Maximum
$200,000	$300,000	$2,200,000	$16,000,000	$270,000,000

What do you observe about this distribution of risk for data breaches? Does the spread look different than the cell phone incident? Are the losses distributed differently?

Notice how different these two distributions look. The mobile phone losses are relatively *evenly distributed*; the gap between the median ($466) and maximum ($2,974) is reasonable, and you can see a gradual progression through the quartiles.

The data breach distribution tells a completely different story. There's a massive jump between the third quartile ($16M) and the maximum ($270M)—a 17× increase. This is the "heavy tail" or "fat tail" distribution that's common in cybersecurity, where most incidents are manageable, but the worst-case scenarios can be catastrophic.

This difference in distribution shape fundamentally changes how we communicate and manage these risks. The mobile phone risk is predictable; the data breach risk has extreme uncertainty in the tail. We'll explore why cyber risks behave this way and what it means for your analysis later in this chapter.

For now, the key insight is that the five-number summary instantly reveals whether you're dealing with a "normal" risk distribution or one of these challenging cyber risk patterns. Most importantly for risk communication, it gives stakeholders an instant view of the shape of risk, which is a great conversation starter on how to respond.

For executive communication, you might prefer showing the 10th and 95th percentiles as "best case" and "worst case" instead of minimum and maximum, but the five-number summary captures the same insights about distribution shape.

WHY YOUR NUMBERS CHANGE EACH TIME

If you've run your Monte Carlo simulation multiple times, you've probably noticed that your results change slightly with each run. This is completely normal and expected.

Monte Carlo simulations use random sampling, so each run draws a slightly different set of scenarios. Think of it like polling—survey 1,000 different people and you'll get similar but not identical results.

Focus on patterns, not precision: If your median bounces between $450K and $480K, your insight is "typical losses around $450–480K," not exactly $463K. Round your numbers for presentations and emphasize the story your distribution tells rather than precise values that will vary slightly each time.

This is the "less wrong" mindset from Chapter 4 in action.

A Quick Word on Average, Mode, and Median

You'll encounter these terms constantly in risk data and executive conversations, so it's worth clarifying what people usually mean.

- **Mean (average):** Most people use this term to mean "mean" (sum divided by count), but it can be misleading when applied to cyber risks. That $12M "average" data breach cost includes some massive outliers that skew the number upward. The median value of $2.2M is often more helpful for planning.

  There are two ways people talk about averages in risk:

  One includes *every year*, even those with no incidents. That's your **expected annual loss**, what you'd plan for across time.

  The other includes *only the years when something actually happened.* That shows the **typical cost per event** when a loss occurs.

- **Mode (most likely):** The value that occurs most often. With some cyber risks, this is usually the smallest number in your range because most incidents are minor, with a few extremely large outliers. It's helpful for describing typical day-to-day experience, but it doesn't help with budgeting for the big ones.

- **Median (P50, sometimes called "typical")**: The 50th percentile; half of all outcomes fall below it, half above. The median is useful for describing a "typical" year or event, especially when the data is skewed by a few large outliers.

For Risk Communication: When someone says, "What's the average cost?" clarify whether they want the mathematical mean (for insurance/budgeting) or the typical case (median). Both are valid, but they tell very different stories about the same risk.

AVERAGE VS. CENTRAL TENDENCY

Earlier in Chapter 4, we explored how ranges and percentiles express uncertainty. This sidebar shows how those ideas carry through into interpreting results.

Central tendency refers to a single number that represents the "middle" or "typical" value in a distribution. Be careful when using the word "average" in risk communication. Most people associate "average" with "mean," but some statistics textbooks still teach that "average" refers to central tendency broadly, which includes mean, median, and mode.

As a distribution becomes more skewed, these three numbers drift apart:

- **Mode**: The most common value; what happens most often.
- **Median**: The middle value; half the outcomes are higher, half are lower.
- **Mean**: The balancing point; the probability-weighted center of all outcomes.

To avoid confusion, specify which measure you're using rather than simply stating "average." Say "the mean is $500K" or "the median outcome is $300K" instead of "the average loss is...." This ensures everyone understands exactly what number you're referencing.

The five-number summary captures all of this without the confusion of terminology, which is why we start there.

GENAI PROMPT: RISK DISTRIBUTION SNAPSHOT

[From the Quant Risk Analysis worksheet that contained your mobile phone risk analysis, copy the raw Monte Carlo simulation data (Sim tab, Expected events/year (λ) column) results into a CSV or Excel file and upload into the prompt]

Attached is a dataset of simulated loss values from a Monte Carlo risk model. Analyze it and return results in two clearly separated sections:

Section 1: Five-Number Summary

- Minimum
- Q1 (25th percentile)
- Median (Q2, 50th percentile)
- Q3 (75th percentile)
- Maximum

Section 2: Central Tendencies

- Mean
- Median (repeat for comparison)
- Mode

Output the results in a clean, labeled table format, with each section clearly separated. Provide a short interpretation of what the numbers imply about risk outcomes (e.g., 'half of the simulated losses are below X').

When Risk Distributions Behave Strangely

Cyber risks often create unusual distributions that can confuse stakeholders if you're not prepared. Here are two common patterns you'll encounter:

Some cyber events create distributions where the minimum, first quartile, median, and third quartile are all zero, but the maximum jumps to a massive, outsized amount. This represents extremely low-frequency, high-impact events: most of the time, nothing happens, but when it does, it could be existential for the company. To communicate this clearly, it helps to show both the event loss distribution (the range of outcomes for a single incident) and the annual loss distribution (how those events add up across a year). The aggregate view makes it clear that even if most years see no events, the rare ones can drive devastating losses.

The communication trap here is obvious: if you report the median, it's zero. Stakeholders will say, "Well, if the typical is nothing, why should we invest in controls?" This is exactly when you need the five-number summary and percentiles to show that while most scenarios are benign, the tail risk could be catastrophic.

At the other extreme, very large companies might see several phishing attempts daily, multiple malware detections, or constant credential stuffing attempts. Each incident incurs a small cost, but the frequency makes the cumulative impact substantial. Here, the mean might be more useful than the median for showing the true cumulative cost of these constant small incidents.

Understanding these distribution patterns prepares you for the visualization techniques in the next section, where you'll learn to present these complex distributions in ways that stakeholders can understand and act upon.

EXERCISE 6-1: BUILD YOUR STATISTICAL RISK SUMMARY

Find the statistical summaries on the Monte Carlo simulation from your mobile phone Excel in the spreadsheet. Alternatively, you can use GenAI prompts to create new summaries.

Your Tasks

- Read and interpret the statistical summaries.
- Write a 30-second explanation of this risk using a few key numbers.
- Draft an answer to "How bad could this get?" using your statistical results.
- Identify which measure best represents the typical cost.
- Check for anomalies: Does your distribution show heavy tails or other unusual patterns?

This exercise prepares you to interpret and communicate risk results to stakeholders in a confident manner.

Key Visualizations That Matter

There are two visualizations I want to demonstrate that are often used to communicate quantitative risk results. Often, they are paired with the summary statistics shown in the previous sections. There are many other visualizations available, such as a tornado diagram, a ridgeline plot, and a box plot; however, the histogram and the loss exceedance curve are the most common in cyber risk analysis. I encourage you to experiment with these and others to find the best that works for you and the people you are communicating with.

Histogram: The Shape of Risk

The histogram illustrates the shape of risk, as shown in Figure 6-1. In quantitative risk analysis, a histogram groups Monte Carlo simulation results into bins and displays them as a bar chart. The x axis shows loss amounts, and the y axis shows how frequently simulated results landed in each loss range.

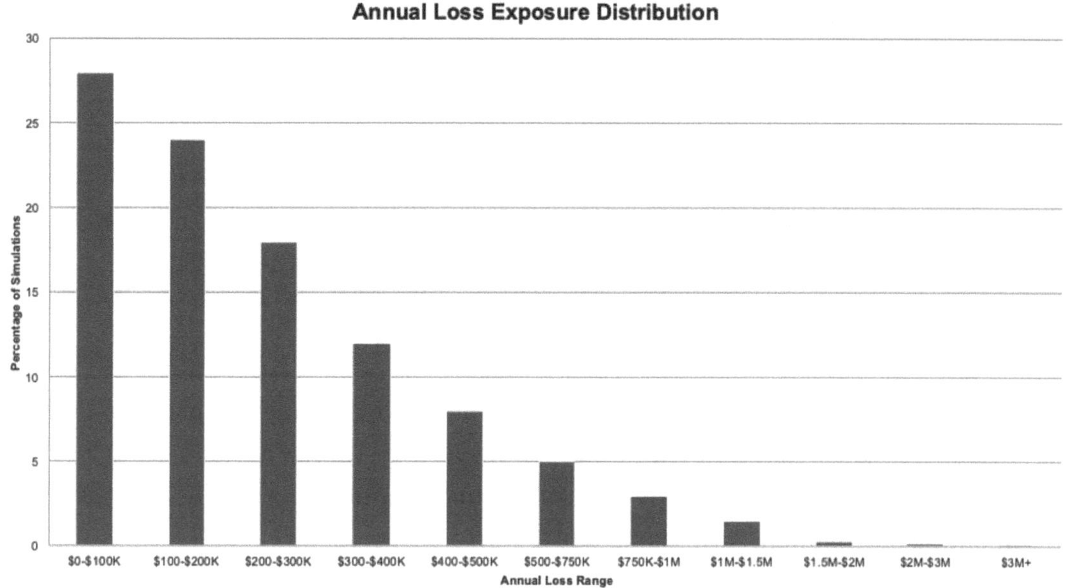

Figure 6-1. *Monte Carlo simulation results graphed on a histogram*

How to Read and Communicate Histograms: Focus on the shape: Where do most losses cluster? How wide is the spread? Are there outlier "tail events"? When communicating, emphasize that this shows the range of financial impacts *if* the risk occurs, not the probability of occurrence itself. For executives, lead with business impact: "Most scenarios cluster around $X, but we need to prepare for outliers up to $Y." The key insight is in the distribution shape. A narrow peak means predictable losses, while a wide spread or long tail indicates high uncertainty requiring different planning strategies.

Benefits

- Shows the complete risk profile at a glance, clearly highlighting both typical outcomes and extreme scenarios
- Familiar format that stakeholders can easily interpret

Key Consideration: The most common mistake is misinterpreting the y axis. It shows how often different loss amounts occurred in your simulation, not the probability of an incident happening. Think of each bar as showing "if something bad happens, here's how bad it's likely to be."

Loss Exceedance Curve, a.k.a. the "What Are the Chances?" Chart

This is my favorite visualization, and I call it the "what are the chances" chart. This might be the most important visualization for executives, but it's also the one that confuses people the most. It would be a wise time investment for all risk managers to learn this visualization inside and out and learn how to narrate it to executives in real time.

Why This Chart Is Difficult (and Why That's OK)

In my experience, people in information security often don't recognize this chart and say they dislike it because they don't know how to interpret it. There's a good reason for this: security professionals think in terms of "Will an attack happen?" while this chart answers "If something bad happens, how bad could it get?"

Step outside of the information security field, though, and people start to recognize this chart immediately. Finance teams encounter this type of graphic in insurance models, executives face it in business forecasting, and anyone who has looked at weather predictions has seen similar probability curves. It is known as a loss curve, an exceedance probability graph, a cumulative distribution function (CDF), and various other terms in other fields.

The Power of This Visualization

This chart answers the question executives care about: "What are the odds we'll lose more than $35 million?" shown in Figure 6-2. It's the same thinking insurance companies use to set premiums and the same logic the C-suite uses for scenario planning. Figure 6-2 is an example of a loss exceedance curve that one might show to executives.

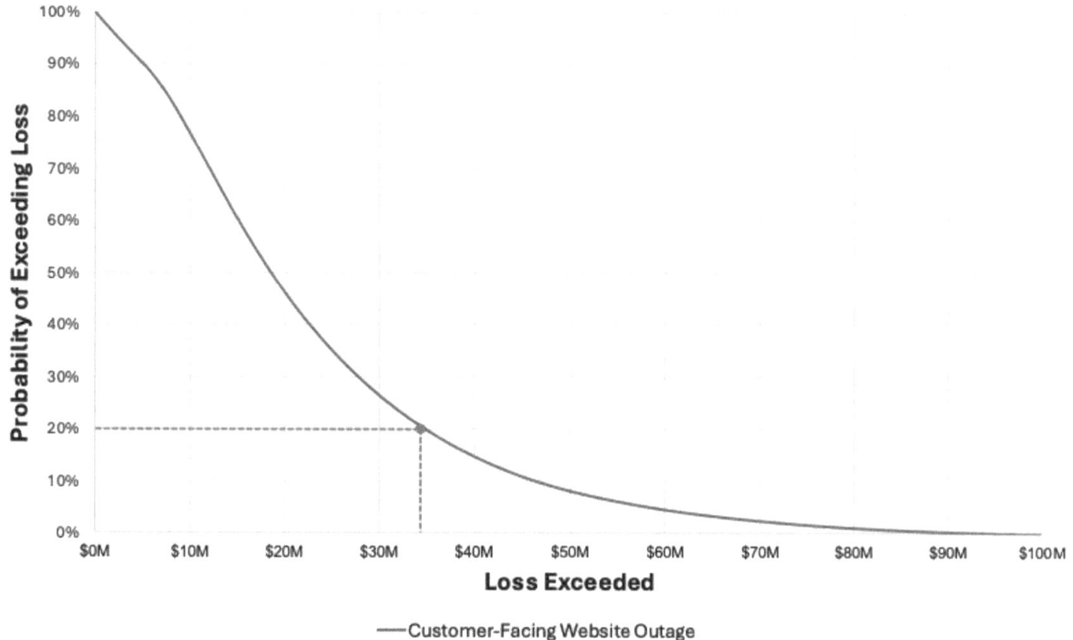

Figure 6-2. *An exec-ready loss exceedance curve showing a ~20% chance of losses exceeding $35 million or more*

How to Read It

- The y axis shows probabilities (0% to 100%).
- The x axis shows dollar amounts.
- The curve shows the chances of losses exceeding any given dollar amount.

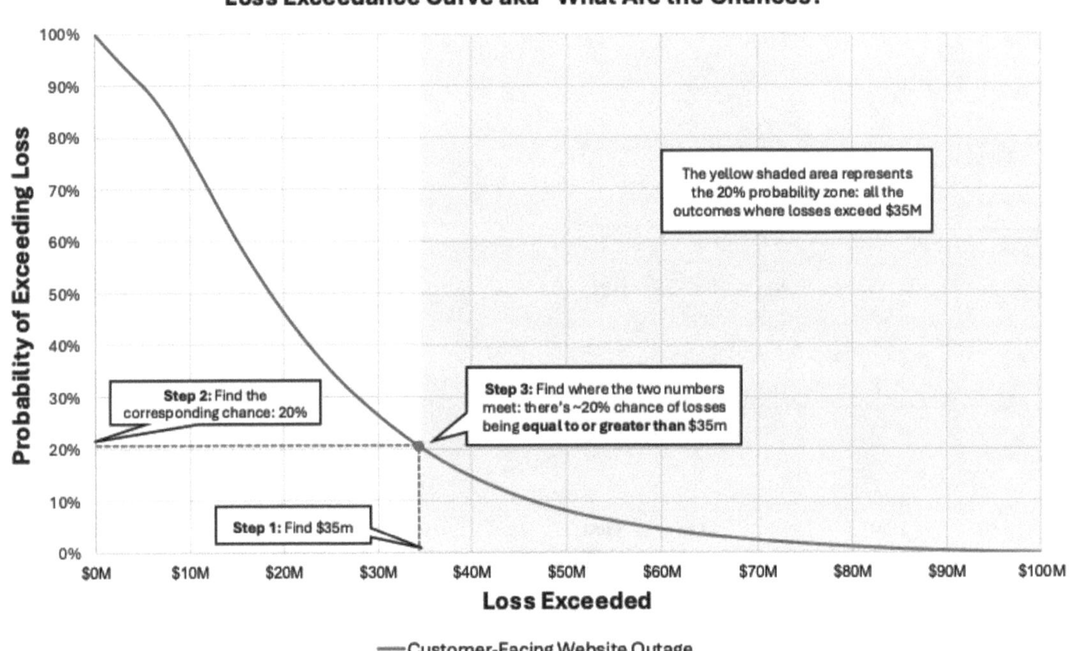

Figure 6-3. *How to read a loss exceedance curve*

Detailed Walkthrough: Follow Along on Figure 6-3

Step 1: Find your dollar amount of interest on the x axis (e.g., $35M).

Step 2: Move straight up from that point until you hit the curve.

Step 3: Move horizontally left to read the probability on the y axis (e.g., 20%).

Interpretation: "There's a 20% chance that losses will exceed $35 million."

Visual Helper: The yellow-shaded area in Figure 6-3 represents the 20% probability zone, which encompasses all outcomes where losses exceed $35M. The larger this shaded area, the higher the probability of exceeding that loss amount.

Common Pitfall: Don't confuse the y axis with the frequency of incidents. The curve shows "if an incident happens, what's the chance losses exceed X amount?", not "how often do incidents occur?" The incident frequency is already baked into your annual loss exposure calculation.

Anchoring a Loss Exceedance Curve to Real Decisions

When presenting a loss exceedance curve (LEC), avoid arbitrary dollar markers. Instead, connect the curve to thresholds that matter to your stakeholders:

- **Risk tolerance:** Ask your board or CFO, "What's the maximum loss we can absorb before it threatens operations?" Use that number as your anchor point.
- **Cyber insurance limit:** Losses beyond the policy limit are uninsured, and the organization bears the full impact. Remember that exclusions and sub-limits (e.g., ransomware or regulatory fines) may reduce the effective coverage.
- **Budget thresholds:** Compare losses to contingency or emergency reserves. If there's a 60% chance of exceeding reserves, planning needs attention.
- **SEC materiality:** For US-based public companies, ask legal, "At what loss level would disclosure likely be required?" There's no fixed dollar rule. Materiality depends on context, but establishing a working threshold makes the curve actionable.
- **Project costs:** Compare loss probabilities to security investments; if there's a 40% chance of losses exceeding a $3M project's cost, the investment looks justified.

Each of these anchors transforms the curve from a probability graph into a decision-making tool.

Creating Loss Exceedance Statements

I always accompany the curve with narrative statements that serve as a voiceover for people who have trouble reading charts:

- "There is a 20% chance that losses will exceed $2 million."
- "We have a 50/50 chance of losses exceeding $500,000."
- "There's only a 5% chance we'd see losses above $8 million."

Start your executive presentation with the loss exceedance statement, then show the curve. This primes their understanding before they see the visual.

GENAI PROMPT: CREATE A HISTOGRAM AND A LOSS EXCEEDANCE CURVE

[From the Quant Risk Analysis worksheet that contained your mobile phone risk analysis, copy the raw Monte Carlo simulation data (Sim tab, Annualized Loss column) results into a CSV or Excel file and upload into the prompt]

Attached is a dataset of simulated loss values from a Monte Carlo risk model.

Create and display:

- A histogram of the loss distribution with appropriate binning, labeled axes, and rounded tick marks.
- A Loss Exceedance Curve (LEC) where the x-axis is loss amount (USD) and the y-axis is exceedance probability (%).
- Generate five clear loss exceedance statements in plain language. Each should follow the format: "There is a X% probability that losses will exceed $Y."
- Choose meaningful thresholds (e.g., 10th, 25th, 50th, 75th, 90th percentiles, or round-number thresholds).

Format all monetary values in millions of USD. Provide a short interpretation of the results: what the histogram shows, what the LEC shows, and how the exceedance statements can be used in decision-making.

Make sure all charts are professional and publication-ready.

The Risk Heatmap: When You Have No Choice

There's an uncomfortable truth that all security risk analysts must live with: the risk matrix or risk heatmap is the *de facto language of risk* in our field. The risk communication methods shown earlier in this chapter are preferable, of course, but there will be times when you are expected to communicate risk via a heatmap.

As the old adage goes, *if you can't beat 'em, join 'em*. Let's make the heatmap better.

First, some grounding. There are two names for the visualization in Figure 6-4:

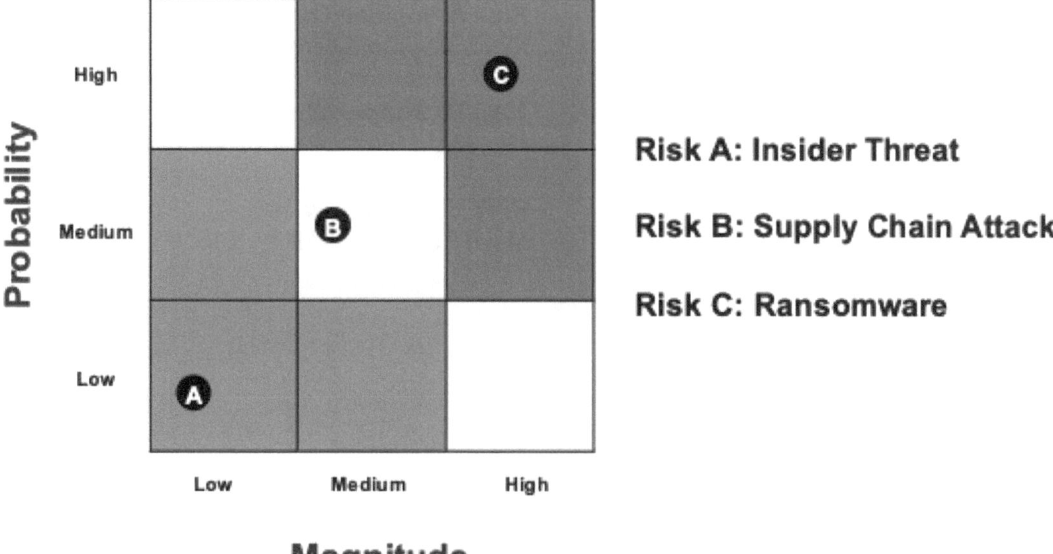

Figure 6-4. *A traditional risk matrix: standard 3×3 grid showing a typical qualitative approach*

The Risk Matrix: This is a *model for assessing risk.* You pick an adjective for impact, pick an adjective for likelihood, and where the two meet on the grid, that's your risk.

The Heatmap: This is a *risk communication tool,* not a model. Risk has already been assessed, and the results are plotted on a heatmap.

We covered the problems with qualitative methodologies and the risk matrix in Chapter 2, but specifically, when it comes to risk communication, the main issues are the following:

- We're not articulating uncertainty.
- We're losing the shape of risk.
- It's too simple. Reducing it down to a single color or point on a grid loses too much information.

Making the Heatmap Better

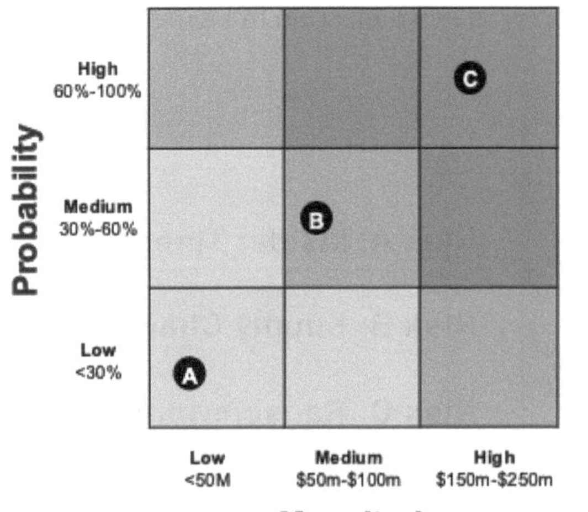

Risk A: Insider Threat
Min $2M | Most Likely $10M | Max $50M

Risk B: Supply Chain Attack
Min $5M | Most Likely $70M | Max $75M

Risk C: Ransomware
Min $1.5M | Most Likely $150M | Max $200M

Figure 6-5. *A quantitatively anchored heatmap*

See the heatmap in Figure 6-5. You'll notice a few changes I've made to encourage people to think quantitatively. If you can implement one or more of these tips, you'll be communicating risk better than the traditional approach shown in Figure 6-4. Here are the key changes I made:

- **Quantitative bins:** Both axes are divided into equal-sized quantitative bins. The y axis uses probability percentages (0–100%) instead of vague frequency categories, and the x axis is scaled by the cost of a single loss.
- **Distribution in the legend:** The heatmap shows where the Most Likely value sits, while the legend shows the full distribution of each risk.
- **Neutral color scheme:** Instead of using red/yellow/green, I'm using shades of blue. This reduces the emotional bias that comes with traditional traffic light colors and forces attention to the legend and actual numbers rather than gut reactions to red/green.
- **Outer bounds anchored in risk capacity:** In my example, $250M represents my fictitious organization's risk capacity. Anything above this amount exceeds the organization's ability to absorb the cost.

Here are additional improvements you can try, not shown in Figure 6-5:

- **Whiskers:** Plot each dot at the median (P50) and add whiskers (like error bars) that extend to the 10th and 90th percentiles or even the 5th and 95th. This helps show uncertainty ranges directly, rather than compressing everything into bins.
- **Scatter view:** Instead of a binned heatmap, you can plot each scenario as a point on a scatter chart, with *frequency or probability* on the y axis and *impact* on the x axis (log scale). Each point can include whiskers to show the range of possible impacts.
- **Iso-value lines:** Add light diagonal "equal loss" lines showing combinations of frequency and impact that produce the same expected loss (e.g., $100K, $1M, $10M). These lines make it easier to compare which risks drive more total exposure.
- **Multiple markers:** If you're plotting only one risk, use three marks: most likely, 10th percentile, and 90th percentile. Use different symbols with a clear legend.
- **Bubble size:** Use bubbles to visualize the range size, letting them span multiple grid boxes. This approach requires careful explanation to avoid confusion, but it can convey uncertainty when properly narrated.
- **White background**: Remove all colors from the grid to further reduce biasing effects.

⚠ RISK PLACEMENT

Risk is a distribution, not a single point. When we plot it on this type of chart, we're forcing it into a visualization that wasn't designed for quantitative risk. You'll need to decide which point on the distribution to use: median, mean, or an outlier such as the 95th percentile. Whatever you choose, be consistent and transparent about your method.

Putting It All Together

A few years back, I was doing my quarterly technology risk update for the C-suite at a large US-based company where I'd built the quantitative risk team. I'd run Monte Carlo simulations on several major technology risks and had loss exceedance curves ready to show the results.

The CISO warned me beforehand: "The C-suite doesn't like numbers. They won't receive it well." I planned to keep the narrative heavy and reserve the quantitative analysis for backup.

I walked in and began discussing some existential risks we were facing, focusing on stories and qualitative descriptions. Five minutes in, the CFO interrupted: "If this is the result of a Monte Carlo simulation, do you have an exceedance probability curve?"

I glanced over at the CISO, the one who told me the C-suite doesn't like numbers.

I threw up the loss exceedance curve, and the entire room lit up. We spent the next 30 minutes having the best risk conversation I've ever had with executives. We discussed investment trade-offs, opportunity costs, insurance levels, tail risk, and everything in between.

What I Learned About Executive Risk Communication

Don't assume executives can't handle numbers. They deal with financial uncertainty every day. The problem isn't the math; it's usually how we present it.

Always have your loss exceedance curve ready. Even if you plan to go narrative-first, executives who understand business risk will often want to see the shape of uncertainty.

Let them drive the conversation. Once you show the curve, executives often ask exactly the questions you hoped they would about probability, impact, and decision options.

Trust your analysis. If you've done the work right, the quantitative story is usually more compelling than the qualitative version.

Presentation Tips

- **Lead with the key insight in titles**: "20% Chance of $2M+ Loss" puts the decision-relevant information first.

- **Round to avoid the appearance of false precision**: "$1.7–3.2M" becomes "$2–3M" for executive discussions.
- **Always present both the typical loss and the outliers (e.g., 90th or 95th percentile**). They spark different, but equally important, conversations. You may decide to address the typical loss directly while transferring risk from the outlier or ensuring cash reserves to withstand it.
- **Include a brief data source note:** "Based on industry benchmarks and expert estimates" or "Derived from internal incident data and external studies".

Know your audience: Every organization is unique, and its organizational culture varies significantly. Your job is to read the room and adapt, but always come prepared with the tools that can elevate the conversation.

Chapter Summary

The Big Idea: Effective risk communication requires selecting the right visualization for your audience and purpose, from histograms for analysts to executive-friendly loss exceedance curves for informed strategic decision-making.

Key Takeaways

- **Master the core visualizations:** Histograms for showing risk shape and loss exceedance curves for executive communication.
- **Loss exceedance curves are your secret weapon** for executive communication because they show the probability of exceeding different loss amounts in language that business leaders understand.
- **Use heatmaps carefully** as communication tools only, never as analytical models, and always anchor them to quantitative data.
- **Supplement visuals with narrative** using loss exceedance statements that translate charts into plain English.
- **Different audiences need different approaches** because security teams may prefer narratives, while executives respond better to loss exceedance curves.

Bottom Line: The goal isn't finding the "right" visualization; it's understanding your audience and helping your organization make better decisions about the risks they face. Meet people where they are, focus on the decisions that need to be made, and choose the communication approach that gets stakeholders to act on the information, rather than agonizing over mathematical perfection.

What's Coming Next

You've learned to turn quantitative results into compelling visual stories. Now you're ready to continue building the foundational blocks for complete risk assessments from start to finish.

In Chapter 7, you'll learn to transform vague worries like "our cloud setup feels risky" into precise, measurable risk statements using the A-T-E framework. You'll discover how to expand those statements into comprehensive assessment scopes that tell you exactly what data to collect, which experts to interview, and how to set clear boundaries on your analysis.

CHAPTER 7

From Risk Statements to Assessment Scope

Make it simple, but significant.

—Don Draper, *Mad Men*

Mid-career, I joined a global retailer that equipped every floor associate with an iPhone-like device for the sales floor: a combination barcode scanner, credit card swiper, and inventory lookup device. Those handheld devices communicated directly with the corporate databases, including in-stock products, payment processing, and even customer profiles.

While helping a few teams clean up and quantify the security risk register, I stumbled on a line item that looked harmless enough: "Lost or Stolen Store Device." Makes perfect sense to whoever logged it, right?

Not quite.

When it came time to present this risk to leadership for quarterly planning, I hit a wall. How do you analyze "Lost or Stolen Store Device"? What's the asset at risk? What kind of loss are we talking about? The statement was so vague I couldn't even begin to collect data or estimate impact.

I called a meeting with the risk owners to get clarity. One question got three different answers:

- **IT's take** (they issued the phones): "The asset is the device. That's a $1K hardware hit. Order a replacement and move on."
- **InfoSec's take** (they secure the data paths): "The asset is the data on those phones: full inventory and maybe cardholder data. We're talking about a potential data breach."

T. Martin-Vegue, *From Heatmaps to Histograms*, https://doi.org/10.1007/979-8-8688-2300-8_7

- **Store manager's take** (they need uptime): "The asset is our point-of-sale capability. No device, no checkout. Customers stack up and sales stall."

Which view was correct? **All of them**. There's an adage in risk management: "Risk is in the eye of the beholder." Each team was looking at the same event but identifying completely different assets at risk, resulting in distinct types of losses. I ended up carving that single, mushy entry into three separate risk statements: (1) device replacement cost, (2) potential PII exposure, and (3) diminished point-of-sale capability. Only then could I run meaningful risk analyses and attach sensible frequency and loss numbers to each scenario.

This is why scoping a risk assessment matters. Before we crunch a single number, we must get clear on what we're analyzing. Do it right, and the rest of the assessment flows. Skip it, and you'll burn hours (or days) chasing the wrong problem, arguing over definitions, and polishing an assessment no decision-maker asked for.

Where This Fits in the CRQ Process

This chapter and the next wrap up risk fundamentals; then, we move into Part 3, which is all about data collection. I'd like to show you where you stand in the process. **This chapter is crucial** for the following six chapters because it is where we identify and define what we will measure and the data we will collect.

- **Chapter 7 (this chapter)**: Scoping a risk assessment
- **Chapter 8**: Decomposing magnitude into measurable pieces
- **Chapters 9–13**: Collecting, vetting, and blending the data your risk assessment scope identified (external research, internal data, expert interviews)

This chapter gets you from confusion to clarity about what you're analyzing. The chapters that follow will show you how to gather the specific data your scope identifies.

Introducing Risk Statements and Risk Assessment Scope

A **risk statement** is a single sentence that captures the essential elements of a risk in a structured format, identifying the threat source, the asset at risk, and the potential impact.

The "Lost or Stolen Store Device" misunderstanding has happened to me many times before and many times since. This is a key lesson I teach anyone I lead on a risk team or anyone I work with on risk assessments: we all need to be on the same page about what we are assessing. To get on the same page, we need to scope the assessment properly. But before you can scope an assessment, you need to start with clear statements.

Many people think scoping an assessment means jumping straight into detailed narratives about how attacks unfold. That's getting ahead of the process.

Here's what works: first, you craft a precise risk statement that everyone can agree on; then, you expand it with all the operational details. Skip the statement step, and you'll end up with beautifully detailed scope documents that different people interpret completely differently.

Think of building a risk analysis like planning a research project:

- **Risk statement**: The research question that defines what you're investigating
- **Risk assessment scope**: The detailed research plan that defines your methodology, boundaries, and what you will and won't study

Just like a researcher needs both a clear question and a detailed study plan, you need both a focused risk statement and a comprehensive scope to do effective quantitative analysis.

EXERCISE 7-1: BRAINSTORM YOUR WORRIES

Take a few moments and brainstorm some generic risks. They don't need to be fully formed yet. They can be worries, findings, gaps, control deficiencies, or something the CTO said to you in the elevator. Write them down.

Examples to get you started:

- "Our cloud setup feels risky."
- "Employees keep clicking phishing emails."
- "That audit finding about password policies."
- "What if our main vendor gets breached?"

Don't worry about structure or precision yet. Just capture what comes to mind.

The Progression: From Worry to Analysis

Every quantitative risk assessment follows the same basic path. You start with something vague and messy: a concern, a finding, something that keeps you up at night. Through the process you'll learn in this chapter, you transform that worry into something you can measure and act on. Figure 7-1 shows this progression.

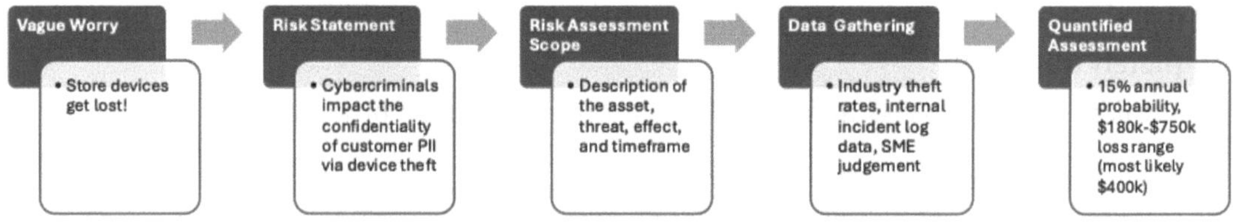

Figure 7-1. *The progression of a vague worry into a quantified assessment*

Each step builds on the previous one. The risk statement gives you clarity about what you're analyzing. The scope defines your boundaries. The data collection focuses your research. The quantified assessment provides the information decision-makers need to act.

The A-T-E Framing

The first step in escaping the swamp of ambiguity is writing a clear risk statement. One sentence, if shaped correctly, carries everything we need to start a conversation about what we mean when we say "risk." It also sets us up for success in the following two stages: building your assessment scope and collecting data.

This approach comes from FAIR (Factor Analysis of Information Risk). FAIR is not just one model, but rather a family of related frameworks and methods. What I'm showing here is FAIR's approach to building risk statements. FAIR utilizes **Asset, Threat Agent, and Effect** as the core components of risk statements, as illustrated in Figure 7-2. I call it A-T-E framing because it's easier to remember, but the concept is identical. There is an optional fourth piece, ***Method***, for times when you want extra detail.

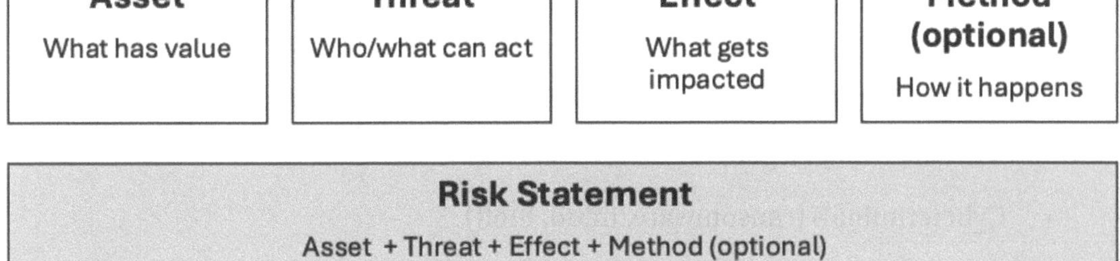

Figure 7-2. *The components of a risk statement*

FAIR's approach to risk statements is worth adopting because it's simple, unambiguous, and uses standard definitions. Whether you ultimately employ FAIR's full quantitative methodology or a different approach, this Asset-Threat-Effect structure compels you to be specific about what you're analyzing.

Asset: What Has Value

First comes the **Asset**, which is the thing that has value to the organization. It can be a system, a database, intellectual property, cash, people, or even something intangible like brand reputation. Start broad: customer data is a fine first cut. Drill down only when the analysis demands it, for example, "Customer personally identifiable information of EU citizens." Begin simple; zoom in later.

Common Assets Most Organizations Have

- Customer data (PII, payment info, contact details)
- Financial systems (accounting, payroll, banking)
- Intellectual property (code, designs, trade secrets)
- Operational systems (email, file servers, databases)
- Physical infrastructure (buildings, equipment, devices)
- Brand reputation and customer trust

Threat: Who or What Can Act

Next, we identify the **Threat**. A threat is any actor or force of nature that can act against the asset and cause harm or loss. Earthquakes, malicious ex-employees, untrained or careless current staff, cybercriminal groups, power outages, and foreign intelligence services all qualify. Most organizations share a core set of threats, such as untrained employees or commodity cybercriminals. Every sector also has its own flavor. A government agency worries about foreign spies; critical infrastructure fears nation-state saboteurs; hospitals lose sleep over ransomware gangs. Keep motive neutral; accidents count too. There are often many threats paired with a single asset. For each asset, there may be more than one threat actor.

Common Threats Every Organization Faces

- Cybercriminals (ransomware, fraud, theft)
- Untrained employees (mistakes, misconfigurations)
- Malicious insiders (data theft, sabotage)
- Natural disasters (floods, earthquakes, storms)
- System failures (hardware breakdowns, software bugs)
- Third-party vendors (breaches, outages, failures)

Effect: What Gets Damaged

Finally, for each asset-threat pair, we spell out the **Effect**. What materializes if the threat acts on the asset? This can be a tough step for beginners, but with practice, it becomes second nature. Start with the standard information security **CIA Triad**: confidentiality, integrity, and availability, and build from there. Consider all the ways the threat actor can target the asset. Just as in the previous step, there may be more than one effect for each **asset-threat** pair.

Effects are very asset-threat specific. **Common ones include**

- **Confidentiality loss:** Data exposed, secrets stolen, privacy breached
- **Integrity loss:** Data corrupted, systems modified, records falsified
- **Availability loss:** Systems down, processes stopped, services unavailable
- **Authentication loss:** Identity compromised, unauthorized access gained

Putting It Together

The result is several crisp, short risk statements. Stakeholders see a risk they recognize. Risk analysts are presented with a problem they can assess.

Using the example above of **Lost or Stolen Store Device** from the beginning of the chapter, we now have:

- "Thieves impact the **availability** of point-of-sale systems."
- "Cybercriminals impact the **confidentiality** of customer PII."
- "Equipment failure impacts the **availability** of payment processing."

Adding Method (Optional)

When needed, add the **Method**. Phishing, zero-day exploits, and forklifts through the data-center wall—knowing "how" sharpens discussions around how to respond to the risk. It is optional; the first three elements already provide a statement that can be quantified.

Adding a **method** to our retail examples gives us even more clarity:

- "Thieves impact the availability of point-of-sale systems **via physical device theft**."
- "Cybercriminals impact the confidentiality of customer PII **by accessing data on stolen devices**."
- "Equipment failure impacts the availability of payment processing **via hardware malfunction**."

The Mad Libs Approach

I call it A-T-E framing because that's the easiest way to think through risk components: Asset ➤ Threat ➤ Effect. But when you write the actual sentence, start with the threat for natural grammar: "[Threat] impacts the [Effect] of [Asset]."

Why the mismatch? Because thinking order and writing order serve different purposes. You brainstorm, starting with what has value (the asset), but readers understand sentences that begin with who's acting (the threat). This template gets you 80% of the way there. Just polish the language for clarity.

ALWAYS CONNECT TO ORGANIZATION OBJECTIVES

Develop risk scenarios that directly align with organizational objectives. Sometimes that means starting with effects first. Start conversations about how damage impacts the company and work backward from there.

GENAI PROMPT: RISK STATEMENT BUILDER

I have a risk concern: [*insert concern*]

Convert this into clear risk statements using A-T-E format:

- Asset: What valuable thing could be harmed?
- Threat: Who or what could act against it?
- Effect: How would it be damaged? (confidentiality, integrity, availability)

Create 1-3 statements formatted as: "[Threat] impacts the [Effect] of [Asset]"

Requirements:

- Be specific enough to measure frequency and impact
- Focus on realistic, plausible scenarios
- If multiple assets/threats are involved, create separate statements
- Include business impact, not just technical details

Now let's practice this approach with your own risk concerns.

EXERCISE 7-2: CREATE RISK STATEMENTS

Grab a few of your worries from **Exercise 7-1** and turn them into fully formed risk statements using the **A-T-E framing**, optionally adding a method. Feel free to do it by hand or with GenAI.

Where to Find Risk Statement Inspiration

Do you need more risk statements beyond your current register? Look to three sources: your organization's strategic objectives (what could prevent achieving them?), industry security news (when you see "Hospital hit by ransomware," ask "Could that happen here?"), and cross-functional conversations with operations, legal, finance, and IT teams about what keeps them up at night. Risk brainstorming workshops, which we'll cover in Chapter 14, bring these perspectives together systematically.

GENAI PROMPT: RISK DISCOVERY ASSISTANT

Scan this [*industry report/news article/incident*] and identify potential risk scenarios for a [*your industry*] organization with [*brief description of your business*].

Create 3-5 risk statements using this format: "[*Threat*] impacts the [*Effect*] of [*Asset*]"

Focus on scenarios that could realistically affect an organization like ours.

Quick Quality Filter

Before investing time in detailed scoping, quickly scan your list for obviously implausible scenarios. Ask yourself: Could this realistically happen at an organization like ours? Remove clear outliers: scenarios that require multiple unlikely events or sophisticated attackers, which don't align with your threat landscape. Don't overthink this step; you can always revisit statements later. Begin with the risks that are most clearly relevant to your environment.

Use these guidelines to evaluate whether your risk statements are worth analyzing:

- Must have an asset at risk.
- Must have a threat that can reasonably act against the asset.
- The event must result in some form of loss.
- A reasonable person would think of the scenario as within the realm of possibility.
- Not only is the event possible, it's plausible.

GENAI PROMPT: QUALITY FILTER HELPER

[paste risk statements]

Take the above risk statements and evaluate them against the General Guidelines below. For each statement, assess:

- Does it have a clear asset at risk?
- Is the threat reasonable and capable of acting against the asset?
- Does the event result in measurable loss?
- Is it within the realm of possibility for a reasonable person?
- Is it not only possible, but plausible?

Provide a confidence rating in the strength of each statement and suggest improvements where needed.

Scoping Your Risk Assessment

Your risk assessment scope is the bridge between identifying a risk and analyzing it. Think of it as a project charter: you're defining exactly what you'll measure and what you won't, which prevents scope creep and ensures stakeholders understand your results. Without a clear scope, you'll waste time collecting irrelevant data, miss critical information, and build models that don't answer the business question. Get this right, and the rest flows naturally.

Your scope must answer five essential questions:

1. **What decision is this informing?** Be specific: "Should we invest $50K in additional WAF protection?" not "assess our web security risk."
2. **What exactly are we measuring?** Expand your asset beyond the risk statement. "Customer payment database containing ~50,000 active credit card records" tells you more about impact than "customer data."

3. **What are we NOT measuring?** Critical for preventing scope creep: "Analysis excludes employee HR database and marketing customer data."
4. **What's our time horizon?** Default to 12 months unless you have a specific reason otherwise.
5. **What specific losses could occur?** This connects to Chapter 8. Based on your asset-threat-effect, identify which loss categories might apply:
   - Productivity loss (operational downtime?)
   - Response costs (incident response needed?)
   - Replacement costs (what needs to be replaced?)
   - Fines and judgments (regulatory penalties?)
   - Reputation damage (customer/brand impact?)
   - Competitive advantage loss (strategic value at risk?)

You'll learn to measure each category in detail in Chapter 8, but identifying them now guides your data collection.

DEFENDING YOUR SCOPE AGAINST "WHAT ABOUTS"

As you circulate your scope for feedback, expect "what abouts"—inevitable scope creep requests. Listen to each one, but bring it back to two things: the risk statement and the business decision.

The opportunity cost matters: Every additional piece of scope costs time, effort, and potentially delays the decision. Before expanding, ask:

- Will this change the decision we're trying to make?
- Could the decision-maker act confidently without this?

How to respond: "That's an interesting point. Let's capture that as a separate risk to analyze later, but for this assessment, we're focused on [restate original scope] because it addresses [the business decision]."

From Scope to Data Collection: Your Translation Guide

Once you've answered the five scoping questions, Table 7-1 shows examples of what data to collect.

Table 7-1. *From scope questions to data collection requirements*

Scope Question	What This Tells You About Data Collection	Specific Data You Need
Q1: What decision?	• Precision level required • Timeline constraints • Key stakeholders	• Decision-maker's risk tolerance • Comparable past decisions • Budget constraints
Q2: Asset and effect?	**For Frequency:** How often does this happen?	**External:** Industry attack/incident rates for this asset-threat combo **Internal:** Your logs, past incidents, vulnerability scans **SME:** Security team likelihood estimates
	For Magnitude: How much impact?	**External:** Industry cost benchmarks **Internal:** Asset value, revenue dependencies **SME:** Business impact estimates
Q3: NOT measuring?	• Data you can skip • Scope boundaries	Keep this list handy when stakeholders request additions
Q4: Time horizon?	• How to annualize data • Seasonal factors	• Historical data covering your timeframe • Planned changes in the next 12 months
Q5: Loss categories?	**For EACH category you identified, you need specific cost data**	Chapter 8 breaks down how to measure: • Productivity loss • Response costs • Replacement costs • Fines and judgments • Reputation damage • Competitive advantage loss For now, just identify which categories apply to your scenario.

Complete Worked Example: From Statement to Data Road Map

Risk Statement: "Cybercriminals impact the confidentiality of the customer payment database via SQL injection."

Scoping the Assessment

1. **What decision is this informing?** Justify $50K WAF investment for Q1 budget approval by CISO.
2. **What asset and effect are we measuring?** Customer payment database (50,000 credit card records) experiencing a loss of confidentiality through unauthorized access. (Excludes marketing database and employee HR data.)
3. **What are we NOT measuring?** This analysis excludes insider threats, social engineering attacks, and our mobile app infrastructure.
4. **What's our time horizon?** Next 12 months, assuming current WAF effectiveness remains constant.
5. **What specific losses could occur?**
   - Response costs (incident response, forensics, breach notification)
   - Fines and judgments (PCI DSS penalties)
   - Reputation damage (customer churn, brand impact)
   - Productivity loss (system downtime during investigation)

The Data Collection Road Map Emerges

Based on this scope, you now know what data to collect:

Frequency Data

- **External**: SQL injection attack rates in ecommerce, industry threat reports
- **Internal**: Vulnerability scan results, WAF logs, past incidents
- **SME**: Security team estimates on current exposure

Magnitude Data (organized by loss category)

- **Response costs**: Incident response hourly rates, notification costs
- **Fines and judgments**: PCI DSS penalty ranges, legal settlement benchmarks
- **Reputation**: Customer churn rates after breaches, brand recovery costs
- **Productivity**: Hourly downtime costs, investigation duration estimates

Notice how identifying specific loss categories in Question 5 directly tells you what data to collect. Chapter 8 will teach you what each category means and how to break it down into measurable components.

What You've Accomplished

Your scope has done three critical things:

1. **Defined boundaries**: What you will and won't measure
2. **Identified loss categories**: The specific types of impact to quantify
3. **Created a data road map**: What information you need to collect

Question 5 drives everything that follows. You know you need response cost data, fine ranges, churn rates, and downtime costs because you identified those specific loss categories in your scope. Chapter 8 teaches you to break down each loss category into measurable components.

GENAI PROMPT: SCOPE ASSISTANT

Create a complete risk assessment scope for: [paste risk statement]

Context: [industry], [org size], [key regulations], [geographic footprint]

Answer these five scoping questions:

1. What specific business decision will this assessment inform?
2. What asset and effect are we measuring? (Be precise about the asset details)
3. What are we NOT measuring? (Clear exclusions)
4. What's the time horizon? (Default: 12 months)
5. What specific losses could occur? (Identify which categories apply: productivity loss, response costs, replacement costs, fines & judgments, reputation damage, competitive advantage loss)

Then create a data collection roadmap showing:

- Frequency data needed (external, internal, SME sources)
- Magnitude data needed for each loss category identified
- Specific questions to ask experts

Be specific and actionable - this will guide my data collection.

Chapter Summary

The Big Idea: Clear risk statements and comprehensive assessment scopes are the foundation of effective quantitative risk analysis. Get this right, and everything else falls into place naturally.

Key Takeaways

- **Start with precise risk statements** using the A-T-E framework (Asset, Threat, Effect) to eliminate ambiguity before you invest time in analysis.
- **Expand statements into detailed scopes** that define exactly what you'll measure, what you won't, and what data you'll need to collect.

- **Protect your scope boundaries** against "what about" requests that can derail focus and timeline.
- **Use the scoping framework systematically** to identify decision context, stakeholder impacts, and data collection requirements.
- **Think like a project manager**. Your assessment scope is the charter that keeps everyone aligned on deliverables and expectations.

Bottom Line: The 30 minutes you spend getting clear on what you're analyzing will save you hours of collecting irrelevant data and arguing over definitions later.

What's Coming Next

You've transformed vague worries into clear risk statements and detailed assessment scopes. Your scope identifies which loss categories to measure and creates a data collection road map.

Chapter 8 breaks down "effect" into specific business loss categories you can quantify. You'll learn what productivity loss, response costs, fines, reputation damage, replacement costs, and loss of competitive advantage mean, as well as how to decompose each one for measurement.

Chapters 9–13 then show you how to collect the data your scope identified: external research, internal data analysis, and expert interviews.

Your scope is the blueprint. Everything that follows builds on what you defined here.

CHAPTER 8

Understanding Loss: The Six Forms

> *The whole is greater than the sum of its parts, but you still need to understand the parts.*
>
> —Often attributed to Aristotle

A few years back, I was working with a company that wanted to assess the risk of data compromise across its AWS infrastructure. When we started discussing magnitude, or how much an incident would cost, the initial approach seemed straightforward: find some industry data on breach costs, adjust and validate it with SMEs, and then move on to the modeling.

The first pass took about ten minutes. I compiled a generalized dollar amount based on publicly disclosed incidents from similar companies, adjusted it with a group of experts at the company, and presented a range that reflected our best estimate. I was careful to note what was included and what wasn't, and the number gave executives a solid directional sense of the financial risk they were facing.

That initial estimate proved to be quite accurate, falling within our 90% confidence interval. For many risk assessments, that's exactly where I would have stopped. One magnitude number, properly scoped and defensible, often provides all the decision-making insight you need.

However, some executives wanted to delve further. They wanted to understand the breakdown: How much of that cost would be attributed to legal fees, lost customers, or incident response? After explaining the time and effort involved, which was about a month of additional data collection, we collectively decided it was worth the investment.

T. Martin-Vegue, *From Heatmaps to Histograms*, https://doi.org/10.1007/979-8-8688-2300-8_8

That decomposition effort paid off in ways we hadn't anticipated. It revealed gaps in our cyber insurance coverage, since policies only cover certain types of losses. It helped us design better controls by pinpointing specific areas for cost reduction. Perhaps most importantly, it created a library of reusable magnitude components, which significantly accelerated future assessments.

The next similar risk assessment took three weeks instead of a month. The next one took two weeks. By the fourth assessment, we had reduced the timeframe to one week, as we could reuse a significant portion of the foundational data collection.

The decomposition framework I used originates from FAIR (Factor Analysis of Information Risk), which is why I recommend that all readers examine FAIR's six forms of loss, even if you don't intend to adopt the full FAIR model.

This chapter explores the concept of breaking down magnitude, the "how much it hurts" aspect of risk, into its component parts. You'll learn about the six forms of loss that organizations experience when things go wrong and when it makes sense to decompose magnitude rather than measure it directly.

When to Decompose (and When Not To)

The six forms framework is powerful, but you don't always need it. For almost any risk scenario, you can derive defensible total loss costs using publicly available data, internal organizational data, and SME estimates. If that aggregate number answers the business question, stop there. Many risk assessments work perfectly well with a single total magnitude estimate.

Decompose when you need to understand

- **Where** losses materialize (identifying insurance gaps, since policies cover specific loss types)
- **When** costs hit (immediate invoices vs. long-term strategic impacts affect cash flow and decision timing differently)
- **What** to control (discovering that 80% of loss is productivity helps you prioritize availability controls over incident response investments)
- **How** losses unfold (understanding the mechanism helps design targeted mitigations)

Skip decomposition when

- The business decision only needs total magnitude ("Is this risk worth $100K to mitigate?").
- Timeline is tight, and directional accuracy is sufficient.
- The breakdown wouldn't change the decision or control strategy.

The opening AWS story shows both approaches: the ten-minute aggregate estimate was accurate and sufficient for initial decisions. We only decomposed when executives needed to understand the breakdown for insurance coverage and control design.

Why Breaking Down Loss Matters

Here's the thing about cyber incidents: they're not just IT problems that stay contained within one team. They're business events that impact every part of an organization, from the call center to the C-suite, encompassing customer relationships and regulatory compliance. Different stakeholders are concerned about various types of losses, and each type of loss necessitates distinct response strategies.

Let's examine this with a simple example of how the same innocent can be viewed through different lenses.

Imagine a ransomware attack that encrypts your customer database for 48 hours. Here's how different people in your organization would think about the impact, illustrated in Figure 8-1.

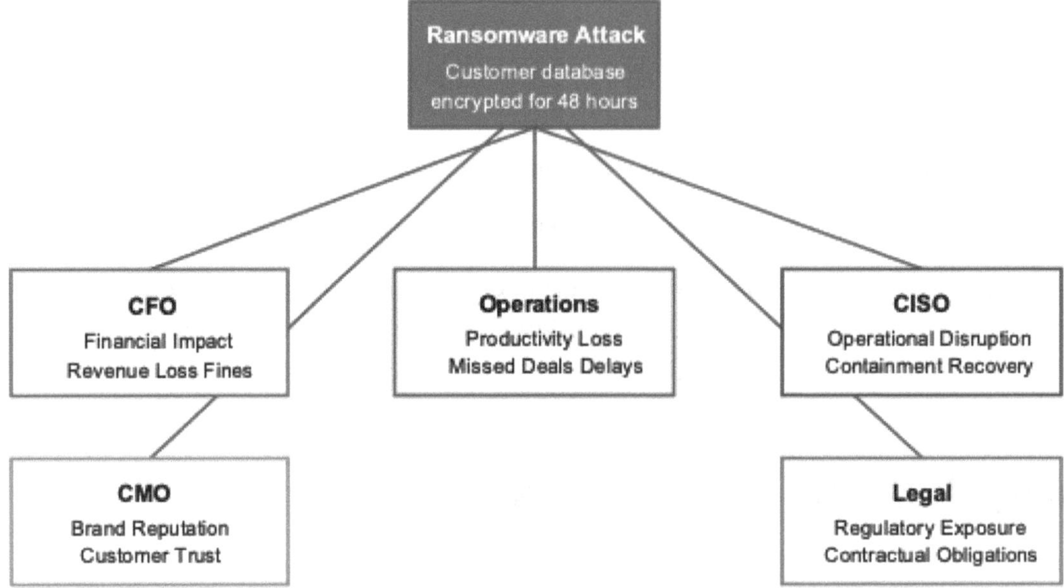

***Figure 8-1.** One ransomware incident creates five different types of perceived loss, each mattering to different stakeholders*

The CFO focuses on the immediate financial hit: "How much will this cost us in lost revenue, incident response fees, and regulatory fines?"

The CISO thinks about the operational disruption: "How long until we're back online, and what will it take to contain this and prevent it from spreading?"

The Chief Marketing Officer worries about long-term reputation: "How many customers will lose confidence in us? What's this going to do to our brand?"

The Chief Legal Officer considers regulatory exposure: "Are we looking at GDPR fines? What about our contractual obligations to customers?"

The Chief Operations Officer calculates productivity loss: "If our sales team can't access customer data, how many deals are we going to miss this quarter?"

Each perspective represents a distinct type of loss, and different stakeholders are concerned with different aspects. The six forms framework helps you answer specific questions about where, when, and how losses occur, questions that a single aggregate number can't address.

Use decomposition strategically: when stakeholders need to understand the breakdown, when you're designing targeted controls, or when you're matching losses to insurance coverage. Otherwise, the total magnitude is enough.

The Six Forms of Loss

Now that you understand why breaking down loss matters, let's explore the framework that makes it practical. The FAIR (Factor Analysis of Information Risk) methodology identifies six primary forms of loss that organizations experience when cyber incidents occur (Jones & Freund, 2014). Think of these as different channels through which a single event can hurt your business.

Developed by Jack Jones, the six forms, as shown in Figure 8-2, of loss provide a practical way to break down the complex and multifaceted nature of cyber incident impact. Each form has its own characteristics, timing, and measurement challenges. A ransomware attack, for instance, might trigger losses in all six categories. Still, the costs would unfold differently: some would be immediate and trackable through invoices, while others would materialize over quarters or years through strategic impacts.

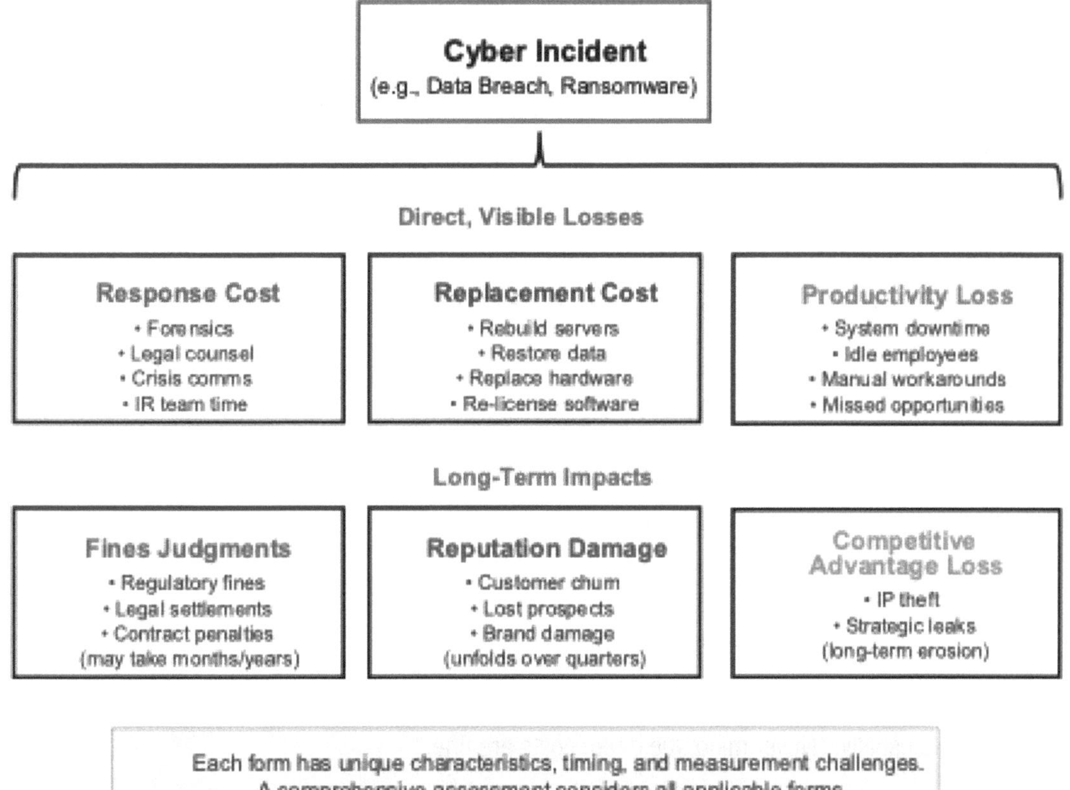

Figure 8-2. *The six forms of loss*

Understanding Measurement Approaches

Some loss forms generate direct costs that appear immediately in accounting systems, including invoices, expenses, and line items that finance teams can track in real time. Others represent long-term impacts that unfold over extended time horizons and require different measurement approaches, such as customer behavior analysis, market studies, or strategic assessments. Both types are measurable; they just require different analytical methods and timeframes.

YOU DON'T NEED TO MEASURE EVERY LOSS FORM

Remember from Chapter 7 that you scope things in and out of your risk assessment based on business needs and feasibility. Some loss forms are straightforward to estimate; others require significant effort that may not be worth the investment.

I've conducted many risk assessments where Competitive Advantage Loss was clearly a possibility following an event, but I scoped it out due to the complexity of measurement. The key is being transparent: for example, stating upfront what's included (Response, Replacement, Productivity, Fines) and what's excluded (Competitive Advantage).

Managing Pushback on Exclusions

When stakeholders question why something is out of scope, I describe exactly what including it would require:

"To properly measure Competitive Advantage Loss, we'd need:

- *Half-day workshop with executive leadership*
- *Purchase competitive intelligence data (~$15K)*
- *Hire a consulting firm for competitive landscape analysis (~$50K)*
- *Add 4-6 weeks to the timeline"*

I've never had an executive take me up on that offer. Once they see the effort required, the response is usually: "Never mind, the direct costs are fine."

Remember: Focus your effort where it drives the business decision. It's better to have three well-estimated loss forms than six poorly estimated ones.

1. Productivity Loss

What it is: The economic impact when employees can't perform their normal duties due to an incident. This includes both direct downtime (people sitting idle) and reduced efficiency from working around problems.

Plain language: This is what happens when your people can't do their jobs because systems are down, data is unavailable, or they're stuck using slow manual workarounds instead of their normal tools.

Examples

- Sales team unable to access CRM during ransomware attack, missing follow-ups and new deals.
- Manufacturing line workers are idle, while control systems are restored after a malware infection.
- Employees manually process orders when the ecommerce platform is compromised.

Measurement approach: Moderate complexity. External downtime cost benchmarks exist, but you need internal operational data (employee counts, processes affected, revenue dependencies). SMEs must estimate the duration and scope of the disruption. Historical outages reveal which teams were affected and for how long, providing crucial calibration for future estimates.

2. Response Cost

What it is: The direct expenses incurred to detect, investigate, contain, and recover from an incident. This covers everything from emergency consultant fees to the time your own teams spend managing the crisis.

Plain language: This is the money you spend cleaning up the mess: forensics experts, legal counsel, crisis communications, overtime pay for your incident response team, and all the coordination work needed to get back to normal.

Examples

- External forensics firm fees
- Legal counsel for breach notification and regulatory guidance
- Crisis communications and public relations support

- Incident response team time and emergency contractor costs
- Credit monitoring services for affected customers
- Executive time spent in crisis management meetings
- Travel expenses for on-site incident response

Measurement approach: Easiest to estimate. Abundant external data on forensics hourly rates, legal fees, and IR costs. SMEs can readily estimate team size and response duration. If your organization has experienced similar incidents, use actual invoices and time logs to calibrate estimates.

3. Replacement Cost

What it is: The expense of rebuilding, restoring, or replacing assets that were damaged, corrupted, or compromised during an incident. This includes both physical and digital assets.

Plain language: This is what it costs to rebuild or replace what was broken: whether that's reformatting infected servers, recreating lost data, or buying new equipment that can't be safely restored.

Examples

- Rebuilding servers from clean backups after ransomware encryption
- Recreating corrupted databases from partial backups and manual entry
- Replacing hardware that can't be safely cleaned of malware
- Re-licensing software that was compromised or needs reinstallation
- Cloud resource costs for emergency restoration and additional compute power

Measurement approach: Straightforward estimation. Hardware/software pricing is publicly available. Internal asset inventory tells you what's at risk. SMEs can assess rebuild complexity and timeline. Past restoration projects provide concrete rebuild timelines and cost baselines.

⚠ DON'T DOUBLE-COUNT RESPONSE AND REPLACEMENT COSTS

When an incident occurs, the same technical staff often performs both investigation activities (Response) and rebuilding work (Replacement). It's easy to accidentally count their hours twice—once under "incident response costs" and again under "system restoration costs," inflating the total magnitude estimate by measuring the same labor in two different categories.

For example, if you estimate 40 hours of security engineer time as Response Cost, then also count those same 40 hours rebuilding servers as Replacement Cost, you've just counted the same $8,000 twice. Your final loss estimate will be artificially inflated.

The key distinction:

Response Cost(Understand and Coordinate)	Replacement Cost(Rebuild and Restore)
Forensic investigation	Rebuilding servers
Incident coordination	Recreating databases
Crisis communications	Replacing hardware
Executive meetings	Re-licensing software
Documentation and reporting	Restoring from backups

Response = Investigation and containmentReplacement = When assets must be rebuilt/ replaced

4. Fines and Judgments

What it is: Legal and regulatory penalties imposed due to the incident, including government fines, lawsuit settlements, and contractual damages from failing to meet obligations.

Plain language: This is what you pay when regulators, customers, or business partners decide you didn't protect their interests adequately and seek financial compensation through legal or regulatory channels.

Examples

- GDPR fines for inadequate data protection.
- HIPAA penalties range from thousands to millions, depending on the breach scope.
- SEC enforcement actions for inadequate cybersecurity disclosure.
- Class action lawsuit settlements from affected customers.
- Contractual penalties for SLA violations during outages.
- State attorney general fines for breach notification failures.

Measurement approach: Moderate complexity. External data on regulatory penalty ranges and settlement amounts is available. Typically, one would need an internal compliance posture and legal exposure assessment from SMEs. There can be a high variance in outcomes, and previous regulatory actions or contract penalties at your organization or similar peer orgs can establish enforcement patterns and penalty magnitudes.

5. Reputation Damage

What it is: The long-term impact on stakeholder trust, brand value, and customer relationships resulting from how the incident and your response are perceived by the market.

Plain language: This is a hit to your organization's reputation, and the business consequences that follow include customers leaving, prospects choosing competitors, and partners reconsidering their relationships with you.

Examples

- Customer churn following breach disclosure
- Difficulty attracting new customers who cite security concerns
- Lost sales opportunities where security becomes a competitive factor
- Reduced employee morale and increased turnover as talent questions company stability
- Stock price decline reflecting a loss of investor confidence
- Partners requiring additional security assurances or contract modifications

Measurement Approach: Higher complexity. Limited external data that matches your specific customer base and market position. Requires sophisticated SME elicitation about customer behavior, churn sensitivity, and recovery timeline. If you've had past incidents, analyze actual customer churn rates, retention impacts, and recovery timelines to establish organization-specific patterns.

6. Competitive Advantage Loss

What it is: The erosion of your organization's strategic market position due to compromised intellectual property, strategic information, or confidential business plans falling into competitors' hands.

Plain language: This is what happens when confidential information that gives you an edge (like product designs, customer lists, or strategic plans) gets stolen and potentially used against you by competitors.

Examples

- Trade secrets or proprietary algorithms exposed and reverse-engineered by rivals.
- Product road maps leaked, allowing competitors to rush competing features to market.
- Customer lists are stolen and used for targeted competitive sales campaigns.
- Merger and acquisition plans disclosed, affecting negotiation positions.
- Pricing strategies revealed, undermining competitive positioning.
- Research and development investments were compromised before the product's launch.

Measurement Approach: Highest complexity. Very company-specific with limited external comparables. Requires deep strategic assessment from SMEs about IP value, competitive dynamics, and market impact. Past IP compromises or strategic leaks provide case studies for estimating market impact, duration, and competitive positioning effects.

SIDEBAR: WHAT ARE "PENANCE PROJECTS?"

After major incidents, organizations often make reactive investments to appease leadership, boards, or regulators—what risk experts Doug Hubbard and Richard Seiersen call "penance projects" (Hubbard & Seiersen, 2023). **These aren't formal loss forms to include in your magnitude estimate**, but they're worth understanding because they represent real money spent to manage perception rather than reduce actual risk."

Example: After Target's massive 2013 data breach that compromised 40 million credit card accounts and 70 million customer records (Reed, 2023), the company invested heavily in cybersecurity infrastructure, including building a state-of-the-art "Cyber Fusion Center" (Chain Store Age Staff, 2015).

While some of these investments likely provided genuine risk reduction, the scale and speed of Target's response had elements of organizational "penance" beyond what a purely risk-based analysis might have recommended.

Track these post-incident expenses separately from your six forms of loss. They're real costs organizations incur after breaches, but they're driven by organizational psychology and external pressure rather than the incident itself.

See Appendix B in the back of this book for a detailed measurement guide for the six forms of loss.

Addressing Executive Questions About Opportunity Cost

Executives often ask: "What strategic work gets delayed when we respond to this incident?" They're not asking for a seventh loss form; they want context about resource trade-offs and strategic impact.

Don't quantify opportunity cost in your magnitude estimate. Instead, present it as supplementary context after showing your six-form results.

Example Framing

"Our quantified loss estimate is $500K–$1.2M across the six forms. Additionally, an incident of this scale would likely require pulling four to six engineers off projects for two to three weeks, potentially delaying product launches."

Key Principles

- Keep the six forms pure. Opportunity cost stays outside formal calculations.
- Frame by consequence (delayed launches, paused initiatives) rather than monetizing hypothetical revenue.
- Acknowledge the speculation; you're describing likely organizational responses based on past incidents, not calculating measurable losses.

This gives executives the strategic context they need without compromising the integrity of your risk model.

Now that you understand the six forms conceptually, here's how to apply them to your risk scenario.

Applying the Six Forms to Your Risk Scenario

After you've completed your risk scope in Chapter 7 and identified which loss categories might apply to your scenario, it's time to quantify them. This section shows you how to move from *I know reputation damage could occur* to *Here's my estimated range for reputation costs.*

Step 1: Triage Which Loss Forms Apply

For your scoped scenario, identify the relevant loss forms in Table 8-1. Include each item that applies to your scenario.

Table 8-1. *Triage applicable loss forms*

☐	**Response cost** → Investigation/containment needed?
☐	**Replacement cost** → Systems/data need rebuilding?
☐	**Productivity loss** → Normal work disrupted?
☐	**Fines and judgments** → Regulatory/contractual exposure?
☐	**Reputation damage** → Will stakeholders know?
☐	**Competitive loss** → Strategic info at risk?

Response cost applies to almost every scenario. The others depend on your specific risk statement and scope.

Step 2: Prioritize Your Effort

Not all loss forms deserve equal analysis time. Just because it can be measured doesn't mean it has to be measured. It's perfectly fine to skip difficult or expensive-to-measure loss forms if you disclose this clearly in the risk report. Plot each applicable form on the grid in Figure 8-3 to decide where to invest your effort.

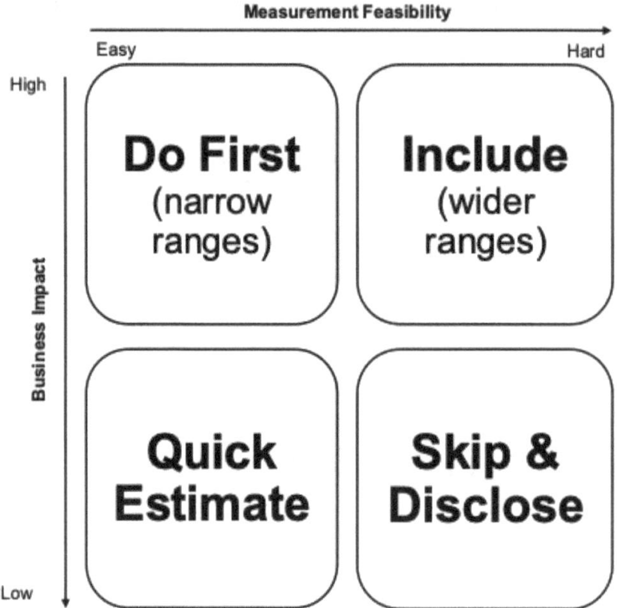

Figure 8-3. *Prioritize your effort*

Example: Ransomware affecting the customer database

- **Response cost** → Do first (high impact, easy to measure)
- **Productivity loss** → Include (high impact, moderate effort)
- **Reputation damage** → Include (medium impact, harder to measure, accept wider ranges)
- **Competitive advantage** → Skip (low impact, hard to measure, acknowledge but don't quantify)

Step 3: Define What Each Loss Form Means for Your Scenario

For each loss form you've prioritized, we need to be specific about what would happen in your organizational context.

Use this scoping framework:

Loss Form	Key Scoping Questions
Response Cost	• Who responds? (internal teams, external consultants) • What activities? (forensics, legal, communications, coordination) • How long? (hours, days, weeks)
Replacement Cost	• What needs rebuilding? (servers, databases, credentials) • What can't be recovered? (requires fresh deployment) • What's the rebuild approach? (from backups, from scratch)
Productivity Loss	• Which employee groups are affected? (sales, operations, support) • What work stops or slows? (specific processes, transactions) • For how long? (outage duration + recovery lag)
Fines and Judgments	• Which regulations apply? (GDPR, HIPAA, PCI, SOX) • What contracts have penalties? (SLAs, customer agreements) • What's the violation severity? (minor breach vs. systemic failure)
Reputation Damage	• Who learns about this? (customers, investors, media) • What's their likely reaction? (churn, hesitation, concern) • How long to recover trust? (weeks, quarters, years)
Competitive Advantage	• What strategic info is at risk? (IP, road maps, customer lists) • Who could exploit it? (direct competitors, new entrants) • What's the competitive window? (before we can respond)

Example: For a SQL injection scenario, scoping Productivity Loss means asking the following:

- Customer service team can't access order history → Which processes stop?
- Sales team can't process new orders → For how many hours?
- Finance can't run reports → Which decisions get delayed?

This specificity directly informs the magnitude estimates you'll develop in Step 4.

Step 4: Estimate and Aggregate

For each loss form you're quantifying, develop three estimates (lower bound, typical, upper bound) that reflect your uncertainty. Wide ranges are honest; narrow ranges you can't defend are useless.

Combining your estimates:

	Lower bound (P5)	Typical (P50)	Upper bound (P95)
Response Cost	$10K	$25K	$50K
Replacement Cost	$5K	$15K	$30K
Productivity Loss	$20K	$60K	$100K
Total Magnitude	**$35K**	**$100K**	**$180K**

Step 5: Validate Your Work

Before finalizing your magnitude estimates, verify:

Completeness

- All applicable loss forms are identified based on your scenario.
- Data sources documented for each estimate.
- Key assumptions stated explicitly.
- Exclusions noted and justified.

Consistency

- Time periods align across all estimates (usually 12 months from your scope).
- No double-counting between categories.
- Ranges reflect appropriate uncertainty levels.
- SME input validates the overall magnitude.

Usability

- Results address the original business question from your scope.
- Presentation format suits your audience's needs.
- Action implications are clear.

GENAI PROMPT: BUILD SIX FORMS OF LOSS

[Insert a scenario: e.g., "a ransomware attack that encrypts our customer database for 48 hours"]

Using the FAIR's Six Forms of Loss framework (Response Cost, Replacement Cost, Productivity Loss, Fines & Judgments, Reputation Damage, Competitive Advantage Loss):

1. Identify which loss forms apply to this scenario and which don't
2. For each applicable form, explain what would happen
3. Determine which forms are worth measuring vs. which to exclude
4. Identify what data sources you'd need for each form you plan to measure

Focus on *what* would happen and *where* to find data, not specific dollar amounts.

You're Done with Magnitude!

Once you complete this process, you have finished the magnitude portion of your risk assessment. Your aggregated ranges (minimum, most likely, maximum) represent the total financial impact if this risk scenario were to occur.

Hold onto this data. When you're ready to build your complete risk model using Monte Carlo simulation, these magnitude estimates will be one of your key inputs. The other key input (frequency) will be covered in the subsequent data collection chapters.

Chapter Summary

The Big Idea: Breaking down magnitude into the six forms of loss provides a structured way to understand where, when, and how cyber incidents impact your business, but *decomposition is optional.* Use it when understanding the breakdown drives better decisions.

Key Takeaways

- **Decompose strategically, not automatically**. A single aggregate magnitude estimate often suffices; decompose only when stakeholders need to understand where losses materialize, when costs hit, or what to control.
- **Master the six forms framework**. Response cost, replacement cost, productivity loss, fines and judgments, reputation damage, and competitive advantage loss capture how incidents create financial impact through different channels.
- **Match the measurement approach to the loss type**. Direct costs (response, replacement, fines) rely on invoices and historical data; long-term impacts (reputation, competitive advantage) require strategic analysis and trend evaluation.
- **Provide context without breaking your model**. Address executive questions about opportunity cost and penance projects as supplementary context, not formal loss categories to quantify.

Bottom Line: You now have a framework for thinking about impact that goes far beyond "high, medium, low." Use it when decomposition adds value; skip it when aggregate magnitude is enough.

What's Coming Next

You've completed Part 2. You've built the foundations of quantitative thinking (Chapter 4), run your first Monte Carlo simulation (Chapter 5), learned to communicate results with powerful visualizations (Chapter 6), mastered the art of scoping assessments (Chapter 7), and decomposed magnitude into the six forms of loss (Chapter 8). You can now think in ranges, run simulations, and present results that drive decisions.

Now you're entering Part 3, and this is where most people get stuck: data collection.

It's the number one obstacle analysts face. You know what to measure and how to communicate it, but finding and trusting the data feels overwhelming. Should you use that industry report? Can you trust your incomplete incident logs? How do you get reliable estimates from busy experts?

Chapter 9 breaks the myths keeping you paralyzed and introduces the three-source model for systematic data gathering. You'll discover that the data you need is closer than you think.

Chapters 10–14 then show you exactly how to find, evaluate, and combine that data:

- Chapter 10: How to vet and trust your sources
- Chapter 11: Mining external research and industry data
- Chapter 12: Extracting insights from internal systems
- Chapter 13: Working effectively with subject matter experts
- Chapter 14: Blending all three sources into defensible estimates

You've learned the methodology. Now you'll learn to feed it with real data that transforms abstract frameworks into defensible dollar ranges.

Part 3 will unstick you. Let's begin.

References

Chain Store Age Staff. (2015,. September 2). *Target opens cyber fusion security center. Chain Store Age.* `https://chainstoreage.com/news/target-opens-cyber-fusion-security-center`

Hubbard, D. W., & Seiersen, R. (2023). *How to Measure Anything in Cybersecurity Risk* (2nd ed.). Wiley.

Jones, J., & Freund, J. (2014). *Measuring and Managing Information Risk: A FAIR Approach*. Butterworth-Heinemann.

Reed, C. (2023,. October 5). *Target data breach: Full timeline through 2023*. Firewall Times. `https://firewalltimes.com/target-data-breaches/`

PART III

Solving the Data Problem

CHAPTER 9

Getting Unstuck with Data

The obstacle is the way.

—Marcus Aurelius

One of the most challenging risk assessments I ever worked on involved a financial institution's massive cloud infrastructure: the scope included everything from internal systems to customer-facing platforms, with threats ranging from cybercriminals to untrained employees. Getting started seemed daunting, especially the data collection phase.

I assigned this project to one of my risk analysts, expecting it would take a few weeks. Instead, I watched them struggle for over a month. They'd find industry reports but question whether they applied to our environment. They'd review our incident logs but worry the data was too sparse. Every data source seemed to create more questions than answers.

I took a step back and worked with them through data gathering step by step: started with what we had, created priors from external sources, and systematically filled in the blanks. The result was a comprehensive, defensible assessment that helped leadership make critical investment decisions. The key wasn't having perfect data from day one. It was having a systematic approach.

If you've watched your analysts get stuck on data collection or if you've felt that same overwhelm yourself, you're in the right chapter.

This is where everything you've learned starts to pay off. In Part 1, you built the foundation for thinking quantitatively about risk. In Part 2, you've built scenarios, defined what you're measuring, and scoped your risk assessment. Now comes the part that stops most people in their tracks: data.

T. Martin-Vegue, *From Heatmaps to Histograms*, https://doi.org/10.1007/979-8-8688-2300-8_9

This chapter bridges the gap between knowing what to measure and *actually* measuring it. You'll learn the three-source model that forms the backbone of Chapters 10–12: how to find and evaluate external data, extract insights from internal sources, and work effectively with subject matter experts. By the end of Part 3, you'll have a systematic approach that prevents the kind of paralysis my analyst experienced.

Data is where many people get stuck. Some find it intimidating, while others fall into common "data myths" that make quantitative risk feel impossible before they even start. Here's the reality: the last decade of cyber incidents has given us mountains of data about what attacks look like. We just need to learn how to see the signal through the noise.

This isn't about becoming a statistician or building perfect datasets. It's about getting unstuck and moving forward with useful, defensible information that drives better decisions. By the end of this chapter, you'll understand exactly what data you need and where to find it.

Before You Search: Seeing the Problem Clearly

When analysts get stuck, it's rarely because they lack data. It's because they don't know which data matters.

I've seen this pattern countless times: someone frames a risk scenario and starts hunting for every number they can find—incident counts, threat feeds, productivity rates, survey data, vendor reports. After two weeks, they're surrounded by documents but still can't answer the question that started it all: *What should I measure?*

Before you go searching, you need to see the problem clearly. The fastest way to do that is to work backward from your decision.

Start with the outcome you care about. In decision analysis, this is called the *figure of merit*, the single quantity your model produces to show how well different choices satisfy what you care about, such as minimizing cost or maximizing ROI. In a CRQ analysis, that's usually *annualized loss exposure (ALE)*, but depending on your context, it could also be *downtime hours* or *the probability of a material event this year*.

Then ask yourself: What drives that number? What has to happen for that outcome to change? Those drivers become your *uncertainties*.

Now ask: Which of those uncertainties are influenced by choices we can make? Those become your *decisions*.

What you're doing here is decomposing the problem: turning a complex tangle of possibilities into a structured chain of cause and effect. Once you've drawn that chain on a whiteboard, a piece of paper, or diagramming software, you've defined the *few things worth measuring*.

This step only takes five or ten minutes, but it can save you hours of wasted research. In decision science, that sketch has a name: an **influence diagram**. It's a simple visual map showing how decisions, uncertainties, and outcomes connect. It's one of the best tools for figuring out which data you need before you start gathering it.

THE QUICK TEST FOR INFLUENCE DIAGRAMS

If changing an input wouldn't meaningfully change your decision, it's not worth chasing data for it.

As decision analyst Robert Brown explains, influence diagrams "visually display the flow of influence (cause, relevance, or correlation) among decisions, uncertainties, and values within a problem" and "clarify the kinds of information needed to think through the problem" (Brown, 2018).

WHAT'S AN INFLUENCE DIAGRAM?

Influence diagrams are decision maps. They show what affects what, without the complexity of a full decision tree. Each shape represents a different type of element in your reasoning:

- **Rectangles:** Decisions you can make
- **Ellipses:** Uncertainties that affect the outcome
- **Trapezoids:** Fixed facts or constants
- **Diamonds or hexagons:** Your objective or key result (like expected loss or ROI)
- **Arrows:** The direction of influence—how one factor conditions another

You don't need special software to use one. Start with your decision at the left, draw arrows to the factors that make it uncertain, and end with the outcome you're trying to predict.

In a CRQ context, that might look like this:

- **Decision:** Invest in ransomware detection technology.
- **Uncertainties:** Attack frequency, probability of payout, cost of recovery.
- **Outcome:** Annualized loss exposure.
- **Objective:** Minimize expected loss or maximize ROI.

Even a rough sketch on a whiteboard clarifies which uncertainties drive your decision and, therefore, where to focus your data collection. A simple example is shown in Figure 9-1. The arrows show conditional influence between decisions, uncertainties, and outcomes.

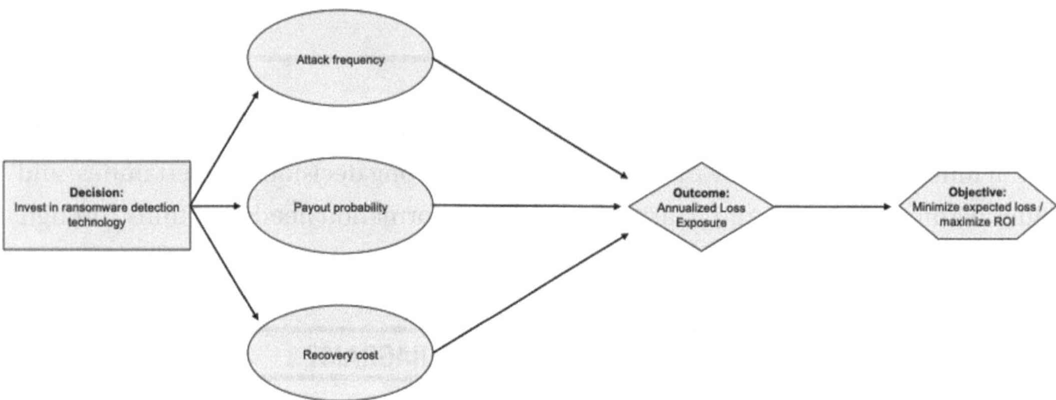

***Figure 9-1.** Simplified influence diagram for a ransomware decision*

GENAI PROMPT: MAP YOUR UNCERTAINTIES

Create an influence diagram for this risk scenario: [*describe your scenario*].

Show the decision I need to make, the key uncertainties that affect that decision, and the final outcome (expected loss, downtime, or another measure of success). Label each node type clearly: decision, uncertainty, and objective, and describe how they influence one another.

Use the output as a first-pass map. Even if it's rough, it will help you focus your data collection on the inputs that truly drive the outcome you're modeling.

Breaking the Data Myths That Keep You Stuck

Let's tackle the biggest misconceptions head-on. These myths sometimes stop people before they even attempt an analysis, but each becomes manageable once you have the right approach to overcome it (see Table 9-1).

Table 9-1. *Breaking the data myths*

Myth	Reality	What To Do Instead
Need lots of data	Need enough to decide	Collect until decision is clear
Need expensive tools	Excel works fine	Start simple, upgrade if needed
Need actuarial tables	Use proxy data	Borrow from similar risks
No incidents = no model	Use industry base rates	Adjust external data to your context
SMEs = garbage in/out	Structured elicitation works	Use ranges, not point estimates
Need an army of people	Focus beats resources	Scope tight, start small

Myth 1: "I Need a Lot of Data"

The Reality: You don't need a lot of data. The goal of a risk assessment isn't to count everything or achieve perfection; it's to reduce enough uncertainty to enable better decisions. Sometimes a better decision only requires a little bit of data, while other times it needs more. In my experience, there can be diminishing returns if you over-collect, and trying to gather all possible data can hinder progress. You might never be done collecting, and you might never get to the decision-making.

Here's what "enough data" looks like: whatever it takes to help a business leader choose between options. Can they decide whether to spend $200K on a new control? Accept the current risk level? Buy more insurance? If your data can inform those choices, you have enough.

In Practice: Collect just enough data to perform the analysis as you have scoped it. If you later need greater precision, you can always dig deeper. Start simple, then iterate.

Myth 2: "I Need Expensive Software and Specialized Tools"

The Reality: Some of the most effective risk analyses are done in Excel with basic functions like RAND() and simple arithmetic. The math behind Monte Carlo simulations is mostly addition, multiplication, and basic statistics. While specialized platforms can add convenience later, they're not required to produce sophisticated, defensible analysis.

Here's what you need: A spreadsheet program and the ability to think in ranges. You can build simulations, calculate percentiles, create loss distributions, and run sensitivity analysis all within Excel or Google Sheets.

In Practice: The value is in the thinking, the methodology, and the conversations an analysis prompts, not the tools. Master the concepts first with simple tools. If your analysis proves valuable and you need more efficiency later, then consider specialized platforms.

Myth 3: "I Need Actuarial Tables"

The Reality: Actuaries lack comprehensive actuarial tables for many types of emerging risks, not just cyber. When they face these situations, they typically use approaches familiar to risk analysts: proxy data, expert judgment, scenario modeling, and simulation techniques.

Here's a technique commonly used in insurance that applies well to cyber risk: **class rating**. Instead of looking for cyber-specific tables, find data about similar organizations. If you're a mid-size healthcare company, look for breach data from other healthcare companies of similar size. If you can't find that, use broader datasets and adjust based on your specific risk factors.

In Practice: You can often borrow approaches from other risk disciplines. Actuaries, epidemiologists, catastrophe modelers, and environmental risk modelers all work with sparse, uncertain data, and many of their methods can be adapted for cyber risk.

SIDEBAR: THE NIRVANA FALLACY

The Nirvana Fallacy is a cognitive bias where people reject an imperfect solution while waiting for a perfect one that doesn't exist. It's named after the Buddhist concept of "nirvana," a perfect, unattainable state.

In risk analysis, the Nirvana Fallacy shows up as

- "Risk quantification is impossible in cybersecurity until we have complete actuarial tables like the life insurance industry has."
- "This industry report doesn't perfectly match our company, so we can't use it for risk modeling."
- "Our SME estimates aren't 100% accurate, so we should stick with qualitative assessments."

The fallacy tricks people into thinking that because a solution isn't perfect, it's not worth pursuing. But perfect data, perfect models, and perfect certainty don't exist in risk analysis or anywhere else.

The antidote: Remember that "good enough to make a better decision" is infinitely more valuable than "perfect but never started."

Myth 4: "No Incidents Means No Model"

The Reality: Most people can buy car insurance even if they've never had an accident. Insurance companies use demographic data, geographic factors, and vehicle characteristics, not just personal claims history.

The same principle applies to cyber risk. Even if you've never had a ransomware incident, you can estimate your risk using industry data, your control posture, and characteristics like sector, size, and technology stack. Here's how: start with a base rate from external sources (like "3% of companies in our sector experience ransomware annually"), then adjust up or down based on your specific situation.

In Practice: External data provides base rates. Internal factors help you adjust those rates. You don't need your own incident history to start.

Myth 5: "Using SMEs Equals Garbage In, Garbage Out"

The Reality: When used with structured elicitation methods, SMEs can be remarkably accurate, especially in domains where data is sparse or problems are novel. Research shows that calibrated expert judgment often outperforms unstructured opinion and, in some contexts, even data-only approaches (Cooke, 1991; Tetlock & Gardner, 2015).

The trick is structure. Instead of asking "What do you think the risk is?" try this: "Based on your experience, what's the lower bound (P5) frequency? The upper bound (P95)? What feels most typical (P50)?" This three-point approach captures uncertainty while leveraging expertise.

In Practice: The problem isn't expert judgment; it's unstructured expert judgment. Simple techniques like asking for ranges instead of point estimates can dramatically improve accuracy.

Myth 6: "I Need an Army of People"

The Reality: You can run effective risk assessments quickly and cheaply, often with just a few people working part-time. The key is starting at the right level of abstraction and resisting scope creep.

Here's a simple approach: pick one well-scoped scenario and spend a few hours gathering data from the three sources (external, internal, and subject matter experts at your organization). That's enough to build a basic model that's far more useful than red-yellow-green ratings.

In Practice: Efficiency comes from focus, not resources. Scope tightly, start simple, iterate as needed.

The next four chapters provide practical techniques to turn theory into practice. You'll learn exactly how to evaluate and trust your data sources (Chapter 10), find and use external data that's useful (Chapter 11), extract insights from internal sources you already have (Chapter 12), and structure expert conversations to get reliable estimates and blend all of the above (Chapter 13).

From Myths to Method: The Three-Source Solution

Each myth we just discussed points to the same underlying problem: risk analysts may not know where to look for data or how to evaluate what they find. The solution is systematic: use three complementary data sources that work together to create complete, defensible risk pictures (Figure 9-2). External data provides industry context, internal data offers organizational specificity, and subject matter experts (SMEs) within your organization deliver forward-looking judgment. Together, these sources create a complete foundation for defensible risk estimates.

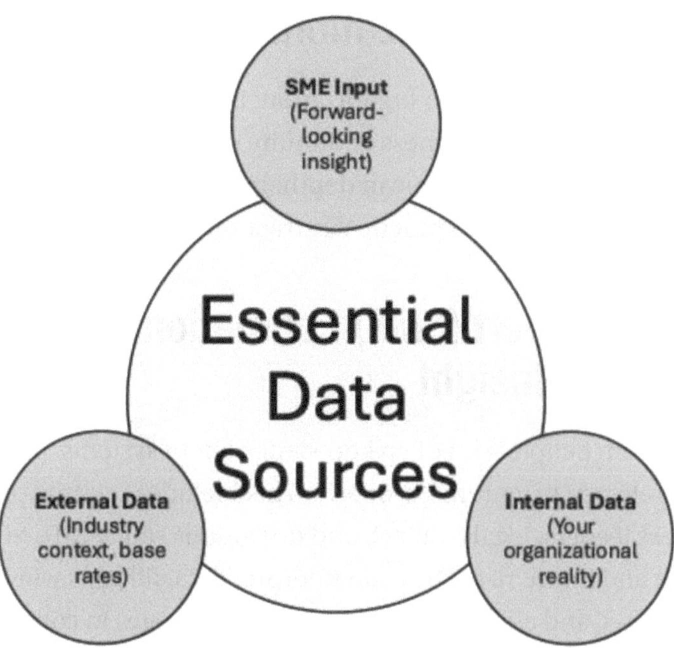

Figure 9-2. *The three essential data sources*

The three sources work together: external data provides context, internal data adds specificity, and expert judgment bridges gaps and looks forward.

Every credible risk assessment draws from as many of these three data types as possible. Think of them as the foundation of a building: for most assessments, all three sources will be available, though occasionally one may not be accessible (e.g., external data for novel threats, internal data for unimplemented systems, or subject matter experts for highly specialized or emerging domains). You can build something with a partial foundation, but the strongest structures rest on all three pillars.

External Data: Context from the Outside World

External data is anything that originates outside your organization but relates to your risk scenario. This includes industry reports, breach databases, regulatory filings, academic research, and threat intelligence. Chapter 11 shows you exactly where to find this data and how to use it.

Internal Data: Your Organizational Reality

Internal data comes from within your organization: incident logs, vulnerability scans, help desk tickets, postmortems, business continuity tests, and financial records tied to past events. Chapter 12 covers this topic in depth, including both typical and atypical data sources that prove useful, plus practical extraction methods.

Subject Matter Expert (SME) Estimation: Forward-Looking Insight

SME input comes from people with deep knowledge about systems, processes, threats, or consequences relevant to your risk scenario. This includes security professionals, engineers, business leaders, legal counsel, and operations staff. SMEs bridge the gap between past data and future risk. They can interpret data, fill gaps where historical information is missing, and adjust estimates based on changes in controls, threats, or business context. Chapter 13 dives deep into this topic.

When building your assessment, external data typically provides your starting baseline, internal data shows how your organization differs from industry norms, and SME input fills gaps and validates your findings.

GENAI PROMPT: FIND RELEVANT DATA SOURCES

To practice applying the three-source model before seeing the detailed examples, use this prompt to brainstorm data sources for your specific risk scenario. Remember to validate any AI suggestions and verify that recommended sources actually exist and are accessible.

I'm assessing [*risk scenario*] for a [*company size/industry*] organization. Help me identify:

- 3-4 external data sources (industry reports, breach databases, academic studies, regulatory data)
- 3-4 types of internal data we might already have (logs, tickets, financial records, past incidents)
- 2-3 job functions or types of subject matter experts to interview and one specific question to ask each

Focus on practical, accessible sources that a risk analyst could realistically obtain.

Here's how the three-source model directly addresses each myth:

- **Myth 1** (too much data): Focus collection on three specific source types.
- **Myth 2** (expensive tools): Data and tools are cheap/free; upgrade only when needed.
- **Myth 3** (actuarial tables): Use external industry data as your foundation.
- **Myth 4** (no incidents): Combine external base rates with internal adjustments.
- **Myth 5** (unreliable SMEs): Structure expert input systematically.
- **Myth 6** (too many people): Each source requires different, manageable effort levels.

How These Sources Work Together: Real-World Examples

Here's how the three sources combine in practice across different risk scenarios.

Example 1: Ransomware Risk Assessment

External data: According to the 2025 Verizon Data Breach Investigations Report, ransomware was involved in 44% of breaches (Verizon, 2025).

Internal data: Your incident logs show no ransomware events in the past three years, but you've had five successful phishing incidents, and your backup testing revealed a 12-hour recovery gap.

SME input: Your incident response lead believes that given your current controls, successful ransomware would likely take 24–48 hours to detect and three to five days to fully recover, with costs primarily driven by business downtime rather than ransom payment.

Combined insight: You might estimate a ransomware incident roughly once every 10–20 years (lower than sector average due to no history, but not zero due to phishing success), with impact ranging from $300K to $3M. The wide impact range reflects uncertainty about incident severity. It could be a small ransomware event affecting a few systems or a major attack that encrypts critical infrastructure and requires extensive recovery efforts.

Example 2: Phishing Success Rate

External data: KnowBe4's 2024 Phishing Benchmarking Report found that 34.3% of untrained employees clicked simulated phishing emails, but that rate dropped to 4.6% after a year of consistent security awareness training (KnowBe4, 2024).

Internal data: Your security team's records show 8% click-through rate on quarterly phishing simulations over the past year.

SME input: Your IT security lead explains that your recent email filtering upgrade and mandatory training likely improved performance, but notes that real phishing attempts are more sophisticated than your tests.

Combined insight: You estimate a 5–15% success rate for real phishing attempts in your environment. Lower than industry average due to good controls and training, but higher than your test results because actual attacks are more convincing. The range reflects uncertainty about attack sophistication vs. your defenses.

Example 3: Cloud Outage Business Impact

External data: While not a perfect match, an older Ponemon Institute study found that data center outages cost between $926 and $17,244 per minute, offering a useful reality check when evaluating other sources (Ponemon Institute, 2016).

Internal data: Customer support tickets from last year's 3-hour AWS connectivity issue show 47 customer complaints and 2 cancellations, representing roughly $8,000 in immediate revenue impact.

SME input: Your VP of Customer Success believes the real impact was higher because most frustrated customers don't complain; they just don't renew. Your DevOps lead points out that you've since implemented better monitoring that would reduce detection time.

Combined insight: Current outage cost estimate of $6,000–$12,000 per hour, most likely $8,000. Internal data provides a good baseline, external data confirms you're in the normal range, and SME input suggests hidden costs but also recent improvements.

Why Multiple Sources Work Better

These examples show why no single source tells the complete story. External data provides context and benchmarks, and starting with it first helps reduce bias in subsequent data collection by encouraging objectivity and preventing you from anchoring on a single internal number or assumption. Internal data provides specificity and organizational reality. SMEs provide forward-looking judgment about changes and hidden factors. Together, they create a more complete and defensible picture than any one source alone, turning abstract industry statistics into actionable, organization-specific insights.

This triangulated approach produces assessments that are defensible, actionable, and far more useful than "high risk" or a red color on a heatmap.

When You Have Limited Sources: A Practical Framework

Not every risk assessment starts with perfect data from all three sources. Here's how to proceed based on what's available.

When You Have Only External Data

Situation: Industry reports and studies, but no internal history or available experts.

Approach

- Use external data as your baseline estimate.
- Use wider uncertainty ranges to account for unknown organizational factors—we'll cover specific adjustment methods in Chapter 10.
- Document assumptions about how your organization might differ from the industry average.
- Plan to refine estimates when internal data or SME input becomes available.

Example: Industry data shows 15% annual phishing success rate. Without internal context, estimate 5–30% for your organization with a note to narrow this range as you gather more information.

When You Have External + Internal Data

Situation: Industry benchmarks plus your own incident logs, metrics, or historical data.

Approach

- Start with an external baseline for context.
- Adjust based on internal data patterns (higher/lower than average, different trends).
- Use internal data to calibrate magnitude estimates (your actual costs vs. industry averages).
- Document what makes your organization different.

Example: Industry average of 15% phishing success, but your logs show 8% in simulations. Estimate 6–12% for real attacks, noting that your training program appears effective, but real attacks are more sophisticated.

When You Have All Three Sources

Situation: External benchmarks, internal data, and access to knowledgeable experts.

Approach

- Use external data for initial context and benchmarking.
- Ground-truth with internal data to understand your specific situation.
- Leverage SME insight to adjust for future changes, hidden factors, and forward-looking risks.
- Create ranges that reflect the consensus or explain disagreements between sources.

Example: Industry 15%, internal data 8%, SME estimates 10–15% for future attacks due to increasing sophistication. Final estimate: 8–15%, with most likely 12%.

QUALITY OVER QUANTITY

One high-quality source often beats three poor-quality sources. A single credible SME with deep knowledge of your environment may provide better estimates than multiple outdated industry surveys.

The goal isn't to use all three sources for every assessment. It's to use the best available sources and be transparent about limitations.

Understanding the Data Spectrum

Before we dive into practical data collection, it's helpful to understand that not all data is created equal. Data falls along two important spectrums that affect how useful it is for risk analysis.

Qualitative vs. Quantitative Data

Qualitative data is everywhere in cybersecurity: descriptive adjectives, arbitrary rankings, opinions, and feelings. You've seen it in the form of "high, medium, low," "red, yellow, green," or "fast, slow." These categories may help structure a conversation, but they are inherently subjective and can vary wildly from one team or one person to the next.

Quantitative data is about numbers: counting, ratios, and measurements. Instead of "a lot of incidents," you have "five security events last month" or "three failed logins from this user in an hour." Quantitative data has the benefit of specificity and repeatability, making it the backbone of defensible risk models.

Subjective vs. Objective Data

Sometimes, the challenge isn't about numbers vs. adjectives; it's about perspective. Here, we encounter the **subjective/objective spectrum**.

Subjective data reflects personal opinions and judgments: "That risk feels high," or "I believe incidents will increase by 10% next year." Subjective data is shaped by experience, bias, and context. SMEs bring valuable insights, particularly in filling gaps where data is sparse or providing context that external and internal data sources might miss. Still, subjective data is most reliable when used alongside other data sources rather than as a standalone foundation.

Objective data is about observations and measurements: "It's 70 degrees today," or "We had one reportable data breach last year." These are concrete observations, less vulnerable to bias and personal interpretation.

The Data Type Matrix

Table 9-2 shows how these concepts work together in practice.

Table 9-2. *Data type matrix*

	Qualitative Data	Quantitative Data
Subjective	• High, medium, low ratings • Interview responses • Risk descriptions	• Expert predictions of breach frequency • SME estimates of downtime duration
Objective	• Incident report narratives • Categorized findings	• Actual incident counts • Measured financial losses • Verified breach statistics

In the following chapters, we'll show you specific techniques for each quadrant: how to structure subjective data, how to validate objective data, and how to extract quantitative insights from qualitative sources.

All types of data have value in risk analysis. While quantitative and objective data often feels more reliable, subjective expert judgment can be remarkably accurate when properly structured. In fact, as you'll learn in Chapter 13, calibrated expert opinions can sometimes outperform other approaches in forecasting, especially when the right elicitation techniques are used (Tetlock & Gardner, 2015). The goal isn't to dismiss any category, but to understand how to extract the most value from whatever data you have.

Addressing AI-Generated and Synthetic Data

With the rise of large language models, you might wonder if AI should be considered a data source for cyber risk quantification. The short answer: **No, it can't be a primary data source.** AI-generated data has three fundamental problems for risk analysis:

It's not grounded in direct observation. GenAI doesn't witness or measure anything. It reflects patterns from training data that may be biased, outdated, or incomplete.

You can't trace the data origin easily. You won't know if output comes from a legitimate research report, a Reddit thread, or a hallucination. Risk models need auditable sources.

There's a risk of circular reasoning. If AI trained on human judgment is used to simulate expert judgment, you create feedback loops that reinforce biases without adding new information.

How AI Can Support Real Data Sources

While AI shouldn't be its own category, it can dramatically accelerate the three core sources:

For external research: AI can help you find and summarize reports in minutes instead of hours. You still need to verify the underlying sources and check for hallucinations.

For internal analysis: AI can extract patterns from logs and tickets faster than manual review. AI is still processing real internal data, just as a human would, but more efficiently.

For expert elicitation: AI can help structure interviews, suggest questions, or challenge assumptions. It's augmenting human judgment, not replacing it.

With that context about AI's role established, let's get practical.

You Can Start Right Now

Here's what I want you to remember: the data you need to get started is closer than you think.

That vulnerability scan in your inbox? Internal data. The Verizon DBIR you skimmed last month? External data. The security engineer who remembers the last major incident? SME goldmine.

The goal isn't perfection; it's **progress**. Start with what you have, express uncertainty as ranges, and build confidence through iteration.

EXERCISE 9-1: IDENTIFY YOUR DATA SOURCES

Scenario: Your organization wants to assess the risk of business email compromise (BEC)—the risk of attackers gaining access to employee email accounts and using them to commit fraud against the company or customers.

Your Task: For each source type, brainstorm what information would be valuable. Don't try to collect the data yet; just identify what you'd look for and where you might find it.

Part A: External Sources

What industry data would help you understand BEC risk? Consider:

- How often do organizations experience BEC attacks?
- What's the typical financial impact?
- What are the common attack methods?
- Which industries or company sizes are most targeted?

Write down: Three to four types of external data that would be useful and where you might find them (industry reports, government studies, security vendor research, etc.)

Part B: Internal Sources What does your organization already track that might relate to BEC risk? Think about

- Email security logs and alerts
- Financial transaction monitoring
- Employee reports of suspicious emails
- Past incidents involving email compromise
- Training records or awareness metrics, like phishing test results

Write down: Three to four types of internal data your organization might have and which teams would own them

Part C: SME Sources

Who in your organization would have insights about BEC risk? Consider people who

- Handle email security and monitoring.
- Investigate security incidents.
- Process financial transactions.
- Train employees on security awareness.
- Understand business processes that could be targeted.

Write down: Two to three people you'd want to interview and one specific question you'd ask each**Reflection Questions**

- How do the three source types provide different perspectives on the same risk?
- Which source type seems most accessible in your organization?
- What gaps do you notice—areas where you'd have limited information?

Chapter Summary

The Big Idea: The data you need to start cyber risk quantification is closer than you think—you just need to know where to look and how to use it effectively.

Key Takeaways

- **Break the data myths** that keep people stuck: you don't need massive datasets, expensive tools, or actuarial tables to begin.
- **Use the three-source model:** External data (industry context), internal data (your reality), and SME input (forward-looking insight) work together to create complete risk pictures.
- **Start with what you have** and improve over time rather than waiting for perfect information.
- **Focus on decision-support**—collect just enough data to help leaders choose between options, not everything possible.

- **Understand the data spectrum** from qualitative to quantitative, subjective to objective—all types have value when used appropriately.

Bottom Line: The goal isn't perfection; it's progress. Start simple, express uncertainty as ranges, and build confidence through iteration.

What's Coming Next

You've broken the data myths and understand the three essential sources: external data for context, internal data for organizational reality, and SME input for forward-looking insight. Now comes the critical question: How do you know if the data you find is actually worth using?

Before you start hunting for industry reports or mining incident logs, you need a systematic way to evaluate what you find. Not all data is created equal. Vendor surveys sit alongside rigorous research, marketing claims masquerade as statistics, and biased sources get shared as frequently as independent studies.

Chapter 10 **teaches you how to vet and trust your data sources.** You'll learn a simple three-step framework to evaluate any piece of information in minutes, distinguish quality research from hype, and adjust your uncertainty ranges based on data reliability. This evaluation skill is the foundation for everything that follows.

References

Brown, R. D. III. (2018). *Business case analysis with R.* Apress.

Cooke, R. M. (1991). Experts in uncertainty: Opinion and subjective probability in science. Oxford University Press.

KnowBe4. (2024). Phishing by industry benchmarking report.

Ponemon Institute. (2016). Cost of data center outages. Vertiv.

Tetlock, P. E., & Gardner, D. (2015). Superforecasting: The art and science of prediction. Crown Publishing Group.

Verizon. (2025). 2025 data breach investigations report. `https://www.verizon.com/business/resources/reports/dbir/`

CHAPTER 10

How to Vet and Believe Your Data

Don't believe the hype.

—Public Enemy

I once inherited a FAIR-based risk program where some of the security scenarios didn't pass a basic reality check. When I dug deeper, I discovered most of the impact estimates were based on a vendor marketing report that turned out to be a poorly designed survey with a tiny sample size and no disclosed methodology. The data wasn't relevant to our company size or sector, but someone had plugged it directly into the model anyway.

I delayed the quarterly risk reports for a few weeks while I rebuilt the analysis with defensible data. When I finally presented the updated numbers, they were dramatically lower than what leadership had been seeing for months. This was a medium-sized company, and it turns out the new analysis showed that risk was elevated by at least $50m per scenario. That is a huge difference for a company of that size. That led to some very uncomfortable questions: "Why were our previous estimates so inflated? How do we know these new numbers are right? What else might be wrong with our risk program?"

Here's the thing: this wasn't malicious or lazy. The analysis was from a smart analyst who hadn't been taught systematic data quality evaluation. If you're reading this chapter, you probably don't want to end up explaining to your CISO why your risk estimates just dropped by 60%.

Until very recently, exhaustive data collection, sourcing, vetting, and analysis were prohibitively difficult, even for large teams with significant resources. The common approach was to utilize limited data sources, which were heavily supplemented by SME estimates. A chapter like this would have been considered too onerous as recently as

T. Martin-Vegue, *From Heatmaps to Histograms*, https://doi.org/10.1007/979-8-8688-2300-8_10

2024. But generative AI has fundamentally changed the landscape. Tasks that used to take analysts weeks—sourcing diverse datasets, cross-referencing multiple studies, and identifying methodological red flags—can now be done in a fraction of the time with AI assistance.

This transformation means the time is now to implement rigorous data vetting and evaluation standards. We can finally afford to be systematic about data quality without the prohibitive time costs. More importantly, using AI-accelerated research with strong vetting processes makes our risk assessments far more defensible to skeptics who question quantitative approaches.

The cyber risk quantification field has developed sophisticated modeling techniques and frameworks, but it has largely ignored the fundamental question of data quality. Most CRQ resources will teach you how to build Monte Carlo simulations or apply FAIR methodology, but they won't tell you how to evaluate whether your inputs are worth modeling in the first place. Other fields like climate science and nuclear safety have solved this problem decades ago with systematic frameworks for tagging data origin and quality.

Every risk analyst faces the same challenge: useful data is everywhere, but so is junk data disguised as research. Vendor surveys with small sample sizes, industry reports with undisclosed methodologies, and expert opinions that turn out to be less than expert all compete for space in your risk model. The difference between building a credible analysis and accidentally misleading your leadership often comes down to one skill: knowing how to evaluate whether a piece of information is worth using.

That skill, data vetting, is what this chapter teaches. You'll learn a simple three-step process to evaluate any data source in minutes and turn questionable information into honest, defensible ranges you can confidently use in your models.

The challenge is bigger than any single analyst. The cybersecurity field now produces massive amounts of data—some excellent, some problematic. LinkedIn polls asking "How much did your last breach cost?" sit alongside legitimate research. Vendor blog posts citing cherry-picked statistics get shared as frequently as peer-reviewed papers. Without evaluation skills, it's hard to distinguish between rigorous research and promotional campaigns dressed up as studies. Every dataset that goes into a quantitative risk assessment should carry its own "nutrition label." Reviewers should be able to see, in seconds, both the number and the story behind it: where it came from, how reliable it is, and what limitations they should know about. That's why we need a systematic screening process.

A Simple Three-Step Evaluation

The solution is systematic data evaluation that an analyst can do in a few minutes. Every data source receives the same treatment: a quick screening to eliminate obvious problems, basic documentation for audit trails, and a quality assessment to establish appropriate uncertainty ranges.

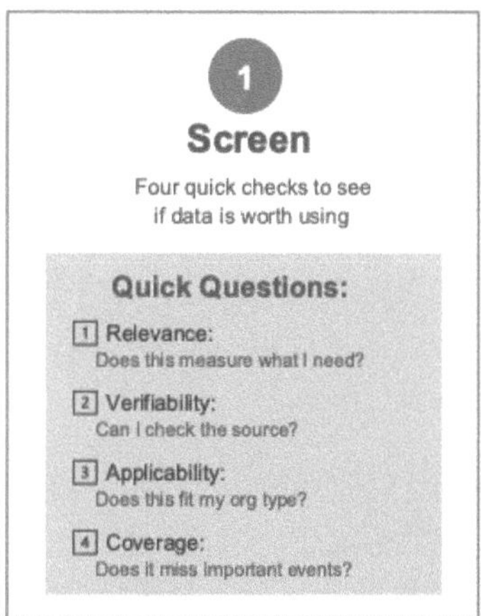

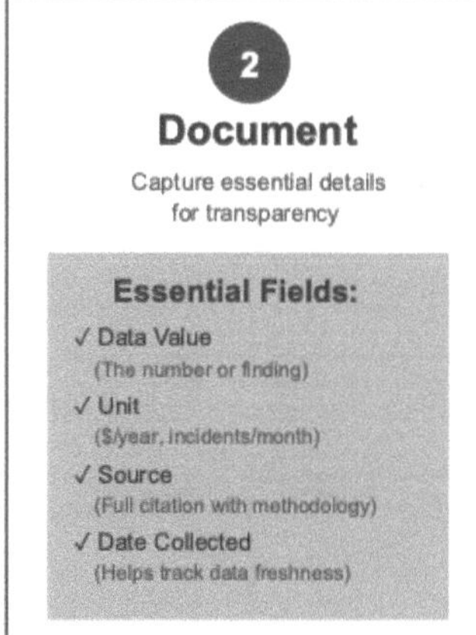

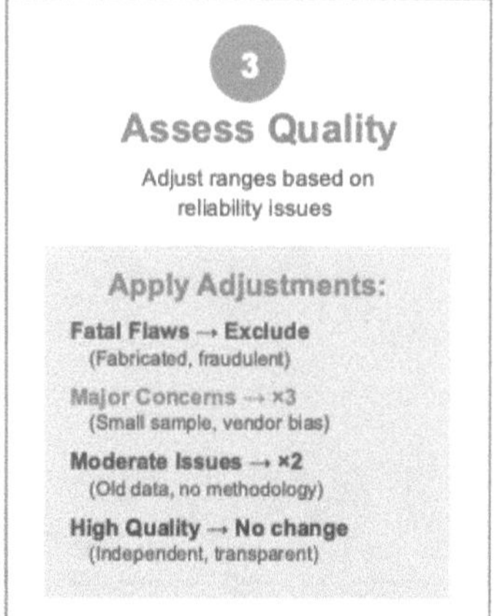

Figure 10-1. *The three-step data evaluation process*

Here's how it works, as seen in Figure 10-1:

- **Step 1: Screen**—Four quick checks to see if data is worth using.
- **Step 2: Document**—Capture essential details for transparency.
- **Step 3: Assess quality**—Adjust ranges based on reliability.

Figure 10-2 illustrates the systematic application of the four screening criteria to determine whether data sources are suitable for use. Keep in mind that we're not trying to *eliminate* all uncertainty. It's about *showing* our levels of uncertainty. Uncertainty can never be eliminated entirely. When data quality is questionable, we widen ranges rather than exclude potentially useful information. When data is strong, we can use narrower ranges with more confidence.

Figure 10-2. *Quality assessment decision tree: apply the four screening criteria systematically to determine if data sources are worth using.*

Let's walk through each step.

Step 1: Screen Your Data

First, before using any data, we need to screen it through these four quick checks. This tells us if we should even use the data in the first place.

Relevance: Does this measure what I'm modeling?

- **Use it**: Downtime hours when measuring outage costs, incident response times for the same incident type, expert estimates with a clear scope that matches your scenario
- **Be skeptical**: Generic risk scores, mixed IT tickets, vague expert opinions

Here's a quick example of how to apply those screening questions to a real-world data source you've almost certainly encountered before.

EXAMPLE: EVALUATING "COST OF A DATA BREACH" TYPE REPORTS

I'm calling this one out because these reports are everywhere. They show up in executive decks, insurance filings, and vendor marketing slides, often cited as if they were definitive. Many readers will encounter them long before they ever build a quantitative model or review peer data.

The problem isn't bad intent. It's weak methodology. Most of these "Ponemon-like" reports rely on small, self-selected samples, opaque survey designs, and results packaged for marketing rather than measurement. That doesn't make them useless, but it does mean they belong in the **low-confidence** tier of this framework.

Treat them as directional input, not calibrated data. They can help shape priors or illustrate trends, but they shouldn't anchor your quantitative model without independent, reproducible data to back them up.

Verifiability: Can I check the source and method?

- **Use it**: Published reports with methodology, timestamped logs, experts with track records
- **Be skeptical**: Random slide deck numbers, missing data with no explanation, unsupported expert claims, industry reports with no methodology

If the source can't be verified, don't discard it immediately. Note it as unverified and use it only as supporting or anecdotal evidence until stronger data becomes available.

Applicability: Does this fit my organization type?

- **Use it**: Same industry/size/region, similar systems, relevant expert experience
- **Be skeptical**: Different sectors, unrelated technology, irrelevant expert background

Coverage: Does this source miss important events?

- **Use it**: Known coverage rates, acknowledged limitations, realistic scope claims
- **Be skeptical**: Public databases missing private incidents, partial logs with no adjustment, claims of perfect visibility

SCIENTIFIC FOUNDATION

This screening approach is adapted from the **Numeral, Unit, Spread, Assessment, Pedigree (NUSAP)** framework (Funtowicz & Ravetz, 1990), used for over 30 years in fields like environmental science, nuclear safety, industrial safety, public health, and many more to evaluate data quality under uncertainty.

Quick Decision Rules

- **Fails 1 criterion**: Use with caution; apply heavy uncertainty ranges (step 3).
- **Fails 2+ criteria**: Exclude and find better sources.
- **Passes all 4**: Move to Step 2 for detailed assessment.

If Data Raises Red Flags

- **First choice**: Find better data that passes all screens.
- **If none exists**: Use SME methods (Chapter 13) instead, possibly using the problematic data as a discussion starter.

GENAI PROMPT: SOURCE SCREENING ASSISTANT

[*paste data source, description, and raw data if possible*]

I'm evaluating this data source for a risk assessment. Please assess it against these four criteria:

1. Relevance: Does this measure what I need for [*specific risk scenario*]?
2. Verifiability: Can the methodology and source be traced and checked?

3. Applicability: Does this fit a [your org size/industry] organization?
4. Coverage: What might this source be missing or excluding?

Rate each criterion as Pass/Fail and explain your reasoning.

Now, practice applying these screening criteria with some realistic examples:

EXERCISE 10-1: SOURCE SCREENING PRACTICE

Evaluate these three sources against the four screening criteria:

- A LinkedIn poll: "How much did your last cyber incident cost?" (47 responses)
- Your company's incident response log from last year's database outage
- Gartner report on cloud security costs (500+ enterprise survey, methodology disclosed)

For each source, determine: Pass or fail on each criterion? Use or exclude?

Check your work with the GenAI prompt preceding this exercise.

Step 2: Basic Data Collection

Data without context is dangerous. This step creates an audit trail that stakeholders can follow, helping you revisit assumptions later when conditions change. Make it a practice to save each data point you collect and each risk measurement in a shared, accessible location. This approach delivers two key benefits: transparency that builds stakeholder confidence and reusability that saves a tremendous amount of time, as similar data points appear across different scenarios and assessments. For each source that passes Step 1, capture these essential elements:

Essential Documentation Fields

Data value: The central figure or finding you're working with (percentage, dollar amount, frequency, or any quantitative claim). See *Appendix C* for a full list of data types and unit examples.

Unit: The measurement scale that makes your data unambiguous (incidents/year, USD loss, probability, etc.).

Source: Full citation with enough detail for someone else to find the exact same information.

Date collected: When you gathered this information (helps track data freshness).

Documentation Template

Table 10-1. *Sample data collection documentation template*

Data Value	Unit	Source	Date Collected
44%	Breaches with ransomware present	2025 Verizon DBIR, Summary of findings, p. 10	1/15/2025
12–24 phishing incidents	Incidents/year	Internal: ServiceNow tickets, category "Phishing," 2023–2024	1/10/2025
\$150K–\$500K (CISO estimate: \$280K most likely)	USD breach cost	SME estimate: CISO based on 2022 incident + legal fees	1/12/2025

What If I Can't Find a Range?

If your source only gives a single number with no range, that's a signal to pay closer attention. Real-world data always has uncertainty. Look for any indication of spread around the main number, whether it's confidence intervals (95% CI: 180K–320K), simple ranges (two to six incidents/yr), or even narrative qualifiers like "order-of-magnitude estimate."

If you still can't find it, don't worry. We'll cover this in the next section.

Documentation Best Practices

- Record sources immediately—don't rely on memory.
- Use full citations, not just URLs that might change.
- Include enough detail for someone else to find the same information.
- Note ranges when available, not just single numbers.

GENAI PROMPT: DOCUMENTATION STANDARDIZER

Create a systematic record for this data source: [*paste source info*]. Output in a table format that can be optionally exported as an Excel file. Format it with these fields:

- Data Value: [the specific number/range]
- Unit: [precise measurement scale]
- Source: [full citation with page/section]
- Date Collected: Today's date

Step 3: Assess Quality and Adjust for Uncertainty

Now comes the critical step: evaluating what you've collected and adjusting for reliability issues. This creates appropriate confidence levels, not artificial certainty. When data quality is questionable, we widen uncertainty ranges rather than exclude potentially useful information. As you learned in Chapter 4, uncertainty doesn't mean we lack data. It means we're defining our confidence in what we do have.

The Simplified Quality Checklist

Use this four-category approach to quickly assess any source's quality factors:

Fatal Flaws (Exclude Immediately)

- Fabricated or completely unverifiable sources
- Fraudulent organizations with known misconduct history
- Synthetic data presented as real incidents
- Marketing surveys disguised as research
- Sources or claims that defy basic logic

Major Concerns (×3 Range Adjustment—or adjust to your comfort level)

- Small sample sizes relative to the population they claim to represent
- Heavy vendor bias (selling solutions to the problem they're measuring)

- Scale mismatches (Fortune 500 data applied to SMB scenarios)
- Cherry-picked timeframes or outlier events
- Geographic/regulatory mismatches (EU data for US analysis)

Moderate Issues (×2 Range Adjustment—or adjust to your comfort level)

- Survey data with undisclosed methodology
- Self-reported incidents without verification
- Data over two to three years old for rapidly evolving threats
- Missing error bounds or confidence intervals
- Moderate sample size limitations

High Quality (No Adjustment Needed)

- Large, representative samples with disclosed methodology
- Independent research from reputable organizations
- Recent data relevant to your context
- Transparent limitations and confidence intervals
- Multiple independent confirmations

These multipliers (×2, ×3) reflect my experience with what creates appropriately conservative ranges for different quality issues. You might find that ×1.5 or ×4 feels right for your risk program and organizational context. The key principle is consistent: lower quality data should result in wider uncertainty ranges. Start with these guidelines, then adjust based on what feels defensible when you present to stakeholders.

Important Rule: Don't stack penalties. Apply only the largest single adjustment needed. If a source has both small sample size (×3) and vendor bias (×2), use ×3, not ×6.

Appendix D has a comprehensive list of quality factors, examples, and range adjustments.

GENAI PROMPT: QUALITY ISSUE DETECTOR

[copy/paste source, source description or document (e.g. doc, PDF)]

Analyze this data source for quality issues. Check for these problems:

- Sample size and methodology transparency
- Potential bias or conflicts of interest
- Relevance and applicability to my context
- Missing context or important limitations

Rate as: Fatal Flaw, Major Concern, Moderate Issue, or High Quality. Describe in detail why you are making this assessment and cite specific examples in the source to back your reasoning.

Range Adjustment Examples

When you identify quality issues, adjust uncertainty ranges to reflect reduced confidence:

How ×2 Adjustment Works

- **Original estimate**: "15–25% annual breach rate."
- **After ×2 adjustment**: "8–40% annual breach rate."
- **You're acknowledging**: "This could be quite different from what the source claims."

How ×3 Adjustment Works

- **Original estimate**: "$500K average breach cost."
- **Convert to range**: "$300K–$700K" (rough estimate).
- **After ×3 adjustment**: "$100K–$1.1M."
- **You're saying**: "This number is highly uncertain."

Here's how quality assessment and range adjustment work together in practice.

Documentation Example

Table 10-2. *Complete documentation example showing quality assessment in practice*

Data Value	Unit	Source	Date Collected	Quality Concerns	Range Adjustment	Use Case
44%	Breaches with ransomware present	2025 Verizon DBIR, Summary of findings, p. 10	5/15/2025	No significant concerns identified	None applied	Primary input for baseline frequency
12–24 phishing incidents	Incidents/year	Internal: ServiceNow tickets, category "Phishing," 2023–2024	4/10/2025	~80% coverage rate, consistent logging	×2 for coverage gaps	Primary input, adjusted for incomplete visibility
$150K–$500K (CISO estimate: $280K most likely)	USD breach cost	SME estimate: CISO based on 2022 incident + legal fees	4/12/2025	Single expert, based on one incident	×2 for limited sample	Supporting estimate, validate with external data

Creating Ranges from Point Estimates

Many sources only provide single numbers: "Average breach cost is $4.2M" or "23% of companies experienced ransomware." But quantitative risk assessment requires ranges to capture uncertainty. Look at the back of the report or the organization's website for any additional data slicing or ranges. If you still can't find anything, you'll need to convert it.

Step 1: Identify What Type of Estimate You Have

- **Mean/average**: Mathematical average (common but problematic in cyber)
- **Mode**: Value that shows up most frequently, sometimes called "Most Likely" (rare but better)

- **Undefined**: Just a number with no explanation (unfortunately common)

Step 2: Convert Using the Appropriate Method

For Averages (Most Common): Cyber data is usually skewed; a few big incidents pull the average up. Don't use the average as your mode/"most likely" value. At this point, there is no choice but to take the data and the report and ask SMEs to apply their best judgment and create a three-point estimate, using the average as a starting point.

Example: "Average ransomware cost is $1.5M."

- Ask SMEs: "What's a realistic low-end cost?" → $200K (5th percentile)
- "What's typical in your experience?" → $800K (median)
- "What's the high-end that's still plausible?" → $5M (95th percentile)

For Point Estimates with No Context: *Example: "12% of healthcare orgs experienced breaches."*

- **Build range around it**: "8–18%" based on SME judgment
- **Apply quality adjustments**: If survey-based, maybe "5–25%"

Step 3: Apply Quality Adjustments to Your New Range

After creating the range, apply any ×2 or ×3 adjustments based on data quality issues identified above.

EXERCISE 10-2: APPLY THE COMPLETE FRAMEWORK

Practice the full three-step process on these three data sources.

Sources to Evaluate

1. **Verizon** 2025 **DBIR finding:** "Ransomware was involved in 44% of breaches" (large annual study, established methodology, publicly available report).
2. **Internal ServiceNow data:** Eighteen phishing incidents logged over 2023–2024, but system only covers about 80% of employees.
3. **CISO estimate:** "Based on our 2022 incident, a breach would cost $280K most likely, could range $150K–$500K" (estimate based on a single past event).

Your Task

- **Step 1:** Apply the four screening criteria.
- **Step 2:** Document each source.
- **Step 3:** Assess quality and determine range adjustments.

Focus on documenting your reasoning: Why did you categorize each source in the Simplified Quality Checklist? What specific factors drove your range adjustment decisions?

Why Range Widening Works: The Scientific Foundation

Range widening isn't punishment for poor data. It's honest uncertainty accounting based on decades of research in decision science. When Douglas Hubbard studied how estimation accuracy relates to data quality, he found that imprecise inputs require more conservative ranges to maintain calibration (Hubbard, 2014).

Calibration means that when you say "90% confidence," you're right about 90% of the time. Well-calibrated risk analysts produce uncertainty ranges that accurately reflect what they actually know vs. what they wish they knew.

This systematic approach to uncertainty comes directly from the NUSAP framework we adapted for screening. NUSAP explicitly encourages mapping the strength of each data component and using that assessment to inform how broadly uncertainty is expressed (Funtowicz & Ravetz, 1990). The ×2 and ×3 range adjustments apply this principle: weaker data components require broader uncertainty ranges.

The Logic

- High-quality data = narrower uncertainty ranges = higher confidence
- Poor-quality data = wider uncertainty ranges = appropriate skepticism
- False precision from bad data = worse than honest uncertainty

Real-World Example: A vendor survey of 47 companies claims "average breach cost is $2.1M." Without quality adjustment, you might use "$1.8M–$2.4M." But the small sample and vendor bias warrant ×3 widening, giving you "$600K–$6.3M," a range that honestly reflects what you actually know vs. what you wish you knew.

This approach prevents overconfident decisions based on shaky foundations while preserving useful signal from imperfect sources.

The Ten-Minute Assessment Method

For each source, spend no more than ten minutes asking

1. **Can I defend this source if challenged?** (Do I know where it came from and how it was created?)
2. **Does this actually measure what I need?** (Is it relevant to my scenario and organization?)
3. **What would make me distrust this number?** (What are the obvious limitations?)

If you can't answer the first two confidently, find better data. The third question guides your range adjustments.

⚠ AVOID THESE DATA VETTING TRAPS

Mistake 1: "This number looks official, so it must be good."

Reality: Marketing surveys often look professional.

Mistake 2: "I'll just use the average as my best estimate."

Reality: Most incidents are below average, while a few large ones pull the mean up.

Mistake 3: "I can't find perfect data, so I won't do the analysis."

Reality: Honest uncertainty beats perfect paralysis.

Mistake 4: "This data is recent, so it must be relevant."

Reality: Recency doesn't equal relevance—fresh data about the wrong scenario is still useless for your analysis.

Mistake 5: "If multiple sources say the same thing, it must be true."

Reality: Industry reports often cite the same original flawed study, creating an echo chamber of bad data.

Mistake 6: "Big sample size automatically means high quality."

Reality: A survey of 5,000 CISOs who self-select to respond is still biased, regardless of size.

Mistake 7: "Academic sources are always more reliable than industry reports."

Reality: Peer-reviewed research can be years out of date or too theoretical for practical risk decisions.

Mistake 8: "I found one great source, so I don't need to validate it."

Reality: Even high-quality sources have blind spots and limitations that matter for your specific scenario.

"Good Enough" Decision-Making

Don't overthink it. You're looking for obvious problems, not conducting a peer review. Perfect data doesn't exist in risk analysis. The goal is appropriate uncertainty, not false precision.

Stop assessing when

- You've identified the main quality issues.
- You know what range adjustment to apply.
- The data answers the core question.
- You can explain the limitations to stakeholders.
- Further analysis won't change your decision (see Value of Information sidebar below).

Dig deeper only when

- Your quality assessment is inconclusive.
- The data doesn't answer your core question.
- You found major red flags that need investigation.
- The decision involves significant budget or risk.
- Conflicting sources give dramatically different answers.

THE VALUE OF INFORMATION: WHEN TO STOP LOOKING

Before spending more time hunting for better data, ask: "Will finding more information actually change my decision?" This concept, called the Value of Information (VoI), is central to Douglas Hubbard's Applied Information Economics approach (Hubbard, 2014).

The Core Principle: Information is only valuable if it could change your decision, and the value depends on how much that decision matters.

If you're deciding between two security controls and already have enough data to make a confident choice, additional research has low VOI.

If you're presenting to the board and your estimates could change budget allocation by millions, high-quality data has high VOI.

If you're doing a quick risk screening for quarterly planning, perfect precision has low VOI.

Sometimes, a single high-quality source beats spending days hunting for the perfect dataset that doesn't exist.

Chapter Summary

The Big Idea: Every piece of data tells a story about its reliability. Learn to read that story so you can build defensible risk estimates from imperfect sources.

Key Takeaways

- **Don't believe the hype**. Learn to distinguish quality research from marketing disguised as data
- **Apply systematic screening** before evaluating quality: Does it measure what you need? Can you verify it? Does it apply to organizations like yours?
- **Use the quality assessment framework** to identify red flags and apply appropriate range adjustments (×2, ×3) that reflect reduced confidence.
- **This applies to ALL data types**: external sources, internal data, and SME input all need systematic evaluation.

- **Transparency about uncertainty is better than false precision.** Wider ranges from poor-quality data honestly reflect what you don't know.

Bottom Line: Every dataset should carry its own "nutrition label" showing where it came from, how reliable it is, and what limitations matter for your analysis.

What's Coming Next

Chapter 11 will take you hunting for external data, showing you exactly where to look, how to extract usable numbers from industry reports, and how to spot the red flags that distinguish quality research from vendor hype.

Time to go find some data.

References

Funtowicz, S. O., & Ravetz, J. R. (1990). *Uncertainty and Quality in Science for Policy.* Springer Netherlands.

Hubbard, D. W. (2014). *How to measure anything: Finding the value of intangibles in business* (3rd ed.). Wiley.

Verizon. (2025). "2025 Data Breach Investigations Report". Retrieved from `https://www.verizon.com/business/resources/reports/dbir/`

CHAPTER 11

Finding and Using External Data

Without data, you're just another person with an opinion.

—W. Edwards Deming

External data refers to any information that did not originate within your own organization. External data is a double-edged sword: it's plentiful, easy to obtain, often free, and, sometimes, can be used directly in risk assessments in varying areas. However, working with it is easily the most complicated part of the three-source model used in this book. Formats are all over the map (large data dumps, PDFs, glossy vendor reports, scraped news feeds, advertisements disguised as research), the reporting goals vary (regulatory compliance, marketing, peer-reviewed research), and the quality ranges from directly usable to "should never have seen daylight." Luckily for risk analysts everywhere, a lot has changed since the olden days of data gathering (the olden days are early 2025, of course). AI can now help you discover relevant sources, extract key statistics, and even assess data quality, turning what used to be a 30-hour research project into a focused 2-hour effort.

In this chapter, you'll learn to find and evaluate external data that measurably improves your risk assessments. We'll cover the five types of external sources, red flags that signal unreliable research, and step-by-step methods for turning industry reports into quantified inputs you can defend to stakeholders.

T. Martin-Vegue, *From Heatmaps to Histograms*, https://doi.org/10.1007/979-8-8688-2300-8_11

LESSONS FROM 1066: THE COST OF IGNORING EXTERNAL SIGNALS

In early 1066, Harold Godwinson ascended to the English throne following the death of Edward the Confessor on January 5th, 1066. At that time, England was relatively peaceful, and Harold's advisors, observing the internal stability, likely developed a sense of security. They hadn't experienced a significant negative event, and the kingdom appeared stable.

However, warning signs were evident.

To the north, Harald Hardrada of Norway was assembling a fleet of approximately 300 ships, preparing to invade England. To the south, William of Normandy was building ships and gathering an army, openly preparing for invasion.

Both men had histories of successful military campaigns. Yet, Harold focused inward, consolidating power and securing loyalty from the English nobility. He didn't fully consider the external threats, creating a critical blind spot.

Then the invasions began.

On September 20th, 1066, Hardrada's forces defeated the English earls Edwin and Morcar at the Battle of Fulford. Five days later, Harold marched north and achieved a significant victory against Hardrada at the Battle of Stamford Bridge on September 25th.

However, shortly after, William landed on the southern coast of England on September 28th. Harold rushed south to confront this new threat and was ultimately killed at the Battle of Hastings on October 14th, 1066. This defeat led to the Norman conquest of England and a profound transformation of its society and governance.

Lesson: Your internal environment might appear calm, but ignoring external indicators, such as competitors experiencing cyberattacks, regulatory actions against peers, or emerging threats in similar technology stacks, can leave you vulnerable. External data provides the foresight needed to anticipate and address risks proactively before they become incidents.

Why Your Organization's Data Only Tells Half the Story

Looking inward, only at the incidents, threats, and controls that have occurred at your company, isn't enough to understand the full risk landscape. Your internal logs might tell you what's happened before, but they won't show you everything that could happen next.

I own a house, and like every other homeowner, I face fire risk. However, I've never had a fire. In risk analysis, we call this "zero incident risk." If an insurer based my premium purely on that personal history, they'd think I carried no risk. But that's not how insurance works.

Instead, my fire policy is priced using demographic and contextual data: where I live, the materials my house is built with, proximity to fire stations, and local incident rates. As we covered in Chapter 9, this approach is known as **class rating** in actuarial science: grouping me with others who share my characteristics to estimate risk. My individual loss history might nudge the price up or down, but the insurer's estimate is built on a broad, population-level picture of similar homes and neighborhoods.

We can apply this exact logic to cyber risk quantification.

Just because your company has never experienced a data breach doesn't mean your risk is zero. It might mean you've been lucky, you're doing things right, or you've experienced one and don't know it. To create a realistic picture of risk, we need to look beyond your walls.

It means pulling data about companies with comparable technology stacks, regulatory environments, geographic footprints, employee counts, and industries. It also means using breach data from competitors, enforcement actions from regulators, and loss studies from insurers. This gives us a **base rate**, the historical frequency observed across a similar population.

This starting estimate is your **prior** in Bayesian terms: your initial belief before you layer in organization-specific information. We'll express the posterior again as P5–P50–P95. You can then revise that estimate using internal data and SME input (the updated estimate is called a **posterior**), as illustrated in Figure 11-1.

Figure 11-1. *How base rates are used in risk analyses*

Base rates are especially valuable when you have little or no internal data. They give you a starting point and support benchmarking, so you can say, "Here's what organizations like ours are experiencing." That level of research lends credibility when presenting to stakeholders because your inputs don't exist in a vacuum.

You'll create different types of base rates, for example:

- **Frequency estimates**: How often certain incidents happen in your sector
- **Magnitude estimates**: Typical financial losses from those incidents
- **Control failure rates**: Rates of things like phishing clicks or patching delays

All of these can be derived from external data. While they're not perfect, they're far better than playing "pick a color" on a risk matrix. Keep in mind, these are starting points that you'll refine as you gather internal data (Chapter 12) and expert judgment (Chapter 13).

Why I Reach for External Data Early

Whenever I start a risk assessment, external data is almost always one of the first places I look, sometimes even before the scenario statement is fully drafted. Here's why external data should be your starting point, not an afterthought:

- **External data grounds your analysis in reality.** At the very start of an assessment, external data helps turn vague concerns into realistic, evidence-based scenarios. Instead of building scenarios around abstract fears ("What if we get hacked?"), you can craft storylines grounded in documented incidents: "Based on three peer company breaches disclosed in SEC filings, here's how a similar attack might unfold in our environment...."
- **External data shows you how real-world incidents actually progress**: who the threat actors are, what initial access methods they use, how long they remain undetected, and what types of damage they cause. It also acts as a reality check for your assumptions. When your estimates are double the industry average, that's either a red flag about your analysis or valuable insight about your unique risk profile.
- **External data builds credibility and provides defensible starting points.** Executives become much more comfortable when they see that inputs weren't invented in-house. Referencing a competitor's SEC filing, an insurance industry loss study, or regulatory enforcement data signals analytical rigor and gives decision-makers something familiar to anchor their understanding.
- **More practically, external data provides the baseline estimates you need when internal data is sparse or nonexistent.** Rather than starting with wild guesses, you begin with industry-grounded numbers that you can then adjust based on your specific context. This transforms your role from "person making up numbers" to "analyst applying industry context to organizational reality."

⚠ USE AI TO ACCELERATE, BUT NOT REPLACE, THIS PROCESS

Generative AI can speed up early-stage research dramatically. A task that once took 30–40 hours can now be done in under an hour—but only if you review and validate the outputs.

Where GenAI excels in external data work:

- Finding relevant sources across the five data types
- Extracting key statistics from long reports and studies

- Converting between units, currencies, and time periods
- Identifying potential quality issues in data sources
- Suggesting organizational context adjustments

Pro tip: Use specific prompts like "Extract all frequency and cost statistics from this breach report, noting sample sizes and methodology" rather than generic requests like "summarize this document."

Critical Cautions

- **Always verify citations**: AI often creates plausible-sounding but nonexistent sources.
- **Check calculations**: AI can make basic math errors in conversions and transformations.
- **Validate quality assessments**: AI may miss subtle bias indicators or methodological flaws.
- **Don't outsource judgment**: AI can suggest adjustments, but can't replace your understanding of organizational context

Bottom Line: AI is excellent at accelerating the mechanical parts of external data collection and transformation, but the critical thinking about relevance, quality, and application to your specific risk scenario still requires human expertise.

The Five Types of External Data: A Taxonomy

You know external data is valuable, but where do you start? With hundreds of potential sources available, from incident databases and threat intelligence to industry surveys and regulatory filings, it's easy to get lost in the noise. This taxonomy provides a road map, organizing external data into five types based on what they reveal and when to use them.

Understanding these categories helps you search more efficiently and evaluate what you find more critically. Instead of randomly hunting for data, you can target the specific type of information your analysis needs: historical incidents, current exposures, expert opinions, analytical insights, or legal precedents.

WHERE TO FIND EXTERNAL DATA

I keep talking about this "external data," but I haven't said where to actually find it. There's not one place to find it. The truth is it's everywhere.

Start with a subject like a loss type, a threat group, a worry, or a specific risk, and use your best search engine and GenAI detective skills. Look through breach databases, regulatory filings, incident reports, and white papers. But don't stop there. Industry conferences, local meetups, and conversations with colleagues are also great ways to discover who's putting out quality research and where to find it.

1. Event-Based Data | *What Happened?*

These are sources that track actual incidents, breaches, losses, and their consequences. It's a look back at what really happened in the world.

Examples: Incident databases, insurance/claims data, regulatory disclosures (like SEC 8-K, GDPR notifications), press coverage, VERIS Community Database, and Privacy Rights Clearinghouse breach reports.

What You'll Find: Information about what happened, where it occurred, and how much it cost. This includes basic facts like dates, affected organizations, and costs, plus details like technical vectors, impact breakdowns, and timelines.

CRQ Use Cases: Build base rates for frequency estimates, calibrate impact models (legal costs, ransom payments, downtime), validate scenario timelines, map incidents to FAIR loss types, benchmark control failures, and identify threat actor patterns.

2. Measurement and Exposure Data | *How Exposed Are We?*

These are sources that quantify vulnerabilities, external-facing systems, and attack surfaces. They help you assess how exposed your organization, or your entire sector, is to specific threats.

Examples: Vulnerability databases (CVE/NVD), internet scanners (Shodan, Censys), external risk ratings, threat intelligence feeds, and patch management reports.

What You'll Find: Counts of known vulnerabilities, vulnerability details, exposed services or ports, patch status, misconfigurations, or threat actor interest. Some data is technical and raw, while other sources provide summarized scores or exposure trends.

CRQ Use Cases: Estimate likelihood before controls are applied, scale exposure to critical assets, benchmark patching windows, identify inherited risks from vendors, prioritize remediation efforts, and inform subject matter expert assumptions for frequency estimates.

3. Opinion, Perception, and Benchmark Data | *What Do People Say?*

These sources reflect what people believe is happening, based on surveys, benchmarking studies, or expert opinions. They capture perception more than reality, but still offer insight into trends, priorities, and self-reported losses or controls.

Examples: Industry surveys (Ponemon, SANS), analyst reports, peer benchmarking studies, ISAC surveys (e.g., FS-ISAC, H-ISAC), and maturity assessments.

What You'll Find: Self-reported incident rates, preparedness levels, spending benchmarks, maturity scores, or perceived risk rankings. Most include charts and summary stats, but quality varies widely.

CRQ Use Cases: Sanity-check internal assumptions, inform stakeholder expectations, support qualitative priors, compare maturity or investment levels, estimate market trends, and guide early scenario design.

⚠ CAN I USE LINKEDIN/X (TWITTER) POLLS AS A DATA SOURCE?

No. Here's why:

1. **No sampling control:** Anyone can respond. There's no way to ensure the audience reflects your population of interest (e.g., CISOs, mid-size orgs, specific sectors).
2. **Massive selection bias:** People who respond are self-selecting, often skewed by who follows the pollster, time posted, or who sees it due to retweets.
3. **No demographic metadata:** You don't know who answered, what region or industry they're in, or whether they understood the question.

4. **No margin of error:** You can't quantify how wrong the results might be.
5. **High potential for trolling or bad-faith responses:** Especially in controversial or "hot take" security topics.
6. **Gimmicks or giveaways:** Especially if there's a drawing or a free gift card for answering. People will say anything for a $5 Amazon gift card.

4. Research and Analysis Data | *What Do Deep Dives Reveal?*

These are sources that conduct in-depth examinations of cybersecurity topics, ranging from peer-reviewed academic studies to highly detailed vendor and law firm reports. They help us understand the "why" behind trends, attacker motivations, and the real-world impact of security incidents.

Examples: Academic research, vendor threat reports (e.g., Mandiant, CrowdStrike, Palo Alto Networks Unit 42), law firm incident digests (e.g., BakerHostetler, Cooley), think tanks (e.g., RAND, ENISA, CSIS), and major analyst firms (e.g., Forrester, Gartner).

What You'll Find: Structured case studies, attacker behavior trends, root cause analyses, legal impacts, cost breakdowns, and, in some cases, attacker economic modeling. Peer-reviewed papers may provide theoretical models or risk models, while law firm and vendor reports often analyze hundreds of real-world cases.

CRQ Use Cases: Calibrate impact scenarios, analyze root causes, identify attacker incentives, support regulatory framing, validate magnitude assumptions, inform downstream risk calculations, supplement Monte Carlo ranges, compare attacker tactics by industry, and identify gaps in internal data.

5. Legal and Enforcement Data | *What Are the Consequences?*

These are sources that track regulatory enforcement, lawsuits, fines, and legal consequences following cyber incidents. They help quantify what happens after something goes wrong, especially the legal, financial, and reputational fallout.

Examples: Regulatory enforcement actions (e.g., SEC, FTC, GDPR fines, NYDFS), lawsuits and settlement databases (PACER, Westlaw), attorney general notifications, law firm reports, consent decrees, legal filings, and breach notification letters.

What You'll Find: Details on fines, legal fees, settlements, court rulings, and timelines between incident, investigation, and enforcement. You may also find commentary on root causes (like MFA failure or delayed notification), legal theories used in lawsuits, and variations across jurisdictions.

CRQ Use Cases: Model legal and regulatory loss types, benchmark enforcement patterns, validate scenario timelines, analyze legal root causes, support compliance-driven risk models, estimate litigation likelihood, and compare sector-specific legal exposure.

Table 11-1. *Common external data sources by type*

Data Type	Where to Start Looking	Key Databases/Sources
Event-Based	Industry reports, regulatory filings	VERIS, SEC 8-K filings, GDPR breach notifications, Privacy Rights Clearinghouse
Measurement and Exposure	Vulnerability databases, scanning services	CVE/NVD, Shodan, Censys, vendor threat intel feeds
Opinion and Benchmark	Industry surveys, analyst reports	SANS surveys, Ponemon Institute, Gartner reports, ISAC publications
Research and Analysis	Academic papers, vendor research	IEEE papers, vendor threat reports, law firm analyses, think tank studies
Legal and Enforcement	Regulatory websites, legal databases	SEC enforcement, FTC actions, GDPR fines, PACER court records

Remember: Once you find potential sources, apply Chapter 10's quality assessment framework before using them in your analysis.

GENAI PROMPT: BRAINSTORM RESEARCH TYPES

I'm researching legal fines, judgments, settlements, and regulatory enforcement actions related to data breaches. Provide a comprehensive and up-to-date list of reliable sources, including U.S. and international regulators, legal databases, breach reporting portals, and industry reports, that track or publish this information. Prioritize sources that include penalty amounts, case summaries, and regulatory bodies involved. Where available, include links to databases or trackers with searchable enforcement records.

AI TRIANGULATION FOR DATA VETTING

When using AI to collect or summarize external data, consider running a *multi-model check*. Ask one LLM to produce a summary or dataset; then prompt a different LLM to critique or verify it. Disagreement signals where human review is needed. This cross-model approach doesn't eliminate bias, but it helps surface hidden assumptions and reduce hallucinations.

Before diving into how to use external data, here are some common mistakes to avoid when working with the sources you've found.

⚠ COMMON PITFALLS TO AVOID

Even though external data is powerful, it's not foolproof. Be cautious about

- **Overreacting to headline events.** A single breach at a peer company doesn't mean the same threat applies equally to you.
- **Using stale or decontextualized data.** A regulatory action from 2019 might not reflect today's enforcement climate.
- **Assuming others' consequences are universal.** Just because a global bank got fined $50M doesn't mean your mid-sized SaaS org faces the same exposure.

Now that you understand the five types of external data and have practiced finding relevant sources, let's explore how to systematically put that information to work in your risk assessments.

EXERCISE 11-1: DATA HUNTING MISSION

Your Mission: Pick one of the risk themes below (or use one from your organization or earlier chapter exercises), and practice finding external data that would inform a quantitative risk assessment.

Risk Themes

- Business email compromise targeting finance employees
- Ransomware affecting critical business systems
- Cloud service outage impacting customer-facing applications
- Data breach involving customer personal information
- Insider threat involving data theft or sabotage

Step 1: Quick Planning

Using your scenario-building skills from earlier chapters, identify what external data you need to answer these questions:

- How often does this happen to organizations like yours?
- What does it typically cost when it happens? (Think about the six forms of loss)
- What types of sources from our taxonomy would be most helpful?

Step 2: Hunt for Sources

Find two to three external sources for your theme. Try to get at least one from different data types (event-based, research, legal, etc.).

Step 3: Quick Quality Check

For each source, note the following:

- What data type is this?
- Does it seem credible? Any red flags?
- How would you use this in a risk assessment?

How to Use External Data

Now that you understand the five types of external data available, let's explore how to systematically put that information to work in your risk assessments. External data serves three key purposes in risk analysis: building realistic scenarios, creating quantitative model inputs, and validating your final results.

The three methods below show you how to accomplish each purpose, plus we'll cover the data transformation techniques you'll need regardless of which method you're using.

Method 1: Building Risk Scenarios and Statements

External data helps you build realistic, evidence-based risk scenarios using the structured format from Chapter 7: Asset + Threat + Effect + optional Method.

When to use: During risk scenario building (Chapter 7), when starting a new risk assessment, or when updating existing scenarios with current threat intelligence.

Step-by-Step Process

1. **Define your asset**: Start with the asset you want to protect; then use external data to understand what similar assets attackers typically target and value.
2. **Research relevant threats**: Find threat intelligence showing which threat actors target organizations like yours: their capabilities, motivations, and recent campaign patterns.
3. **Ground effects in real cases**: Use external data on actual incident impacts: financial losses, business disruption duration, regulatory penalties, and recovery timelines from peer organizations.
4. **Document attack methods (optional)**: Look for incident reports showing how similar attacks actually unfold: initial access vectors, lateral movement techniques, and exploitation methods.
5. **Validate timeframes**: Base your assessment period on documented threat patterns: campaign seasons, disclosure timelines, or regulatory cycles.
6. **Assemble your structured scenario**: Combine external insights into the Chapter 7 format with specific, evidence-based components.

Example using Chapter 7 structure, supplemented with external research:

- **Asset**: Customer payment database containing 50,000 credit card records
- **Threat**: Cybercriminal groups seeking financial data for resale (based on published threat intelligence)
- **Effect**: $2.8M–$8M in response costs, regulatory fines of $500K–$2M, 7–14 days business disruption (based on peer company SEC filings and PCI penalty guidelines)
- **Method**: SQL injection via unpatched web application vulnerabilities (CVE data shows this vector in 40% of similar breaches)

GENAI PROMPT: EXTRACT RISK SCENARIOS FROM INDUSTRY REPORTS

I've uploaded [*industry report/threat intelligence/incident database*] in the prompt and need to extract relevant risk themes for my organization. Analyze this document and help me build evidence-based risk scenarios:

My organization context:

Industry: [*your industry*]

Size: [*employee count/revenue*]

Technology profile: [*cloud-first/hybrid/legacy*]

Extract and organize:

- Relevant incident patterns: Which incidents in this report match organizations like mine? Group by risk theme (ransomware, BEC, cloud outage, etc.)
- Threat-actor-asset combinations: For each relevant incident, identify: What assets were targeted? Which threat actors were involved? What methods did they use?
- Impact data: Extract specific cost figures, disruption timelines, and recovery details for incidents at similar organizations

- Prioritized scenarios: Rank the top 3-5 risk scenarios by relevance to my organization profile
- Structured output: For each priority scenario, format using Asset + Threat + Effect + Method structure with specific data from the report

Cite page numbers and specific sections for each data point you extract, and flag any gaps where additional external research would be helpful.

Method 2: Creating Quantitative Model Inputs

External data provides the baseline estimates that anchor your risk models in industry reality before you add organization-specific adjustments.

When to use: Building frequency and magnitude estimates for new risk models, establishing defensible starting points when internal data is sparse, or creating industry-grounded baselines.

Step-by-Step Process

1. **Identify the data you need**: List what you need to estimate: annual frequency, incident duration, response costs, regulatory penalties, and business disruption costs
2. **Find relevant industry benchmarks**: Search for sources matching your sector, size, and risk profile. Target recent studies with high-quality data (Chapter 10).
3. **Extract relevant statistics**: Gather specific data points from your sources. For example:
    - Incident frequencies (15% of healthcare orgs experienced ransomware in 2024)
    - Cost ranges (Average breach response: $2.8M, range $1.2M–$8.5M)
    - Duration data (Median recovery time: 12 days)
    - Penalty amounts (GDPR fines averaged €2.4M for healthcare violations)

See Method 4 if these statistics need transformation before use in your model.

4. **Apply quality adjustments**: Use Chapter 10's framework to adjust for data limitations: ×2 range widening for medium quality sources, ×3 for low quality.

5. **Document your inputs**: Record original statistics, quality assessments, adjustments made, and key limitations for transparency and future updates.

Example Transformation

- **Raw external data**: "Average breach response cost: $4.5M" (vendor survey, n=200)
- **Quality assessment**: Survey-based with potential vendor bias = ×2 range adjustment
- **Model input**: Response cost range of $2.25M (P5)–$9M (P95), typical is $3.6M (P50), noting industry average with uncertainty adjustments for survey limitations

GENAI PROMPT: EXTRACT QUANTITATIVE MODEL INPUTS

I've uploaded [*industry report/study*] and need to extract specific quantitative data for my risk model. Please analyze this document and help me find model-ready inputs:

My risk scenario: [*brief description of what you're modeling*] **My organization:** [*size/industry/context*]

Extract these specific data types:

1. **Frequency statistics**: Find percentages, incident counts, or rates related to my scenario. Include the sample size and time period for each statistic.
2. **Cost data**: Extract cost ranges, averages, or case study amounts. Note what's included/excluded in each figure (direct costs only, total business impact, etc.).
3. **Duration data**: Look for timeline information – detection times, recovery periods, business disruption lengths.
4. **Penalty/fine amounts**: Find regulatory enforcement amounts, settlement figures, or legal costs.

For each data point, provide:

- The exact statistic with context
- Sample size and methodology quality indicators
- Page number/section where found
- What transformation might be needed (currency conversion, time period adjustment, etc.)
- Quality assessment notes (survey vs. measured data, potential bias, sample limitations)

Flag any statistics that seem unusable due to quality issues or context mismatches.

Most frequency estimates can be gathered with the tools above. For more complex scenarios, consider this advanced technique:

ADVANCED TECHNIQUE: BETA DISTRIBUTION MODELING

For situations where extracting frequencies described in Method 2 doesn't apply, like when you have incident counts but unknown or highly uncertain denominators, statisticians sometimes use *beta distribution modeling*.

Tools like Excel add-ins and resources like Hubbard and Seiersen's *How to Measure Anything in Cybersecurity Risk* make this technique quite accessible.

However, Method 2, combined with the quality adjustments (Chapter 10) and SME elicitation techniques (Chapter 13), covers the majority of real-world external data situations. For a beginner's toolkit, you have everything you need to get started effectively.

Advanced practitioners who encounter edge cases can explore beta distributions later, but these core methods will handle most of what you'll face in practice.

Method 3: Validating and Stress-Testing Results

External data serves as your reality check, ensuring your risk assessment results reflect industry patterns rather than spreadsheet errors or organizational blind spots.

When to use: After completing your initial risk model, when results seem unusually high or low compared to intuition, or before presenting findings to stakeholders.

Step-by-Step Process

1. **Compare loss estimates to published ranges**: Check if your results fall within documented incident costs from SEC filings, insurance claims, or regulatory settlements.
2. **Benchmark frequency against industry norms**: Verify your incident rates align with sector-specific breach databases, threat intelligence, or peer disclosure patterns.
3. **Test scenario plausibility**: Ask whether your risk scenario would seem realistic to external observers familiar with your industry's threat landscape.
4. **Investigate significant outliers**: If your estimates are 2–3× higher or lower than industry averages, determine whether this reflects genuine organizational differences or analytical errors.
5. **Update with current intelligence**: Refresh your validation using recent threat reports, enforcement actions, or incident disclosures to catch evolving risk patterns.

Example Validation Catch

- **Risk assessment result**: Ransomware frequency of 2.1 incidents per year.
- **External validation**: Suppose industry data showed the financial services sector averages 0.3 incidents per year.
- **Investigation result**: Error found in frequency calculation; corrected estimate of 0.4 incidents per year aligns with industry patterns while reflecting slightly higher exposure due to legacy systems.

GENAI PROMPT: VALIDATION RESEARCH STRATEGY

I need to validate my risk assessment results against industry benchmarks. Help me plan a systematic validation approach:

My assessment results:

- Risk scenario: [*brief description*]
- Annual frequency estimate: [*X incidents per year*]
- Financial impact range: [*$X - $Y per incident*]
- Organization context: [*size/industry/specifics*]

Help me identify:

1. **Benchmark sources to check**: What specific databases, reports, or studies should I search for validation data on this scenario?
2. **Key validation questions:** What specific questions should I investigate to validate each estimate?
3. **Red flags to watch for:** What would indicate my estimates are unrealistic (too high/low relative to industry norms)?
4. **Research strategy:** What's the most efficient sequence for finding validation sources?
5. **Quality criteria:** How should I evaluate whether benchmark sources are suitable for comparison?"

Method 4: Transforming Raw Statistics

Most external data requires conversion before it becomes usable in risk models. This method provides tools for the most common transformations you'll encounter. Use only the steps that apply to your specific statistic.

When to use: You've found relevant statistics, but they're in percentages, cover different time periods, or lack the context needed for direct use in your model.

Transformation Tools

If you need the denominator—Look in methodology sections or footnotes for total population ("23% of 500 surveyed companies" = 115 incidents from 500 companies).

WHAT'S A DENOMINATOR?

It's the bottom part of a fraction that tells you the whole picture. If 42 companies experienced data breaches, that means very different things depending on whether those 42 came from a pool of 100 companies (high frequency) or 10,000 companies (low frequency).

Without the denominator, you can't calculate meaningful frequency estimates for your risk model.

If your statistic is a percentage—Convert directly to frequency (23% of companies = 0.23 incidents per org per year, assuming a one-year observation).

If you need to calculate per-organization rates—Divide incidents by population size (342 breaches ÷ 8,500 companies = 0.04 per year).

If your data covers multiple time periods—Normalize to annual rates: quarterly data ×4, multi-year studies ÷ number of years.

If adjusting for currency—Convert using exchange rates from when the study was conducted (€2.4M using 2022 EUR/USD rate of 1.05 = $2.52M).

If adjusting for inflation—Use the study-year FX rate; then inflate to current dollars with a transparent index (e.g., CPI) and show the year.

If clarifying scope—Identify what's included/excluded in cost figures; then adjust or note limitations (e.g., study includes only direct response costs, excludes lost revenue which may underestimate total impact by 40–60%).

If you need to adjust for your context—Make directional adjustments based on organizational differences:

- Smaller organizations often have lower absolute costs but higher relative impact.
- Higher-risk industries may warrant increased frequency estimates.
- Legacy technology environments typically face higher vulnerability-based risks.

If you need uncertainty ranges—Convert point estimates to ranges reflecting data quality and organizational variability. Reference Chapter 10's quality framework for appropriate adjustments.

Validation check—Does your final number make intuitive sense? Is it within an order of magnitude of similar studies? If dramatically different, double-check your transformations.

Simple example: *Raw statistic:* "15% of healthcare organizations experienced ransomware in 2024"; *Applied tools:* Percentage conversion (15% = 0.15 per year) + range creation (0.10–0.25 reflecting uncertainty)

Don't range-widen for quality and then widen again for the same limitation when adding organizational context.

Common Transformation Pitfalls

- **Currency timing errors**: Using current exchange rates for historical data.
- **Double-counting adjustments**: Applying both organizational and quality adjustments to the same number. For example, don't widen ranges once for quality, then again for the same limitation when adding organizational context.
- **Scope mismatches**: Comparing studies that measure different cost components.
- **Unit confusion**: Mixing per-incident and annual figures.

GENAI PROMPT: HELP ME TRANSFORM THIS STATISTIC

I found this statistic, but I can't use it directly in my risk model:

The statistic: [*paste exact text from source*]

Source: [*name/date of report*]

What I need: [*frequency per year/cost estimate / etc.*]

Help me figure out:

1. What information might be missing from this statistic (like total population, time period, etc.)?
2. What conversions do I need (percentage to frequency, currency, time period, etc.)?
3. Walk me through the transformation step-by-step
4. What should I watch out for with this type of data?

Consider these common transformations:

- Converting percentages to annual frequencies
- Adjusting for different time periods
- Currency and inflation adjustments
- Finding missing denominators
- Creating uncertainty ranges from point estimates

Method 5: Extracting Magnitude Data

External data provides the cost baselines that ground your impact estimates in industry reality. This method shows you how to systematically extract and organize magnitude data using the six forms of loss framework from Chapter 8.

When to use: You need cost estimates for your risk model, want to validate internal cost assumptions, or need industry benchmarks for different types of losses.

Step-by-Step Process

1. **Reference the forms of loss**: Use the work from Chapter 8 to guide your search—response costs, business disruption, asset replacement, regulatory fines, competitive advantage loss, and reputation damage.

2. **Search by loss category**: Work through each loss form systematically. Look for incident response studies (response costs), downtime research (business disruption), enforcement databases (regulatory costs), etc.

3. **Extract relevant cost data**: Gather specific ranges and breakdowns:

   - Response costs (e.g., Average IR cost: $275K, range $150–$400K)
   - Disruption costs (e.g., $50K per hour of downtime for mid-size retail)
   - Regulatory penalties (e.g., GDPR fines: €500K–€20M for data breaches)

4. **Apply quality adjustments**: Use Chapter 10's framework: high quality sources use as-is, medium quality sources get ×2 range adjustment, low quality get ×3 adjustment.

5. **Update your worksheet systematically**: Add ranges, quality notes, source citations, and gap indicators for what still needs internal data or SME input.

6. **Document limitations**: Note what's included/excluded in cost figures, organizational context differences, and areas needing local customization.

Example extraction: Loss category; response costs

- **External data**: $150K–$400K (Security Vendor Study 2024, Quality: Medium)
- **Applied adjustment**: $75K–$800K (×2 range widening for survey limitations)

GENAI PROMPT: EXTRACT AND CATEGORIZE ALL COSTS

Extract all cost-related data from this document and categorize it for risk modeling:

Source material: [*upload document or paste text*]

Do the following:

1. **Find all cost figures** (ranges, averages, case studies, penalties, etc.)
2. **Categorize each cost** into logical groups (response costs, business impact, regulatory penalties, etc.)
3. **Note key details** for each: what's included, sample size, time period, organization type
4. **Flag quality concerns** (survey vs. actual data, small samples, potential bias)
5. **Suggest gaps** where cost categories might be missing

Focus on costs that would be relevant for cyber risk assessments at organizations similar to mine: [*brief context*]

Now that you have the tools to extract and transform external data, let's practice putting it all together.

EXERCISE 11-2: COMPLETE EXTERNAL DATA WORKFLOW

Using the external data sources you found in Exercise 11-1, practice Methods 1 and 2 to build a structured risk scenario and extract quantitative inputs.

Part A: Build Your Risk Scenario (Method 1)

Using your external research, create a risk statement with the A-T-E framework:

- **Asset**: What gets targeted based on your research?
- **Threat**: Which threat actors from your sources?
- **Effect**: What realistic impacts did you find?

Part B: Extract Model Inputs (Method 2)

Mine your sources for quantitative data:

- Find frequency statistics (percentages, incident counts).
- Extract cost figures (ranges, averages).
- Note duration data (recovery times, detection periods).
- Apply basic conversions using Method 4 tools if needed.

Deliverables

- **Risk scenario**: One completed risk scenario (Chapter 7)
- **Key inputs**: Annual frequency range, cost range, duration estimate
- **Source notes**: Where each number came from

Chapter Summary

The Big Idea: External data provides the industry context that transforms generic risk concerns into evidence-based assessments—but only when you know how to find quality sources, extract usable statistics, and ground your analysis in organizational reality.

Key Takeaways

- **Start with the taxonomy**. Use the five data types as your research road map rather than hunting randomly for sources.
- **Build scenarios from evidence**. Ground your risk statements in documented incidents, threat patterns, and actual impact data from peer organizations.
- **Transform systematically**; most external statistics can't be used directly; apply the conversion tools based on what your specific data needs are.
- **Validate against industry norms**. Use external benchmarks to reality-check your results and catch analytical errors before presenting to stakeholders.
- **External data is your foundation, not your destination**. Establish defensible baselines that you'll customize with internal data and expert judgment.
- **Document everything**; capture source details, quality assessments, and transformation logic for transparency and future updates.

Bottom Line: External data gives you the industry context to move beyond organizational blind spots, but success requires systematic collection, critical evaluation, and appropriate transformation of raw statistics into reliable model inputs.

What's Coming Next

Chapter 12 takes you inside your organization to find the data that's most relevant to your specific environment. You'll learn how to extract frequency and magnitude insights from logs, incident reports, and operational records—even when that data is messy, incomplete, or scattered across different systems.

Time to look inward.

CHAPTER 12

Your Best Evidence: Finding and Using Internal Data

Insufficient facts always invite danger.

—Mr. Spock

The next essential source of risk data is **internal data**, which is information generated within your own organization. Unlike external data, which provides context and baseline estimates, internal data serves as your anchor, grounding your risk estimates in the specific systems, controls, weaknesses, and operational realities of your environment. It's your most tailored and organizationally relevant source of evidence.

Years back, I started a new job at a financial services firm and was tasked with developing a quantified "Top 5" list of risks for the C-suite. Data breaches dominated the news that year, particularly at US-based banks and lenders. Executives sought to understand how data breach risk compared to other risks within the organization, as well as how our risk posture aligned with that of our peers.

I applied the techniques from the previous chapter to establish an initial base rate of data breach risk, which represented the risk faced by firms like ours in the sector. Next, I wanted to update that number based on new information. That new information was, primarily, internal data.

There were three primary things I was interested in learning that would cause my initial base rate to move: Have we experienced more or fewer reportable data breaches than our peers? Was our control environment better or worse than our peers'? Would the cost of a data breach, considering various factors, be about the same as our peers' or different?

T. Martin-Vegue, *From Heatmaps to Histograms*, https://doi.org/10.1007/979-8-8688-2300-8_12

With that in mind, I set out to gather as much data as possible from telemetry, previous assessments and audits, incident logs, postmortems, red teaming exercises, bug bounty submissions, control evaluations, and other relevant sources.

What I discovered was eye-opening. Our incident history was better than the industry average, but our control environment had some concerning gaps that were outside of standards. Most importantly, our potential breach costs would likely be significantly higher than those of our peers due to our specific customer base and regulatory environment. By the time I finished the analysis, my final risk estimate had moved substantially from where I started, and the internal data was what made that adjustment possible.

This chapter will show you exactly how to gather, evaluate, and use internal data the same way I did at that financial services firm. You'll learn where to find this data within your organization, how to extract meaningful insights from messy sources, and how to combine it with external benchmarks to build more accurate, defensible risk models.

Why Internal Data Matters

You've seen how internal data can update your external base rates, as in my financial services example. Now let's explore the full scope of what internal data can do and where to find it in your organization.

Examples of What Internal Data Looks Like

- Vulnerability scan results showing exposure trends or high-risk assets
- Penetration test and red team findings, which highlight real paths an attacker could take
- Incident response tickets and root cause analyses from past events
- Security team risk write-ups, including risk registers or assessment summaries
- Postmortems from outages or security incidents
- Tabletop and simulation exercise outcomes, especially those tied to loss estimates or impact
- Business continuity or disaster recovery assessments, often linked to downtime estimates

- IT asset inventories, which help estimate the blast radius or exposure surface
- Security control telemetry (e.g., blocked phishing attempts, alerting volume, patch coverage)

Used correctly, this data provides direct insight into how often things go wrong, how quickly you recover, and how prepared you are for various threat scenarios. It's your best chance to estimate frequency, duration, and exposure tailored to your business.

For Example

- If your internal data shows you average three security incidents per year that require containment and cleanup, that's a strong basis for modeling scenario frequency.
- If your average downtime from a critical system failure is four hours and your business units report $250,000/hour in lost productivity, that's a concrete internal estimate of loss magnitude.
- If you've had two high-severity phishing incidents in the past 18 months, you now have a data-driven case to model future credential compromise risk.

The limitations (and why the three-source approach matters): Internal data isn't perfect. It may be scattered across tools, teams, or departments. It may be incomplete, especially if incidents weren't well documented or loss estimates weren't captured. It may also be biased or have poor coverage. For example, if only "serious" events are logged, you'll miss low-level but frequent problems.

That's exactly why internal data shouldn't stand alone and needs to be cross-checked with external data and expert judgment, whenever possible. When combined with the other sources, internal data helps illuminate the organization's risk surface. It lets you move from "what could happen to someone" to "what's likely to happen to us."

Why stakeholders trust it: I've presented the results of quantitative risk assessments more times than I can count. Nearly every time, engineers, executives, and peers come in with a healthy dose of skepticism. That's not a problem; it's a necessary step in any risk assessment. The best way to respond is with data they recognize: actual numbers from their own environment, tied to incidents they remember, backed by systems they use.

Internal data becomes the bridge between theory and operations. It helps you shift from "What tends to happen in the industry?" to "What's actually happened here?" That shift turns abstract models into something decision-makers can act on.

Types of Internal Data Sources

Your organization generates risk-relevant data across dozens of systems and processes. The key is knowing where to look and what each source can tell you about frequency, magnitude, or control effectiveness. Table 12-1 maps the most common internal data sources to their practical applications in cyber risk quantification, also illustrated in Figure 12-1.

Table 12-1. *Common internal data sources, where to find them, and CRQ applications*

Main Data Source	Examples	CRQ Applications
Security Detection and Intelligence	EDR alerts, SIEM logs, vulnerability scans, IDS/IPS data, threat intel feeds, IOC matches, attribution data, attack campaign tracking	Frequency (threat detection patterns), Scenario Building (attack pattern analysis), Contextual (threat landscape understanding)
Incident Response and Crisis Management	Incident reports, postmortems, forensic analyses, crisis communication logs, stakeholder notification records, media monitoring	Frequency (incident volume tracking), Magnitude (loss analysis, response costs), Scenario Building (incident pattern calibration), Contextual (response coordination effectiveness)
Helpdesk and Ticketing Systems	Phishing tickets, malware reports, outage logs	Frequency (incident volume, cause analysis)
Business Continuity and Recovery	BCP test results, disaster drills, RTO performance, backup test results, recovery time measurements, data restoration logs, failover testing	Magnitude (downtime estimates, recovery timelines), Control Evaluation (recovery capability assessment)

(*continued*)

Table 12-1. *(continued)*

Main Data Source	Examples	CRQ Applications
Financial, Legal, and Litigation Records	Downtime cost estimates, legal fees, insurance claims, lawsuit records, settlement amounts, legal discovery costs, regulatory penalty histories, litigation timelines	Magnitude (loss quantification, legal consequence measurement), Contextual (organizational risk exposure)
Asset and Infrastructure Data	CMDBs, asset inventories, application catalogs, cloud service logs	Frequency (exposure surface mapping), Magnitude (asset classification for impact), Control Evaluation (coverage gap analysis)
Compliance, Audit, and Control Performance	Audit findings, control tests, SOC and PCI reports, regulatory examination findings, compliance test results, and regulatory correspondence	Control Evaluation (control strength assessment), Magnitude (regulatory risk exposure), Contextual (compliance maturity)
Identity and User Behavior	Access logs, MFA usage, DLP alerts, insider threat flags	Frequency (access risk patterns), Control Evaluation (identity control effectiveness)
Awareness and Culture	Phishing test results, training completion rates, and employee security surveys	Frequency (human error rates), Control Evaluation (training effectiveness), Contextual (security culture maturity)
Risk and Governance	Risk register entries, exception logs, and past scenario models	Scenario Building (baseline modeling), Contextual (trend comparison, risk appetite)
Change and Project Data	Change logs, DevOps metrics, and control project statuses	Frequency (operational risk, deployment issues)
Third-Party and Vendor Management	Breach notification records, regulator inquiries, subpoenas, SLAs, vendor questionnaires, vendor security assessments	Frequency (vendor incident patterns), Magnitude (external legal and contractual impact)

(continued)

Table 12-1. *(continued)*

Main Data Source	Examples	CRQ Applications
Network and Infrastructure Monitoring	Network flow data, bandwidth usage, system performance metrics, capacity planning data	Frequency (system failure patterns), Magnitude (performance impact), Contextual (resilience baselines)
Customer/ External Impact	Customer complaints, service desk escalations, SLA breaches, customer churn data	Magnitude (business impact measurement), Contextual (reputation effects)
Security Testing and Validation	Bug bounty results, red team exercises, tabletop exercise outcomes, pen test reports	Scenario Building (exploitability validation), Control Evaluation (response capability testing), Contextual (security posture assessment)

Figure 12-1. *Fifteen places to look for internal data sources*

The great thing about internal data is that you don't need all of these sources to get started. Even two or three categories can provide enough insight to improve your risk estimates meaningfully. Start with what's most accessible in your environment and build from there.

YES, YOU HAVE INTERNAL DATA (EVEN IF IT'S UGLY)

People I talk to about incorporating internal data into their risk assessments usually fall into two camps: they think they don't have enough data to get started and don't know where to find it, or they're completely overwhelmed by the amount of data their organization produces.

Both problems have the same solution: **start with your scenario, not your data.** This is why we built scenarios in Chapter 7 before diving into data collection. When you know exactly what risk you're modeling, you can focus on the specific data sources that matter most, rather than trying to analyze everything at once or giving up because you think you don't have anything useful.

The list in Table 12-1 can help you get started, but focus on low-hanging fruit that gives you the most uncertainty reduction for effort expended. You don't want to spend weeks cleaning up, normalizing, and analyzing a dataset just to find out that it doesn't really illuminate the risk landscape much, and a much easier data source did the job just fine.

Start small and targeted. Pick one or two data sources that directly relate to your scenario and see what insights emerge. Expand later once you've proven the value of the approach.

Leverage GenAI. If your organization permits AI usage on internal data, AI-based tools can sift through mountains of data, including telemetry, vulnerability scans, unstructured text in memos and reports, incident logs, and much more. These tools can find patterns, extract context, assess relevance, and pair findings with risk scenarios. Many of the quantitative risk objections I've heard over the years ("not enough data" or "too much data") are becoming moot in the age of AI-assisted risk analysis.

Where to Find It (and Who to Ask)

Finding internal data isn't about building a new pipeline. It's about tracking down what already exists, which is usually scattered across systems, logs, and ticket queues. The speed at which you can collect this data and the depth available are, unfortunately, very organization-dependent. The fortunate among us may be able to type a well-crafted GenAI prompt into an AI-enabled enterprise search tool and obtain most of what they need in no time. Others may need to spend a bit of time channeling their inner Sherlock

Holmes: going out to talk to people who know what data sources exist, asking (or begging) for access, and getting help interpreting what they find. For the latter group, this section is for you. You just need curiosity, persistence, and a few well-aimed questions.

Who to Ask

These are some of the teams illustrated in Figure 12-2, sitting closest to the data you want. They may not always own it directly, but they'll know where it lives or who to nudge.

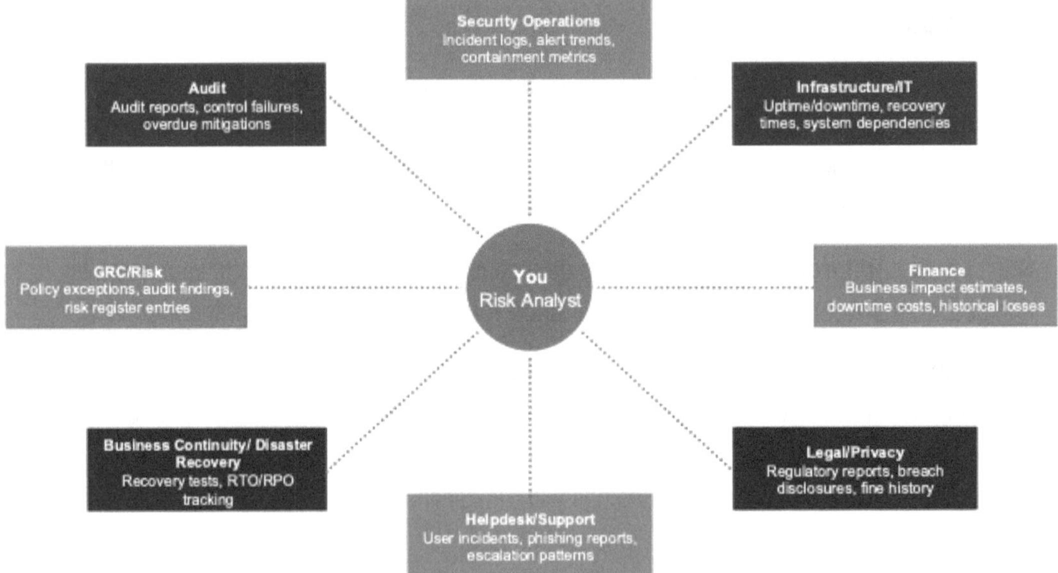

Figure 12-2. *Some teams to ask for data and what to ask for*

- **Security operations (SecOps):** Incident logs, alert trends, containment metrics, SIEM data, threat intelligence feeds, forensic reports
- **Infrastructure/IT:** Uptime and downtime records, recovery timelines, system dependencies, performance metrics, capacity planning data
- **GRC/Risk:** Policy exceptions, risk register entries, control mappings. Internal Audit: Audit findings, control efficacy work

- **Finance:** Historical losses, materiality thresholds
- **Legal/privacy:** Regulatory reporting, breach disclosures, fine history
- **Helpdesk or support:** User-reported incidents, phishing complaints, escalation patterns
- **Business continuity/disaster recovery:** Recovery testing results, scenario outcomes, RTO/RPO tracking, business impact estimates
- **Vendor/third-party risk:** SLAs, vendor assessments, supplier breach notifications, vendor security questionnaires
- **Security testing/AppSec:** Pen test results, bug bounty findings, red team exercise outcomes, vulnerability remediation timelines

DON'T ASK FOR "DATA"

Ask for timelines, logs, summaries, or reports that show what happened when something broke. Specific questions get better results. Try to speak the language of the team you are interacting with.

Starter Questions and Scripts

Knowing *who* to talk to is one thing. Knowing *what* to ask is another. Use these starter scripts to gather data without spinning your wheels. They're designed to be copy-pasted, adapted, and sent as Slack messages, emails, or hallway drive-bys.

To Security Ops or Detection Engineers

"Do we have any records or logs that show how often [threat or incident type] was detected in the last year? I'm working on a risk scenario and want to get a handle on frequency."

"Do we track how long it usually takes to contain a confirmed incident, from detection to mitigation?"

"Any dashboards that show alert volumes over time or by severity? Even just the raw numbers would help."

To IT or Infrastructure

"Do we track how long it usually takes to recover from a system outage or security incident? Even rough timelines would help."

"I'm trying to model the impact of downtime. Do we have actualized RTOs or any real recovery data from past outages?"

"Can I see any recent reports on unplanned downtime or service interruptions, especially the ones that required escalation?"

To Audit

"I'm reviewing risk exposure related to [scenario]. Are there any recent audit findings, risk acceptances, or policy exceptions tied to this area?"

"Is there a central place where we track control failures or overdue mitigations?"

"Any reports or spreadsheets from past audits that include likelihood or impact estimates?"

To Finance

"Do we have any cost estimates or financial impact numbers from past incidents: downtime, legal costs, penalties, anything like that?"

"Has anyone modeled or tracked how much a major outage or breach actually costs us?"

"Do we track payouts for cyber insurance claims, or set aside contingency budgets for security-related events?"

To Support or Helpdesk

"Do we track how many phishing reports or malware tickets come in each month? And do we log how long it takes to close them?"

"Is there a ticket category for security-related issues? I'd love to see counts or trends over time."

"Have we ever done a review of the most common types of end-user security complaints or escalations?"

To Everyone

"I'm trying to build a risk scenario and don't want to waste time chasing the wrong data. If you had to tell me one system, report, or person to talk to about this topic, who would it be?"

"Is there anything you or your team use to track incidents, patterns, or lessons learned, even if it's not formal?"

"If I wanted to know what usually goes wrong in [system/process], what would you point me to first?"

WHEN PEOPLE SAY NO (AND WHAT TO DO ABOUT IT)

Some people will be less than enthused to help with your data requests. Here's how to handle common pushback:

"I don't have time for this."

- Offer to do the work yourself if they can just point you to the right system or reports.
- Ask for just ten minutes to understand what data exists, not necessarily to get it all immediately.
- Come back during their slower periods or offer to help with something they need.

"That data is confidential/sensitive."

- Clarify exactly what you need (often it's trends or counts, not sensitive details).
- Ask about anonymized or aggregated versions.
- Involve your manager or their manager if the data is genuinely critical to a risk assessment.

"We don't track that," or "That data doesn't exist."

- Ask what they *do* track that might be related.
- Probe for informal tracking, spreadsheets, or institutional knowledge.
- Ask who else might have similar data on the same risk.

"I'd need approval from [higher authority]."

- Offer to help draft the request or provide context about why it matters.
- Ask who specifically needs to approve and what information they'd need.
- Consider involving your leadership to make the request peer-to-peer.

"Audit just came through last month."

- Explain that you're doing risk analysis, not audit compliance: "I'm trying to understand how often things happen and what they cost, not whether controls exist on paper."

- Clarify the difference: "Audits check if you have the right processes. Risk analysis estimates what could go wrong and how much it might cost if it does."
- Emphasize forward-looking value: "This helps us make better decisions about where to invest our security budget, not just pass the next audit."
- Frame it as complementary: "This actually makes audits easier because we'll have better data about what our real risks are."

Remember: You're trying to improve organizational risk management. Most people want to help once they understand the purpose and see that you're not trying to create busy work for them.

Coverage Rates

You learned the core data quality evaluation framework in Chapter 11. Apply those same principles to internal data. However, there is one additional aspect of internal data evaluation that deserves special attention: coverage rate. A coverage rate measures the percentage of your environment that is reflected in the data. For example:

- If you're using detection logs, what portion of your endpoints or assets are covered by the logging tool?
- If you're analyzing tickets or response events, are all business units represented or only a few?
- Is this data specific to one region, team, or system, and are you trying to generalize it beyond that scope?

Coverage rate helps you avoid drawing conclusions from a skewed sample. If your dataset only covers 40% of your environment, you need to be explicit about that and adjust your frequency estimates accordingly.

What to do: Address poor coverage in one of three ways: (1) Find complementary data sources with better coverage, (2) scale your estimates mathematically only if you're confident about both the coverage rate and that your logged incidents are representative, or (3) use SME input to validate coverage assumptions and identify what goes unreported. The SME piece is particularly important. They might say, "Yes, we only log about half" or "actually, minor phishing attempts never get logged, but major ones always do," which fundamentally changes how you'd adjust.

WHY COVERAGE RATES MATTER SO MUCH

Imagine a fire marshal walks into an apartment building and inspects installed ten smoke detectors. All ten are in perfect working order. Based on that inspection, things look great: safe building, responsive residents, no action needed. The report will reflect that ten out of ten detection controls are in place.

But then you learn something else.

There aren't supposed to be ten smoke detectors in the building. There are supposed to be 50. That means the building is missing 40 detectors that weren't inspected. Suddenly, the "ten out of ten working" stat doesn't feel so great, illustrated in Figure 12-3. Not only is it a misleading statistic, but without the full picture, we're missing the fact that the apartment building is at elevated risk if a fire broke out.

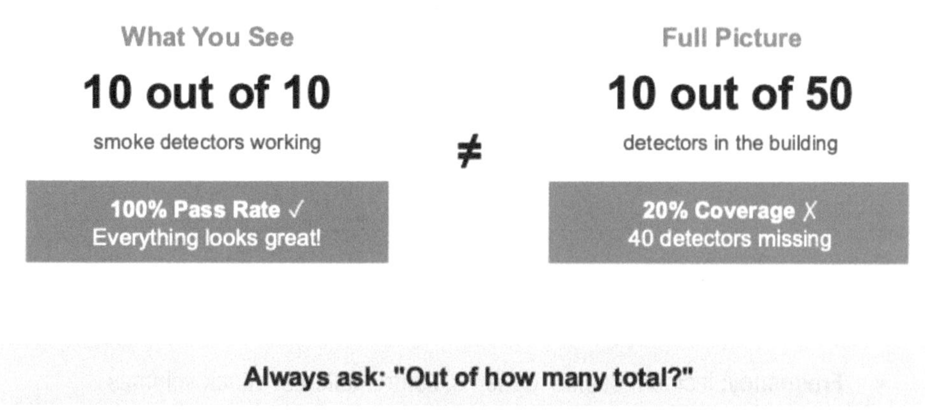

Figure 12-3. *Why knowing the coverage rate matters*

This is the importance of **coverage rate**. If you're gathering data for a risk model, it's not enough to know how many alerts were closed, how many systems were patched, or how many users clicked a phishing link. You also need to know: Out of how many?

- If your vulnerability scan shows 500 issues across 100 assets, how many assets were scanned out of the total number of assets at the organization?
- If your alert volume is trending down, is that across the whole environment or just the parts where logging is enabled?

- If your ticket closure time is improving, does that reflect the whole organization or just one business unit?

Coverage rate is the denominator. It's what turns metrics into meaningful signals. Without it, your data can't tell the whole story, no matter how good it looks on the surface.

🤖 GENAI PROMPT: EXTRACT CRQ-RELEVANT DATA FROM INTERNAL DOCUMENTS

When analyzing internal documents for risk quantification, use this prompt to identify and extract usable data. Always verify a sample manually to catch errors, especially for financial figures or critical metrics.

I need to analyze the attached document for cyber risk quantification (CRQ). Do the following:

1. **Identify Data Types Present**

   List what types of data the document contains (incidents, audits, costs, timelines, vulnerabilities, testing results, etc.)

2. **Classify Internal Data Sources**

   Categorize by team/source (SecOps logs, audit findings, financial records, BC/DR testing, etc.)

3. **Extract CRQ Elements**

   Pull all relevant quantification data:

   - **Frequency:** Incident counts, patterns, control failures, attack volumes
   - **Magnitude:** Direct/indirect costs, downtime impact, financial losses
   - **Control/Response:** Detection/containment/resolution times, team effort, control effectiveness
   - **Exposure:** Affected systems, vulnerability counts, blast radius
   - **Context:** Root causes, threat actors, contributing factors

4. **Provide CRQ Insights**

   Briefly explain how this data could be used in risk models (e.g., "Supports frequency estimation for ransomware" or "Provides magnitude inputs for outage scenarios")

Format as a structured table. Mark unavailable information as "Not specified" rather than guessing.

From Raw to Useful: Prepping Internal Data for CRQ

You've done the hard part: tracked down data, sifted through logs, and reviewed countless dashboards. Now it's time for the fun part: turning the data into inputs for the risk quantification model.

This section shows how to take the data you've collected and transform it into estimates for the three core CRQ components: **scenario definition, frequency, and magnitude.** We'll also use internal data to provide **context** for the overall risk landscape.

HOW TO PRACTICE THE FOLLOWING METHODS

As with all the techniques in this book, I strongly encourage you to practice them on your own. However, unlike other chapters, this one deals with data that comes from inside your organization and may be confidential, regulated, protected by attorney-client privilege, or all of the above. The section later in this chapter, "Ethical Considerations and Privacy," elaborates on these concerns.

I still want you to practice, so there's a downloadable AI-generated incident log that replicates what an incident response team might log in a typical organization. You can find it at `www.heatmapstohistograms.com` in the Tools & Downloads section. You can use this dataset, or even better, use GenAI to create your own based on the metadata your team actually tracks.

Method 1: Use Timestamped Records to Estimate Frequency

If you have incident logs, alerts, or tickets with time stamps, you can calculate how often something happens.

How to Do It

- Count the number of relevant events.
- Define the time window (e.g., 12 months).
- Divide or scale events by time to get an annualized rate.
- Adjust for partial coverage if the data only reflects part of the environment.

Examples

- 12 phishing incidents over 8 months → ~18 per year (12 ÷ 8) × 12 = 18 incidents per year
- 3 unplanned website outages over the last 5 years → ~0.6 per year (3 ÷ 5 = 0.6 outages per year)
- 2 insider-driven data exfiltration events over the past 9 years → ~0.22 per year (2 ÷ 9 ≈ 0.22 incidents per year)

Remember: these calculations give you point estimates. You'll need to convert them into ranges using SME input or the quality adjustment methods from Chapter 11. Define the range as a lower bound, typical, and upper bound, a.k.a. P5, P50, and P95, so your inputs align with the modeling approach introduced earlier.

EXERCISE 12-1: ESTIMATING FREQUENCY

Note: Use the sample incident dataset available at

`www.heatmapstohistograms.com`

- Sort the spreadsheet by **Incident Type**. Pick one type (like "Phishing" or "System Outage"); then count how many times it occurred during the time period.
- Since the data covers a seven-month window (January–July 2024), you'll need to **annualize the frequency** using this formula: **Annualized Frequency = (Events ÷ 7) × 12**.

- This gives you a normalized event rate you can use in your risk model.
- While you're doing your analysis, the Information Security manager approaches you with a problem. There was a training issue with some of the junior analysts, and it was discovered that some incidents were not logged. After discussion, it's estimated that **about 10% of incidents were not logged**, meaning the incident list has about a **90% coverage rate**.
- Adjust your data for this coverage rate: divide your frequency estimate by 0.9 to account for missing incidents.
- The manager seemed sure, but not 100% confident about the coverage rate. Using the quality adjustment methods from Chapter 11, **apply a ×2 range widening** to reflect uncertainty about coverage and data quality. The adjustments are for uncertainty, not strict math corrections.
- You now have an annualized frequency estimate with appropriate uncertainty ranges for your chosen incident type.
- Note that the above adjustments are for uncertainty, not strict math corrections.

Method 2: Extract Event Durations to Estimate Downtime, Incident Response, and Recovery Windows

Look for start and end times in tickets or postmortems. This information helps you estimate how long incidents actually take, from detection to containment to full recovery. That duration becomes a key input for modeling downtime, labor costs, and lost productivity.

How to Do It

- Obtain a list of incidents with corresponding timeline data.
- Break down the incident timeline into stages: detection, containment, resolution.
- Calculate **minimum, most likely, and maximum** recovery times to understand the range.

Use this data to help inform your forms of loss (Chapter 8). Here are key cost categories to consider:

- Response costs from labor, paired with hourly wage (security, IT, legal, communications)
- Revenue loss per hour for customer-facing services
- Third-party fees (e.g., outside counsel, PR, contractors)
- Penalty multipliers for violations tied to duration (e.g., SLA fines)

Example: Over the past five years, your company experienced eight significant system outages, with recovery times captured in postmortems and incident ticketing. You calculate

- **Lower bound (P5):** Two hours (minor service disruption with rapid recovery)
- **Typical (P50):** Six hours (typical recovery with coordinated response)
- **Upper bound (P95)**: Four days (complex outage involving multiple systems and coordination with outside firms)

GENAI PROMPT: ESTIMATE DOWNTIME, INCIDENT RESPONSE, AND RECOVERY

Note: Use the sample incident dataset available at `www.heatmapstohistograms.com`.

1. Find the column that contains duration data. Focus on incidents that caused system downtime or required significant response effort. **Hint:** Look at the "Analyst Notes" column. Use GenAI to help you find patterns.
2. Group incidents by severity level (Low/Medium/High/Critical).
3. For each severity level, identify the minimum, median (most likely), and maximum duration values.
4. Calculate response costs for information security incident responders:
    - Extract team size information from the analyst notes (look for phrases like "3 SOC analysts," "4 network engineers")

- Use an average weighted hourly wage of $150/hour for security team members
- Apply your duration values (min/median/max) to calculate cost ranges: (Team Size × Duration × $150/hour)
- You now have a range for the Response Costs category in your magnitude analysis

5. Calculate business impact from downtime:

- For incidents that affected multiple users, use an estimated downtime cost of $8,000/hour (adjust this figure based on your organization's typical hourly revenue and the systems affected)
- Apply your duration values to calculate impact ranges
- This gives you estimates for the Business Disruption category in your magnitude analysis

You have now practiced Method 2 and created magnitude estimates using simulated internal data.

Note: You may want to weight your final estimates based on the frequency of each severity level.

Method 3: Define Scenarios Based on Repeating Patterns

Use documented incidents to discover causes, effects, threat paths, and consequences. Use this information to improve your risk scenarios.

How to Do It

- Look for patterns, repeatable conditions, or unique factors in postmortems or incident write-ups.
- Document threat vector, asset class, control state, and outcome.
- Use this to create credible, concrete risk scenarios.

Examples

- Three separate cloud breaches stemmed from the same third-party misconfiguration. Use this to model a scenario where a vendor exposes sensitive data via cloud storage.
- Two separate BEC incidents involved finance employees falling for credential phishing and having mail forwarding rules set up without detection. Use this to model a scenario where a phishing attack leads to unauthorized access and silent data exfiltration from a corporate email account.

GENAI PROMPT: PATTERN RECOGNITION FOR RISK SCENARIOS

Upload incidents into the GenAI prompt

Analyze the attached incidents and identify common patterns that could inform risk scenarios. For each pattern you find, provide:

1. **Common elements**: What threat vectors, asset types, or failure modes repeat across incidents?
2. **Root cause patterns**: What underlying conditions or control gaps enabled these incidents?
3. **Impact patterns**: What types of losses or consequences occurred consistently?
4. **Scenario framework**: Write a risk scenario statement based on this pattern using this format:
   - **Asset**: What specific system, data, or resource was affected?
   - **Threat**: What actor or force caused the problem (e.g., cybercriminals, untrained employees, system failures)?
   - **Effect**: What aspect of security was compromised - confidentiality (data exposed), integrity (data corrupted), or availability (systems down)?
5. **Format**: "[Threat] impacts the [Effect] of [Asset]

Focus on patterns that appear in two or more incidents rather than one-off events. Present your findings in a structured format that I can use in a risk assessment.

Method 4: Model Control Conditions from Exceptions and Audit Findings

Scenarios depend on whether key controls are working or not. Internal data shows where they're failing. Failing controls, especially newly failing ones, give you a signal to adjust frequency and/or magnitude upward in your risk models.

How to Do It

- Review exceptions, audit reports, or known control gaps.
- Use this information to adjust the frequency and magnitude numbers in your risk analysis, as appropriate.

Examples

- You just discovered that 80% of systems are exempt from MFA. This raises the likelihood of account compromise in insider threat scenarios.
- Your fraud detection vendor just went out of business, and it will take at least a month to onboard a new one. This increases the frequency of successful fraud cases, and more events may slip through without detection. It may also increase magnitude, since a delayed response usually means higher losses, more remediation effort, and more customer impact.

GENAI PROMPT: DERIVE CONTROL GAPS FROM INCIDENT DATA

Upload incidents into the GenAI prompt

Analyze the incidents attached to identify control gaps and failures. Group your findings by control gap type, not by individual incident. Only derive gaps explicitly seen in the incident data. Do not extrapolate.

For each control gap you identify, provide:

1. **Control Gap Name:** (e.g., "MFA Not Enforced," "Patch Management Delays," "Email Filtering Bypassed")

2. **Gap Category:**
   - Preventive Controls: Failed to stop incidents from occurring
   - Detective Controls: Failed to identify threats quickly
   - Response Controls: Failed to contain or mitigate effectively
   - Recovery Controls: Failed to restore operations efficiently
3. **Root Cause Type:**
   - Technical: System misconfiguration, software bugs, hardware failures
   - Process: Missing procedures, inadequate workflows
   - People: Training gaps, policy violations, human error
   - Vendor/External: Third-party failures, supply chain issues
4. **Supporting Incidents:** List the incident IDs where this gap contributed to the problem
5. **Risk Impact:** How does this gap affect the frequency or magnitude of future incidents?

Ethical Considerations and Privacy

Quantitative risk analysis requires deeper data access than traditional assessments. While red-yellow-green methods might review summary reports, CRQ often involves years of incident logs, detailed postmortems, and sensitive operational data. This increased depth requires extra care.

Key Considerations

Attorney-client privilege and PII protection: Flag anything that appears protected but isn't clearly marked. I've found names, contact info, and customer data accidentally embedded in logs and analyst notes. Always escalate these discoveries and follow your organization's data retention policies.

GenAI and data privacy: If using AI for cleanup or analysis, use only enterprise-grade tools that meet your organization's security policies. This isn't just best practice; it may be a compliance requirement. Regulators like FINRA and the SEC expect firms to supervise technology use, including GenAI.

Access permissions: Just because you can access HR systems, email logs, or monitoring tools doesn't mean you should without explicit approval. Get proper signoff when in doubt.

Reporting on teams: When data reveals repeated failures in specific departments, be direct but thoughtful. Risk assessments should inform, not shame.

Regulatory compliance: Industries subject to GDPR, HIPAA, or SOX have specific limitations on data use, even internally. Check with legal or compliance teams when uncertain.

Transparency in analysis: Always include an assumptions and disclaimers section explaining data limitations, coverage adjustments, and modeling decisions. This builds trust, invites feedback, and often surfaces better data from stakeholders who weren't initially involved.

Remember: Cleaning messy data and adjusting for gaps is standard analytical practice. The key is being transparent about your methods and limitations.

Protecting Results As They Circulate

When it's time to share your assessment, respect confidentiality. If your results are abstracted enough from the source data, it may not be a problem. But for deep-dive assessments, especially ones tied to active incidents, legal matters, or regulatory issues, double-check that your outputs are tagged and handled appropriately.

If you've used privileged or confidential data to produce the results, make sure that protection carries forward. That includes slides, summaries, and anything shared with stakeholders. If there's any doubt, loop in privacy, compliance, or legal before circulating. That's part of doing the job responsibly.

Chapter Summary

The Big Idea: Internal data serves as your anchor, grounding risk estimates in your specific operational reality, but only when you know how to find it, evaluate its quality, and transform messy organizational records into usable risk inputs.

Key Takeaways

- **Start with your scenario, not your data**. Let your risk assessment scope guide what internal sources to prioritize rather than trying to analyze everything at once.

- **Master the four transformation methods.** Convert timestamped records to frequency estimates, extract duration data for magnitude analysis, identify patterns for scenario building, and model control conditions from audit findings.
- **Apply targeted quality evaluation.** Focus especially on coverage rates and common challenges like reporting bias, definitional drift, and data locked behind organizational silos.
- **Use the systematic approach to data collection.** Know who to ask, what questions to get results, and how to handle pushback when people say no.
- **Leverage GenAI responsibly.** Use approved, enterprise-grade tools to accelerate pattern recognition and data extraction, but always validate outputs and follow your organization's privacy policies.
- **Practice ethical data handling**, respect attorney-client privilege, protect PII, get proper approvals, and be transparent about data limitations and analytical adjustments.

Bottom Line: Internal data provides the organizational specificity that transforms generic industry baselines into actionable, credible risk models that stakeholders recognize and trust.

What's Coming Next

Chapter 13 introduces the third essential data source: subject matter experts. You'll learn how to structure expert judgment, run effective elicitation sessions, and combine SME insights with the external and internal data you've already collected to create complete, defensible risk assessments.

CHAPTER 13

Your Secret Weapon: Subject Matter Experts

It's tough to make predictions, especially about the future.

—Yogi Berra

Earlier in my career, I worked on a risk assessment focusing on customer data systems. The external data appeared typical for the sector, with low breach frequency and standard impact ranges. The internal data was even more reassuring. Their customer database had zero reported incidents in five years, good audit results, and all the right controls on paper.

I was about to quickly wrap this up and move on to bigger and badder risk scenarios when I scheduled a quick validation session with our senior database administrator. I expected a 15-minute confirmation that would wrap up the assessment.

Instead, she frowned when I shared the findings. "Zero incidents?" she asked. "That's not right."

It turns out the database system had terrible logging. Three times in the past 18 months, they'd discovered unauthorized access attempts that bypassed their monitoring entirely. None of it was included in the official incident reports because "nothing was actually taken," and the attempts were detected through manual review, not automated detection.

That 15-minute conversation completely flipped my risk assessment. What appeared to be a well-controlled environment was, in reality, a significant issue with multiple unaddressed exposures. The historical data wasn't lying; it was just a victim of a horrible coverage rate and poor incident reporting processes.

T. Martin-Vegue, *From Heatmaps to Histograms*, https://doi.org/10.1007/979-8-8688-2300-8_13

The SME provided the forward-looking context that saved my analysis. Without her insight, I would have delivered a dangerously inaccurate assessment to leadership. To recover, I led a formal elicitation workshop with her team to create realistic and credible frequency numbers. I also added questions about coverage rates of controls to my risk assessment toolbox to every single risk assessment after, as discussed in Chapter 12.

This is why **subject matter experts** are the third essential source of risk data. These are the individuals within your organization who possess in-depth knowledge of the systems, processes, threats, or consequences relevant to a specific risk scenario. They're not just security professionals; they might be engineers, IT leads, legal counsel, product managers, or business unit leaders. There are people whose experience touches a dimension of the risk you're analyzing.

This is where we move from the **past** to the **future**. As Shakespeare said, "*Past is prologue*," and that's a good way to think about both external and internal data. They are records of what has already happened. They don't predict the future directly. They give us a foundation, but not a forecast.

Always remember that risk analysis is a **forecast**. Risk analysis is about what might happen in the next year, not what already happened last year. So how do we turn past into prologue? That's the role of subject matter experts.

SMEs help us look forward. While traditional forecasting methods like time series analysis work well on stable historical data, they sometimes don't tell the full picture in technology risk, where attacker tactics, control effectiveness, and organizational priorities evolve quickly.

Think of your **risk scenario** as both a road map and a set of guardrails. You're not looking for one person who can inform every aspect of the scenario from start to finish. Instead, you'll consult multiple experts who each provide insight into a piece of the puzzle: frequency, exposure, impact, or control performance.

By the time you engage your SMEs, you've already grounded the scenario. You have **external base rates** (Chapter 11) that show what tends to happen across the industry and among your peers. You've paired that with **internal operational data** (Chapter 12) that reveals what has happened within your organization. Now you're handing them that context and asking for a forward-looking, 12-month forecast:

- "Here's what tends to happen in our industry, and here's what's happened to us. Does this scenario still feel realistic for our environment?"

- "Do we have any controls, security projects, or initiatives in flight that could reduce the frequency or magnitude of this risk?"
  - **Examples**: New MFA rollout, EDR deployment, security awareness training, improved monitoring
- "Are there any business changes or emerging conditions that could increase our exposure?"
  - **Examples**: Mergers and acquisitions, new cloud migrations, planned system upgrades, expanding to new markets, control budget cuts, degraded or failing controls, newly identified sophisticated threat actor groups targeting our sector
- "Given all of this context, what's your estimated range for [frequency/magnitude] over the next 12 months?"

This structured approach transforms subjective judgment into defensible analysis. **Expert elicitation**, a formal discipline for synthesizing expert judgments when other forms of data are unreliable or insufficient, is well established in domains such as nuclear safety, structural engineering, and environmental risk assessment (Cooke, *Experts in Uncertainty*, 1991; see also Cooke & Goossens, 2008)

Some in cybersecurity dismiss SME input as "garbage in, garbage out." But that criticism misunderstands how judgment works. The issue isn't that SMEs are subjective; it's whether their subjectivity is **calibrated, structured, and challenged**. We'll go deeper into how to do that later in this chapter.

For now, simply know that when used effectively, SMEs provide the final, forward-looking component in a defensible risk model. They help you connect the dots between what has happened and what's likely to happen next.

Experts Are Not a Monolith

The "garbage in, garbage out" objection assumes that all SMEs are the same and provide poor quality estimations. Subject matter experts *are not* all the same. They fall along a spectrum of usefulness, reliability, and structure. Table 13-1 and Figure 13-1 provide a framework and overview for considering the different types of SME judgment, how to elicit and interpret their input, and how to enhance it when necessary.

The Five Types of SME Input

Table 13-1. *The five types of SME input, examples, and how to uplevel*

Type	Definition	Example	When to Use	How to Improve
1. Unaided Guess	Raw, unstructured opinion with no evidence or expertise necessarily involved	"I'd say ransomware risk is high right now. Just a feeling."	Early ideation, scenario brainstorming	Don't use as final input. Probe for reasoning or redirect toward aided estimation.
2. Aided Estimation	Opinion supported by data, experience, or domain knowledge	"Our threat intel shows increased activity in our sector. I'd estimate higher-than-normal ransomware risk this quarter."	Low-stakes models, rough sizing	Ask for range estimates and reasoning behind the number.
3. Calibrated Expert	Domain expert with training or experience in expressing uncertainty as ranges	"Likelihood of successful phishing in the next year: 15% to 35%, typical around 25%."	Model inputs (e.g., FAIR)	Requires ongoing practice to maintain calibration. Consider pairing with other experts, though this may introduce groupthink risks.
4. Expert Aggregation	Structured combination of judgment from multiple domain experts	"Delphi group consensus after three rounds: 20–40% chance, typical around 30% chance of ransomware this year, based on known control gaps."	High-importance models, scenario validation, when individual expert bias is a concern	Use structured methods like Delphi. Works best with 5+ experts and multiple rounds.

(continued)

Table 13-1. (*continued*)

Type	Definition	Example	When to Use	How to Improve
5. Prediction Market	Forecasting the market where participants buy and sell shares based on event outcomes	"Internal market indicates 12% probability of insider incident in Q4."	Strategic forecasting	Rarely implemented due to infrastructure needs and cultural barriers. Requires critical mass and careful design.

Note This classification framework is informed by principles from structured expert judgment, calibration theory, and forecasting research, particularly *Superforecasting* (Tetlock & Gardner, 2015), Cooke's Method (Cooke, 1991), and the Delphi technique (Rowe & Wright, 1999), but the specific categorization and terminology used here are my own, designed for practical application in cybersecurity risk programs.

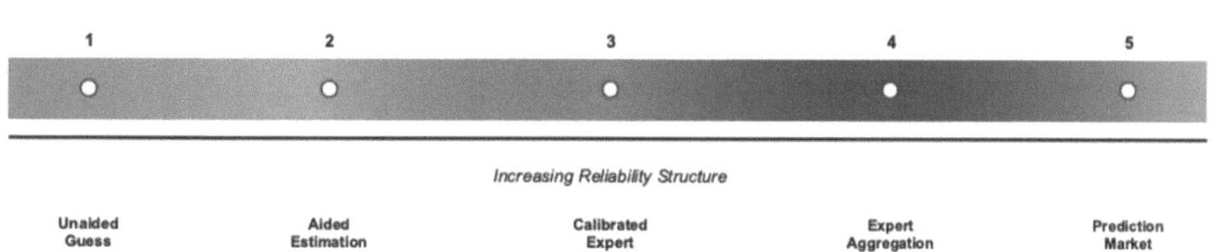

Figure 13-1. *Overview of the types of subject matter experts*

- **Moving up isn't automatic**: While you can add structure to improve SME input, true calibration requires ongoing practice and feedback loops that are difficult to maintain in most organizations.
- **Higher isn't always better**: A single well-calibrated expert (Type 3) may outperform a poorly structured group (Type 4) if the group suffers from groupthink or anchoring.

- **Prediction markets are rare**: While theoretically powerful, internal prediction markets for cyber risk are uncommon in practice due to cultural, technical, and participation challenges. For those interested in the concept, see Good Judgment Open (gjopen.com).

Expert Calibration and Why Cyber Risk Is Different

Subject matter experts can often outperform data when they have the full picture: technical knowledge, lived experience, and context that data alone can't provide. Research shows that experts produce highly accurate predictions when they receive constant feedback and face consequences for being wrong. Meteorologists compare their forecasts to actual weather daily. Bookmakers lose money on bad odds. Card players lose games. This feedback loop, combined with real consequences, builds calibration: when your stated probabilities match actual frequencies over time (Tetlock & Gardner, 2015; Murphy & Winkler, 1984).

We lack these feedback loops in cyber risk, as illustrated in Figure 13-2. We might estimate ransomware likelihood and never see an event. Major cyber incidents are actually rare, despite headlines. At the individual level, feedback is too slow or infrequent to build natural calibration. Some analysts go entire careers without experiencing a major incident they've modeled.

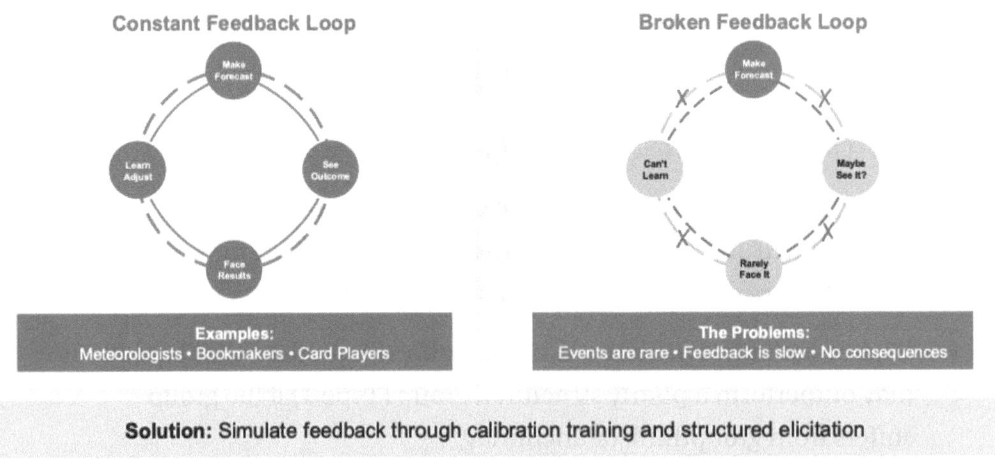

***Figure 13-2.** Constant feedback loops can result in natural calibration*

The feedback loop can be simulated through specially crafted trivia exercises. Participants aren't graded on getting answers right, but on accurately estimating their confidence. Done regularly with feedback, this builds calibration (Hubbard, 2014). Some people are naturally calibrated or maintain it through hobbies like fantasy football or poker. For most of us, it requires discipline.

The challenge is that Calibration requires ongoing individual discipline and organizational commitment that most can't sustain.

RUNNING A FULL CALIBRATION WORKSHOP

How to run a full calibration workshop and ongoing exercises to keep people calibrated is outside the scope of this book. If you are interested in doing this, an in-depth overview can be found in *How to Measure Anything in Cybersecurity Risk* by Douglas Hubbard and Richard Seiersen. Additionally, Hubbard offers virtual calibration training that risk analysts and SMEs can take at `www.hubbardresearch.com`.

Three Practical Strategies for Working with Uncalibrated Experts

Ideally, we'd calibrate all our SMEs through ongoing training and practice. However, throughout my entire career, I've conducted only a handful of full calibration workshops. They work brilliantly in the moment, but people leave the company, fall out of practice, or simply don't have time for regular calibration exercises.

There is some good news, however. You don't need perfectly calibrated experts to get defensible estimates. You just need structure. Here are three career-tested strategies that produce reliable SME input without requiring formal calibration training.

Strategy 1: Ask Multiple Experts

Each SME brings their own worldview, biases, expertise, and blind spots. By gathering estimates from multiple experts and aggregating them systematically, individual errors tend to cancel each other out, while the signal strengthens.

Why this works: Groups of forecasters often outperform individuals. Even when no single person gets it right, the mathematical average or median frequently lands closer to reality.

Practical Guidance

- **Minimum viable:** Two experts with direct experience (enough to start)
- **Better:** Two to four experts with different perspectives (technical + operational + business)
- **Optimal:** Five to seven experts with systematic aggregation

Covered in detail: "Aggregating Expert Opinion" section later in this chapter

Strategy 2: Structure the Elicitation Process

You can't easily change how people think about probability, but you can change how you ask questions. Structured methods of eliciting expert opinion in interview settings, like the Delphi technique, prevent common bias traps: anchoring, groupthink, and dominant voices drowning out minority opinions.

Why this works: The structure does the heavy lifting. Private estimates before group discussion, systematic revelation of ranges, and documented rationale transform gut feelings into defensible analysis.

Practical Guidance

- Always ask for ranges (P5, P50, P95), never point estimates.
- Collect independent estimates before group discussion.
- Capture the reasoning behind every number.

Covered in detail: "Mini-Delphi Method" section later in this chapter

Strategy 3: Prime Them Quickly

A ten-minute calibration exercise before elicitation gets experts thinking probabilistically. It's not perfect calibration, but it dramatically improves estimate quality by teaching under- and overconfidence and teaching the difference between "best guess" and "confidence interval."

Why this works: Most people give ranges that are too narrow because they confuse "my best guess plus/minus a little" with "90% confidence interval." A quick warm-up resets expectations and makes them comfortable with wider, more realistic ranges.

Practical Guidance

- Takes only ten minutes, no formal training required.
- Use two to three trivia questions to teach confidence.
- Focus on ranges, not right answers.
- Do this immediately before gathering estimates.

Covered in detail: "The Ten-Minute Calibration Primer" section below

The Ten-Minute Calibration Primer

This quick exercise primes SMEs to think probabilistically and recognize their own overconfidence. It takes ten minutes, requires no formal training, and can be done informally right before you elicit forecasts. Even the saltiest systems engineer shouldn't balk at three trivia questions.

The goal is to get them comfortable expressing uncertainty as ranges rather than point estimates and to show them that their "confident" ranges are usually too narrow.

How to Run It

Step 1: Cover the Basics (two minutes)

Explain three key concepts:

- **Possibility vs. probability:** Binary thinking ("will this happen?") vs. probabilistic thinking ("how likely is this?").
- **Ranges vs. point values:** Instead of "the project will take six months," try "90% confident it will take four to eight months."
- **What 90% confidence means:** If you're truly 90% confident, you should be wrong only one time out of ten.

WHAT DOES GOOD CALIBRATION LOOK LIKE?

- **Well-calibrated:** When you say *90% confident*, you're right about nine out of ten times. Your ranges are appropriately sized: wide enough to capture uncertainty but narrow enough to be useful.
- **Overconfident (most common):** You're wrong more often than expected because your ranges are too narrow. You say "5-7 incidents per year" when reality could be 2-12. You miss the actual outcome and make decisions based on false precision.
- **Underconfident (rare):** You're right more often than expected because your ranges are too wide. You say "0–100 incidents per year" when reality is likely 3–8. Your estimate is technically correct but useless for decision-making. If everything is "somewhere between nothing and everything," stakeholders can't act on it.

The goal isn't to be correct all the time; it's to give ranges that are both realistic and useful. Most people struggle with overconfidence, which is what this exercise addresses.

Step 2: Run Quick Calibration Questions (five to eight minutes)

Ask them to give a range they're 90% sure contains the correct answer. Emphasize that if they're well-calibrated, they should be wrong about one time out of ten. Here are a few examples of questions. Feel free to use your own.

Question 1: "How tall is LeBron James?"

- **Correct answer:** 6'9" (or 6 feet 9 inches).
- **Teaching moment: Watch for overly narrow ranges like "6'7"–6'9"" vs. appropriately wide ranges like "6'6"–6'11"."**

Question 2: "What year was the first iPhone released?"

- **Correct answer:** 2007.
- **Teaching moment:** Even for recent events, a 90% confidence range might be 2004–2010, not 2006–2008.

Question 3: "How many time zones does Russia span?"

- **Correct answer:** 11 time zones.
- **Teaching moment:** For unfamiliar facts, a truly 90% confident range might be 8–15, not 9–12.

Step 3: Reveal and Discuss (two to three minutes)

After each question, reveal the answer and ask who got it right (whose range included the correct answer). Most people give ranges that are too narrow because they confuse "my best guess plus/minus a little" with "90% confidence interval." A 90% CI should feel uncomfortably wide. That's the point. If your range feels tight and precise, you're probably overconfident.

This exercise nudges them into the right mindset: embracing wider ranges that reflect their true uncertainty. Now you're ready to gather estimates for your risk scenario.

Selecting the Right SMEs

You don't need a perfect panel of colleagues to get started. While multiple SMEs generally produce better results by bringing different perspectives and reducing individual bias, don't let the search for the ideal group prevent you from moving forward with useful input.

How Many Experts Do You Need?

- **Absolute minimum:** One expert with direct experience (not ideal, but sometimes it's all you have, it's enough to start and improve later)
- **Minimum viable:** Two experts with direct experience (enough to start with reasonable confidence)
- **Better:** Two to four experts with different perspectives (technical + operational + business)
- **Optimal:** Five to seven experts with systematic aggregation

Each expert brings their own worldview, biases, expertise, and blind spots. Blending their answers (covered later in this chapter) typically produces more reliable estimates than relying on any single perspective. Keep in mind that using multiple experts reduces individual error; however, relevance beats quantity. Three incident responders who've handled ransomware will give you better input than ten executives who've only read about it.

What Makes a Good SME for CRQ

Look for these characteristics when selecting experts:

- **Direct operational experience** with the system, process, or threat you're modeling
- **Recent exposure** to the risk scenario, when possible (within the past two years)
- **Willingness to express uncertainty** rather than false confidence
- **Business context understanding**, not just technical details

A good SME can also explain why the number moves. They can tell you what makes the estimate higher, what makes it lower, and what conditions drive that variation. They understand how the system behaves in the real world.

If your SME cannot explain why they believe their estimate or cannot describe the reasoning behind the range they chose, you may need to probe deeper or find additional input. The best experts can talk through their assumptions and acknowledge what they do not know. A reliable SME is also someone who is not directly incentivized by the outcome of the estimate. Incentives shape how people see risk. A control owner may lean toward a lower estimate, while someone trying to justify a project may lean higher. If you have to use someone with a clear stake in the outcome, acknowledge it up front and ask them to describe how that incentive works for them. Also, avoid using the final decision-maker as your SME. Decision owners often carry strategic or political pressures that can influence their forecast even if they do not intend to.

THE IKEA EFFECT

When running elicitation workshops, watch out for the **IKEA effect**, an unintentional bias where people overvalue things they helped build. It's named, of course, after the furniture retailer. If you've ever spent an hour building a wobbly IKEA bookshelf, you probably felt oddly proud of it anyway. That's the IKEA effect.

The same bias shows up in risk workshops. When people are estimating the likelihood or impact of security failures, they may downplay the probability of something going wrong with a system, process, or control they designed. Not because they're lying, but because it's hard to imagine your own work failing.

Facilitator Techniques to Reduce This

- **Frame it as forecasting, not auditing**: "We're trying to predict what might happen, not evaluate what you've built."
- **If people get defensive, step back**: "This isn't about blame or performance reviews. We're just modeling future scenarios."
- **Normalize uncertainty**: "Every system has some failure rate. We're trying to estimate what that looks like for planning purposes."
- **Bring in a cross-functional group** that includes both insiders and outsiders to the system in question.
- **Use the Mini-Delphi method** to collect independent estimates before group discussion.

Your bedside manner matters. People need to feel safe expressing uncertainty about their own work. If the room feels like an audit or performance review, you'll get defensive answers instead of honest estimates.

Structure and diversity help break the bias, but facilitation style determines whether people contribute insight or defend their past decisions.

Running Effective SME Workshops

By now, you know what to ask SMEs. It's the same data you've been collecting from external sources and internal systems. SMEs just add the final layer: forward-looking judgment and organizational context.

Present what you've found; then ask them to reality-check it. Don't ask them to estimate from scratch. Show them the industry data, show them your internal findings, then ask: "Does this make sense for us? What would you adjust?"

This works better because it gives them something concrete to react to instead of starting with a blank page.

For Frequency Estimates

- "Industry data shows X-Y incidents annually. What range feels right for our environment? Why?"
- "Our internal logs show Z incidents over 18 months. Based on that and current conditions, how would you adjust that up or down?"
- "Given our controls and threat landscape, what's the lower bound, typical, upper bound (P5, P50, P95) frequency?"

For Magnitude Estimates

- "External studies suggest external forensics firms would charge us between $X and $Y for this type of incident. Does that match your experience?"
- "Our last incident cost $C. What range should we use going forward?"
- "What cost categories are we missing?"

For Control Effectiveness

- "This data assumes standard controls. How do ours actually perform?"
- "What's changed since this data was collected?"

For Scenario Validation

- "Does this attack path reflect how incidents actually unfold here?"
- "What would make this scenario more or less likely in our environment?"

Remember: SMEs aren't starting from scratch. They're refining what you've already built.

GENAI PROMPT: SME INTERVIEW SCRIPT GENERATOR

I'm conducting expert elicitation for a cyber risk assessment. Generate 6-8 structured interview questions that will help me gather reliable frequency and magnitude estimates while avoiding common bias traps.

Risk scenario: *[paste your risk scenario here]*

Expert background: *[describe their role/expertise]*

What I need: Frequency estimates (incidents per year) and impact ranges (cost per incident). The script should ask the SME to decompose the factors that make up magnitude in their area of expertise and provide estimates.

Include questions that:

- Ask for ranges, not point estimates
- Probe for the reasoning behind their estimates
- Address uncertainty appropriately
- Avoid leading or anchoring language

Format as a ready-to-use interview script with follow-up prompts.

Let's put these learnings into practice.

EXERCISE 13-1: SME ELICITATION QUESTION DESIGN

Your Task: You're planning a workshop to estimate phishing success rates. First, identify the problems with each question; then write three good ones from scratch.

Part A: Fix These Bad Questions

- **Question 1:** "What's our phishing risk?"
- **Question 2:** "Are we likely to get phished this year?"
- **Question 3:** "How much would a phishing incident cost us?"

Answer Key

Question 1 Problem: Too vague; doesn't specify frequency vs. magnitude, timeframe, or what "risk" means.

Sample fix: "In a typical 12-month period, what's your range for successful phishing incidents that compromise at least one employee account?"

Question 2 Problem: Forces binary yes/no instead of capturing uncertainty ranges.

Sample fix: "How many successful phishing incidents do you expect in a typical year? Give me your lower bound, typical, upper bound (P5, P50, P95) estimates."

Question 3 Problem: No scope defined; doesn't specify incident severity or cost categories.

Sample fix: "For a typical phishing incident that compromises one employee email account, what's the total cost range, including response time, IT cleanup, and business disruption?"

Structured Workshops: The Mini-Delphi Method

If you can get 5+ SMEs in a room (or on a call), structured workshops produce the highest-quality estimates with the least post-processing. When done correctly with the ten-minute calibration primer and proper facilitation, you can often use the outputs directly in your model without requiring additional adjustments.

If you can't get everyone together, the distributed elicitation approach, covered later, works well, although it requires additional quality controls.

Delphi originated at RAND Corporation in the 1950s by Norman Dalkey and Olaf Helmer as a systematic way to capture expert judgment for forecasting. RAND's 1969 memorandum, *The Delphi Method: An Experimental Study of Group Opinion* (Dalkey & Helmer, 1969), reported formal experiments evaluating the technique after its initial development.

The full Delphi technique involves multiple rounds of anonymous surveys. Experts see aggregated results from previous rounds and can revise their estimates (Dalkey & Helmer, 1969). It's been used for everything from technology forecasting to medical consensus-building.

Delphi can take weeks and multiple survey rounds. For cyber risk workshops, we need something faster that captures the same benefits.

Delphi solves three key problems:

1. Dominant voices drowning out valuable minority opinions
2. Anchoring bias, where the first estimate shapes everyone else's
3. Social pressure to conform rather than express genuine beliefs

The Mini-Delphi Format

At the Beginning of the Workshop

- Share context (worksheet, business objective, known data from external and internal sources, gaps you're trying to fill).
- Explain what you'll be asking for (90% ranges, not point estimates).
- Optionally include two to three calibration trivia questions to warm people up.

During the Session

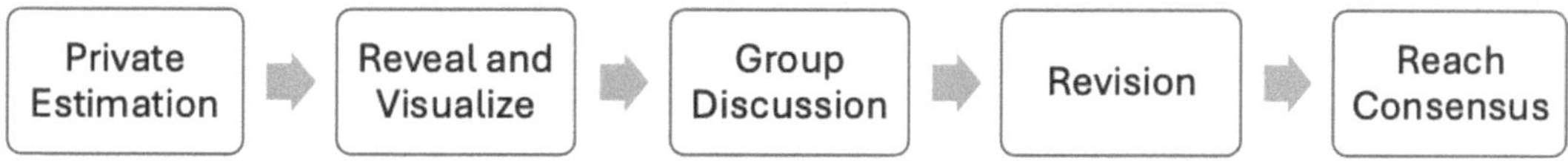

Figure 13-3. *Overview of steps when holding a Mini-Delphi style elicitation workshop*

Round 1: Private Estimation

Ask everyone to write down their range for the first variable silently. For example: "What's the annual frequency (range) of successful ransomware incidents in our environment?"

No discussion. No talking. Just write.

AN ADVANCED WAY TO ELICIT PERCENTILES

Advanced elicitation methods used in structured expert judgment and applied forecasting often start with percentile anchors rather than asking for a simple range. A simple range, sometimes called a naive range, is when you ask an SME for their lower bound, upper bound, and typical value without any additional structure. People tend to make these ranges too narrow because they anchor on their "best guess" and adjust only slightly up or down.

A more advanced approach uses a thought experiment instead of asking for a range directly. This involves asking for a **lottery comparison** to anchor each percentile using a lottery comparison. A lottery comparison is a forced-choice question that helps an SME reveal the value where their uncertainty really sits. For example, to elicit a P95 or P5 value, you can ask:

"What number makes you unsure whether the outcome is higher than that value or whether you should take a 1-in-20 lottery instead?"

The point where they feel indifferent becomes their percentile anchor.

You can use the same idea for the midpoint. To anchor the P50, ask for the number where they feel genuinely torn about whether the actual outcome will come in higher or lower, vs. taking a coin toss.

These comparisons help people separate their intuition from their confidence, and they tend to produce wider and more realistic bounds than asking for a range directly. After this, you still follow the usual Mini-Delphi flow: group discussion, then private revision.

A full description of this method can be found in Robert Brown's *Business Case Analysis with R: Simulation Tutorials to Support Complex Business Decisions (2018),* which provides a detailed walkthrough of percentile elicitation using structured lotteries.

Round 2: Reveal and Visualize

Collect the ranges, anonymize them, and display them all at once on a board, screen, or shared doc.

Round 3: Group Discussion

Facilitate a quick discussion. Where's the disagreement? Who's high and why? What data or experience are people leaning on?

Don't let this turn into a debate. You're collecting information about why people think what they think, not trying to reach a consensus yet.

Round 4: Revision

Invite people to update their ranges if they want. Still privately, but no pressure to change.

Round 5: Reach Consensus

Record the final range for each participant and the group consensus if you're aggregating. Document the rationale.

Repeat this cycle for each major variable. You'll get better estimates and richer reasoning with this structured rhythm than from a freeform discussion.

Controlling for Group Bias

The Mini-Delphi structure handles most bias issues. Watch out for these additional pitfalls:

- Don't put a CISO or SVP at the top of the Zoom grid. They'll shape the tone unintentionally.
- If someone dominates the discussion, redirect: "Let's hear from others before we continue."
- Don't let early speakers anchor the conversation. Stick to the private-first structure.

Capture Rationale, Not Just Numbers

Every range needs a short "why." Ask the participants, "What's your range, and what experience or evidence made you pick it?"

Capturing rationale helps you

- Reuse SME inputs later.
- Spot patterns in how people think.
- Defend assumptions to stakeholders.
- Course-correct if new data emerges.

No one remembers why they said "two to ten" six months ago. Document it while it's fresh.

GENAI PROMPT: MINI-DELPHI WORKSHOP AGENDA

Design a 90-minute Mini-Delphi workshop agenda for eliciting expert estimates on [*risk scenario*] from [*number*] participants.

Workshop goal: Gather frequency and magnitude estimates for [specific risk]. Magnitude estimates should be decomposed into loss forms by the participants, where possible. Participants: [describe expertise levels and roles] Format: [in-person/virtual]

Include:

- Detailed timing for each phase
- Facilitation tips for each section
- Bias mitigation techniques
- Materials needed
- Sample questions for each estimation round
- How to handle common problems (anchoring, groupthink, dominant voices)

Make it actionable for someone who hasn't run this type of workshop before.

Distributed Elicitation Best Practices (Work with What You Have)

Most of the time, it's challenging to gather five or more experts in a room. People are busy, schedules don't align, or you need input from someone in a different office or time zone.

Distributed elicitation works. You gather the same structured input through one-on-one meetings, email exchanges, Slack conversations, or online forms. The process requires more discipline from you as the facilitator, plus some additional quality controls after you collect the estimates.

Step 1: Structure Your Request

Prepare a standard package before contacting any SME. Include the following:

Context Setting

- Brief scenario description
- What decision does this assessment support
- Available context and data (external and internal data, collected into a nice report)
- How their input will be used

Estimation Framework

- Quick explanation of ranges vs. point estimates
- What 90% confidence means
- Examples of what you're looking for

Specific Questions

- Use the same prompts for every SME.
- Always ask for lower bound, typical, upper bound (P5, P50, P95) estimates.
- Ask for their reasoning behind each estimate.

Step 2: Choose Your Delivery Method

- **One-on-one meetings** are most effective for complex scenarios. You can probe their reasoning in real time and clarify any confusion immediately.
- **Structured email or Slack** works for straightforward requests. Include all context in a single message. Make it easy for them to respond.
- **Online forms** (like Google Forms) provide the most scalable option for large groups. They ensure consistent formatting across all respondents.

Step 3: Quality Control During Collection

Watch for these red flags:

- Point estimates instead of ranges
- Unreasonably narrow confidence intervals
- Missing reasoning or explanations
- Estimates that seem copy/pasted from external sources
- Rationale that is obviously AI-generated

When you spot problems, follow up. Ask clarifying questions. Gently push for broader ranges if experts appear overly confident.

Step 4: Apply Range Adjustments

You're working with uncalibrated individual estimates. Apply the quality framework from Chapter 10. Individual SME estimates typically warrant some range adjustment unless

- The expert has demonstrated calibration through training or practice.
- They provided detailed evidence-based reasoning.
- Their estimate aligns closely with other data sources.

The following section covers how to aggregate multiple SME estimates into a single input for your model.

Aggregating Expert Opinion

You've gathered estimates from several experts. Now turn those different three-point estimates (P5, P50, P95) into a single input for your model. Aggregate the percentile points separately. In Excel, use the AVERAGE() or MEDIAN() functions across each percentile level.

Use MEDIAN() if your SMEs went through calibration. Use AVERAGE() for uncalibrated experts since biases tend to cancel out in groups.

Before you aggregate, look at the spread first. Check for

- **Tight clustering:** Most estimates within 20–30% of each other (good to aggregate)

- **Bimodal distribution:** Two distinct camps suggesting different assumptions (investigate before aggregating)
- **Wide scatter:** May need more structured elicitation
- **Outliers:** 3× higher or lower than others (investigate these)

When you find outliers, check if they misunderstood the question, possess unique insight others lack, or are guessing vs. drawing on experience.

A SIMPLER METHOD FOR AGGREGATION

Another option is to keep the widest reasonable range from all SME estimates. Take the lowest P5 across experts, the average P50, and the highest P95. This preserves the full spread of what the group thinks is possible.

Use this when the experts disagree or when the scenario is uncertain and you do not want to narrow the range too quickly. You can always tighten it later with discussion or better data. Averaging or using medians is still the default, but this wide-range method is useful when you want to see the full uncertainty before you blend it.

Aggregation Example

Five SME estimates for annual phishing success rate range from “3–18%, typical 8%” to “2–30%, typical 10%.” The expert with the widest range is new to the organization. The one with higher estimates knows about recent control gaps. Using median aggregation: 5–22% with 12% as the typical value.

When Simple Aggregation Doesn’t Work

Sometimes the spread is too wide for simple averaging. Model multiple scenarios when experts disagree by more than 5× on key parameters, when they’re clearly modeling different scenarios, or when disagreement reflects genuine uncertainty. Model both conservative and optimistic cases; then present both to stakeholders.

Three Applications of SME Input

SME judgment fits with your risk assessment in three main ways. Select the approach based on the data you have and the model you're trying to create.

Application 1: When Data Doesn't Exist

Use when: No historical data is available from external or internal sources, or the data exists but is too expensive or difficult to obtain.

The approach: Ask for a range that captures uncertainty. Walk them through three questions: the low end (rare but possible), the middle (most typical), and the high end (still realistic but uncommon)—P5, P50, P95. Give them time to think. If they give you a point estimate, redirect: "That's helpful. What would be the range around that?"

Key Prompts

- "What's the low end? Maybe a 1-in-20 outcome?"
- "What's your best guess for the typical case?" (P50)
- "What's the high end that wouldn't shock you?"

Tools: Mini-Delphi workshops or structured one-on-one elicitation.

Application 2: When Data Needs Context

Use when: You have data from external sources or internal systems that need adjustment or interpretation.

The approach: Present the data first; then ask the SME to review and verify it. Don't ask if the data is right or wrong. Ask how it applies to your specific situation. Listen for organizational factors, recent changes, or environmental differences that the external data can't capture.

Key Prompts

- "This data says X. Does that match your experience?"
- "If you had to give a realistic range around this number, what would it be?"
- "What makes us higher or lower than this industry average?"

Common Applications

- Converting industry averages into organization-specific ranges
- Adjusting external data for your company size, sector, or controls
- Adding uncertainty bounds to point estimates from reports

Application 3: When Modeling Future Changes

Use when: You need to estimate how planned changes, new controls, or evolving threats will affect risk going forward.

The approach: Focus on specific changes rather than general risk levels. Describe the current scenario; then walk through how a proposed change affects each part of the risk. Ask them to think through implementation realistically, not just design intent. Get ranges for effectiveness rather than binary yes/no answers.

Key Prompts

- "If we implement [new control], how much would that reduce frequency or impact?"
- "How will [planned change] affect our risk profile over the next 12 months?"
- "What's the range of effectiveness we should expect from [control/process]?"
- "How might [emerging threat/technology change] shift these numbers?"

Common Applications

- ROI analysis for proposed security investments
- Modeling risk changes from business initiatives (cloud migration, M&A)
- Adjusting estimates based on threat landscape evolution
- Forecasting control degradation or improvement over time

Historical data and current benchmarks can't tell you how future changes will affect risk. Only SMEs bridge that gap with forward-looking judgment.

WHEN SMES STRUGGLE WITH RANGES: ALTERNATIVE TECHNIQUES

Some experts freeze when asked for ranges. They are strong in their domain but have trouble thinking in percentiles or confidence intervals. In these cases, alternative techniques can help capture their judgment without requiring statistical fluency.

One option is to walk through the extreme outcomes. Start with the worst case, and ask the SME what would need to happen for that outcome to occur. Then ask for the value that would surprise them if it were even worse. That becomes the high-end estimate. Do the same for the best case to anchor the low end. Once both extremes are clear, it is usually easier for the SME to choose a typical value. This works well for people who think more naturally in scenarios than in probability terms.

Two other methods, curve sketching and the chip method, also help SMEs express uncertainty visually. With curve sketching, the SME draws the shape of the distribution they believe is most realistic. With the chip method, they distribute tokens across outcome bins to show which values they think are more or less likely. Both techniques turn mental models into structured input without requiring them to name percentiles directly. For detailed instructions, see `www.heatmapstohistograms.com` in the Tools & Downloads section.

You now have all three pieces of the CRQ data puzzle: external data from Chapter 11, internal data from Chapter 12, and SME input from this chapter. Each source gives you valuable information, but most risk analysts struggle with the next step: How do you blend these three different types of inputs into a single estimate for your model? The next chapter shows you exactly how to systematically combine external data, internal evidence, and expert judgment into defensible estimates you can use in your risk assessments.

Chapter Summary

The Big Idea: Subject matter experts aren't just gap-fillers when data is missing. They provide forward-looking insight and organizational context that no external dataset can capture.

Key Takeaways

- **Use three practical strategies when formal calibration isn't feasible.** Ask multiple experts to reduce individual error, structure the elicitation process with methods like Mini-Delphi, and prime participants with a ten-minute calibration exercise before gathering estimates.
- **Start with a minimum of two experts, but don't wait for the perfect panel.** Two SMEs with direct experience give you enough to start with reasonable confidence. One expert works, though you'll need additional quality controls.
- **Match the SME application to your data situation.** Elicit estimates from scratch when no historical data exists, use SMEs to interpret and adjust existing data for your environment, and leverage their judgment to model how future changes will affect risk.
- **Structure beats calibration in practice.** Mini-Delphi workshops with private estimation rounds, systematic aggregation of multiple estimates, and documented rationale produce defensible results without requiring ongoing calibration training that most organizations can't sustain.
- **Aggregate systematically, not casually.** Use the median for calibrated experts or the mean for uncalibrated groups. Always examine the spread first and investigate outliers before combining estimates into a single model input.

Bottom Line: The goal isn't eliminating expert judgment bias. It's structuring that judgment to get defensible estimates that reflect real operational knowledge. SME input is the third essential data source, providing the forward-looking context that historical data alone cannot capture.

What's Coming Next

You now have all three data sources: external benchmarks, internal evidence, and expert judgment. Most risk analysts struggle with the next step: How do you blend these three different inputs into a single estimate for your model? Chapter 15 shows you exactly how to systematically combine them into defensible estimates you can use in your risk assessments.

References

Brown, R. D., III. (2018). Business case analysis with R: Simulation tutorials to support complex business decisions. Apress.

Cooke, R. M. (1991). *Experts in uncertainty: Opinion and subjective probability in science.* Oxford University Press.

Cooke, R. M., & Goossens, L. H. J. (2008). *TU Delft expert judgment data base. Reliability Engineering & System Safety.*

Dalkey, N. C., & Helmer, O. (1969). *The Delphi method: An experimental study of group opinion* (RAND Research Memorandum RM-5888-PR). Santa Monica, CA: RAND Corporation.

Hubbard, D. W. (2014). How to measure anything: Finding the value of intangibles in business (3rd ed.). Wiley.

Murphy, A. H., & Winkler, R. L. (1984). Probability forecasting in meteorology. *Journal of the American Statistical Association, 79*(387), 489–500.

Rowe, G., & Wright, G. (1999). The Delphi technique as a forecasting tool: Issues and analysis. *International Journal of Forecasting,* 15(4), 353–375.

Tetlock, P. E., & Gardner, D. (2015). *Superforecasting: The art and science of prediction.* Crown Publishing Group.

CHAPTER 14

How to Blend Data

When the facts change, I change my mind. What do you do, sir?

—John Maynard Keynes

The Problem Every Analyst Faces

This is the moment every risk analyst, beginner or experienced, eventually reaches. You've spent a good amount of time collecting data for your analysis. You've looked at base rates from competitors and industry peers, pulled internal logs and telemetry, and talked to subject matter experts who helped you interpret what all that data means. You haven't done this just once; you've done it several times for a single analysis: once for the frequency of loss events and, then again, sometimes six more times, for each of the six forms of loss on the magnitude side.

Some of that data looks clean and ready to plug straight into your model. Other parts don't agree with each other. Some even contradict themselves. And that leaves you staring at a pile of data, wondering what to do next.

That's where this chapter comes in.

By now, you've gathered external data in Chapter 11, explored internal data sources in Chapter 12, and worked with subject matter experts in Chapter 13. You've also learned in Chapter 10 how to evaluate and adjust data for quality, bias, and coverage. Now you've reached the last step where everything comes together. This is where you make sure that what goes into your FAIR or other CRQ model is coherent, reconciled, and defensible. It's the moment where all the work you've done so far becomes something usable.

And for that, we're going to take a little help from an eighteenth-century Presbyterian minister.

T. Martin-Vegue, *From Heatmaps to Histograms*, https://doi.org/10.1007/979-8-8688-2300-8_14

What an Eighteenth-Century Minister Can Teach Us About Risk Analysis

In the early 1700s, an English Presbyterian minister named Thomas Bayes unknowingly changed the course of many fields, including decision science and risk management. He wore many hats; he was a theologian, philosopher, and mathematician, and he gave us a way to think about uncertainty that still shapes modern decision-making. His insight was simple yet profound: when new evidence appears, don't discard what you already know. Instead, update it. Start with a belief, add new information, and see how that changes your understanding of the world.

That's the foundation of Bayesian reasoning. It's also what we do in risk analysis every day, whether we know it or not.

A NOTE ON BAYESIAN REASONING

This chapter uses the "Bayesian reasoning" conceptually, not as a mathematical derivation. You won't see equations here; instead, you'll learn a structured way of updating beliefs using evidence, consistent with the **Bayesian mindset**.

The Reality of Data Collection

In previous chapters, I've described the risk assessment process like this:

You begin with what you can know about the world before looking at your own organization. That means starting with the base rate. The base rate gives you a population-level baseline, a reference point for how often an event happens across similar companies or industries. It doesn't tell you what will happen inside your environment, but it sets the stage for everything that follows.

From there, you look inward. Internal data gives you evidence about how your organization behaves relative to that baseline. It adds specificity and realism, showing how your systems, people, and controls shift the picture. Last, you bring in subject matter experts. They add context that no dataset can. SMEs add information about things that are changing, controls that are planned, and threats that haven't appeared in the numbers yet.

That's the ideal. But every analyst knows the ideal is rarely what happens. Sometimes the base rate you need doesn't exist, or the external data is too expensive to obtain. Maybe you could get it through a subscription or a research engagement, but the budget isn't there. Other times, internal data is incomplete or fragmented across systems. Occasionally, there are no SMEs who know enough about the scenario you're analyzing. Or they're simply not available. I've had situations where no amount of persistence, or homemade cookies, could get a half hour on anyone's calendar.

These are the natural constraints that shape the work of a risk analyst. The danger is getting stuck trying to collect everything before you move forward. That's what leads to analysis paralysis: the belief that you can't begin until the picture is perfect. That mindset completely defeats the purpose of adopting the *less wrong* philosophy from Chapter 4.

The *less wrong* mindset gives us permission to move forward even when the data isn't perfect. It's about progress through iteration. Bayesian reasoning fits beautifully into that idea. It gives you a way to take the evidence you have, whether it's one source or all three, and move ahead with a belief grounded in data. When new evidence appears, you update your belief and continue refining your analysis.

Combining the less wrong mindset with Bayesian reasoning is one of the most practical and powerful ways a risk analyst can work within the realities of everyday corporate life. It keeps you from chasing perfect data and lets you make better, evidence-based decisions while staying flexible enough to change your mind when the facts change.

Let's try a simple exercise to see how Bayesian reasoning works in real life.

EXERCISE 14-1: SIMPLE BAYES UPDATING

We're going to do a simple exercise with the weather. Try to do this tomorrow morning when you first wake up. You want to know what the weather will be like so you can decide how to dress, whether to wear a coat or a raincoat, bring an umbrella, or choose between walking to the grocery store or driving.

Step 1: When you first wake up, before checking any weather information or looking outside, form a belief about how the weather will be for the entire day (morning to evening): temperature, sunny or overcast, dry or wet. Write down your beliefs and what decision you'd make: what to wear, what to bring. This is your **prior**.

Step 2: Look out the window. Observe the sky, see if the ground is wet, and try to sense the temperature through the glass. Think again about how the day might turn out, and update your belief. Would you change your decision? This is your **posterior**: an updated belief after new evidence.

Step 3: Go outside briefly. Notice the actual temperature, wind, and humidity—the things you couldn't sense from inside. Think again about how the rest of the day will go and what decision you'd make. Your belief from **Step 2** is now your new **prior**, and **Step 3** gives you a new **posterior**.

Step 4: Check the weather forecast on your phone. Use this to update your belief again and make your final decision about how to prepare for the day. Your belief from Step 3 is now your **prior**, and Step 4 is your latest **posterior**.

Step 5: At the end of the day, you now have perfect information about what happened. Ask yourself:

- Did each new piece of information help you make a better forecast and decision (like how to dress or whether to bring an umbrella)?
- Was there a point where you could have stopped collecting data because you had enough to make your decision?
- If each step had taken ten minutes of your time, when would you have stopped collecting information?

The connection to risk analysis: This is exactly how you'll combine risk data. Start with external base rates, update with internal evidence, and refine with expert input. Each source improves your estimate without requiring perfect information.

When to Use Bayesian Reasoning

You won't always use this framework, and that's by design. Bayesian reasoning is a tool, not a rule. The decision to apply it depends on the question you're trying to answer, the value of additional information, and the data you have.

Sometimes you will have all three kinds of data: external, internal, and SME input. Other times, you will have only one or two. The goal is not to fill every box. It is to use what you have in a structured, transparent way. If your sources line up cleanly, you do not need to blend them. You are done.

In practice, you will see two paths. On the first path, the blending happens in the room. Your SMEs review external base rates, consider internal evidence, and provide calibrated ranges in a structured session. Their output already reflects the updates you need, and your job is to document how each source influenced the result and to note any overlaps or gaps.

On the second path, inputs arrive separately or point in different directions, or you are missing one or more data types. In that case, you perform the blending yourself. Start from the strongest available baseline, update with internal evidence, refine with SME context if you can get it, and record how each step moved your belief. Either path is valid. What matters is that your reasoning is visible.

GENAI PROMPT: BAYES IN PLAIN ENGLISH

Explain Bayes' Theorem to a CISO using a phishing example, without equations, in under 150 words

Bayesian Thinking As a Mental Model

You don't have to be a statistician to use Bayesian reasoning. The math exists for people who need it, but what matters most for a risk analyst is the mindset. Bayesian reasoning is a way to structure how you think about uncertainty. It's not about equations; it's about staying honest with yourself about what you know, what you don't, and how new information should change your view.

That mindset can transform how you approach risk analysis. It keeps your attention on what matters, avoids the trap of "boiling the ocean," and sidesteps the most common mistakes analysts make when they first start working quantitatively: believing they need to collect every possible piece of data before they begin, thinking their analysis isn't valid unless it's perfect, or getting stuck in endless research instead of making progress.

Bayesian reasoning also helps guard against the cognitive biases that creep into almost every analysis: overconfidence, anchoring, and the IKEA effect, where we overvalue something simply because we built it ourselves.

The model itself is simple. You start with a belief about the world, which we call a **prior**. Then you gather evidence: new information, observations, or data. You update your belief in light of that evidence, and that updated belief becomes your **posterior**. The next time you revisit the question, today's posterior becomes tomorrow's prior. You're always learning, always updating, never claiming to have the final answer.

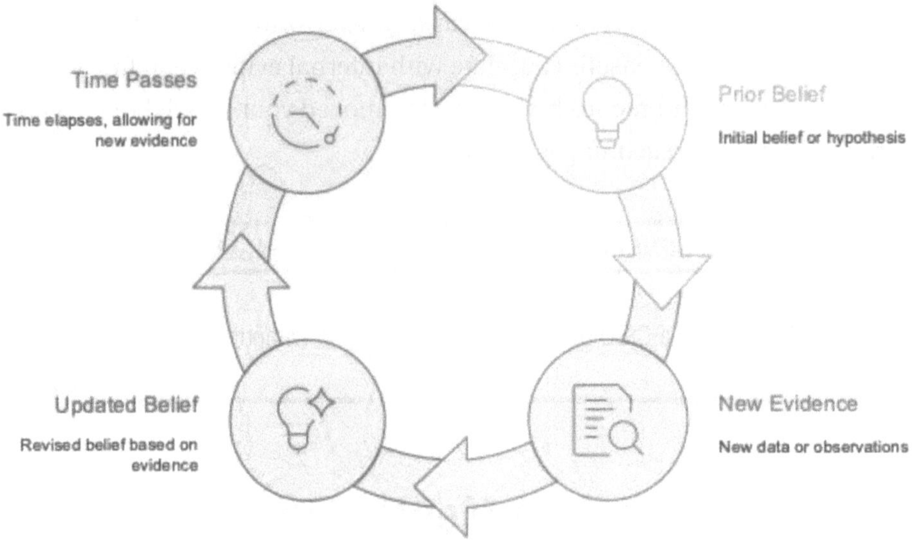

Figure 14-1. *Bayesian updating is cyclical*

Imagine you're assessing the likelihood of a data breach at your company. You start with a prior: based on industry reports, maybe a 10% annual chance of a significant breach. Then new evidence comes in: your security team reports three times more phishing attempts this quarter, and a scan finds unpatched systems. You update your belief upward, maybe to 15%. A month later, you run phishing training, patch everything, and see real improvement. That's new evidence, so you update again, maybe back down to 12%. This cycle is illustrated in Figure 14-1.

What matters is the process, not the specific numbers. You started with imperfect information, made a decision, gathered new evidence, and refined your view. You didn't wait to collect "all the data." You used what you had, stayed open to new inputs, and kept improving.

That's what Bayesian reasoning looks like in practice. It's simply disciplined humility.

RISK ANALYSTS INTUITIVELY DO THIS

This same iterative refinement is already embedded in how most risk analyses evolve over time. Each new scenario, control change, or incident effectively updates a prior belief about loss frequency or magnitude.

Why Bayes Matters for Data Blending

Most analysts feel forced to choose one source over another. Bayesian reasoning gives you a better frame: start with your best available belief, and update it as new evidence appears. Each source does not replace the last. It refines it.

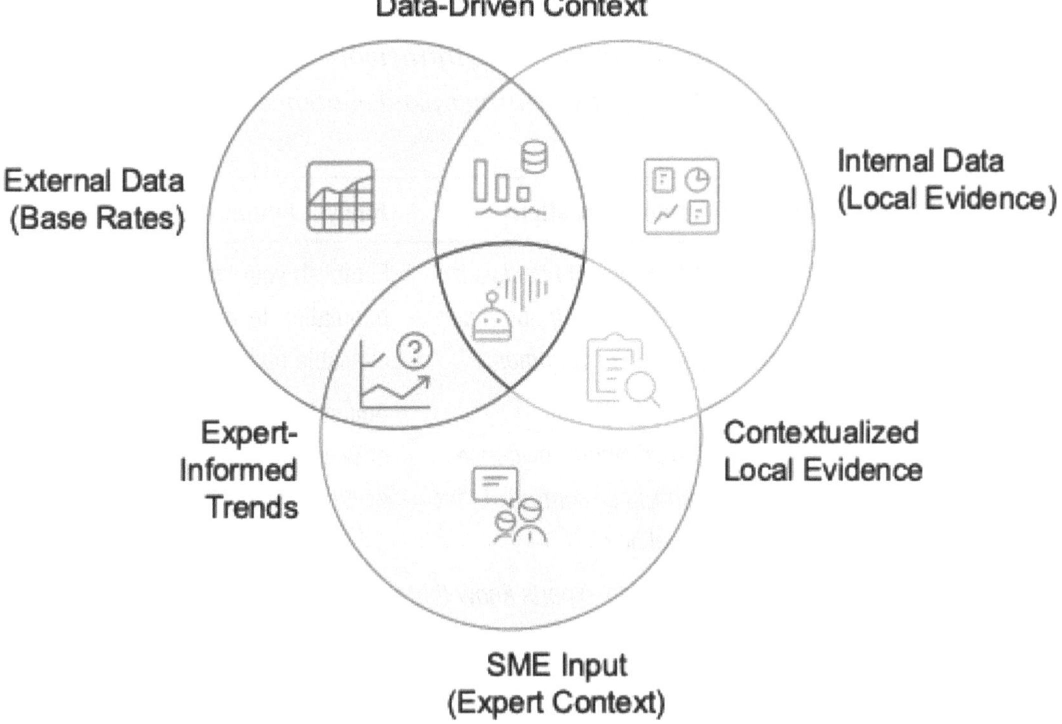

Figure 14-2. *The three sources of data blend together to provide additional context*

In practice, you may have three sources, as seen in Figure 14-2, or only one or two. That is fine. The point is not completeness. It is transparent reasoning with what you have.

The next section shows a simple sequence you can apply in any order, depending on what evidence is available. Use it to turn mixed inputs into a single, defensible estimate.

The Four-Step Bayesian Blending Process

Here is how to apply Bayesian thinking to combine your sources into a single, defensible estimate you can use in your risk model. You begin with the strongest available baseline and then update that belief as you layer in additional evidence. If you have all three sources, great. If you do not, you still follow the same reasoning pattern and document what is missing. An overview is shown in Table 14-1.

Table 14-1. *The four-stage Bayesian blending framework. Each step refines, rather than replaces, what came before, transforming mixed evidence into a coherent, defensible estimate.*

Stage	Evidence Source	Guiding Question	Analyst Action / Outcome
Prior	External base rate or the strongest available baseline	*"What would I believe if I knew nothing about our specific environment?"*	Establish your starting belief: the population-level expectation or best available baseline.
First Update	Internal data	*"How does our organization's evidence confirm or contradict that baseline?"*	Adjust the belief upward/downward or widen uncertainty based on local evidence quality and coverage.
Second Update	SME input	*"What do experts know that the data can't yet show?"*	Add forward-looking judgment to account for upcoming control or threat changes.
Posterior	Combined estimate	*"Given everything, what should we now believe?"*	Derive the final, defensible range for modeling: transparent, traceable, and updatable.

Step 1: Choose Your Strongest Available Baseline (Your Prior)

Often, this is a credible external base rate. That gives you a population-level starting point. If a good base rate does not exist or is out of reach, use the best available baseline.

Acceptable baselines, in order of preference:

- A large, recent, transparent external dataset
- An adjacent or analogous external dataset when a direct one does not exist
- Well-scoped internal history that is relevant to the scenario
- A clearly documented SME baseline when data is unavailable

When using external data, look for

- Large and representative samples
- Recent publication dates
- Transparent methodology
- Independent research

Apply your quality adjustments first. If Chapter 10 led you to widen uncertainty by a factor, use the adjusted range as your starting point. The spirit here is simple: this is what you would believe if you knew nothing else about your specific environment.

Step 2: Ask What Your Internal Data Says (First Update)

Now compare your organization's evidence to the baseline. Does it confirm, contradict, or refine the baseline?

Use it to move the estimate when

- Incident logs show a higher or lower frequency than the baseline.
- Loss records suggest a different magnitude than published studies.
- Control telemetry changes the exposure picture.

Account for coverage and quality. If logging is partial or the period is short, reflect that as wider uncertainty rather than a hard shift. You are asking, "Given the baseline and the internal evidence, what should I now believe for this environment?"

If you do not have usable internal data, say so, keep the prior, and carry that uncertainty forward.

Step 3: Get the SME Reality Check (Second Update)

Present the baseline and the internal evidence to your SMEs and capture their forward-looking adjustments.

Useful Prompts

- Does this baseline feel right for us and why?
- What does our internal data miss that you know from operations?
- What upcoming changes would shift this estimate over the next 12 months?
- Where would you put low, typical value, and high (P5, P50, P95)?

When SMEs give you a range, ask them what conditions would produce the low value, the typical value, and the high value. Their short explanations reveal the causal factors behind the numbers and help you see which part of the external baseline best applies to your environment. You're not asking for additional estimates; you're asking for context that makes the update defensible and prevents double-counting internal data.

Be explicit about overlap. If an SME is relying on the same internal dataset you already used, note it and avoid double-counting. Treat their input as a refinement rather than a brand-new piece of evidence.

If SMEs are unavailable, document the assumptions you would have tested with them and flag triggers to revisit the estimate later.

Step 4: Document Your Bayesian Reasoning

Write down how each source moved your belief and why. This is your audit trail and your future update guide.

Your note should include

- **Prior**: The baseline you started with and why it was chosen
- **First update**: How internal evidence shifted or widened the range
- **Second update**: How the SME context refined it further
- **Final posterior**: The range you will use in the model
- **Assumptions and triggers**: The conditions that would cause you to revisit this number

The power of Bayesian blending is that it turns "garbage in, garbage out" into "transparent in, defensible out." You do not need perfect sources. You need honest, traceable reasoning about imperfect ones. Each source may be limited on its own. Combined thoughtfully, they produce something stronger and more useful than any single input. Here's what good documentation looks like when you apply Bayesian reasoning in a real assessment in Table 14-2.

Table 14-2. *Example of a transparent audit trail showing how evidence shifts beliefs through successive updates*

Step	Description	Example Entry
Prior	Starting belief and rationale	"23% industry phishing rate; widened to 15–30% for survey uncertainty."
First Update	Internal evidence adjustment	"One confirmed incident/18 months $\approx$ 10–22% annual probability; limited logging coverage."
Second Update	SME refinement	"Control improvements $\rightarrow$ 8–20%, P50 $\approx$ 12%; forward-looking view."
Posterior	Final modeling input	"Use 8–22% (P50 = 12%); revisit after next two quarters of data."
Assumptions/ Triggers	Conditions for re-evaluation	"Training stable; logging $\geq$ 95%; revisit if BEC activity spikes."

Worked Example: Phishing Frequency

Let's see Bayesian blending in action.

Scenario: Estimate the organization-level frequency of at least one successful phishing incident in the next 12 months.

Step 1: Establish Your Prior (External Baseline)

An industry study reports that 23% of companies in our sector experienced at least one successful phishing incident in the past year. Assuming our organization is typical of that population, this implies a prior probability of roughly 23% that *we* would experience at least one such incident in a given year. Because the data is survey-based, we use Chapter 10 to widen the range to 15–30% to account for quality and reporting uncertainty. This represents our prior belief before considering internal evidence.

Step 2: First Update (Internal Evidence)

Now we compare our organization to that baseline. Our ticketing and incident records for the past 18 months show three phishing emails that bypassed filtering and reached users and one confirmed successful incident with credential capture. Logging coverage is about 80% across relevant mailboxes and business units.

Two quick adjustments keep us honest.

First, we need to stay consistent on the unit of measure. The external prior is the chance our company has at least one successful incident this year, so we need to interpret internal evidence in the same unit.

Second, coverage matters. With one confirmed success in 18 months and partial visibility, a reasonable internal update is that our organization's annual chance of at least one success falls somewhere around 10% to 20%, with a wide interval to reflect thin data and incomplete coverage. These values are illustrative; the point is how you reason through evidence.

Internal evidence points slightly below the industry prior, but with high uncertainty due to sample size and coverage. We record 10% to 22% as a working internal view, median at 15%, and carry forward the uncertainty rather than declaring a precise number.

Step 3: Second Update (SME Input)

We present the external prior and our internal evidence to the SME group: security awareness, email security operations, and incident response. The awareness team reports that training coverage expanded six months ago, and phishing-simulation click rates dropped significantly. Email operations notes a recent filtering upgrade and tighter tuning against attachment-borne campaigns. Incident response cautions that threat patterns shift quickly and that business email compromise attempts often spike during seasonal vendor payment cycles.

The SME consensus is that the industry number feels high for us, given recent control changes, but that internal data probably understates risk because of logging blind spots and because simulations are not the same as real attacks. The group proposes an 8–20% range, P50 at 12%, as a forward-looking estimate for the next 12 months, with a plan to revisit after two quarters of improved logging. We record these numbers as the current best estimate.

The complete process is shown in Figure 14-3.

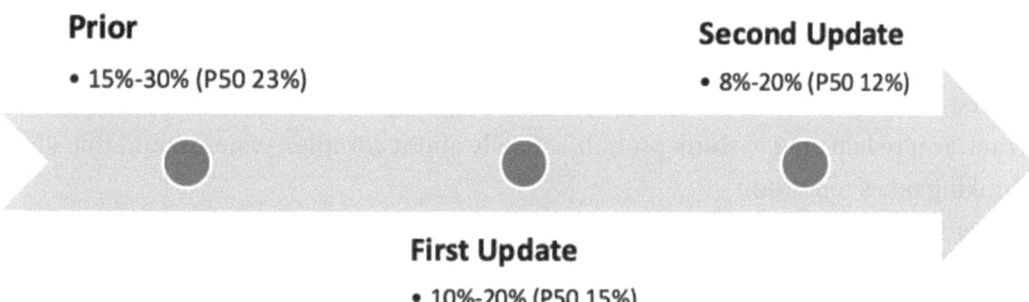

Figure 14-3. *Refining estimates through updating*

Step 4: Document Your Bayesian Reasoning

Final estimate for modeling: 8–22% chance of at least one successful phishing incident in the next year, P50 at 12%.

- **Prior (external):** 23% survey point widened to 15–30% for quality limits.
- **First update (internal):** One confirmed success in 18 months with ≈80% coverage supports a 10–22% range, midpoint ≈15%, reflecting thin data and possible undercount.

- **Second update (SME):** Control changes and operational context support 8–20%, midpoint 12%, with an explicit plan to revisit after logging improves.
- **Assumptions and triggers:** Training and filter efficacy remain stable; logging coverage reaches ≥95%; any material change in attack mix or a confirmed BEC attempt triggers a refresh.

What You Just Did

You blended three different kinds of evidence without discarding any of them. The population base rate set the context, internal records provided a local reality check, and SME judgment added forward-looking insight that data could not yet show. You did not pretend to eliminate uncertainty; you managed it. You showed your work, aligned units, and created an audit trail that others can follow, challenge, or update.

Building Confidence over Time

Your first few assessments using Bayesian blending might feel uncertain, and that's normal. You're learning to think probabilistically about complex systems, and that kind of thinking takes repetition.

Over time, something shifts. As you apply this approach again and again:

- Your Bayesian intuition sharpens. You start recognizing which priors are strong and which are fragile.
- You develop better judgment about how much each update should move your belief.
- You build a library of vetted priors that you can reuse and refine rather than reinventing them.
- Stakeholders begin to trust your analyses because they can see the reasoning behind them.

Most importantly, you stop feeling paralyzed by imperfect data. Instead of waiting for the perfect dataset, you learn to make sound, defensible decisions with the information that's available.

That is the gift Reverend Bayes gave us three centuries ago: a way to reason honestly under uncertainty without demanding certainty first.

Chapter Summary

The Big Idea: Bayesian reasoning provides a structured approach to combining external, internal, and expert data into a unified, coherent view of risk. It replaces "pick a number" analysis with transparent, evidence-based reasoning that adapts as new information appears.

Key Takeaways

- **Bayesian reasoning isn't only about equations**. It's also a mindset for updating beliefs as evidence accumulates.
- **Start with your strongest available baseline** (often an external dataset); then refine it with internal data and expert judgment.
- **Use transparent documentation** to show how each source shifted your belief and why; that audit trail is what makes your analysis defensible.
- **You don't need perfect data**—just disciplined logic and honesty about uncertainty.
- **The "garbage in, garbage out" problem disappears** when your reasoning is visible, traceable, and open to revision.
- **With practice**, Bayesian blending sharpens intuition, builds stakeholder trust, and accelerates decision-ready analysis.

Bottom Line: Blending data isn't about averaging numbers. It's about systematically updating your beliefs using evidence. The result is a defensible, auditable estimate that grows stronger over time and aligns perfectly with FAIR and modern CRQ principles.

What's Coming Next

In **Chapter 15**, we set everything in motion. You'll take the blended estimates from this chapter and use them in a complete cyber risk quantification analysis, building full scenarios, running Monte Carlo simulations, and turning probabilistic reasoning into actionable decisions.

PART IV

Risk Assessment in Action

CHAPTER 15

Extending This to CRQ

I love it when a plan comes together.

—Hannibal, *The A-Team* (1980s TV)

When I was learning quantitative risk, before I ran my first analysis, I felt like I understood the individual parts, but I didn't understand how they all fit together. It was like the time I dumped the contents of the IKEA *Storklint* six-drawer dresser onto my living room floor, only to realize the instructions were missing.

I could clearly identify every piece: the panels, the top, the back panel, the handles, the screws, and the nails. But how did it all fit together?

If this book, especially Chapters 7 through 14, feels like that IKEA *Storklint* dresser dumped across your living room floor with no instructions, congratulations. You just found the instructions. And, just like IKEA furniture, you may still be a little confused even *with* the instructions. You might have to take half of it apart because something is upside down, then put it back together. That's perfectly fine. You're on the right track and moving forward.

Before we begin, let's calibrate where we are.

This chapter will show you how to assemble all the pieces of a quantitative risk analysis. Everything up to this point, including this chapter, applies to any flavor of quantitative risk. You can use it for cyber, technology, or even operational risk.

It's also broad enough to strengthen any model, whether you are using FAIR, the techniques from Doug Hubbard's books, your own approach, or something else. If you never move beyond this chapter, that's perfectly fine. You'll still be able to run credible, defensible risk analyses.

If you want to use FAIR, think of this chapter as the foundation. The next chapter, Chapter 16, will show how what you build here maps neatly into the FAIR model. Everything in this chapter is fully compatible with FAIR, but can easily be integrated into any other new or existing CRQ program.

T. Martin-Vegue, *From Heatmaps to Histograms*, https://doi.org/10.1007/979-8-8688-2300-8_15

The Baby-Steps Map

At its simplest, assembling a risk analysis is this, seen in Figure 15-1.

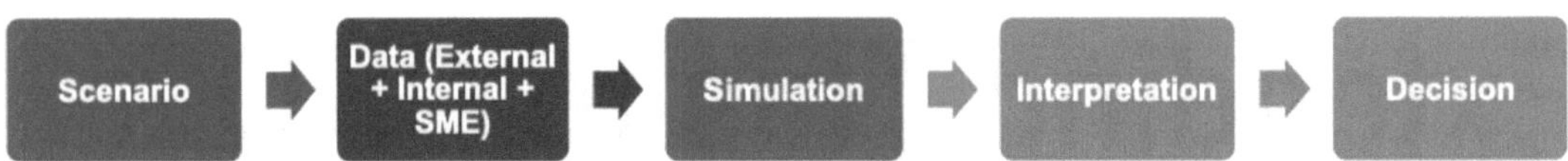

Figure 15-1. *The CRQ assembly map*

The rest is just practice.

Do these in order, and don't worry if it still feels slow or mechanical at first. That's how every modeler starts.

1. **Write One Crisp Risk Scenario (A-T-E)**

   See Chapter 7.

   - Describe a plausible event in one paragraph: the Asset, the Threat, and the Effect.
   - Define your timeframe, scope, and what is out of scope.
   - If another person could picture the same event, your scenario is ready.

2. **Pick the Relevant Loss Forms**

   See Chapter 8.

   - Choose one or two loss forms that matter most.
   - Keep it manageable. The goal is to learn the process, not cover every possible impact.
   - Most analysts start with productivity and response loss.

3. **List the Minimum Data You Need**

   See Chapters 9 and 10.

   - Ask yourself, "What do I need to estimate frequency and magnitude?"

- Jot down external, internal, and expert sources that could answer those questions.
- Don't collect yet. Just identify what's required.

4. **Grab an External Base Rate**

   See Chapter 11.

   - Look for industry benchmarks or research reports that approximate how often events like yours occur.
   - Treat these as a starting point, not the truth.
   - Note the quality of each source using the confidence grades you learned earlier.

5. **Pull One Internal Signal**

   See Chapter 12.

   - Find something observable in your environment that relates to the scenario.
   - It could be an incident count, an audit finding, or a system log pattern.
   - This anchors your analysis to real organizational experience.

6. **Ask One to Three SMEs for a Range**

   See Chapter 13.

   - Talk to people who understand the process or system best.
   - Ask for low, typical, and high estimates (P5, P50, P95).
   - Document what they assumed when giving those numbers.

7. **Vet and Adjust Your Data**

   See Chapter 10 again.

   - Check for consistency and bias.
   - Apply the widening rules for lower-confidence sources.
   - Ask: "Would someone else believe this range if they saw the sources?"

8. **Blend Your Three Sources**

   See Chapter 14.

   - Combine external, internal, and SME data into a single range for frequency and magnitude.
   - Record how each changed your belief.
   - This becomes your model input.

9. **Drop the Ranges into the Spreadsheet**

   See Chapter 5.

   - Use your preferred tool to perform a Monte Carlo simulation (simulate thousands of possible outcomes).
   - Don't worry yet about fine-tuning.
   - You're just generating the shape of possible loss.

Go to `www.heatmapstohistograms.com` in the Tools & Downloads section, and download the risk analysis spreadsheet for Chapter 15. It's the same as the one for Chapter 5, but adjusted to better handle CRQ results in the millions of dollars. Alternatively, you can *vibe code* it:

GENAI PROMPT: CRQ RISK ANALYSIS

I'm learning cyber risk quantification and want to run a simple Monte Carlo simulation.

Use these inputs to estimate annualized loss exposure:

Frequency range (events per year)

- P5: [insert value, for example 0.05]
- P50: [insert value, for example 0.10]
- P95: [insert value, for example 0.20]

Magnitude range (loss per event in USD)

- P5: [insert value, for example $250,000]
- P50: [insert value, for example $600,000]
- P95: [insert value, for example $1,500,000]

Do the following:

1. Choose the best distribution for both frequency and magnitude.
2. Simulate 10,000 trials.
3. For each trial, combine frequency and magnitude to get the total annual loss.
4. Return a **five-number summary**
5. Calculate the **mean**, **mode, median (P50), and P95**.
6. Generate a short text interpretation in plain language, such as:

   "Typical annual loss is about $X with a Y percent chance of exceeding $Z."
7. Plot a simple histogram of simulated losses.
8. Plot a loss exceedance curve.

---

10. **Interpret the Results**

    See Chapter 6.

    - Review your histogram, five-number summary, and loss exceedance curve.
    - Check for logic: Are results in the right order of magnitude?
    - Translate findings into plain language: "We expect about X per year, with a Y percent chance of exceeding Z."

EXERCISE 15-1: DO THIS ON YOUR OWN

Take one or more of the risk scenarios you built in Chapter 7 and follow the steps above to perform a complete, end-to-end risk analysis.

IS IT THAT SIMPLE?

Some early FAIR practitioners, myself included, learned the model in a different era. I was doing my first assessments in the mid-2010s, when most of us collected a handful of inputs, interviewed some SMEs, and dropped ranges into a spreadsheet. That was the norm. It worked well enough, and for many decisions it still does.

In this chapter, I am asking you to do more. The three-source model, the vetting framework, and the blending step are new for many analysts. These ideas add cognitive load. They ask you to slow down, to check assumptions, to compare sources, and to be deliberate about uncertainty. That is intentional.

There are two reasons for this. First, I do not want us taking shortcuts in the rush to implement CRQ. Shortcuts make your results harder to defend, and they make it harder to repeat or explain an assessment later. Second, we now have AI-assisted workflows that remove most of the busy work. AI can scrape data, summarize reports, draft questions, and organize evidence in minutes. That gives you more time to think, to review, to challenge your inputs, and to improve the quality of your decisions.

So yes, the basic process is simple. You can collect a few data points, talk to a few SMEs, and get a directional answer in an afternoon. But you now have the tools to slow down where it matters and raise the quality of your work without slowing down your overall pace.

Running a What-If Analysis

Running a what-if analysis is a simple and high-value add-on to any risk assessment. It requires only a small amount of extra effort but delivers insights that decision-makers and stakeholders care about.

The concept is straightforward. You run two (or more) versions of the same analysis and compare them.

- **Baseline risk:** The first model represents risk as it currently exists, given current controls, the threat environment, data volume, and other relevant factors.
- **After risk:** The second model represents a possible future state where one or more risk factors have changed.

An example plotted on a loss exceedance curve is shown in Figure 15-2.

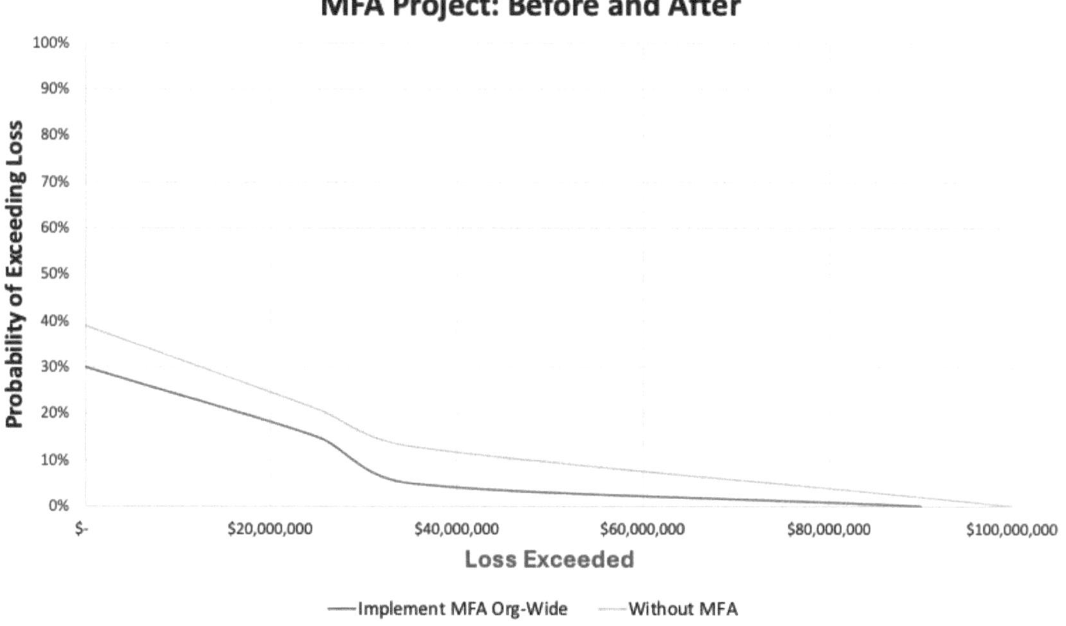

Figure 15-2. *Example loss exceedance curve of how an org-wide MFA implementation reduces risk*

This is one of the most common analyses I perform. You can do it with the spreadsheet example in this book by taking your model from Exercise 15-1, copying the sheet, and changing one variable.

Try adjusting

- The **frequency** input (how often the event might occur)
- The **magnitude** input (how much it costs when it happens)
- Or both together

Some common what-if scenarios I've modeled include

- Implementing a new control, such as MFA
- Automating failover for a critical service
- Expanding into a new market or region
- Increasing vendor or cloud dependencies

- Scaling user volume or transaction load
- Removing an existing control to free up resources
- Accounting for new regulatory fines or penalties
- Improving data quality or monitoring coverage

Each of these tells a different story about how your risk might shift if the environment, your operations, or your assumptions change.

A what-if analysis helps you see not only *what* could change your risk, but *how much* it would matter if it did. It is an easy way to explore uncertainty and test the sensitivity of your model without adding more math or tools.

In Chapter 18, we will build on this idea by introducing **The Six Levers That Move Risk**, a structured way to think about all the forces that push your curve up, down, left, or right. What-if analysis is your first step toward mastering those levers.

Return on Security Investment (ROSI)

At some point in every analysis, someone will ask the question that matters most: "If we spend this money, what actually changes?" That is where Return on Security Investment, or ROSI, comes in.

ROSI sounds like a financial term, but in security, it means something different. In business, Return on Investment, or ROI, measures how much profit an investment earns. You spend one dollar, you make one dollar and a quarter, and your ROI is 25%.

Security does not work that way. We rarely *make* money from security. We avoid *losing* it. The "return" we measure is loss avoided, not profit gained. When we use the phrase "security investments," we are using the term informally. In finance, an investment generates profit. In security, the economic value comes from reducing expected loss.

Even though security does not generate revenue, improving cost efficiency still contributes to economic profit over time. Avoided loss becomes money the company keeps, and money the company keeps improves long-run financial outcomes. The improvement is probability weighted rather than guaranteed, but it still matters.

How ROSI Works

In a risk model, ROSI simply compares two versions of the same scenario, just like we did earlier, with one extra step:

1. **Baseline risk:** What expected loss looks like today
2. **After risk:** What expected loss looks like after a control is in place

The difference between the two is the expected annual loss avoided. Divide that reduction by the cost of the control, and you get the ROSI ratio.

ROSI = (Mean Loss Before – Mean Loss After) ÷ Cost of Control

A ROSI of 1.0 means you avoid one dollar of expected loss for every dollar you spend. That is the break-even point. A ROSI above 1.0 means the control is cost-effective because it avoids more expected loss than it costs. A ROSI below 1.0 means you may be spending more than the loss you are reducing.

This simple version of ROSI is all you need for most day-to-day decisions.

ROI VS. ROSI (AND WHY FINANCE USES A DIFFERENT STRUCTURE)

Finance ROI uses a different formula. It subtracts the cost of the investment before dividing:

ROI = (Gain minus Cost) ÷ Cost

Security uses ROSI because our return is avoided loss, not profit. If you ever need to translate a ROSI result into finance language, you can express it using a net version that mirrors the ROI structure:

ROSI (net) = (Mean Loss Avoided minus Cost of Control) ÷ Cost of Control

In this form, the break-even threshold is zero instead of one.

You do not need this version for operational CRQ work. Use it only when a CFO or finance leader asks for “ROI” in the traditional sense. When a decision moves to the executive or financial level, the organization may also use **NPV** (Net Present Value, a way to compare costs and benefits over time) or **IRR** (Internal Rate of Return, a way to compare returns across projects). You do not need to calculate these for everyday risk analysis. It is enough to know they exist and that finance teams use them for long-term or capital-intensive decisions.

Think of ROSI as your operational tool. Think of ROI, NPV, and IRR as the tools you switch to when a decision rises to the financial leadership level.

How to Explain ROSI to Finance

Finance teams think in terms of profit, cash flow, and return on capital. The simplest way to bridge the gap is

"ROSI shows how much expected loss we avoid per dollar spent. If you want it in traditional ROI form, we can restate it as net benefit divided by cost."

That one sentence translates the analysis into the structure finance already uses.

For readers who want to go deeper into how ROSI fits into multi-year capital planning alongside NPV, IRR, and the Gordon–Loeb model, the FAIR Institute provides an extended treatment of these methods in its white paper on measuring cyber risk reduction.

Why We Use the Mean

When calculating ROSI, use the **mean** (the average outcome from all simulated trials).

The mean represents the long-term expected loss—what you would expect to happen if you repeated the same year thousands of times.

That's why it's the best fit for ROSI, which is essentially a **budgeting decision**: "How much risk do we expect to reduce each year for this investment?"

If you base ROSI on P95, you'll make every investment look better than it really is, because you're assuming every year is almost catastrophic.

If you use the median, you'll understate risk, because you're ignoring the rare but painful years that drive long-term loss.

The **mean** balances both. It shows what happens over time, not just in a good or bad year. The differences between the three are demonstrated in Table 15-1.

***Table 15-1.** Three ways to report risk and when to use them*

Metric	What It Means	When to Use It	Notes
Mean	The long-term average loss	ROSI and cost–benefit decisions	Sensitive to large outliers but best for overall exposure
Median (P50)	The most typical year	Communicating what's "normal"	Doesn't reflect rare but costly years
P95	A bad but plausible year	Stress tests and resilience planning	Too conservative for ROSI; overstates benefits

A Simple Example

Let's say your model shows that average annual loss drops from $600,000 to $400,000 after adding automated failover.

The program costs $100,000 a year.

ROSI = (600K - 400K) ÷ 100K = 2.0

That means for every dollar spent, you reduce two dollars of expected loss. This value **is the ROSI ratio**: the simplest expression of how much benefit you get per dollar invested.

Understanding the ROSI Ratio

The ROSI ratio tells you how much value you get for what you spend.

It looks like a single number, but it carries a story, as seen in Table 15-2.

Table 15-2. *Understanding the ROSI ratio*

ROSI Ratio	What It Means	How to Use It
> 1.0	The investment reduces more loss than it costs	Usually worth considering
≈ 1.0	Break-even	Double-check assumptions or combine with other benefits
< 1.0	Costs more than the modeled benefit	Consider alternatives or non-quantitative justification

You can also flip the equation to show **cost per dollar of loss avoided**:

Cost Efficiency = Cost ÷ (Mean Loss Before – Mean Loss After)

Both approaches describe the same trade-off.

If your ROSI is **2.0**, then your cost per dollar of loss avoided is **0.5**: you spend 50 cents to save a dollar.

If your ROSI is **0.8**, then your cost per dollar of loss avoided is **1.25**: you spend a dollar and a quarter to save a dollar.

Both tell the same story. Use whichever version your audience prefers.

! ROSI IS A DECISION SUPPORT TOOL, NOT A PROMISE

It simplifies a complex judgment into something you can talk about in a meeting.

Some investments with low ROSI may still be mandatory (e.g., regulatory controls or customer requirements). Others may have high ROSI but be hard to implement. The point is not to let the number decide for you, but to use it to guide discussion.

Account for Control Success Probability

Not every control works perfectly every time. Some are hard to deploy, some depend on users doing the right thing, and some simply fail in certain conditions. When estimating ROSI, it helps to adjust the benefit based on how often the control works in practice.

A simple way to do this is to ask an SME:

> "Out of 10 or 100 times this control is needed, how often does it work?"

If they say the control succeeds about 80% of the time, then only 80% of the modeled loss reduction should count toward the benefit. For example, if your model shows a $200,000 annual reduction in expected loss and the control is successful 80% of the time, the adjusted benefit is $160,000.

This keeps you from overestimating the value of controls that are unreliable or inconsistent and helps avoid enthusiasm bias.

ROSI vs. Risk Reduction

ROSI is helpful, but it's not the only way to talk about value. Sometimes, it's clearer to skip the ratio and show results directly in dollars, as seen in Table 15-3.

Table 15-3. *ROSI vs. risk reduction*

Metric	Description	Example
ROSI	Ratio of benefit to cost	"Every dollar spent reduces two dollars of loss."
Risk Reduction	Dollar value of benefit	"Expected loss drops by $200,000 per year."

Both are valid.

Use **ROSI** when you are comparing options or need a simple ratio to talk about value for money.

Use **risk reduction** when you just need to show impact in dollars. When you escalate a decision to finance or the board, you can translate ROSI into traditional ROI, NPV, or IRR if they ask for it.

Closing the Loop

You just built your first complete quantitative *cyber* risk analysis. You learned how to take a clear scenario, add data from multiple sources, run a simulation, and translate the results into business language that leaders understand.

From here, you can already do more than most risk teams ever attempt. You can measure uncertainty, test assumptions, and show how decisions change risk in dollars and probability instead of color and intuition.

If you stopped here, you'd have everything you need to run credible, defensible CRQ analyses in any domain. But if your organization already uses FAIR, or you plan to introduce it, you're ready for the next step.

The next chapter will show how everything you built here maps directly into the FAIR model. You'll see how each element you just assembled fits within FAIR's structure, giving you a shared language to scale your work across teams.

For now, take a moment to appreciate what you've built.

This is the point in the IKEA project where the dresser stands on its own, and it finally looks like the picture on the box.

Where to Go from Here: The Bigger Field

There's a memorable exchange of dialogue from the last installment of the *Star Wars* prequel series, *Revenge of the Sith.* Emperor Palpatine tells Anakin about a power so great it can even save people from death. Anakin asks where he can learn this power. The Emperor replies, "Not from a Jedi."

I think of that line every time someone asks me how to learn cyber risk quantification:

Not from a cybersecurity book.

Cybersecurity gives us the problems, but the solutions come from broader disciplines that have studied uncertainty for centuries.

CRQ isn't a subfield of cybersecurity. It's an age-old business forecasting applied to technology. Quantifying uncertainty connects you to a much older lineage of statisticians, forecasters, actuaries, economists, and decision scientists who have been wrestling with the same questions for hundreds of years.

If you want to keep learning, here are some directions worth exploring.

Books That Build Judgment and Intuition

- ***Against the Gods: The Remarkable Story of Risk*** by Peter L. Bernstein: The historical and philosophical backbone of modern risk thinking
- ***Fooled by Randomness*** by Nassim Nicholas Taleb: A philosophical, sometimes provocative exploration of probability, luck, and overconfidence
- ***How to Measure Anything*** by Douglas Hubbard: A foundational text on measurement and uncertainty, not just for technology
- ***Mistakes Were Made (But Not by Me)*** by Carol Tavris and Elliot Aronson: A sharp, accessible look at self-justification, cognitive dissonance, and why smart people cling to bad decisions
- ***Superforecasting*** by Philip Tetlock and Dan Gardner: How to improve calibration and probabilistic reasoning in real life
- ***The Flaw of Averages*** by Sam L. Savage: Why relying on single-point estimates can lead to wrong decisions and how to fix it
- ***The Signal and the Noise*** by Nate Silver: How to separate meaningful signals from noise in data and prediction
- ***The Wisdom of Crowds*** by James Surowiecki: Why collective judgment often outperforms experts and how to make it work
- ***Thinking, Fast and Slow*** by Daniel Kahneman: A masterclass in human bias, intuition, and why we misjudge probability
- ***Thinking in Bets*** by Annie Duke: How to make better decisions when you can't be certain of the outcome

Fields That Share DNA with CRQ

- **Actuarial science:** The original discipline of quantifying financial and operational risk long before cybersecurity existed
- **Behavioral economics:** How incentives, bias, and cognitive shortcuts shape risk decisions

- **Decision science:** The formal study of how people make choices under uncertainty (Ron Howard, Howard Raiffa)
- **Expert judgment and elicitation:** The science of extracting, calibrating, aggregating, and validating expert knowledge when data is sparse or uncertain (Cooke Method, structured interviews, Delphi)
- **Forecasting:** Using data, models, and probability to predict future outcomes (weather, supply chains, macro trends)
- **Metrology:** The science of measurement: how we define, evaluate, and improve measurements, especially when data is imperfect, indirect, or hard to observe
- **Superforecasting:** Human-driven predictive judgment using calibration, feedback, and prediction markets (Good Judgment Project, Tetlock, Metaculus)
- **Systems thinking:** Viewing risk as the emergent property of interconnected parts, not isolated events

Communities Worth Following

- **FAIR Institute:** The largest community for cyber risk quantification
- **SIRA (Society of Information Risk Analysts)**: The intellectual crossroads of applied risk, statistics, and decision analysis
- **Good Judgment Open/Metaculus:** Forecasting platforms that sharpen calibration and probabilistic thinking

Chapter Summary

The Big Idea: Quantitative risk analysis is not complicated once you see how the pieces fit together. By following a simple, repeatable process: scenario, data, simulation, interpretation, you can turn uncertainty into structured, decision-ready insight.

Key Takeaways

- **You can build a complete CRQ model** using only a clear scenario, three data sources, and a spreadsheet.
- **The goal is not precision but structure.** The point is a consistent way to express risk in dollars and probability, not to chase decimal points.
- **A quick what-if analysis shows you what matters.** It reveals which factors move your risk and how much they matter.
- **ROSI connects risk reduction to cost.** It translates your model results into a language business leaders already understand and can be translated into traditional ROI when you work with finance.
- **CRQ reframes risk conversations.** You move from "Is this risky?" to "How much risk are we willing to accept, and what are we getting for it?"

Bottom Line: You now have every part of a working quantitative risk analysis. You can describe a scenario, collect data, blend sources, run a simulation, test assumptions, and show clear trade-offs in business language. This is the foundation of all modern CRQ, regardless of framework.

What's Coming Next

In Chapter 16, you'll see how everything you built here fits inside the FAIR model. We'll map your inputs, outputs, and terminology to FAIR's structure so you can scale your work across teams and programs without changing the underlying logic.

You've built the engine. Next, we'll install it in the FAIR chassis.

CHAPTER 16

Extending to FAIR

> *You've taken your first step into a larger world.*
>
> —Obi Wan Kenobi

I was walking down the street one afternoon with a colleague from the GRC team of a company where I once worked.

I'd implemented FAIR successfully at a few previous organizations, and this company wanted to apply it to some very specific use cases within their risk program. As we talked, I mentioned how quantitative methods can work well across many kinds of operational and technology risk.

He gave me a puzzled look and said, "I don't like FAIR. Every time I've ever seen FAIR used, the numbers come out way too high."

I looked at him and asked, "Too high compared to what?"

He paused. "I don't know," he said. "They just feel too high."

I then asked, "Have you ever run another quantitative model to compare?"

He hadn't. He just knew the results *felt* off.

That conversation stuck with me because it captures how many people misunderstand FAIR. They think they know what it is, or what it's supposed to be, but they've never actually tested it or compared it against anything else.

FAIR is probably the most widely recognized quantitative risk framework in cybersecurity. It's also the most misunderstood.

What FAIR Is (and Isn't)

FAIR, short for *Factor Analysis of Information Risk*, was developed in the early 2000s by Jack Jones while he was Chief Information Security Officer at Nationwide Insurance (Freund & Jones, 2014).

T. Martin-Vegue, *From Heatmaps to Histograms*, https://doi.org/10.1007/979-8-8688-2300-8_16

Jones has described how the framework began with a simple executive conversation about budget and accountability. After presenting a request for additional funding, he was asked two direct questions: *How much risk do we have?* and *How much less risk will we have if we approve the spend?* (Freund & Jones, 2014).

He realized that, despite long experience in information security, there was no structured way to answer either question. That gap between intuition and measurable evidence sparked the creation of FAIR, a model designed to express information-risk uncertainty in quantifiable, business-relevant terms (Freund & Jones, 2014).

When most people hear FAIR, they picture the classic tree diagram shown in Figure 16-1. *Loss Event Frequency* is decomposed into sub-components on the left, and *Loss Event* Magnitude is decomposed on the right. This is the classic FAIR model, but not the whole story. FAIR began as a single model; it has since grown into a family of connected frameworks and an active global community.

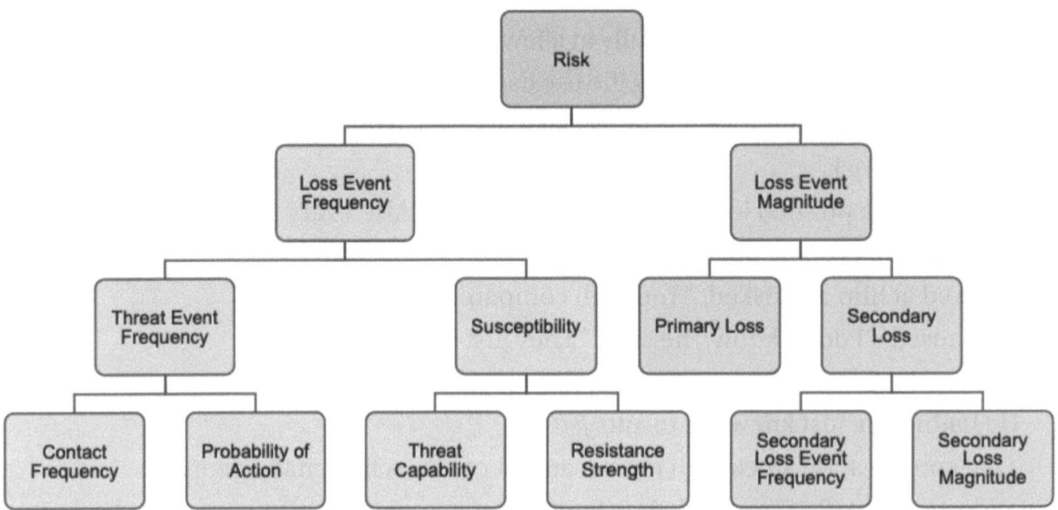

Figure 16-1. *Full FAIR model. (Adapted from Risk taxonomy (O-RT), version 3.1 (The Open Group, 2021))*

WHAT FAIR ISN'T

- Not a product or tool.
- Not a replacement for judgment.
- Not limited to cybersecurity.
- It's a structured way to answer the same questions Jack's executives asked:

  How much risk do we have, and what do we get if we spend the money?

The Open FAIR Standard

FAIR, as a standard, began with **The Open Group**, which still maintains the **Open FAIR Risk Taxonomy** and **Risk Analysis Standards.** Originally published in 2014, these documents define the original model: the structured breakdown of how frequency and magnitude combine to produce risk.

That simple relationship turned vague words like *likelihood* and *impact* into measurable components. It gave security and risk teams a shared language, and it remains the formal specification behind every FAIR-based model today.

The Open Group maintains the formal Open FAIR standards and continues to extend the broader body of knowledge through white papers, guides, and methodological work, including its efforts in Zero Trust and enterprise risk management. The FAIR Institute, founded by Jack Jones, builds on that foundation by developing applied frameworks such as FAIR-CAM, FAIR-MAM, and FAIR-TAM for practitioners.

The Rise of the FAIR Institute and the New Family of Models

Around 2016, FAIR's creator, Jack Jones, and collaborators founded the FAIR Institute, a research-driven, not-for-profit (FAIR Institute, n.d.), to carry the work forward. That community began extending the original model into specialized models that connect risk analysis to real-world management decisions. Table 16-1 shows the different standards, frameworks, and models.

Table 16-1. *The current FAIR ecosystem*

Organization/ Standard Body	Name	Type	Description
The Open Group	Open FAIR Risk Taxonomy (O-RT)	Standard	Defines the Open FAIR model; formerly called the "ontology."
The Open Group	Open FAIR Risk Analysis (O-RA)	Standard	Defines the process for risk analysis.
FAIR Institute	FAIR Model	Standard	Defines the FAIR model; not a formal standard, distinct from the Open Group versions
FAIR Institute	FAIR-CAM (Controls Analytics Model)	Standard	Maps controls into FAIR factors to model how controls affect risk.
FAIR Institute	FAIR-MAM (Materiality Assessment Model)	Framework/ Model	Adds materiality/financial/regulatory terms to FAIR. Can optionally replace the six forms of loss.
FAIR Institute	FAIR-TAM (Third-Party Assessment Model)	Framework/ Model	Extends FAIR into third-party and supply chain risk.
FAIR Institute	FAIR-CRMP (Cyber Risk Management Program)	Standard	Integrates FAIR within ongoing risk governance programs (emerging).
FAIR Institute	FAIR-AIR (AI Risk Playbook)	Playbook	Applies FAIR logic to AI/model risk.

Note Information compiled from The Open Group (2021) and FAIR Institute. See the References for full citations.

Together they form what practitioners now call the **FAIR ecosystem**: a living, modular architecture linking data, controls, and decisions. FAIR exists today in two closely related but distinct forms.

- The **Open Group** maintains the *formal* Open FAIR standards, which define the official taxonomy and analysis process used for certification and auditability.
- The **FAIR Institute**, co-founded by Jack Jones, builds on that foundation through applied frameworks such as FAIR-CAM, FAIR-MAM, and FAIR-TAM.

These community-developed models expand FAIR's reach into areas like controls analytics, third-party risk, and financial materiality, but they do not replace the Open FAIR Standards.

The FAIR Institute has been instrumental in bringing CRQ to the mainstream. Among other contributions, it provides

- Education and certification (for FAIR practitioners) beyond just taxonomy
- Research and community (connecting practitioners, cross-industry sharing)
- Frameworks/models built on or compatible with FAIR (e.g., controls modelling, materiality modelling, third-party risk modelling)
- Resources and tools to integrate FAIR into modern practice (data, metrics, AI integration)

The State of Risk Management Before FAIR

To understand what Jack built, you have to understand what he was reacting to. In the 1990s and early 2000s, information security risk management was mostly qualitative, with a few rare exceptions.

Organizations used arbitrary scales, inconsistent definitions, and a lot of guesswork dressed up as expertise. What little quantitative guidance existed told you to measure things like "exposure factor" or "asset value," but with no clear definitions or context.

As we covered in Part 1 of this book, it's no wonder people thought quantitative risk analysis was impossible. Jack saw that the field wasn't broken because of math; it was broken because of *thinking*.

Jack Jones' Three Big Contributions

1. Precise Definitions

FAIR cleaned up the language. It provides precise, unambiguous definitions for terms like *risk, threat, loss event, asset,* and *Susceptibility*.

Jack uses a favorite analogy in speeches when describing the state of the information security profession. He asks a series of questions to the audience:

- "How many of you would want to ride a space mission?" Typically, a few hands go up.
- Then he asks, "How many of you would want to ride on a mission if the scientists and engineers who designed the spacecraft and planned the mission couldn't agree on the definition of mass, weight, and velocity?"

He then points out to the audience that that's exactly what our profession is doing every day. We're taking our stakeholders on that very mission when we can't agree on basic nomenclature.

If you compare definitions of "risk" across standards, the inconsistency is striking. NIST (2012) calls it a function of likelihood and impact. ISO 31000 (2018) defines it as the effect of uncertainty on objectives. COSO (2020) frames it as "the possibility that events will occur and affect the achievement of strategy and business objectives." GDPR (2016) focuses on the likelihood and severity of harm to the rights and freedoms of individuals. PCI DSS (2022) uses the word "risk" extensively, but never defines it at all, treating "risk" as shorthand for non-compliance. The Open FAIR Taxonomy set out to fix that by defining risk in measurable terms, "the probable frequency and probable magnitude of future loss" (The Open Group, 2021).

2. A Framework for Critical Thinking

Second, Jack introduced a **framework for thinking** about risk.

Before FAIR, a "risk workshop" meant people sitting in a room, listing anything that worried them, and then playing Pick-A-Color. We still do that, but at least there's an alternative. Half the items that come out of such workshops aren't risks; they could be threats, control gaps, vague concerns, or something else entirely. FAIR brought structure. It forced analysts to decompose problems into an asset, threat, and effect. It made risk a reasoning problem, not a coloring exercise.

3. Measurement and Actuarial Logic

Finally, Jack introduced concepts from **metrology** (the science of measurement) and **actuarial science** into information risk management. These ideas existed in academia, but few had made them usable in day-to-day security programs.

FAIR bridged that gap. It gave *practitioners* a way to reason probabilistically and quantitatively without needing to be statisticians.

At a dinner years later, Jack Jones and I explained FAIR to a colleague who is an expert in quantitative enterprise risk management. After listening, he said, “So it’s just actuarial techniques applied to information risk?” Exactly. FAIR didn’t invent quantification; it *operationalized* it for information systems.

How FAIR Works (in Plain English)

If you’ve walked through the exercises in this book, you already know the basics of FAIR.

At its simplest, FAIR expresses **risk** as the combination of

- **Loss Event Frequency (LEF)**: How often losses are expected to occur
- **Loss Magnitude (LM)**: How large those losses are likely to be

Earlier in this book, we called those simply *frequency* and *magnitude.* It’s the same thing, even measured the same way: as ranges articulated in years, not probabilities.

If you stop right there, you’ve already done a FAIR-compatible risk assessment. But FAIR goes further by showing how to break those top-level factors into measurable parts. That decomposition is one of FAIR’s biggest contributions to risk analysis.

This layered structure is the real power of FAIR. It lets you find *data that exists* instead of lamenting data that doesn’t. Every security team has different telemetry. FAIR gives you multiple entry points for quantification so you can start wherever your evidence lives.

FAIR can feel complex at first, especially when implemented through enterprise tooling or governance processes. But at its core, it's simply a structured way to express what you already know about frequency and impact. Start simple, expand only when your data justifies it.

Decomposing Loss Event Frequency

You can think of **Loss Event Frequency** as a function of how often threats act and how often attempts succeed. In the FAIR model, those subcomponents are **Threat Event Frequency (TEF)** and **Susceptibility.**

- **Threat Event Frequency:** How often a threat actor acts against an asset, whether or not the attempt succeeds
- **Susceptibility:** How likely the asset is to experience loss given the threat's capability and the strength of controls resisting it

---

Note We use Susceptibility (synonym in the Open FAIR standard for Vulnerability) to emphasize the probabilistic nature of resistance.

This is useful because organizations often have data that fit one level but not another. Maybe you know how many phishing attempts occurred last year, but not how many succeeded. FAIR's decomposition lets you work with the data you have.

If you lack data even for Threat Event Frequency, FAIR allows another layer of decomposition:

- **Contact frequency**: How often a threat comes into contact with the asset
- **Probability of action**: How likely the actor is to act once contact occurs

Each layer lets you substitute available data for missing pieces while keeping the logic consistent. Susceptibility can also decompose into **threat capability** and **resistance strength.**

GENAI PROMPT: IDENTIFY DATA FOR FREQUENCY

Given a risk scenario where [*describe scenario*], list the kinds of data that could estimate Threat Event Frequency (TEF) and Vulnerability in a FAIR-based risk assessment. For each, note whether the data is internal or external, how often it is updated, and where one could find it.

Decomposing Loss Magnitude

We've already covered this in Chapter 8. FAIR divides **Loss Magnitude** into **Primary Loss** and **Secondary Loss.**

- **Primary Loss:** The direct, immediate cost of the event
- **Secondary Loss:** The indirect or long-tail fallout—regulatory fines, customer churn, reputation damage, or legal costs

In this book, we explored those concepts through the six forms of loss, which align directly to FAIR's magnitude side.

EXERCISE 16-1: DRAW YOUR FIRST FAIR MODEL

Goal: Practice connecting a simple risk scenario to FAIR's core structure.

Scenario: A financially motivated threat actor is likely to attempt a phishing campaign against finance staff. A successful compromise could lead to ransomware encrypting shared drives and disrupting access to financial systems.

Step 1: Start Simple

Draw three boxes: **Risk → Loss Event Frequency (LEF) → Loss Magnitude (LM).**

Write one sentence for each:

- **LEF:** "How often could ransomware from this group encrypt our shared drives?"

  Example answer: "We've had one major ransomware event in the past three years, and similar companies see a few per year."

- **LM:** "What would it cost each time it happens?"

  Example answer: "We'd lose two to three days of productivity and pay recovery and IR costs around $250K."

Step 2: Add One Layer

Under LEF, add **Threat Event Frequency (TEF)** and **Susceptibility.**

Ask yourself:

- **TEF**: How often do attackers try this?
- **Susceptibility**: When they try, how often does it succeed?

Step 3: List New Data You'd Need

Examples: Phishing attempts per year, click-through rates, backup success, MFA coverage.

Step 4: Reflect

What did adding TEF and Susceptibility show that the simple LEF and LM view missed?

Using Only As Much FAIR As You Need

If there's one message to take from this chapter, it's that you can use as much or as little of FAIR as you need.

That's one of its greatest strengths. It's modular. Choose the pieces that fit your program and ignore the rest. You don't have to "go full FAIR" to get value from it. The principle works with the FAIR ecosystem shown in Table 16-1 and with the FAIR model itself, in Figure 16-1.

Throughout this book, I've used parts of FAIR even though this isn't a FAIR book. The point isn't whether you follow FAIR line by line. The point is whether you're thinking clearly about the components of risk.

Some practitioners treat FAIR dogmatically, forgetting that its real power lies in critical thinking and adaptation, in using the parts that help you reason better about uncertainty, not from following the model for its own sake. FAIR, Hubbard's models, and other quantitative frameworks all rest on the same foundation: probabilistic reasoning, measurement under uncertainty, and structured decision-making. They work together because, at the end of the day, it's all just math applied to uncertainty.

The deeper you go in the model, the more data and effort you need. If you already have strong loss frequency data, you don't need to decompose it further just to say you did. Use the level of the model that matches your available data and the decision you're trying to support.

GENAI PROMPT: PICK YOUR FAIR DEPTH

Here is the data I have for a risk analysis: [*paste or describe*]. Suggest the simplest FAIR decomposition that makes sense given the available data. Explain which FAIR factors to include and which to omit.

Here are three examples of mix-and-match approaches that work in practice. Think of them as "choose your own adventure" paths through FAIR, depending on what data you have and the decision you're trying to make.

Example 1: Use Top-Level Inputs Only

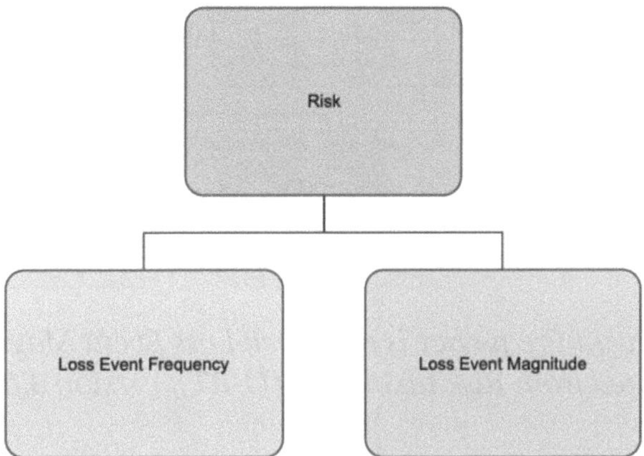

Figure 16-2. *Using FAIR at the Loss Event Frequency and Loss Event Magnitude level. (Adapted from Risk taxonomy (O-RT), version 3.0.1 (The Open Group, 2021))*

If you already have high-quality data for Loss Event Frequency and Loss Magnitude and the decision at hand doesn't require further decomposition, stop there, as seen in Figure 16-2. For instance, the Cyentia IRIS reports provide excellent aggregated data at those levels. I've run analyses using only those two inputs with great success. There's no reason to decompose frequency into more detail if the data is already solid.

Example 2: Fully Decomposed Magnitude

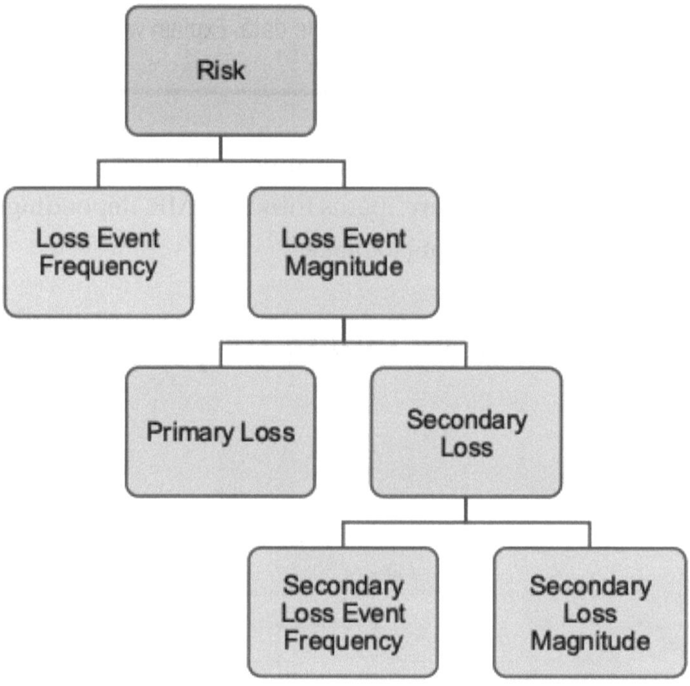

Figure 16-3. *Loss Event Frequency is top-level; Loss Event Magnitude is fully decomposed. (Adapted from Risk taxonomy (O-RT), version 3.0.1 (The Open Group, 2021))*

Sometimes you have reliable data for how often losses occur but want more precision in how you describe their cost. That is especially common in data breach scenarios. The industry now has solid frequency data and increasingly detailed magnitude data, including secondary losses. Each year, this gets easier to obtain as the risk analyst can use AI tools to scan news stories, public databases, and regulatory filings such as 8-K and 10-K forms to extract information about fines, legal actions, and total incident costs. In those cases, it often makes sense to keep frequency at the top level and break magnitude down further, as demonstrated in Figure 16-3.

GENAI PROMPT: EXTRACTING MAGNITUDE DATA FOR DATA BREACH

You are an analyst assisting with a quantitative risk assessment. Your task is to collect verified, factual data on publicly reported data breach incidents that include financial impact details.

Follow these rules strictly:

- **No estimates, projections, or AI-inferred numbers.** Only include values explicitly stated in reliable, published sources.
- **No speculation.** If a cost or loss figure is unclear or disputed, omit it and note that it was unavailable.
- **Check for hallucination.** After retrieving each figure, recheck the source text to confirm the value exists verbatim.
- **Verify every citation.** Only use data from primary or verifiable sources such as
    - Regulatory filings (e.g., SEC 8-K, 10-K, or enforcement documents)
    - Court records or settlement documents
    - Reputable investigative journalism (e.g., Reuters, Bloomberg, WSJ, The Register, SC Media)
    - Company press releases or investor statements

For each incident, extract:

1. Organization name and industry
2. Year of incident
3. Description (one sentence)
4. Reported **primary losses** (response, legal, downtime, restoration)
5. Reported **secondary losses** (fines, lawsuits, regulatory actions, customer churn, reputation impact)
6. Source and publication date
7. Verification note (e.g., "Confirmed in 8-K filed Feb 2024")

Present the results in a table with one row per incident.

Convert values to USD if necessary, and flag any record where cost data cannot be confirmed verbatim.

Example 3: Decompose Threat Frequency Using Control Data

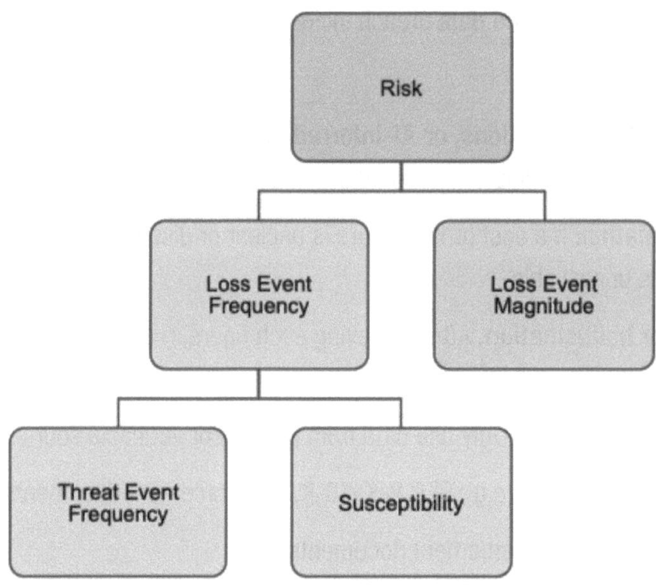

Figure 16-4. *Decomposing Loss Event Frequency enables control evaluations. (Adapted from Risk taxonomy (O-RT), version 3.0.1 (The Open Group, 2021))*

Other times, the data you have is upstream. You might have detailed threat activity data, such as phishing attempts, but limited insight into success rates. In that case, use a control evaluation framework like FAIR-CAM (one of the frameworks listed in Table 16-1) to derive Susceptibility based on control strength. You can decompose Threat Event Frequency and vulnerability further while keeping the rest simple, shown in Figure 16-4.

Practical Tips for Using FAIR Depth Wisely

The examples above are just starting points. You can mix and match levels depending on your data and the decision your analysis is meant to support. The decision context should always be your north star for how deep to go.

A Few Tips

- **Let data guide depth.** If you already have solid evidence for Loss Event Frequency, there's no reason to break it down further. If magnitude is the uncertainty, focus your decomposition there instead.
- **Remember: every layer adds two parts**. When you decompose Loss Event Frequency, you now have to estimate both Threat Event Frequency and Susceptibility. Go deeper only if you can meaningfully inform both sides.
- **Avoid unnecessary layers.** Contact Frequency and Probability of Action are useful for teaching but rarely practical in live analyses. Most real-world models stop at LEF or TEF/Susceptibility.
- **Keep it decision-driven.** Always ask, "Will this extra layer help us make a better decision?" If not, stop where the data and purpose align.

The point isn't how many FAIR factors you use. The point is whether the model helps a real decision get made faster, with more clarity, and less guesswork. FAIR is a toolkit, not a test of purity. Use only as much as you need to get the job done.

Mapping Data to the FAIR Ontology

For each dataset, ask: Does it tell me **how often** something happens, **how bad** it is when it does, or **who else reacts**?

FAIR Element	Question It Answers	Example Data Sources
Threat Event Frequency (TEF)	How often do defined threat communities attempt something that could cause loss?	SIEM/IDS/IPS logs of confirmed attack attempts, phishing/fraud attempts per year, external threat intel and industry reports (DBIR, ENISA, etc.) scoped to your scenario
Contact Frequency (CF)	How often do they have the opportunity to interact with the asset?	Firewall/WAF/VPN logs showing access to exposed services, scan/activity against public apps, identity/access data showing who can reach what (opportunity, not necessarily malicious)
Probability of Action (PoA)	Given contact, how often do they try something harmful?	Threat profiling, adversary behavior reports, red team exercises, and honeypot data showing the proportion of probes that escalate to attempts
Susceptibility (Vulnerability)	Given an attempt, how likely is it to result in loss?	Pen test success rates, exploit success vs. failure in incident/IR data, control coverage and configuration metrics (interpreted as resistance strength vs. expected threat capability)
Loss Event Frequency (LEF)	How often do we experience actual loss events in this scenario?	Confirmed loss-causing incidents in IR/GRC/ticketing systems; may be derived from TEF × Susceptibility, where internal history is thin
Primary Loss Magnitude (PLM)	What are the direct costs per loss event?	IR labor hours × rates, forensics and legal invoices, downtime × business impact, replacement/rebuild costs from finance and ops
Secondary Loss Event Frequency (SLEF)	How often does a Primary Loss trigger secondary fallout?	Historical rate of regulatory investigations, lawsuits, major customer notifications, and adverse media events, conditional on similar incidents
Secondary Loss Magnitude (SLM)	How big are the secondary costs when they occur?	Past fines and settlements, customer churn analysis, revenue or market-cap impact, and extended PR/brand remediation costs

Mapping This Book to FAIR

Everything in this book can be applied within FAIR without modification. Each chapter connects naturally to a different part of the FAIR model or workflow.

- **Chapter 4** and **Chapter 6** fit directly into FAIR's structure of frequency, magnitude, and loss communication.
- **Chapter 7** borrows FAIR's logic for defining assets, threats, and loss events.
- **Chapter 8** is borrowed from FAIR and aligns with FAIR's *magnitude* side.
- **Chapter 10** supports every level of the FAIR ontology by helping you evaluate and calibrate data quality.
- **Chapters 11–13** are framework-agnostic but map cleanly to FAIR's data inputs for frequency and magnitude.
- **Chapter 14** complements FAIR's reasoning process by showing how to combine multiple evidence sources into a single, defensible estimate.

Regardless of which version of the model you use, the workflow is the same: Collect data (Chapters 11–13), vet and normalize it (Chapter 10), then blend sources as shown in Chapter 14.

Every step supports FAIR analysis directly.

Common Missteps and Overuse

1. Confusing Taxonomy with Analysis

Some practitioners treat FAIR's taxonomy as the analysis itself. They believe they must measure all 12 factors in the model to "do FAIR." You don't. Use only the levels your data can support. Two factors: Loss Event Frequency and Loss Magnitude are enough.

2. FAIR As Religion

This happens in both directions. Some people who love FAIR think it's the only correct way to analyze risk. Others reject it entirely because they find its practitioners overzealous. Both miss the point.

If you learn FAIR, you'll benefit from the community, training, and career opportunities. It's where the momentum is. But your long-term aspiration should be to become a *modeler*, not a *"FAIR person."* That means building, adapting, and sometimes developing your own models. FAIR is the starting line, not the finish.

3. Using FAIR to Debate Definitions

Early in my career, I wasted time arguing that "ransomware isn't a risk, it's a method" or that "vendors aren't risks, they're entities." I stopped doing that years ago. I don't debate definitions anymore. I focus on the decision to be made, the story behind it, and the data that informs it. Once the decision context is clear, the formal risk statement emerges naturally. I also have the bonus that people seem to like me more and groan less when I enter a room if I'm not constantly saying, "Well, actually..." (again, the "less wrong" mindset).

DON'T LET THE MODEL GET IN THE WAY OF THE DECISION

FAIR is a tool for understanding uncertainty, not winning arguments about terminology.

If a conversation about risk turns into a debate over whether something is a "threat event" or a "loss event," stop and ask: What decision are we trying to make?

The right level of modeling is the one that supports that decision. More precision doesn't always mean more value.

FAIR is successful when it drives clarity in action, not when it proves you're right about a definition.

How to Get Started with FAIR

If you've read this far, you've already started. Every concept in this book, frequency, magnitude, ranges, calibration, and data sources, is usable in the FAIR model. The only thing left is to connect the labels.

Still, if you want to go further and use FAIR formally, here's how to begin.

1. Pick One Scenario

Choose something small and concrete: a ransomware incident, a data breach, or a system outage. You don't need an enterprise scope to start.

2. Translate Your Work into FAIR Language

Your "frequency" becomes **Loss Event Frequency**.

Your "magnitude" becomes **Loss Magnitude**.

That's it. You're already at the top level of FAIR.

3. Reuse What You Built in Earlier Chapters

The data you collected, external, internal, and SME, fit directly into FAIR's subfactors. You don't need new sources; you just map them to where they belong.

GENAI PROMPT BOX: MAP MY DATA TO FAIR

Given this list of risk data sources [*paste table*], classify each according to the FAIR ontology: Loss Event Frequency (LEF), Threat Event Frequency (TEF), Vulnerability, Primary Loss Magnitude (PLM), Secondary Loss Event Frequency (SLEF), and Secondary Loss Magnitude (SLM). Explain your reasoning in one sentence per item and output a clean, labeled table for Excel.

Highlight any missing FAIR components and suggest additional data that could fill them.

4. Estimate Ranges and Simulate

Use the same calibrated ranges (P5, P50, P95) and Monte Carlo simulation from Chapters 9 through 14. Those are FAIR-standard techniques.

5. Add Depth Only When Needed

If your data supports it, go one level deeper, such as Threat Event Frequency, Susceptibility, or Secondary Loss. If not, stay simple. You're still "doing FAIR."

6. Document and Iterate

Write down your assumptions, sources, and logic. That transparency is what makes FAIR auditable and repeatable.

By reading this book, you've already learned FAIR; you just learned it in plain English first.

Beyond FAIR

FAIR gives you structure, but it is not the whole story. Most of what you have learned in this book, structured data gathering, vetting, blending, and validation, sits outside FAIR. Those ideas did not exist when the framework was created, but they make it stronger. They turn a theoretical model into something living, testable, and scalable.

We now work in a world with more data, better telemetry, and AI tools that can automate the work we used to do manually. The next generation of FAIR practitioners will not start from spreadsheets and calibration training. They will start with AI that can surface, clean, and test data faster than any of us ever could. That does not make our judgment less important. It makes it more important because someone still has to know when the answers make sense.

That is what this book is about. It is a bridge between generations of practice, from the FAIR we learned by hand to the FAIR that will be powered by machines. The same reasoning and discipline still apply, but the tools have changed. As AI takes on more of the heavy lifting, our role shifts from gathering data to guiding, training, and double-checking the systems that do it for us.

If this book does its job, it will help the next wave of risk professionals use FAIR not just as a model but as a foundation. FAIR gave us language and structure. The work ahead is to extend it with better data, better validation, and smarter tools, so the next generation can reason about risk with the clarity, speed, and confidence the field has always needed.

Chapter Summary

The Big Idea: FAIR gives structure, clarity, and definitions to the messy parts of risk. It is the first model to break cyber risk into measurable components that anyone can analyze in the same way. FAIR is Jack Jones's major contribution: a clear, defensible way to reason about uncertainty that removes guesswork and vague language from risk management.

Key Takeaways

- **FAIR defines risk precisely.** Risk is the probable frequency and probable magnitude of future loss. This clear definition anchors everything else and eliminates the confusion found in many other standards.
- **FAIR decomposes risk into measurable parts.** Loss event frequency, loss magnitude, susceptibility, threat capability, resistance strength, and the six forms of loss give you a structured map of how risk actually works.
- **FAIR replaces fuzzy terms with real concepts.** Instead of "likelihood," "impact," or color ratings, FAIR uses probability, ranges, and specific loss categories. These concepts help you measure uncertainty instead of labeling it.
- **FAIR links analysis to decision-making.** FAIR shows leaders where losses come from and what levers they can pull to reduce them.
- **FAIR creates a shared language across teams.** The model gives analysts, engineers, auditors, and executives the same vocabulary. This reduces misunderstandings and leads to clearer, more consistent decisions.

Bottom Line: FAIR is the structure behind modern CRQ. It is the model that turns risk into something measurable, explainable, and repeatable. By mapping your CRQ work into FAIR, you anchor your analysis to Jack Jones's original insight: risk can be understood and managed only when its parts are clearly defined. FAIR brings that clarity to everything you do next.

What's Coming Next

In Chapter 17, we will walk through a complete examples of a risk assessment using real scenarios and real data. You will see how to apply the model end-to-end and how it changes the way organizations make decisions.

References

Committee of Sponsoring Organizations of the Treadway Commission. (2020). Compliance risk management: Applying the COSO ERM framework. COSO. https://www.coso.org

European Union. (2016). *Regulation (EU) 2016/679 of the European Parliament and of the Council of 27 April 2016 (General Data Protection Regulation). Official Journal of the European Union, L 119.* https://eur-lex.europa.eu/eli/reg/2016/679/oj

FAIR Institute. (2025). Factor analysis of information risk (FAIR) standard (Version 3.0). FAIR Institute. https://www.fairinstitute.org

FAIR Institute. (n.d.-a). *FAIR-CAM™: Controls Analytics Model.* Retrieved November 11, 2025, from https://www.fairinstitute.org/fair-controls-analytics-model

FAIR Institute. (n.d.-b). *FAIR-MAM™: Materiality Assessment Model.* Retrieved November 11, 2025, from https://www.fairinstitute.org/fair-materiality-assessment-model

FAIR Institute. (n.d.-c). *FAIR-TAM™: Third-Party Assessment Model.* Retrieved November 11, 2025, from https://www.fairinstitute.org/fair-third-party-assessment-model

FAIR Institute. (n.d.-d). *FAIR-CRMP™: Cyber Risk Management Program.* Retrieved November 11, 2025, from https://www.fairinstitute.org/blog/announcing-fair-cyber-risk-management-program-fair-crmp-standard-v1.0

FAIR Institute. (n.d.-e). *FAIR-AIR™: Artificial Intelligence Risk Playbook.* Retrieved November 11, 2025, from https://www.fairinstitute.org/blog/fair-artificial-intelligence-ai-cyber-risk-playbook

FAIR Institute. (n.d.-f). *About the FAIR Institute.* Retrieved November 11, 2025, from https://www.fairinstitute.org/about

Freund, J., & Jones, J. (2014). *Measuring and managing information risk: A FAIR approach.* Butterworth-Heinemann.

International Organization for Standardization. (2018). *ISO 31000:2018 Risk management—Guidelines.* ISO. https://www.iso.org/standard/65694.html

National Institute of Standards and Technology. (2012). *Guide for conducting risk assessments* (NIST Special Publication 800-30 Rev. 1). U.S. Department of Commerce. https://doi.org/10.6028/NIST.SP.800-30r1

Payment Card Industry Security Standards Council. (2022). *Payment Card Industry data security standard: Requirements and testing procedures* (Version 4.0). PCI SSC. https://www.pcisecuritystandards.org/document_library

The Open Group. (2025a). *Risk Analysis (O-RA), Version 2.1* (The Open Group Standard, Document No. C250). The Open Group. https://publications.opengroup.org/c250

The Open Group. (2025b). *Risk Taxonomy (O-RT), Version 3.1* (The Open Group Standard, Document No. C251). The Open Group. https://publications.opengroup.org/c251

CHAPTER 17

How to Run a Complete CRQ Assessment (A Full Walkthrough)

> *One thing a person cannot do, no matter how rigorous their analysis, is draw up a list of things that would never occur to them.*
>
> —Thomas Schelling

This chapter walks through one complete CRQ analysis from start to finish. It is intentionally deep rather than broad. Instead of giving you several lightweight examples, I want to show you a full, real-world workflow, step by step, so you can repeat it in your own environment.

Additional sample scenarios and industry variations will be available on the book's companion site at heatmapstohistograms.com.

Could It Happen Here? Modeling a Ransomware Event

It started with a news alert on a Tuesday morning.

You are the quantitative risk lead at a US-based mid-sized fintech-style financial services provider. A company almost identical to yours, same industry, similar size, and same technology stack, had been hit by ransomware. Their customer-facing platform was offline for three days. Customers vented on social media. Analysts speculated on the financial hit. Within hours, your CFO forwarded the article with a short note:

T. Martin-Vegue, *From Heatmaps to Histograms*, https://doi.org/10.1007/979-8-8688-2300-8_17

"If this happened to them, could it happen to us? What would it cost? Are we doing enough to mitigate this kind of risk?"

That single question triggered the analysis you are about to walk through.

This is not a postmortem. We are not reconstructing what happened in their environment. We are performing a forward-looking quantitative risk assessment. The goal is to estimate our potential exposure if we suffered a ransomware incident similar to our competitor. It raises a meaningful question, *could this happen to us?,* and one we can answer with evidence, ranges, and structured reasoning.

When a competitor suffers a ransomware incident, I do not want to treat it as a one-off story. I want to know whether it reflects a broader pattern in our sector. One of the quickest ways to do that today is with a targeted GenAI search that pulls together recent ransomware activity among peer organizations.

GENAI PROMPT: SECTOR RANSOMWARE SIGNAL FINDER

I want to stay ahead of ransomware trends in my sector so that I can brief leadership before a headline forces the conversation. Search credible, verifiable reporting for ransomware incidents in the past twelve months that match my organization's profile. Focus on incidents at companies similar in size, industry, technology stack, and regulatory environment.

My organization is a financial services company based in San Francisco with about one billion dollars in annual revenue. We operate primarily in California and use AWS for production and enterprise workloads.

Return:

1. A list of the most relevant ransomware incidents affecting peer organizations
2. A short summary of each incident
3. The primary loss drivers (availability, response, data loss, reputation)
4. Any observable patterns or trends within the sector
5. Why each incident is relevant to us
6. Links to the original sources

Only include incidents with reliable reporting or clear evidence. Do not invent sources.

Step 1: Framing the Scenario

As described in Chapter 7, the first real and most important step in any risk analysis is developing a realistic and properly scoped scenario. The news story gave us a threat, a rough sense of impact, and a clear signal that leadership is concerned. That may not feel like much, but it is more than enough to start.

In practice, I would talk with a few people in engineering and operations to identify the most likely entry point for ransomware in our environment. The goal is to keep the scenario high-level so it stays meaningful to executives while still being specific enough to model.

After a short set of conversations, we aligned on the following A-T-E structure, in Table 17-1.

Table 17-1. *Risk analysis scope for a ransomware incident*

Scoping Element	Description
Asset	Customer-facing production services and data hosted in AWS
Threat	External actor deploys ransomware after gaining unauthorized access
Effect	Multi-day outage with partial encryption of production systems and potential data loss

To close the loop, I brought this back to the CFO to confirm it reflected the concern behind the original question. It did. Modeling this scenario would give a defensible estimate of our exposure and help them understand whether our security investments are sufficient.

This is also a natural moment to identify the decision this analysis will inform, as described in Chapter 19. The decision is

Based on the estimated annualized loss exposure and the causal factors driving it, what kinds and levels of resilience and credential-hardening improvements should we implement in FY 2026?

See Chapter 7 for how to scope scenarios using the A-T-E framework.

Step 2: Setting the Stage—From Headline to Hypothesis

The news story gave us enough information to frame the problem, but not enough to model it. Reporters described an attacker using stolen automation or developer tokens to access a peer company's cloud environment, encrypt storage, and take services offline for about three days. There were hints of partial data loss and a multi-million dollar financial hit, but there was no underlying data, no breakdown of losses, and no visibility into their controls.

That is useful context, but it is not evidence.

The purpose of the headline is to shape the initial hypothesis we want to test. It helps us ask questions such as

- What type of ransomware event are we comparing ourselves against
- Which assets appear to matter most
- What type of access would the attacker need
- How severe the business disruption might be
- What a plausible version of this event would look like in our environment

These clues help refine the scenario we scoped in the previous section. We are not using numbers from the news article as inputs. The inputs for the model come later, when we gather and vet external data, internal signals, and SME input, as covered in Chapters 10 through 14.

For this analysis, we start with a simple and defensible set of assumptions:

- A cloud-hosted production environment
- Privileged access gained through credential compromise
- Encryption of data causing a two- to three-day outage
- Some possibility of partial data loss
- No catastrophic multi-week rebuild

These assumptions give us a clear hypothesis to test: If a similar event happened here, what would our exposure look like?

What Data We Need for This Scenario

Before we start collecting evidence, we need to be clear on what data this scenario requires. Our scope defines everything. Once we settled on a ransomware event that affects customer-facing production systems in AWS, with privileged access gained through compromised credentials and a multi-day outage, the data requirements became clear.

For **frequency**, we need evidence that helps us answer two questions:

1. How often do organizations like ours experience ransomware events?
2. How do our internal controls, history, and architecture make this event more or less likely?

That means we look for external rates from high-quality studies, internal telemetry on credential and access protections, and SME insight into plausible attack paths.

For **magnitude**, we use the six forms of loss from Chapter 8 as our structure. In this scenario, five of them are in scope: response, replacement, productivity, fines and judgments, and reputation. The sixth, competitive advantage, is scoped out because this event does not materially change our strategic position. Some of these require internal data, such as restore times or contractual obligations. Others benefit from external anchors, such as typical loss ranges reported in security research and studies.

This gives us a clear shopping list. The model only needs two things: how often this event could happen, and how large it could be. Everything we collect next is aimed at those two questions.

GUARDRAILS AGAINST SCOPE CREEP

At this stage, the biggest threat isn't *bad data*. It's the *scenario mutating into something it isn't*. A single headline can turn into five different risk assessments if we're not careful.

To keep the analysis on track, only three things are allowed right now:

1. **What the scenario is:** A clear A-T-E everyone can picture the same way
2. **What the scenario is not:** Explicit exclusions so we don't drift into new threat models
3. **What we need next:** Only the evidence required to estimate frequency and magnitude

If someone adds a detail, ask

"Does this change the decision we're supporting?"

If not, it goes in the parking lot.

Step 3: Collecting and Vetting the Data

Good analysis is built one input at a time. For each part of the model, we follow the same cycle you learned in Part 3: begin with a strong external anchor, refine it with internal telemetry, and shape it into a realistic range with SME judgment. Every new piece of information is screened using the Chapter 10 criteria of relevance, verifiability, applicability, and coverage. This ensures we widen uncertainty where the evidence is weak and tighten only when we can justify doing so.

The simplest way to see this in action is to start with frequency. Once we know how often this kind of event could occur, we will estimate the magnitude using the six forms of loss.

Estimating Frequency

External Baseline

We begin with the question:

> *For a company like ours, how often do ransomware events occur in a typical year?*

To answer it, I used GenAI to research and find external sources. It found many reports, blogs and news stories, but I narrowed it down to two reports: the Cyentia IRIS Ransomware 2024 report and the Verizon DBIR 2025 report. Both meet the High Quality criteria from Chapter 10. They are transparent about their methods, have strong sample sizes, and cover industries similar to ours.

The Cyentia IRIS report gives us the clearest external baseline. According to IRIS, organizations in the one billion to ten billion dollar revenue band have an upper bound probability of about 9–10% of experiencing at least one ransomware event in the next 12 months. Screening the source using the Chapter 10 criteria confirms it as High Quality. Following the approach from Chapters 10 through 14, we treat the external estimate as the midpoint, widen the range based on evidence quality, shift it using internal telemetry, and shape the boundaries using SME judgment.

- **P5**: 0.05 events per year
- **P50**: 0.10 events per year
- **P95**: 0.15 events per year

This becomes our external prior. The data collected for this scenario is summarized in Table 17-2.

Table 17-2. *External data collected for our scenario*

External Signal	Observation	Why It Matters	Quality Category
Annual ransomware event probability (peer-sized organizations)	8–12% per year (IRIS Ransomware 2024)	Establishes the external baseline for frequency	High Quality
Typical ransomware loss (all forms combined)	$1.4M (IRIS Ransomware 2024)	Provides scale for magnitude; used as a sanity check, not an input	High Quality
95th percentile ransomware loss	~$50M (IRIS Ransomware 2024)	Helps shape the upper bound of SME ranges	High Quality
Ransomware involvement in breaches (all industries)	44% (Verizon DBIR 2025)	Confirms the significance of ransomware as a top incident pattern	High Quality
Credential misuse (initial access vector)	Credential abuse is the most common initial access vector in breaches (DBIR 2025)	Validates our scenario's entry point (compromised access)	High Quality
Sector context (Financial Services)	15% of incidents involve ransomware (IRIS Ransomware 2024)	Helps calibrate frequency slightly downward for our sector	High Quality

Internal Refinement

Next, we look inward. Following the guidance in Chapter 12, we narrowed our internal data collection to a small set of relevant signals that have good coverage across the enterprise and directly inform either frequency or magnitude for this scenario. We reviewed last year's Internal Audit report covering the in-scope systems, a NIST CSF self-assessment conducted by the Information Security team, and three years of security incidents recorded in JIRA. We found high MFA adoption for administrators, high backup success rates, and no ransomware events in the last three years.

GenAI helps here, too. With a few prompts, it can surface control adoption rates across industries from research institutes, vendors, and nonprofit reports. These benchmarks give us context for how much to narrow the range around our external estimate or whether to shift it slightly.

Here is what we gathered so far from internal telemetry, in Table 17-3. We are not ready to blend yet. We will hold these signals for the next step when we combine them with external data and SME judgment.

Table 17-3. *Internal signals relevant to the scenario*

Internal Signal	Observation	Why It Matters	Quality Category
MFA coverage (administrators)	95%	Reduces likelihood of credential misuse	High Quality
Backup success rate	97%	Strong indicator of recovery capability	High Quality
Median restore time	18 hours	Anchors outage duration estimates	High Quality
95th percentile restore time	32 hours	Sets upper bound for restoration time	High Quality
Historical ransomware incidents (three years)	0	Suggests lower local frequency	High Quality
Legacy access token (privileged)	Present	Creates a realistic attack path	Moderate Issues
Security incidents (JIRA, three-year window)	No confirmed malware or crypto locker activity	Helps calibrate frequency downward	High Quality
Internal Audit report (last year)	In-scope systems compliant with key access controls	Reinforces posture strength	High Quality
NIST CSF self-assessment	Partial gaps in identity and access management	Helps shape SME interpretation and tail bounds	Moderate Issues

Before we use these signals in the model, we tag each one with a Quality Category. This comes from the screening process in Chapter 10. High-quality evidence is observable, relevant to the scoped asset, and backed by strong telemetry or documentation. Moderate Issues means the evidence is useful but incomplete or forward-looking, so we keep the range wider to avoid overconfidence.

Finally, we speak to engineering and operations SMEs. We bring them the external baseline and internal telemetry and ask the structured questions from Chapter 13: Does this feel right? What would surprise you on the low end? What would surprise you on the high end? What would need to happen for the tail of this distribution to occur?

As usual, the conversation is not perfectly linear. One SME believes the frequency should be lower based on our strong credential protections. Another raises concerns about the legacy access token in one subsystem. A third shifts into "what-if" scenarios that are technically possible but do not match the scope of our A-T-E definition. This is normal. SME workshops often drift into imaginative territory or into past incidents that feel familiar but are not relevant to the modeled scenario. Chapter 13 covers this in detail. The analyst's role is to acknowledge input, bring the discussion back to the scoped event, and separate insight from noise.

With a bit of guidance, we refocus on what matters. The SMEs converge on a shared view: a ransomware event in any given year is unlikely but not negligible. Our controls make opportunistic attacks harder, but a motivated actor with access to credentials could still cause harm. They also point out that while most detection rules are strong, some lag current attacker techniques. This helps us shape the distribution's boundaries, especially in the upper tail.

As discussed in Chapter 13, SME input is essential but carries natural uncertainty. SMEs provide insight, not telemetry. They can describe plausible attack paths and identify weak spots, but they cannot give precise probability estimates. They also disagree, anchor on recent incidents, and sometimes over-extrapolate from isolated experiences. This is why we tag SME-derived inputs as Moderate Issues. The Quality Category does not reflect the capability of the people. It reflects the limitations of human judgment, as you learned earlier in the book.

Following the blending method from Chapter 14, the external base rate is our prior. Internal telemetry is the first update. SME input is the second update that shapes the tail and prevents us from becoming overconfident. We are not replacing earlier estimates. We are refining them in light of expert insight that sits in context, not in code.

After incorporating the SME input, we arrive at a frequency estimate shown in Table 17-4 that reflects everything we know about this scenario and this environment.

***Table 17-4.** Final frequency estimate*

P5	P50	P95
.04	.08	.13

This is our blended posterior. The earlier tables for external data and internal telemetry form the audit trail that shows how we moved from a 10% industry base rate to a narrower and slightly lower local estimate between 4% and 13%, centered around 8%.

Estimating Magnitude: The Six Forms of Loss

Magnitude follows the same pattern as frequency. For each loss form, we begin with external anchors, refine them using internal data, and shape the boundaries with SME judgment. We then vet what we found using the criteria from Chapter 10 and apply the quality category to determine how wide the range should be.

To keep this example readable, we will walk through two loss forms in detail. These show the full thought process of the three-source model. After that, we summarize the remaining forms more briefly.

Response (Full Walkthrough)

We start with external anchors. IRIS provides sector-wide ransomware loss data, including typical losses and tail losses. We do not use these numbers directly, but they give us a realistic sense of scale. This keeps us from anchoring our ranges too low or too high.

Next, we refine using internal data. Our internal labor rates, IR staffing patterns, and historical incident workstreams tell us what response looks like for us, not the industry as a whole. This is exactly the distinction from earlier chapters: external data gives shape, internal data gives scale.

Finally, we bring in SMEs. We guide the conversation the way Chapter 13 teaches:

- "What happens in a good response?"
- "What slows things down?"
- "What would surprise you on the high end?"
- "Has this ever gone differently than expected?"

SMEs help us set the boundaries. They identify coordination bottlenecks, cross-team delays, and tasks that scale with outage severity. Two SMEs initially disagree, which is expected. One anchors on a recent near miss, the other on an older multi-week incident. We bring them back to the scoped scenario and align on plausible bounds.

Because this estimate blends external research and SME judgment, we tag it as having **Moderate Issues**. The final data we collected in Table 17-5 is very useful, but not perfect.

Table 17-5. *Response costs estimate*

P5	P50	P95
$400K	$700K	$1.2M

Productivity (Full Walkthrough)

Productivity loss starts with a simple question from Chapter 8:

"How much money does the business lose when systems are down?"

We could not find any relevant external data, so we turned to internal telemetry. Restore times tell us how long we would realistically be offline. Revenue-per-day and customer usage patterns help translate hours into financial impact.

Next, SMEs shape the boundaries. We use the elicitation methods from Chapter 13 to keep the conversation grounded:

- "Which systems generate the most business value?"
- "How quickly do customers notice?"
- "What do manual workarounds look like?"
- "What would surprise you on the high end?"

As expected, the discussion drifts. One SME imagines a catastrophic multi-week rebuild, which is out of scope. Another describes an outage that only affects internal tools, which would reduce loss but does not match the threat scenario. We tighten the conversation and bring them back to the A-T-E definition.

Because this estimate combines internal data with forward-looking assumptions, we tag it as having **Moderate Issues**. The final data we collected is in Table 17-6.

***Table 17-6.** Productivity costs estimate*

P5	P50	P95
$500K	$900K	$2M

Replacement (Short Form)

Replacement costs draw mainly on internal evidence. Engineering provides reliable estimates for rebuilding cloud infrastructure and restoring critical configurations. These tasks are well understood and repeatable, so we tag this loss form as **High Quality** in Table 17-7.

***Table 17-7.** Replacement costs estimate*

P5	P50	P95
$200K	$400K	$800K

Fines and Judgments (Short Form)

Here, we start with external research on enforcement actions and translate it using our own contractual obligations and regulatory environment. Legal SMEs help us interpret vague public cases into concrete ranges that fit our business. This mix of external anchors and documented internal terms makes the evidence **High Quality** in Table 17-8.

***Table 17-8.** Fines and judgments costs estimate*

P5	P50	P95
$0K	$250K	$1.5M

Reputation (Short Form)

Reputation loss is the most uncertain. External research provides broad patterns of churn and brand impact, but internal sales and customer success teams provide the context that matters. Because this loss form depends on customer behavior that has not yet occurred, we tag it as having **Moderate Issues** in Table 17-9.

Table 17-9. *Reputation costs estimate*

P5	P50	P95
$0K	$500K	$3M

Blending the Evidence for Magnitude

Just as in Chapter 14, each loss form moves through the same cycle: external anchor, internal refinement, SME shaping, and an adjustment based on the quality of the evidence. The blended ranges below in Table 17-10 are the posterior for each loss form.

Table 17-10. *Final magnitude ranges by loss form (P5-P50-P95)*

Loss Form	P5	P50	P95
Response	$400K	$700K	$1.2M
Replacement	$200K	$400K	$800K
Productivity	$500K	$900K	$2.0M
Fines and Judgments	$0	$250K	$1.5M
Reputation	$0	$500K	$3.0M

These ranges reflect the outcomes and purpose of Chapter 10's vetting framework. Strong evidence narrows uncertainty; weaker evidence widens it. The result is not one number, but a defensible range that communicates our uncertainty.

Consolidating Loss Forms into a Single Magnitude Input

Some CRQ tools model each loss form separately and add them during the simulation. The spreadsheet from Chapter 15 uses a simpler structure: it expects **one magnitude distribution per event**, expressed as P5, P50, and P95.

To use our five loss-form estimates in that model, we combine them into a single set of inputs.

This is not a perfect mathematical combination. We are not convolving distributions. We are creating a **defensible approximation** that preserves the scale and uncertainty of the blended loss forms. Adding the P5, P50, and P95 values across loss forms is an approximation. In practice, the P5 of the total is not just the sum of the individual P5 values unless every loss form moves in perfect sync. Most events do not work that way. This shortcut produces a wider range, which is fine for early analyses and helps keep the example easy to follow.

1. Add the P5 values across the loss forms.
2. Add the P50 values.
3. Add the P95 values.

This gives us an approximate total loss per event.

Table 17-11. *Combined magnitude estimate (for spreadsheet input)*

Bound	Approximate Sum Across Loss Forms
P5	$400K + $200K + $500K + $0 + $0 = **$1.1M**
P50	$700K + $400K + $900K + $250K + $500K = **$2.75M**
P95	$1.2M + $800K + $2.0M + $1.5M + $3.0M = **$8.5M**

These are the values you will enter into the spreadsheet:

- **Magnitude P5:** $1.1M
- **Magnitude P50:** $2.75M
- **Magnitude P95:** $8.5M

This becomes the **per-event loss distribution** used by the simulation.

In a more advanced CRQ tool, each loss form would be modeled separately. For teaching purposes, and for analysts doing their first quantitative assessment, a single magnitude distribution maintains clarity while still capturing the right order of magnitude and uncertainty.

SAVE EVERYTHING. YOUR FUTURE SELF WILL THANK YOU

Good analysts save every piece of vetted data because most of it can be reused in future risk assessments.

Years ago, I was modeling a ransomware event almost identical to the example in this chapter. We collected restore times, MFA coverage, backup success rates, contractual obligations, IR staffing patterns, and a ton of incident data, both internal and sector-based. At the time, it felt like we assembled that evidence only for this one scenario.

Six months later, we ran a data breach analysis. Suddenly, all those inputs mattered again.

- **Restore times** shaped productivity loss for a system-availability breach.
- **Backup success rates** helped us estimate recovery likelihood after an exfiltration incident.
- **MFA coverage** became part of the frequency estimate for credential-stuffing and unauthorized access events.
- **Incident response labor patterns** reappeared in every scenario involving containment, investigation, or customer notification.

None of that work had to be redone. Because we documented the previous analysis, our subsequent analysis started halfway done.

Data collected for one scenario almost always accelerates the next. Make sure you build a reusable library of vetted data like internal baselines, SME judgments, external research, incident data, sector anchors, and anything else you can get your hands on. Over time, your analyses become faster, more consistent, and far more defensible because you are drawing from a growing body of evidence rather than starting from zero each time.

How to Save It (Without Buying Anything)

Start simple. You don't need a full platform to manage evidence. Focus on *doing* it, with a good structure and consistency.

Here are three free or nearly free ways to store your growing library of vetted data:

1. **Excel or Google Sheets (Start Here)**

   Create a tab for each category:

   - External signals
   - Internal telemetry
   - SME inputs
   - Loss-form examples
   - Quality categories

   Include

   - The data
   - Source link or documentation
   - Date collected
   - Notes on how it was used
   - GenAI prompts you may have used to gather, vet, or refine the data

   This is perfectly sufficient for your first year of CRQ.

2. **Airtable (Low-Friction, Highly Flexible)**

   Airtable's free tier works surprisingly well for CRQ evidence:

   - Tables for external data, internal telemetry, SMEs, and loss-form ranges
   - Tags for Industry, Asset, Threat, Loss Form
   - Attachments for PDFs, screenshots, or SME interview notes
   - Filters for searching quickly across past analyses

   This becomes your "CRQ evidence library" and scales nicely as you run more assessments.

3. **Notion (Free for Personal Use)**

   Great if you want something more narrative:

   - A page per analysis with embedded tables
   - "Evidence blocks" that link to reusable data points
   - Versioning built in
   - Full search across everything

   Notion works well for analysts who prefer writing out context.

My rule of thumb: If you spent more than five minutes finding it, collecting it, vetting it, or debating it...save it for next time.

Step 4: Building the Model

At this point, we have everything we need to quantify the scenario. The modeling steps were covered earlier in Chapter 15. Now we use that same spreadsheet, enter the blended frequency range and the combined magnitude range from Step 3, and run the simulation.

The inputs are simple:

- The blended frequency range
- The combined magnitude range for per-event loss (P5, P50, P95)

After you enter the P5, P50, and P95 values into the spreadsheet, the spreadsheet converts them into distributions, runs the simulation, and produces annual loss estimates. Your job is to interpret the output.

Summary Statistics from the Model

Reference back to Chapter 6, where we learned the five-number summary and other ways to report risk results.

Table 17-12. *Five-number summary for the ransomware scenario*

Minimum	First Quartile	Median	Third Quartile	Maximum
$80,729	$227,497	$306,151	$410,297	$1,074,731

These are the additional outputs most CRQ analyses report:

- **Expected (mean) annual loss:** $332K
- **Annual probability of loss greater than $1M:** 0.01%
- **P90 annual loss:** $520K
- **P95 annual loss:** $592K

These statistics tell us the shape of the risk more than they tell us a single "answer." Most simulated years cluster between **$200K and $400K** in annual loss. A few years produce a higher six-figure loss. Only 1 out of 10,000 simulations exceeded **$1M**. In this environment, ransomware behaves more like a low-frequency, moderate-impact risk, not the catastrophic budget-killer people sometimes imagine.

No single number tells the story on its own. The value is in seeing how the outcomes spread out: most years look uneventful, some are more painful, and a very small number stretch into the high end.

Loss Exceedance Curve (LEC)

Before we interpret the results, it helps to see the LEC itself. This is one of the most useful views in a CRQ analysis because it shows how often annual loss crosses thresholds that matter to the business.

Figure 17-1 shows the probability that annual loss will exceed different financial levels, based on 10,000 simulation runs.

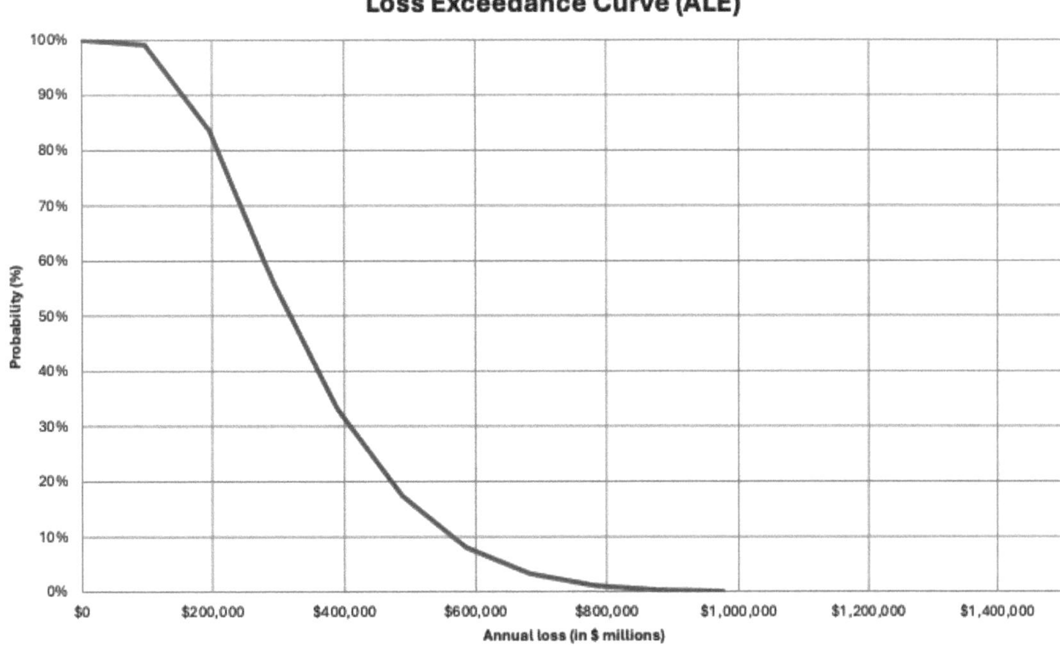

Figure 17-1. *Loss Exceedance Curve for the ransomware scenario*

The Loss Exceedance Curve shows the probability that annual loss will exceed different financial thresholds. It helps leaders understand not just the typical outcomes, but how often losses cross levels that matter to the business.

For this scenario, the LEC tells a clear story.

We have a high likelihood of moderate annual loss and an extremely low likelihood of severe loss:

- There is about an 84% chance that annual loss will exceed $200K.
- A little over half of simulated years exceed $300K.
- Only 27% of years exceed $400K.
- Fewer than 12% exceed $500K.
- And only 0.01% of years exceed $1M.

This curve falls quickly and then flattens, which is typical for low-frequency ransomware events with constrained magnitude. The vast majority of simulated outcomes sit in the lower-to-mid six figures. The right tail exists, but it is short, and only a single simulated year crossed the million-dollar mark.

What this pattern shows is that the risk is predictable in most years, with a narrow band of plausible losses. There is still tail risk, but it is not dominated by catastrophic loss in this particular environment. For the CFO, this curve makes the trade-off clear: controls that reduce downtime or improve credential protections primarily compress the middle of the distribution, not a long catastrophic tail.

If we wanted to explore which assumptions matter most, we could run a few simple what-if tests or look at a tornado diagram. Chapter 15 showed how a what-if analysis works: you change one input, rerun the model, and compare the curves. A tornado diagram is just a visualization that does the same thing on a single chart. It shows how much the output moves when you adjust one input at a time, with the biggest bars at the top and the smallest at the bottom. Some inputs move the curve a lot, others barely move it at all, and that usually points directly to the controls worth improving.

Turning the Analysis into a Decision

When I walk into the CFO's office with this analysis, the goal is simple: help them make a good decision without dragging them through how the sausage was made.

So, I sit down, hand a one-pager over, and say something like

"Here's the picture. Most years, this doesn't happen. In the years when it does, the financial hit lands in the mid-six figures, sometimes a little higher. The million-dollar years are rare. Not impossible, but rare."

They usually lean in at this point, not because of the number, but because the uncertainty is finally concrete. That is the whole point of everything we did in the earlier chapters: building scenarios clearly, vetting data, widening ranges when the evidence was weak, narrowing them when we had good telemetry, and grounding SME input to keep it realistic. All that discipline is what lets us sit in this room and talk about the risk without hand-waving.

The CFO asks the same question every CFO asks:

"So...are we good?"

This is where a risk analyst becomes a strategic partner, not a reporting function.

"We're mostly good," I say. "The likelihood is low, and the tail is short. But there are three places where we can tighten things up that make a measurable difference."

"Here's the good news," I tell the CFO. "There are a few practical things we can do to take a meaningful chunk of this risk off the table. None of them are major projects, and all of them directly reduce the outcomes you saw in the model."

Then I pause and give the headline, not the technical detail:

"They target the weak access paths, they help us spot trouble earlier, and they shorten recovery when something goes wrong."

That is all the CFO needs.

They nod. They understand the shape of the decision. And that is when I say:

"I'll work with the CISO on what those improvements look like in practice and what they cost. We'll bring you options."

Later, in the follow-up with the CISO, we get more specific:

- Remove the legacy access path.
- Improve detection around credential misuse.
- Tighten and automate recovery steps.

But that part is for the security team, not the CFO. I don't give them the Monte Carlo. I don't talk about P95 or vetting or distributions.

Those were for me.

What I give them is the decision:

"We can take a meaningful amount of this exposure off the table for a reasonable investment. If we do these three things, the story looks better a year from now."

That is the moment CRQ pays for itself.

Not in the model.

But in the clarity that lets a leader decide with confidence.

By the end of the conversation, they walk away with three things:

- We understand the risk.
- We understand what drives it.
- And we know what to do about it.

That is what this entire chapter has been building toward: taking a messy, uncertain problem and turning it into something the business can act on. When we do this well, risk analysis stops being a reporting exercise and becomes a strategic capability. It gives leaders clarity, not comfort; choices, not checkboxes; and a way to steer the organization with evidence rather than instinct.

THE FIRST RULE OF CRQ

There's a line in the 1999 movie *Fight Club*:

"The first rule of Fight Club is: you do not talk about Fight Club."

I have my own version of that rule, and it surprises people:

The first rule of CRQ is: do not talk about CRQ.

At least not in the room where a decision is being made.

I learned this the hard way. Once, I walked into a C-suite level meeting and started explaining FAIR, inputs, distributions, Monte Carlo…and I could watch the energy drain out of the room. Eyes glazed over. Someone checked their phone. Once you lose the room, you do not get it back.

Executives do not want a tour of the method. They want to know:

- **What is our exposure?**
- **What drives it?**
- **Are we good?**
- **What should we do next?**

That is the whole conversation.

If they *ask* to go deeper into the model, great. Walk them through it. But do not lead with it. CRQ is the engine behind the analysis, not the meeting.

Chapter Summary

The Big Idea: A full CRQ analysis is not complicated once you see how the pieces fit together. When you move through a simple sequence of steps—scenario, data, ranges, simulation, interpretation—you turn an open-ended question into something a business can act on. The value is not in the math. It is in the clarity you create.

Key Takeaways

- **You can build a complete analysis** with a clear scenario, the three-source model, vetted ranges, and a basic spreadsheet.
- **The end goal is structure, not precision.** You are creating a consistent way to express uncertainty in dollars and probability, not chasing perfect numbers.
- **The insight comes from how the distribution behaves.** It shows the range of possible outcomes, how the tail behaves, and where uncertainty sits.
- **CRQ changes the conversation.** You go from debating fears and opinions to comparing trade-offs the same way the rest of the business does.
- **A good analyst is not just producing numbers.** You are helping leaders make a clearer, faster, and more defensible decision.

Bottom Line: By now, you have seen how a full CRQ assessment comes together. Not as a checklist, but as a way of thinking. You watched a vague, slightly anxious leadership question turn into a structured scenario, a set of vetted inputs, and a clear picture of exposure. You saw how evidence, judgment, and simple tools can turn uncertainty into something the business can work with. Many of the myths we covered earlier in the book should feel less intimidating now. CRQ is not complicated once you see it in motion. It is a straightforward, honest way to reason about risk, and once you use it, it is hard to go back to the old way of doing things.

What's Coming Next

Now that you can run a complete analysis, the next question is simple. How do you make this work inside a real organization?

Chapter 18 looks at what happens when CRQ meets people, process, politics, and culture. You will learn how to introduce this approach without friction, how to build allies, how to keep momentum, and how to make CRQ feel like a natural part of decision-making instead of an add-on.

References

Cyentia Institute. (2024). *Information Risk Insights Study: Ransomware.* Cybersecurity and Infrastructure Security Agency (CISA). https://www.cyentia.com

Verizon. (2025). 2025 Data Breach Investigations Report. Verizon Enterprise Solutions. https://www.verizon.com/business/resources/reports/dbir/

PART V

Making It Stick

CHAPTER 18

CRQ in the Org

> *Experience is simply the name we give our mistakes.*
>
> —Oscar Wilde

Before we dive in, it's worth clarifying what this book covers and what it doesn't.

From Heatmaps to Histograms is about risk analysis, not full-scope risk management. The focus has been on how to frame problems, collect data, and build models that improve decisions. Broader management topics such as risk appetite, governance structures, policy frameworks, and control treatment planning are important, but they belong to the practice of managing risk, not analyzing it. This chapter connects those two worlds. It shows how analysis fits inside a living organization and how to make quantitative reasoning part of everyday decision-making without turning it into a bureaucracy.

A Tale of Two CRQ Programs

I'd like to tell a tale of two CRQ programs, as seen in Figure 18-1. I've built many over the years—most very successful, others not so much. I want to tell you about the least successful and the most successful.

T. Martin-Vegue, *From Heatmaps to Histograms*, https://doi.org/10.1007/979-8-8688-2300-8_18

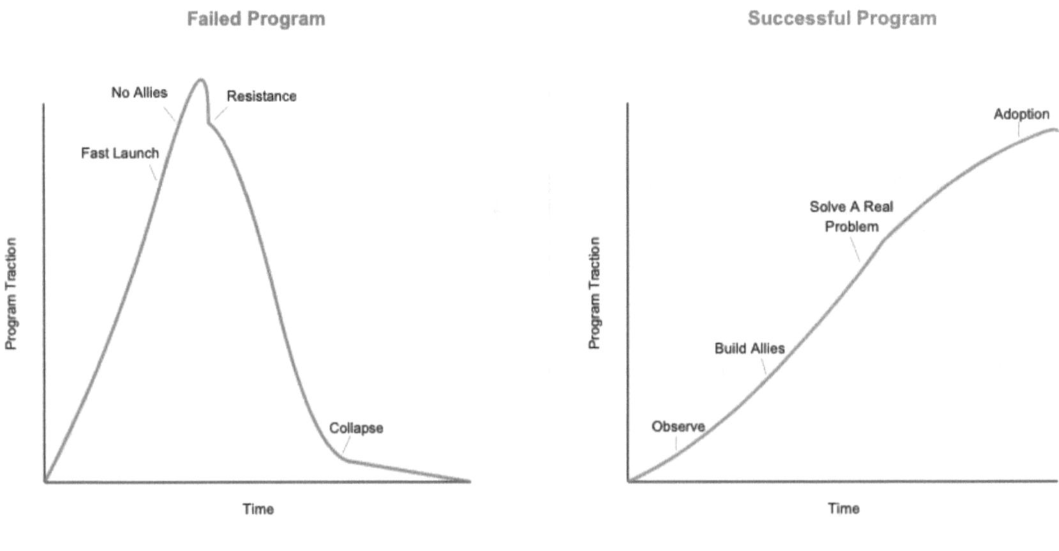

Figure 18-1. *Two CRQ programs: one prioritized for speed (left) and the other for long-term success (right)*

Let's start with the least successful.

It was early in my career, right after I convinced my boss to send me to a two-day FAIR training course. I came back completely hooked. I thought, *this is it.* This is the right way to do risk. Qualitative methodologies, I'd come to realize, were fatally flawed and borderline professionally dishonest. In many ways, I still stand by that (but I've tempered the way I talk about it a bit).

When I got back to work, I walked in like a zealot. I told everyone that from now on, everything would be quantitative. The policies, the risk register, the metrics, everything. I was ready to rebuild the entire program in a week. People listened politely and went back to their day. No traction, no interest, and no allies. My proselytizing lasted about three days. I was right, but it didn't matter. I may as well have been preaching heliocentrism in a medieval cathedral. That era of my life was short-lived, but it taught me something that stuck with me for the rest of my career: conviction alone doesn't build programs. Culture, pacing, and relationships do.

Since then, I've built several programs, most of which have been successful. Now, let me tell you about the most successful one.

This was at a large technology company that wanted to move from compliance theater to genuine, data-driven decision-making. When I arrived, the "risk program" was 30 or 40 lines in an Excel sheet that was updated once a quarter to keep the auditors happy. Leadership wanted more. They wanted quantified risk that could drive real investment decisions.

The first thing I did was...*nothing.* I didn't touch the risk register. I improved small things, like validating risks and updating owners, but otherwise left the existing qualitative program alone. That restraint was deliberate. I'd learned the hard way not to burn the ships.

Instead, I started meeting and talking to people. I looked for the person or team with a real problem, a high-stakes decision they couldn't get traction on. Eventually, I found one: a team managing a security problem with hundreds of millions in potential exposure and weekly realized incidents, but couldn't get any traction or funding to mitigate the risk. They were stuck and needed a better way to make their case.

I ran two analyses. The first was a baseline analysis showing the current risk—risk as it looked *today*. The numbers were eye-opening. Enormous realized losses and escalating exposure. The second analysis was *hypothetical* and modeled what would happen if we invested in one additional headcount and a vendor solution for real-time monitoring and mitigation. The model showed a 70% risk reduction for an investment of about $2 million. That is a stellar return on investment.

I showed the analysis to the risk owner, who was thrilled. We packaged it into a short report, and leadership approved the budget almost immediately. Within a year, the measured reduction matched our forecast. It was a big win.

That success became the proof point. I brought it to other team leads and said, "Here's what we did for them. Want to see if we can do something similar for you?" One analysis became 2, then 15. Each one solved a tangible business problem. All the while, the qualitative register remained quietly in the background, updated and fulfilling its regulatory obligations. When the time was right, I flipped the entire program to FAIR. I didn't have to sell it. Everyone already wanted it.

This experience taught me that CRQ isn't a revolution you declare. It's a conversation you sustain. The difference between my failed and successful programs wasn't math. It was empathy, pacing, and timing. The most successful CRQ programs don't replace the old system overnight. They work within it, show quick wins, and invite people along the way. The rest of this chapter is about how to do exactly that: how to make CRQ stick inside an organization and become part of how decisions get made every day.

Why CRQ Programs Fail (and How to Avoid It)

After running enough of these programs, you start to see the patterns. Some teams take off. Others stall or fade away after the first few analyses. A few never make it past the kickoff meeting. The failures aren't random. They follow a pattern that shows up at three levels: individual, team, and organization, as illustrated in Figure 18-2.

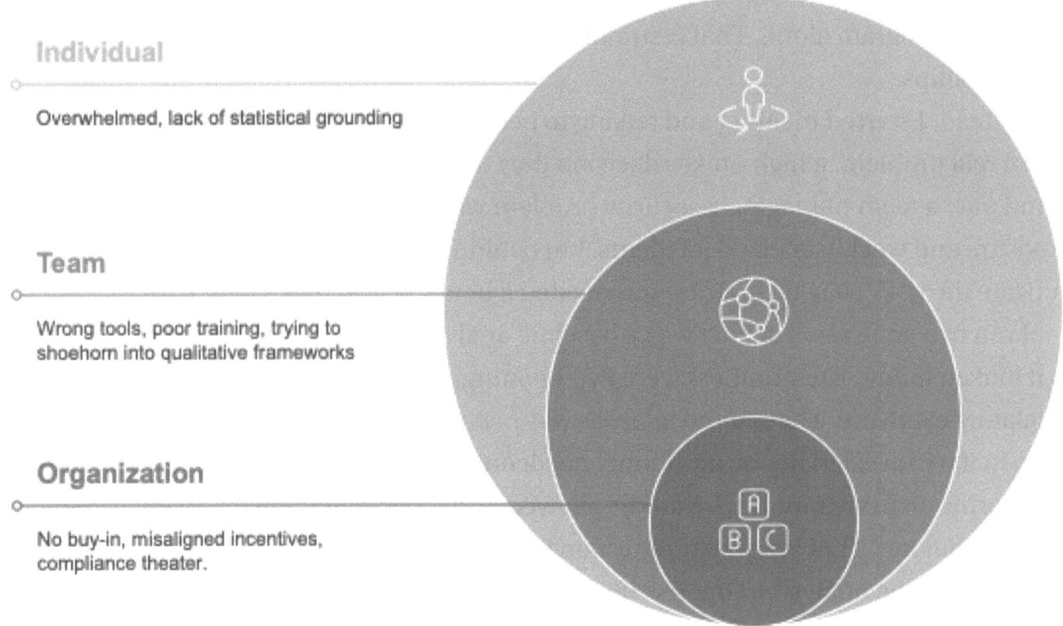

Figure 18-2. *CRQ programs can fail at three levels*

The Individual Level

This one usually starts with enthusiasm. Someone takes FAIR training, reads *How to Measure Anything in Cybersecurity Risk*, or sees a conference talk that finally makes the math click. They're excited. They build a model, plug in numbers, and start sharing histograms with anyone who will look.

But the excitement fades fast when nobody else understands what they're seeing. The analyst starts to feel isolated, frustrated, and eventually burned out. Most of these early efforts fail not because the person is wrong, but because they don't have the foundation or patience to meet others where they are.

At the individual level, CRQ programs fail when analysts try to substitute conviction for influence. They get stuck on the math and skip over storytelling, alignment, and decision context. They also tend to underestimate the extent to which the work actually requires statistical literacy, data wrangling, and communication skills. Quantification without understanding the models, quality checks, or context does not build confidence. It erodes it.

How to avoid it: Start small and humble. Pick one decision that matters and model it well. Show your uncertainty rather than hide it. Find a peer who can review your work and keep you honest. Last, remember that every successful CRQ program is built by someone who learned how to translate probability into a language their stakeholders already speak.

The Team Level

The next pattern happens when a small group of change agents tries to scale too quickly. They have the right intent but the wrong architecture. Maybe they use the wrong tools, bolt quantitative methods onto a legacy qualitative framework, or skip essential pieces like vetting data or learning risk communication because "we'll fix it later." The result is a model that looks sophisticated but collapses under scrutiny.

The team-level failure usually sounds like this: "We built a Monte Carlo simulation, but leadership didn't buy it." What that really means is the team built a model without building credibility. They ran a CRQ process, but not a CRQ *program*: one with data governance, reproducibility, documentation, and a repeatable workflow that others can trust.

Sometimes the opposite happens. The team over-engineers everything. They spend months building infrastructure, taxonomy, and tooling before a single business problem gets solved. By the time their first model is ready, everyone else has moved on.

How to avoid it: Treat CRQ as a service, not a product. Every model should answer a real question with a decision owner and a timeline. Get results out fast, even if they're rough, and iterate. Use the lightest tools possible until you've proven demand. A spreadsheet that drives one funded decision is worth more than a polished platform nobody uses. Build credibility first; the rest can follow.

The Organizational Level

The biggest failures start here. These are the programs that never had a chance because the culture, incentives, or governance were misaligned from the start. The symptoms are familiar: risk lives in a silo, reporting serves auditors instead of decision-makers, and leadership treats CRQ as a compliance checkbox rather than a management tool—something that informs strategy or drives investment.

Failure often happens when CRQ is rolled out as a sudden replacement for qualitative scoring. Replacing subjective rankings is the goal, and everyone knows the current method is flawed. The mistake is expecting the organization to leap straight to the future without a bridge. When CRQ arrives as a band-aid that gets ripped off instead of a path forward, it triggers an immune response. Other teams feel judged, not invited. They shut down cooperation, withhold data, or quietly wait until the quant team runs out of air.

Misaligned incentives make all of this worse. If green dashboards are rewarded more than honest uncertainty, anything that reveals more risk gets treated like a problem. Leaders start asking why the numbers went up rather than what they imply. The same thing shows up in how risk mitigation is rewarded. Teams earn praise for reducing risk even when that reduction costs more than it saves. This reflex drains budgets, crowds out smarter investments, and erodes credibility.

CRQ reframes incentives around efficiency. The goal becomes getting the most loss reduction per dollar instead of stacking more controls simply to show activity. A program that rewards optimization instead of "risk to say we did it" earns more trust and eventually earns more funding, too. That is when CRQ shifts from a reporting exercise into a performance engine.

Many organizations stumble not because the math is wrong but because ownership is unclear. Security teams feel responsible for reducing risk, yet the authority and responsibility to accept or transfer risk sits with the risk owner, usually someone outside of the Security org. When no one is accountable for acting on the numbers, risk quantification becomes a spectator sport. The results look interesting, but nothing changes.

Before building models, make decision rights explicit. Who decides, who implements, who monitors, and who pays the bill. Governance clarity is what turns quantification into management. Without it, the program stays stuck in analysis. With it, the organization starts improving decisions, not just measuring them.

How to avoid it: Anchor CRQ to real business outcomes. Don't call it a program at first. Call it a decision support capability or a forecasting service. Tie every model to a choice leadership already cares about: funding, insurance, budget allocation, or strategic risk appetite. Show how the results make existing processes easier, not obsolete. And build allies early, especially in Finance, Operations, and Legal, because they already understand trade-offs, materiality, and the power of numbers.

Seeing the Whole Pattern

Most failed CRQ programs collapse because of impatience, isolation, or misaligned incentives. The successful ones do almost the opposite. They start small, stay connected, and grow through proof, not persuasion. They treat quantification as a shared language, not a crusade.

I've come to see these patterns as predictable, not personal. Every analyst, every team, every organization starts somewhere along this maturity curve. I've said throughout this entire book that the goal isn't perfection; it's progress. The real measure of success isn't how many Monte Carlo simulations you've run. It's whether your organization is making better, more transparent decisions than it did a year ago.

How to Make CRQ Work Inside an Organization

If the first half of this chapter is about why CRQ programs fail, this half is about how they survive. Every successful program I've seen shared the same pattern. They didn't start with a tool, a framework, or even a mandate. They started with a decision. Someone had to choose between options under uncertainty, and a model helped them do it better. That's where it begins.

Quantitative risk programs thrive when they solve real problems for real people. The analyst isn't trying to convert anyone to a new religion. They're trying to make it easier for a decision-maker to say yes or no with confidence. An overview of this process is in Figure 18-3.

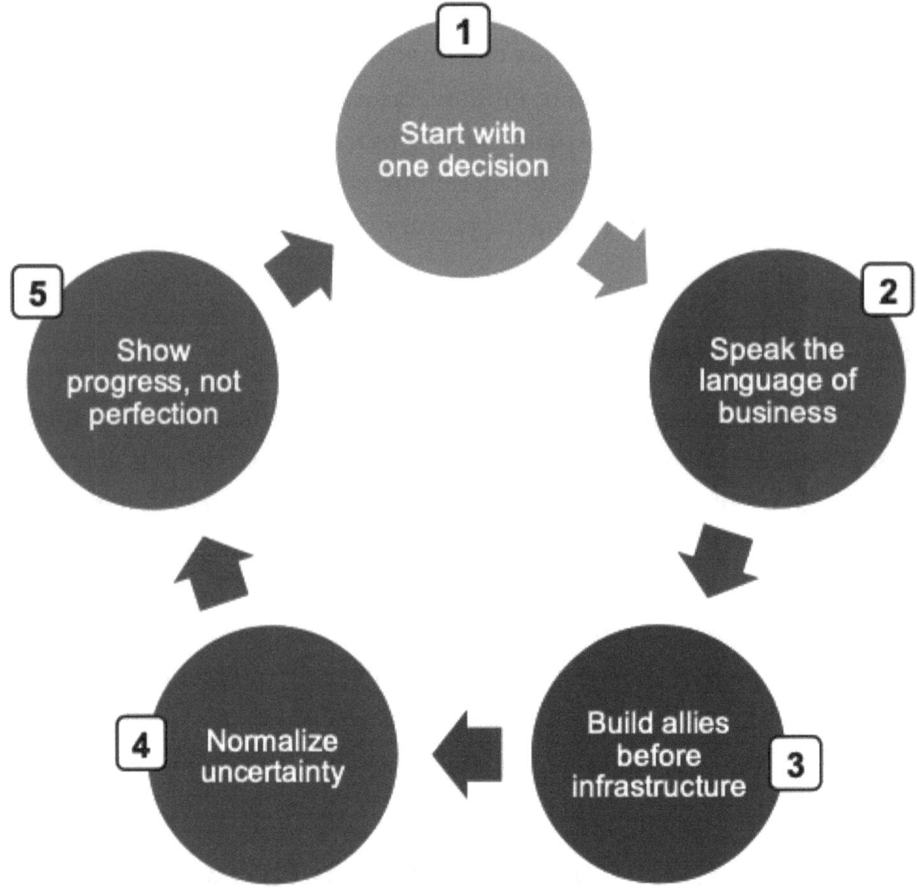

Figure 18-3. *Steps to make a CRQ program succeed*

1. Start with a Single Decision

Find a decision that's stuck: an investment, a controversial control, or a risk that keeps getting downgraded because "it hasn't happened yet." These are goldmines for demonstrating value. When someone in your organization can't get traction on a risk conversation, CRQ is often the missing language that unblocks it.

You don't need a sweeping charter. You need one win. A single well-framed analysis that results in a better, faster, or more defensible decision will teach the organization more about CRQ than a dozen training sessions.

2. Speak the Language of the Business

Most executives already think in probabilities, trade-offs, and financial outcomes, in their own way. They live in a world of forecasts, budgets, and market risk. The problem is not that they fail to understand uncertainty. It is that we often describe it in a language that does not translate. When we frame a risk in terms of threat actors, zero-days, or nation-state operations, they cannot connect it to business outcomes.

They know risk, but not *our* risk. Saying "There is a 20% chance we will lose more than $10 million this year" feels concrete and familiar. Saying "The threat landscape has evolved; *Fancy Bear* and *Stone Panda* are targeting peer companies..." does not. When you express uncertainty in the financial terms the business already uses to weigh opportunity and cost, the conversation changes. CRQ stops sounding like security theory and starts sounding like decision support.

3. Build Allies Before Infrastructure

Before you bring on a pricy CRQ vendor, find allies who can champion your work. Finance is often the best starting point because it already deals with uncertainty and expected value. Audit, compliance, and legal teams are natural partners, too, since they can directly connect their work to yours.

Bring them examples. Show them how a simple quantitative model can support choices they already face: insurance coverage, vendor risk, or capital allocation. When they start using your outputs in their own decks, you've succeeded.

4. Integrate Gently with Existing Processes

Replacing a qualitative program overnight almost never works. Coexist for a while. Translate a few items in the risk register into quantitative form and show the contrast. When leadership starts using your quantified entries to make real decisions, others will want the same thing. Eventually, you can flip the register completely. By that time, nobody will call it a "transition." It will just feel like progress.

5. Normalize Uncertainty

One of the quietest culture shifts a CRQ program brings is the idea that uncertainty isn't failure. It's honesty. People accustomed to heatmaps are used to pretending the world is certain enough to fit in red, yellow, and green boxes. CRQ asks them to be transparent about what they don't know. Over time, that shift changes the conversation from arguing over colors to discussing probability, tolerance, and trade-offs. That's a sign of maturity.

6. Show Progress, Not Perfection

You can't build a mature CRQ program in one quarter. What you can do is show that each quarter, your models get more calibrated, your data gets better, and your decisions start to lead to better outcomes. Visible improvement is what earns executive patience and funding. CRQ is iterative by nature. You don't need to be perfect to be credible. You just need to be transparent, improving, and consistent.

When CRQ is done well, it stops being a security project and becomes part of how the business thinks. Risk quantification becomes less about models and more about shared reasoning. People start asking for the data before you bring it to them. That's when you know it's working.

Keeping It Going

When a CRQ program finally clicks, it's tempting to think the hard part is over. You've built credibility, solved real problems, and earned trust. But risk doesn't hold still. The world keeps changing, and the math moves with it. Controls age. The business shifts. Threats evolve. Even the definition of "too much risk" can change after a new regulation or board directive.

Once CRQ becomes part of how your organization makes decisions, the next challenge is keeping it calibrated. A good program doesn't just model today's environment. It keeps its bearings as conditions shift around it. This is where ongoing monitoring matters, not in a dashboard sense but in a strategic one.

The following section outlines six quiet but powerful forces that move your risk estimates over time. Think of them as the hidden gears underneath every risk model. When they change, your analysis should too.

The Six Levers That Quietly Change Your Risk

Back in 2011, I was a mid-level risk analyst at a regional bank. Each quarter, I refreshed our "existential technology risk" deck for the C-suite and board: classic red, yellow, green heatmaps. I turned reds to yellows, yellows to greens, and everyone applauded:

"Look at the ROI on our security spend. Risk keeps going down!"

The big logical fallacy we committed was treating controls as the only thing that moved risk. If we spent money, risk went down. That was the assumption. Anything else was unthinkable.

Something happened that entirely changed my thinking. Operation Payback occurred, which was a series of massive DDoS attacks against the US financial system. Suddenly, our exposure felt higher, but how do you show that with a traffic light? We had no way to reflect real-world spikes without cranking a color back up, undermining our own narrative.

That moment made something clear: controls are just one lever, and often not the biggest one. Most changes in risk come from forces far outside your walls.

Since then, I've seen six quiet but powerful levers reshape risk across industries and incident types. These shifts don't always show up in your dashboards, but they absolutely move the math. Controls are only the first.

Let's walk through all six and break down what each one does to the two things that matter most in risk. Figure 18-4 provides an overview, with detailed breakdowns following.

Lever	Frequency (F)	Impact (I)
1. Internal Security Posture & Controls	▼ with new controls, skills, data reduction ▲ with control decay, obsolescence, asset growth	▼ with effective controls, simplification ▲ with gaps, obsolescence, asset growth
2. Business & Operating Model Changes	▲ with M&A, new markets, vendors ▼ with divestitures, simplification	▲ with acquisitions, regulation-heavy pivots, vendor risk, macroeconomic shifts ▼ with reduced scope
3. External Threat & Regulatory Landscape	▲ with adversary innovation, geopolitics ↔ with regulatory changes	▲ with stronger adversaries, regulations, geopolitical risk
4. Incidents & Near Misses	▲ or ▼ depending on learnings	▲ or ▼ depending on learnings
5. Visibility & Models	◇ may go up or down with better telemetry or quant models	◇ may go up or down with better telemetry or quant models
6. Risk Appetite, Governance & Insurance	↔ no change in actual frequency	Perceived ▲ when tolerance drops / coverage tightens Perceived ▼ when tolerance rises / coverage broadens

Legend: ▲ increases ▼ decreases ↔ no direct change ◇ could swing either way

Figure 18-4. *Overview of the six levers that quietly change risk*

Below, arrows show where each lever usually nudges those numbers: ▲ = up, ▼ = down, ↔ = no direct change, ◇ = could swing either way.

1. Internal Security Posture and Control Effectiveness

This category is obvious because we all know that investments in controls (should) drive down risk, but consider the entire internal security posture when assessing or reassessing risk.

New Controls
Switching to passkeys, finally enforcing SSO, MFA on admin accounts, encryption, tokenization, etc. (frequency ▼, impact ▼) .

Control Failure or Decay/Configuration Drift
A TLS certificate expires, the "temporary" allow-all rule you added for troubleshooting never gets removed, or the nightly backup job has silently failed for weeks. Nothing outside changed, but weak points opened inside (frequency ▲, impact ▲).

Control Obsolescence As Threats Adapt
SMS codes were fine until SIM-swap kits became a click-to-buy service; an on-prem IDS can't see into your encrypted traffic; SHA-1 signatures are now crackable on a laptop (frequency ▲, impact ▲).

Headcount and Skill Shifts
Your only cloud-security engineer leaves, and the backlog of misconfig alerts piles up (frequency ▲, impact ▲). Hire a seasoned DevSecOps lead, and those arrows reverse (frequency ▼, impact ▼).

Asset and Data Growth
You spin up dozens of new microservices, start logging user biometrics, or expose an API. More entry points and more valuable data (frequency ▲, impact ▲). On the other hand, the strategic removal/deletion/deduplication of sensitive data, tackling tech debt, and then risk moves (frequency ▼, impact ▼).

2. Business and Operating Model Changes

M&A/Divestitures

Acquiring a fintech in Brazil brings unfamiliar tech stacks, inherited vulnerabilities, and new privacy laws like LGPD into scope (frequency ▲, impact ▲). Spinning off a legacy division can reduce surface area and regulatory complexity (frequency ▼, impact ▼).

Market Pivots
Launching a consumer mobile app or expanding into healthcare or education introduces highly regulated data, public-facing attack surface, and more determined threat actors (frequency ▲, impact ▲).

Third-Party and Supply Chain Exposure
Every external dependency adds risk, whether it's a vendor, an API, or an open source library. A new SaaS provider might have weak access controls. A payment or logistics API could be misconfigured or leak data through logs. An open source package may be maintained by a single volunteer and pulled into your environment without anyone noticing. You rarely control how these systems are secured, monitored, or updated, but their risk becomes yours (frequency ▲, impact ▲).

Macroeconomic Shifts: Inflation, Recession, and Currency Swings
Economic changes don't always make attacks more likely (frequency ↔), but they often make them more expensive to handle (impact ▲). Inflation drives up the cost of cloud services, incident response, legal counsel, and regulatory penalties. During recessions, security budgets can get cut, slowing down hiring, delaying upgrades, or pausing key projects. That can create longer-term blind spots or gaps in coverage that attackers may eventually exploit, especially if teams are forced to do more with less.

3. External Threat and Regulatory Landscape

Threat-Actor Capability Shifts

Attackers don't just evolve; sometimes they leap ahead. Periodically, adversaries outpace defenses, yours and your vendors'. We've seen technology change with evolving ransomware, deepfake voice scams, and AI-generated phishing kits. When offensive tools get cheaper, faster, and more effective overnight, it becomes harder to keep up (frequency ▲, impact ▲).

Geopolitical Volatility
Wars, sanctions, and political instability can disrupt trusted vendors, force reliance on unfamiliar or less secure suppliers, and expose your business to nation-state threats. Operating in sensitive regions or serving customers in politically tense areas increases the chance of being targeted, whether directly or as collateral. When incidents do happen, they often carry heavier legal, financial, and reputational consequences (frequency ▲, impact ▲).

Regulatory Shifts and Pressure

New laws, regulations, and guidance like GDPR, SEC breach disclosure rules, and DORA don't necessarily make incidents more likely (frequency ↔), but they increase what it costs. One incident can now trigger multi-country investigations, fines, and reputational damage (impact ▲).

Non-traditional Adversaries and Information Misuse

Not every threat actor is a criminal or state-sponsored hacker. Competitors, researchers, analysts, journalists, or even social media influencers may legally (sometimes illegally) access exposed data, screenshots, or misconfigured assets. Some chase scoops; others chase clout or market edge. They may operate entirely within the law, but the reputational and strategic fallout they trigger can be severe. If your systems are too open, or your data too discoverable, you could be making it easy for someone to exploit your own transparency (frequency ▲, impact ▲).

4. Incident and Near-Miss Learnings

Real events and close calls expose gaps in your assumptions. You might have believed an attack was unlikely or that the damage would be minor, but then something like the Colonial Pipeline ransomware incident shows how wrong that can be. Or maybe your own systems narrowly avoid failure from a threat you never even modeled. These situations often reveal that risk was underestimated, pushing both frequency and impact higher. Occasionally, a post-incident review shows the opposite: you were overprepared, and the risk can be revised down (frequency ▲ or ▼, impact ▲ or ▼).

5. Improved Visibility

Visibility and Data Quality Improvements

Better tools and scanning often uncover risks you didn't know were there. Finding an exposed S3 bucket, a forgotten VPN endpoint, or a misconfigured role means your environment wasn't as locked down as you thought (frequency ▲, impact ▲).

Model Upgrade from Qualitative to Quantitative

Switching from a heatmap to a model like FAIR doesn't change the actual risk, but it gives you a more accurate view. With better inputs and sharper methods, the way stakeholders perceive risk might go up or down or stay the same; it just depends on what the data shows (frequency ◇, impact ◇).

6. Risk Appetite, Governance, and Insurance Terms

Changing Risk Appetite, Governance, and Insurance Terms

The threat landscape may stay the same, but your tolerance for loss can shift. A new board directive, regulatory pressure, or cyber insurance rider might lower the acceptable loss threshold from $10 million to $2 million. That doesn't change the actual impact of an event, but it does change which risks are now considered material and require action. Likewise, if the business grows significantly, it may tolerate the same events without triggering a response (frequency ↔, impact actual = same, perceived ▲ or ▼).

Leadership and Governance Changes

A new CEO or board may bring a very different attitude toward risk. The organization might shift from risk averse to risk seeking, or the other way around. This doesn't change the loss amount of any given event, but it shifts how risk is interpreted, prioritized, and whether a given loss is acceptable or not. You may need to reassess risks against a new benchmark (frequency ↔, impact actual = same, perceived ▲ or ▼).

A Quick Check As You Reassess

If any of these levers have shifted since your last assessment, expect the math to move. Update the model and your assumptions before the headlines do it for you. The next time you revisit a scenario, ask these six questions:

- Have our controls aged, drifted, or become obsolete?
- Did the business itself morph: new products, new markets, new vendors?
- Have attackers leveled up, or has the legal/regulatory landscape changed?
- What did the last incident or near-miss teach us about our priors?
- Do we see the system more clearly today (telemetry, better models)?
- Did the definition of "too much risk" just change?

If even one answer is "yes," the math moved. That's not a failure of the model; it's proof the model is alive and working.

Keeping CRQ Alive

Every CRQ program eventually reaches the point where the work feels stable. The models run smoothly, the results are trusted, and the conversations are healthy. However, that stability can be an illusion if you don't treat your risk program as something that is constantly evolving. The forces underneath your analysis, the Six Levers, never stop moving. Controls drift. Businesses evolve. New laws appear. Leadership changes its definition of acceptable loss. If you are not watching those shifts, your models will start to lag behind reality.

That's why the best CRQ programs behave more like living systems than static tools. They monitor, learn, and adapt. They invite disagreement instead of defending certainty. They treat a new data point, a near miss, or a regulatory change as a signal to revisit the data, not as an interruption to the process. When you reach that level, your organization stops seeing risk quantification as a project and starts seeing it as a habit of thought.

Every program moves through stages to get there. Early CRQ efforts often focus on building credibility and proving value. Mature programs shift from proving to improving, embedding quantification directly into business decisions. Table 18-1 shows some of the differences between early-stage and mature programs.

***Table 18-1.** Early stage vs. mature risk programs*

Characteristic	Early-Stage	Mature
Purpose	Reporting to auditors	Supporting business decisions
Communication	Color dashboards	Probabilistic narratives
Data Use	Static snapshots	Continuous feedback
Leadership View	Experimental	Integral to planning

If the Six Levers seem daunting, the solution is to build a simple but robust program of metrics that tracks them automatically. AI makes this possible in a way that was never realistic before. In the past, I could monitor a few of these changes manually each month. Now, with AI assistance, it is easy to automate much of that monitoring. You can flag changes in threat data, financial exposure, or business context without spending hours hunting through reports.

Leverage AI as much and as often as you can. Use it to summarize incidents, detect data drift, surface anomalies, and even write the first draft of your reassessment plan. AI will help you keep your program alive in another way, too. It removes the last practical excuse not to use CRQ. Executives will start demanding the clarity that quantitative models and automation can deliver. They will stop settling for colors when numbers are available.

Looking back, that was the difference between the program that failed and the one that worked. The first was built on conviction and speed. The second was built on relationships, patience, and curiosity. The successful program did not need to announce itself. It simply kept solving real problems, one decision at a time. Over time, those small wins added up to something much larger: a culture of reasoning about risk instead of reacting to it.

That is the real endgame of CRQ. Not a perfect model. Not a universal taxonomy. But a durable way of thinking that helps the organization face uncertainty with clarity. The tools will evolve. The data will change. New frameworks will appear. The discipline stays the same. Quantification is simply how you make that discipline visible.

When your models start to feel alive, when they respond to changes in the world the same way your organization does, you will know you have crossed the threshold. CRQ is no longer something you run. It's part of the very culture of the organization.

Chapter Summary

The Big Idea: Building a successful CRQ program is just as much about momentum and patience as it is about math. Programs thrive when they grow patiently, earn allies, and adapt to constant change.

Key Takeaways

- **Most CRQ failures stem from culture, pacing, and incentives, not modeling errors.**
- **Start with one real decision that matters**, show clear value, and build credibility through proof, not persuasion.
- **Meet executives in the language they already speak**: trade-offs, costs, and outcomes. Translate uncertainty into financial terms.

- **Coexist with qualitative processes at first**; success will make the case for broader adoption.
- **Treat uncertainty as information, not failure**. Normalize it and use it to drive better questions.
- **Maintain your program with simple, repeatable metrics** tied to the Six Levers of risk change.
- **Use AI** to automate monitoring, detect data drift, and surface early warning signals. It removes the last excuse not to quantify.
- **The real measure of maturity** is when CRQ becomes a habit of thought across the organization, not a standalone project.

Bottom Line
CRQ succeeds when it evolves with the organization it serves. Move slowly, build trust, automate where you can, and let quantification become the shared language of how your company thinks about uncertainty.

What's Coming Next

In **Chapter 19**, you'll learn how to use CRQ to make better, faster, and more defensible decisions. You'll see how to identify the decisions worth quantifying, frame them around real options and preferences, and guide trade-offs between cost, control, and risk tolerance. By the end, you'll understand how CRQ transforms risk analysis from a reporting tool into a decision engine that shapes how the organization thinks and acts.

CHAPTER 19

Making Better Decisions with CRQ

> *The quality of a decision cannot be judged by its outcome, but only by the process by which it was made.*
>
> —Ron Howard

Back in Chapter 4, we learned that the goal of quantification is not to be perfectly right. It is to be less wrong. Everything you have learned since then gives you permission to iterate. You have modeled data, blended evidence, and turned a big, messy ball of uncertainty about the future into something tangible: numbers, ranges, and curves.

This chapter shows you what all that effort was for.

If you think back to Exercise 14-1, you used observable data to make a simple but familiar decision about what to wear for the weather. You looked outside, gathered evidence, updated your belief, and made a choice: jacket, raincoat, umbrella, or none of the above. That exercise was never about the weather. It was about the essence of risk analysis: using imperfect information to make better decisions under uncertainty.

That is the point of everything we have done. The risk management function exists for one reason: to help people choose wisely when the future is uncertain. To help them make the best choice with the information available, not to eliminate uncertainty entirely.

As with many of the lessons in this book, the way forward does not come from information security standards or frameworks. It comes from decision science, a field that studies what makes some choices better than others. When we center our analyses around decisions rather than data, we find clarity again.

T. Martin-Vegue, *From Heatmaps to Histograms*, https://doi.org/10.1007/979-8-8688-2300-8_19

I have been in many moments where my team, or I, started to lose the plot with executives. The analysis became too abstract, too distant from the choice on the table. The fix was always the same: pause and return to the decision itself. What are we choosing between? What does success look like? What information do we already have?

Sometimes that decision is small, like how to allocate this quarter's resources or what the engineering team should focus on next week. Other times it is existential, like how much to keep in cash reserves, whether to acquire a company, or how much risk to transfer through insurance.

The scale changes, but the principle never does. Risk analysis is just decision analysis by another name. The real purpose of decision analysis is clarity, because a good analysis removes noise so the decision-maker can see the choice more clearly. Every decision begins with a simple question: Why choose at all? Something in the environment has changed, or a constraint has appeared, that forces a choice. In that sense, risk management is really decision management. Our work only matters when it informs what people choose to do next.

Clearing the Fog

Most organizations still approach risk analysis backward. They start with reports, dashboards, and frameworks rather than decisions. The result is a flood of information that looks like accountability but rarely changes outcomes. Risk assessments become artifacts instead of tools.

When you peel back the layers, you find that many programs are designed to display risk, not to reduce uncertainty. Heatmaps and red-yellow-green charts may impress in meetings, but they do not help anyone decide what to do. They create the illusion of control without providing a basis for action.

True risk analysis is about decision quality. It exists to clarify choices, not to create dashboards. Until a risk program centers on decision-making, all the math, tooling, and metrics in the world only make the fog thicker.

If most risk programs are built backward, what does it look like to get it right? That brings us to the true purpose of risk assessment.

The True Purpose of Risk Assessment

Risk analysis is not a performance metric or a compliance ritual. Its purpose is to inform a choice under uncertainty. Every activity, such as identifying scenarios, estimating loss, and gathering data, should support a specific decision someone needs to make.

When an analysis fails to connect to a decision, it becomes busywork. Teams spend hours ranking vulnerabilities or scoring risks that never influence a plan, budget, or control.

The goal is not to eliminate uncertainty but to manage it. Quantitative methods make uncertainty discussable and measurable, allowing decision-makers to compare options on equal footing. To see how CRQ supports better choices, we first have to understand what a decision really is.

We have been taught that good risk management means reducing risk. In reality, the goal is optimization: balancing protection, performance, and opportunity so the organization gets the most value from every dollar.

CRQ enables that shift. Once you can measure exposure in financial terms, you can ask better questions: How much protection is enough? Where are we overspending for marginal benefit? Where could we safely take on more risk to gain efficiency?

That is what separates a mature program from a compliant one. Optimization, not reduction.

What Makes a Decision?

Decision science pioneer Ron Howard describes a decision as a commitment to an irreversible allocation of resources made in pursuit of a goal (Howard & Abbas, 2016). It is a practical definition because it reminds us that the point of analysis is action.

Every meaningful risk analysis begins and ends with a decision. You can identify vulnerabilities, model probabilities, and create loss exceedance curves, but if there is no choice to be made, the exercise has no direction.

Decisions are the anchor of risk analysis because they give the work purpose. They tell you why you are modeling uncertainty and what the analysis is supposed to influence. The mistake many organizations make is to start assessing risk before understanding the decision the assessment is meant to support. That almost always leads to reports that look impressive but fail to change anything.

The structure of a good decision was formalized more than 50 years ago by Howard, who defined three ingredients that must be present before a real decision can exist: **choice, preference, and information** (Howard & Abbas, 2016). You can picture them as the three corners of a triangle. The decision-maker uses *logic* to evaluate the components, both together and individually.

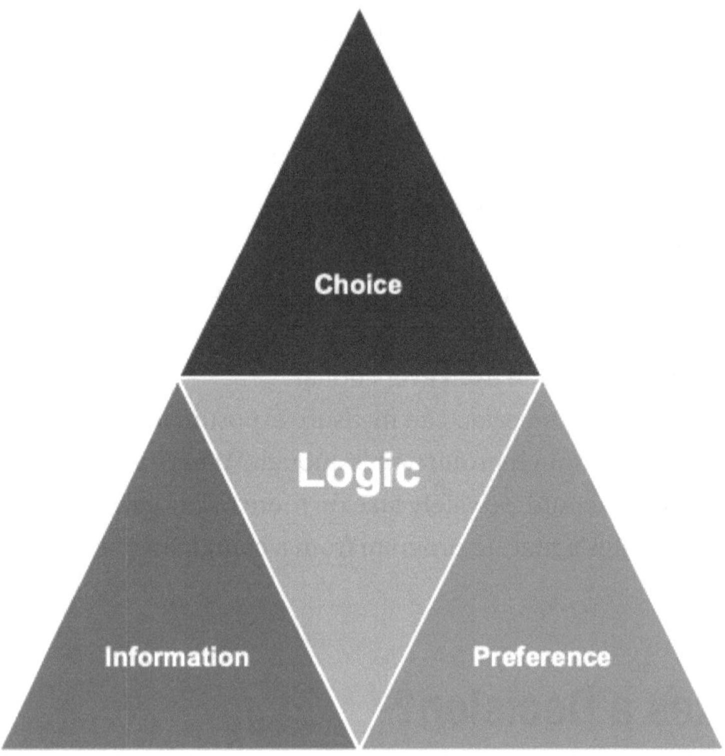

Figure 19-1. *The components of a decision*

Choice

A decision only exists when more than one course of action is possible. "Should we migrate to the cloud or stay on-premises?" is a decision. "We are migrating to the cloud; what are the risks?" is not.

Before you start modeling, identify the real options on the table. Sometimes this exercise exposes that there is no choice at all; someone has already decided, and what they are calling a "risk assessment" is really a request for validation. When that happens, redirect the conversation toward decision quality: *If the direction is fixed, what variables can we still influence?* That keeps the work relevant.

Preference

Even with options, a decision is impossible without a sense of what outcome matters most. Preferences express what the decision-maker values, such as security control strength, cost savings, speed to market, regulatory compliance, or a mix of them. Before you compare alternatives, you need clarity on the objective the decision is meant to satisfy. Without a clear objective, preferences drift, and the analysis loses direction. In practice, that means clarifying objectives before defining the options. Only then can you compare alternatives in a structured way.

Ask explicitly: *What does success look like?* In practice, that question uncovers hidden motives and trade-offs. One stakeholder might prefer resilience over savings; another might prefer convenience over resilience. Understanding those priorities determines how you scope the analysis and what metrics matter. CRQ adds clarity by quantifying those trade-offs instead of treating them as abstract goals.

Information

The third ingredient is information: the evidence available to compare options. This is where risk analysis earns its keep. The job is not to predict perfectly but to make the information component strong enough that choices and preferences can be weighed rationally.

Information can come from internal data, external benchmarks, or subject matter expertise. The question is not *Do we have perfect data?* but *Do we have enough information to make this choice better than guessing?* When you reach that threshold, it is time to model.

The Decision Check

When you combine these three elements, choice, preference, and information, *now* you have a *real* decision. If any piece is missing, you do not. You have a meeting agenda item disguised as a risk assessment.

Before starting any CRQ project, pause and test for the presence of each element:

1. **What are the actual options?**

   If there is only one, it is an implementation plan, not a decision.

2. **What outcome matters most?**

   If the stakeholders cannot answer, the analysis will drift.

3. **What information already exists?**

   If a data gap exists that prevents you from moving forward, focus first on evidence gathering, not modeling.

If you cannot answer all three, do not begin the analysis yet. Clarify the decision first. This ten-minute exercise saves weeks of unfocused modeling later.

Once you know the three ingredients of a real decision: choice, preference, and information, it is easy to spot when any of them is missing. What is harder is knowing what to do next.

Sometimes the correct answer is not to push forward with a risk analysis at all, but to pause and ask a different question.

Alternatives to the Risk Assessment

It may seem counterintuitive coming from a quantitative risk analyst, but quantitative risk analysis is not always the most appropriate tool for making security decisions. When someone asks me to conduct a risk analysis, the first thing I do is ensure it's the right fit for the question at hand. Over time, I've learned that sometimes the most helpful thing we can do is pause and consider whether another method would serve better. Quantitative risk analysis is powerful, but it's not the only way to make a sound, defensible decision.

Here are a few examples of analyses in Table 19-1 I've been asked to perform and how I've redirected the request.

Table 19-1. *Alternatives to risk analysis*

If You Are Asking For...	What You May Need Instead
Document a decision already made	Decision log
Could this threat group break in?	Threat modeling or red team
What is the impact if a system goes down?	Business impact analysis
What happens if ransomware hits us?	Tabletop exercise
Which vulnerabilities should we prioritize?	Vulnerability management and threat intelligence
Are we compliant with regulation X?	Gap assessment or audit
Prove the program is effective	Metrics and KPIs
Where are we most exposed?	Attack surface mapping
Compare vendors	Third-party risk management
Forecast budget needs	Scenario planning or financial modeling
Help us choose between two strategies	Decision matrix or multi-criteria decision analysis
Where are our process weaknesses?	SWOT or root cause analysis
Justify an initiative to executives	Business case
Estimate the cost of an incident after the fact	Post-incident review
Show how we compare to peers	Benchmarking

These tools are not dead ends. They are on-ramps. A tabletop may surface uncertainty about the probability and magnitude of ransomware losses. Scenario planning may expose unclear alternatives or competing preferences. A gap assessment may highlight trade-offs between risk reduction and business friction.

Each of these is an opportunity to turn the conversation into a quantitative risk analysis once the uncertainty is clear and the decision is tied to objectives.

The real payoff is cooperation. Working with continuity teams on a business impact analysis, with compliance on a gap assessment, or with finance on scenario modeling creates shared language. It shows that security is not a critic on the sidelines but a partner helping the business connect the dots. That is how we expand influence and make risk analysis something the whole organization values.

Once you have ruled out the wrong tools, you are ready to use the right one. When the problem is tied to a real decision, when uncertainty matters, and when information can be improved enough to guide that decision, that is where quantitative risk analysis shines. The next section explores how CRQ supports real-world choices, helping teams allocate resources, justify investments, and make confident, defensible decisions when the future is uncertain.

Use Cases for Quantitative Risk

One of the most exciting things about cyber risk quantification is the range of new use cases it unlocks for better decision-making. While most people think of it as just a way to "put numbers on risk," it opens up entirely new ways to guide strategy, investments, and operations.

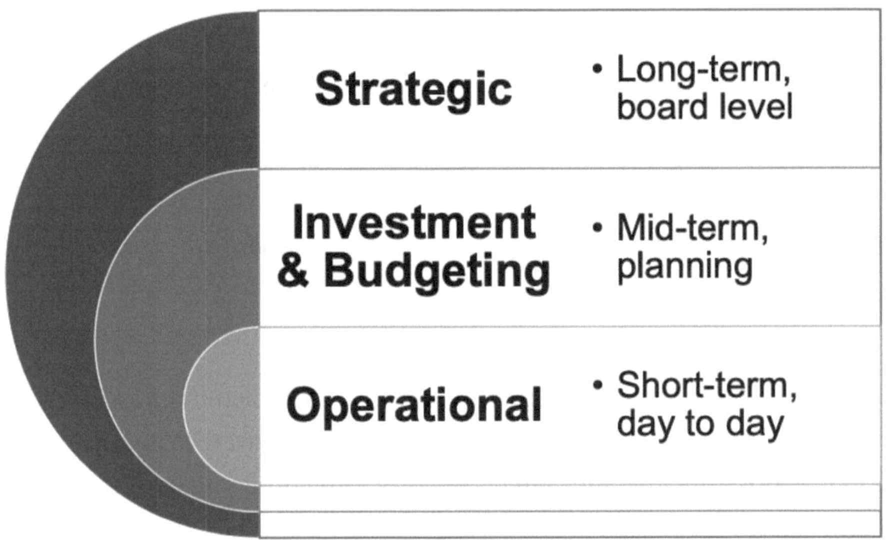

Figure 19-2. Use cases for quantitative risk

Operational Decision-Making

Risk Ranking and Prioritization

The most apparent and foundational use case is risk ranking. This means taking a portfolio of risks (whether threats, vulnerabilities, or projects) and sorting them by probable risk. It helps your team prioritize which risks to remediate first.

Yes, qualitative risk analysis also does this, but only in broad buckets: high, medium, and low or red, yellow, and green. When you have a list of 100 risks, this type of categorization just isn't enough. In fact, it's impossible. Every "high" or "red" risk gives you exactly one data point to compare against other risks, which flattens out important differences.

Quantitative methods offer far more granularity and nuance. When you work with ranges instead of single ratings, you can see the complete picture of each risk. A risk that could happen once per year could warrant a very different response than something that happens once every 20 years, even if both end up with similar overall loss exposure numbers. By enabling you to pull apart these nuances, you can have much richer conversations about what to do about risk and which controls might deliver the most significant return.

Even better, quantitative methods let you test those controls in hypothetical scenarios before you commit any resources.

Identifying and Prioritizing Control Gaps

After running several quantitative assessments across different domains or asset classes, you can start to see patterns where some risks are well-controlled while others need attention. While qualitative methods can identify control gaps, quantitative analysis helps you prioritize them by actual business impact.

Quantitative risk analysis can highlight where your controls are weak, redundant, or overbuilt. It helps you identify inefficient areas where you're spending too much for too little risk reduction and where you might be exposed without realizing it. This makes it easier to rationalize your control stack based on data rather than gut feel.

Investment and Budget Decisions

Adding or Removing Controls

This is my favorite use case because it's where quantification shows its value. It enables unambiguous, defensible decisions about which security controls are worth the cost.

You begin by measuring the baseline risk (where things stand today). Then you create a forecasted, hypothetical model that reflects the addition or removal of a control. This might include a new tool, a vendor, added headcount, or a new security project. Comparing the two scenarios shows you the projected risk reduction and supports smarter, more informed investment decisions.

Every treatment decision is a trade-off among cost, residual risk, and time. CRQ makes those trade-offs visible rather than gut calls. A mitigation that saves $2M in expected loss but costs $3M to deploy is mathematically worse than doing nothing; a cheaper control that trims $500K of exposure for $100K in spend is a clear win.

When leaders see the trade-offs quantified, the conversation changes from "What should we do?" to "Which option fits our appetite and resources best?"

Project ROI and Budget Justification

Once you have modeled the "before" and "after" risk scenarios, you can calculate the return on investment. If you know the cost of the control or project, you can estimate the value of the risk reduction it delivers.

This transforms budget conversations from "we need this for security" to "this investment will reduce our expected annual losses by $X, which makes it worth the $Y cost." You're speaking in business terms that finance and operations teams understand, making it much easier to justify security spending and align road maps to measurable outcomes. It also gives leadership teams the rational basis for making a trade-off between spending money here on security vs. other areas where limited resources might provide higher rates of return.

Strategic Decision-Making

Insurance Analysis

This use case is always popular with executives. A good quantitative risk model helps determine whether certain risks should be insured and, if so, how much coverage is appropriate.

The focus here is on risks that either pose an existential threat to the organization or that exceed what your company can comfortably absorb financially. By assessing top-tier risks, you can have structured conversations about premiums, policy limits, deductibles, and whether you're over- or under-insured.

Third-Party Risk and M&A

Vendor onboarding, mergers, and acquisitions can all rapidly alter your risk landscape, sometimes overnight. That makes them ideal candidates for quick, quantitative assessments.

By modeling how the addition of a third party or acquisition target changes your risk posture, you give executives something they value: the ability to move quickly without flying blind. Even lightweight assessments in this category can be highly impactful.

Emerging Risk Analysis

Every organization faces new threats and regulatory changes that didn't exist before. How do you evaluate the risk of new AI regulations changing how you can process customer data? What about novel attack vectors that exploit technologies your company just adopted?

Quantitative analysis provides a framework for evaluating unfamiliar risks using data rather than speculation. You can model different scenarios based on similar historical precedents, even when the specific threat is new. Sometimes the result is "Yes, this is a big deal, and we need to act." Other times, it's "No, based on what we know, this isn't something to worry about." Either way, you're giving decision-makers clarity on unfamiliar territory.

Exotic and Low-Probability/High-Impact Risks

Then, there are the oddball scenarios that keep your CEO or board members awake at night. What if a solar flare disrupts global satellite communications for weeks? What if a coordinated attack on submarine internet cables cuts off entire regions? What if quantum computing suddenly makes current encryption obsolete overnight? These are plausible and probable scenarios that often seem too unlikely to plan for but could pose an existential risk to the organization if they occur.

Quantitative analysis helps you put these exotic risks in perspective. The risk analyst can help the CEO or the board members sleep easily at night if the risk is not plausible. On the other hand, it may reveal soft spots in the organization's resilience plans. The analysis opens up further conversations around contingency preparations, insurance types, and financial reserves. These analyses are great conversation starters around existential risk. Sometimes these nightmare scenarios are nothing to worry about, more manageable than they appear, and others genuinely deserve attention.

Risk Appetite and Board-Level Reporting

Another important use case is aligning your risk portfolio with the organizational risk tolerance. Boards and executives are often asked to weigh in on risk decisions without a clear view of how close the company is to its stated risk limits.

Quantitative models help clarify that picture. Instead of showing executives color-coded heatmaps, you can show them how much risk the company is carrying compared to what they said they're comfortable with. This leads to more productive board conversations because everyone is reacting to the same numbers, not just subjective color categories.

Fast vs. Focused vs. Deep-Dive Assessments

Not every decision deserves a full-court press of an analysis. Some just need a quick, credible answer; others are big enough to justify days or weeks of analysis. The art of risk quantification is knowing which is which.

When I am short on time, have an impatient executive, or the question is narrow, I do what I call a **fast assessment**. One scenario, a few reasonable inputs, and a quick SME gut-check. Think of it like checking the weather before leaving the house. You are not trying to model the entire atmosphere; you just need to know if you should bring an umbrella. Examples include deciding which of two top risks to brief to leadership or estimating whether ransomware or data theft is more likely this quarter.

When a decision will influence budgets or priorities, I shift to a **focused assessment**. These take a few days instead of a few hours. I blend external data with internal evidence, test a few what-ifs, and see how sensitive the results are to key assumptions. This level is ideal for validating insurance limits, comparing control investments, or testing remediation plans.

Then there are **deep dives**, the long hikes of risk analysis. These are for high-stakes, strategic questions, like assessing cloud migration risk, M&A due diligence, or prolonged business disruption. Here, you use every tool available: full blended data, decomposed loss forms, and multiple sensitivity analyses. It takes longer, but it gives decision-makers confidence in big calls.

The goal is not to analyze everything equally. It is to right-size the work so that effort matches impact. Fast assessments keep the program nimble; deep dives build confidence when the decisions really matter. An overview of the three types can be found in Table 19-2.

***Table 19-2.** Fast vs. focused vs. deep-dive assessments*

Type	When to Use	Effort	Example
Fast	Quick, tactical choices	Hours	Compare top risks, brief leadership
Focused	Budget or priority decisions	Days	Validate insurance, test control benefit
Deep-Dive	Strategic or enterprise-level calls	Weeks	Cloud migration, M&A diligence, existential threats

Assessment Granularity

There is no "right" or "wrong" level of granularity in a risk assessment. You simply need to right-size the work to the decision at hand. Every level, from broad and strategic to narrow and technical, answers a different question for a different audience.

You can start at the top and work your way down. A broad **data breach assessment** that includes all data types, systems, and threat actors is a perfectly legitimate place to begin. It helps you quantify the organization's top risks—the ones the board, executive team, and cyber-insurance underwriters care about. It answers the question, *"How bad could a data breach be for us?"*

From there, you can narrow the focus to **data breach of customer PII stored in AWS**. Now you're answering a different question: *"Where does our exposure live?"* These mid-level analyses are valuable to CISOs, CTOs, and security leadership. They connect directly to budgeting, prioritization, and control investment. Run a few of these for different data sets or systems, and you start to see the full shape of your organization's breach exposure.

Then you can zoom in even further, to **data breach of customer PII from a cybercriminal group exploiting SQL injection in AWS S3**. That's a highly specific, technical question, the kind security engineers and architects need to answer to guide daily work. It's not for the board, and that's the point. Different audiences, different questions, same discipline.

Each level has value. They are not in competition; they're nested, as illustrated in Table 19-3. The broad view informs strategy. The middle connects strategy to operations. The deep view drives technical improvement. When choosing granularity, focus on its *relevance*. Always choose the highest level of abstraction needed to decide.

***Table 19-3.** Levels of risk granularity*

Level	Example Assessment	Primary Audience	Decision Focus
Strategic	Data breach across all data types, systems, and threat actors	Board, executives, insurers	Understand top enterprise risks and overall exposure
Operational	Data breach of customer PII stored in AWS	CISO, CTO, security, and legal leadership	Prioritize controls, plan investments, allocate resources
Tactical	Data breach of customer PII via SQL injection in AWS S3	Engineering, AppSec, red/blue teams	Test defenses, guide mitigation, inform technical design

Results into Action: Risk Treatment Options

Quantifying risk is only half the work. The next step involves using the results to shape decisions. Every analysis ends with a choice, and that choice usually falls into one of five treatment paths. None of them is inherently right or wrong. Each represents a different way of managing uncertainty and aligning with the organization's priorities and appetite for risk. In most risk frameworks, this is called *risk treatment,* in other words, *what are we going to do about this risk?*

The first option is **acceptance**. Sometimes the modeled loss falls within tolerance, or the cost of further reduction simply outweighs the benefit. In those cases, acceptance is not neglect; it is an informed decision. The exposure is documented, monitored, and made visible. Quantification helps articulate exactly how much risk is being accepted rather than letting that decision live in the margins as an adjective.

The second option is **mitigation**, which focuses on reducing either the likelihood or the impact of a loss event. This is where most security investments live. Controls, processes, and training all serve as mitigation tools. Quantification helps determine when a control is worth its cost and how much it changes the expected loss. It turns mitigation from a checklist activity into an investment decision.

A third option is **transfer**, which shifts some or all of the financial impact to another party through insurance or contracts. Transfer is useful when losses are plausible but infrequent, the kind of events that can be insured rather than entirely prevented. CRQ helps by quantifying what coverage levels make sense and what portion of risk the organization should retain.

You can also **avoid** risk altogether by changing or discontinuing the activity that creates it. Avoidance is rare in practice but powerful when the exposure clearly outweighs the value of the underlying business activity. Quantification helps clarify that trade-off by showing what is being gained or lost.

Finally, there is the option to **increase** exposure intentionally. This may seem counterintuitive, but sometimes taking on more risk enables greater agility, efficiency, or opportunity. Quantification helps identify situations where additional exposure is a rational choice rather than a gamble.

WAIT, WHAT? INCREASE RISK?

Yes! Sometimes that is the right answer.

Risk management is not about driving exposure to zero. Mature programs evolve from box-checking exercises into living, decision-optimizing systems that help the organization allocate resources where they matter most.

Increasing risk can be a rational, data-driven choice when the trade-off creates greater value elsewhere. Examples include

- **Outsourcing** a function that raises outage or breach exposure but saves millions in operating cost
- **Removing or relaxing controls** that frustrate customers or drive cancellations
- **Taking on technical debt** to move faster toward a market opportunity

Both the *ISO 31000* framework (International Organization for Standardization, 2018) and *Risk Analysis: A Quantitative Guide* by David Vose (2008) recognize *increase risk* as a legitimate treatment option when it is done consciously and transparently.

Incorporating risk analyses that capture real business trade-offs shows that your program is not just about reducing risk but about enabling better decisions. It demonstrates the ability to weigh options, quantify consequences, and make choices that move the business forward. An added benefit is cultural: your security team stops being seen as the "team of no," a real business blocker, and becomes the team that says, "Sure, let's do it safely and with eyes open."

Our goal as security professionals is not to eliminate risk. Our goal is to make every decision deliberate, proportional, and transparent. By expressing each treatment option in measurable terms—how much risk remains, what it costs to change it, and what benefit the change delivers—you move from intuition to evidence. Each choice becomes an intentional expression of strategy rather than a reaction to fear.

What to Present to Executives: The Decision Support Package

A risk analysis becomes useful only when the decision-makers can act on it. That means giving them a decision support package that answers four questions:

1. **What decision is on the table?**

   Make the choice clear and list the real alternatives.

2. **What changes across the options?**

   Show the baseline and how each option shifts the probable loss, using ranges, not points.

3. **What is the trade-off?**

   Lay out the cost, benefit, and exposure in financial terms so leaders can compare options fairly.

4. **What do you recommend and why?**

   Offer a clear point of view that ties back to the model and the organization's objectives. Don't be afraid to be opinionated.

You don't need to take them through every step you took. Give them what they need to make a clear, confident call.

Chapter Summary

The Big Idea: Every credible risk assessment exists to support a decision. CRQ delivers value when it helps clarify choices, express preferences, and provide just enough information to act with confidence.

Key Takeaways

- **Decisions give risk analysis purpose:** A risk assessment without a decision is motion without direction.
- **Every decision needs three ingredients:** A choice to make, a preference among outcomes, and information to guide that choice.
- **Start with the decision check:** Use it before every CRQ to confirm what question you are really answering.
- **Turn awareness into trade-offs:** CRQ aligns security actions with business objectives.
- **Scale your effort to the stakes:** Right-size your analysis to match the decision's impact.

Strive for better, not perfect. The goal is progress toward better decisions, not flawless models.

Bottom Line: The purpose of CRQ is to enable clear, defensible decisions. A good analysis tells leaders what their options are, how those options differ, and what each one costs in risk terms. When done well, CRQ shifts the conversation from "what's our risk?" to "which trade-off are we choosing, and why?"

What's Coming Next

You have now reached the point where method becomes mindset. The final chapter looks beyond models and simulations to the future of our profession: how AI, automation, and human judgment will shape the next generation of risk analysts. You will see how the skills you have built here extend far beyond quantification itself and into the larger purpose of the work: protecting not just data, but reasoning.

References

Howard, R. A., & Abbas, A. E. (2016). Foundations of decision analysis (1st ed.). Pearson Education.

International Organization for Standardization. (2018). *ISO 31000:2018 Risk management - Guidelines.* ISO.

Vose, D. (2008). *Risk Analysis: A Quantitative Guide* (3rd ed.). John Wiley & Sons.

CHAPTER 20

The Future of CRQ (And Yours Too)

The future is already here — it's just not evenly distributed.

—William Gibson

We've come a long way together.

When you opened this book, we started in a world of heatmaps: of red, yellow, and green certainty that felt safe but said very little. We asked a different question: What if risk could be measured, reasoned about, and communicated in a way that truly helped people make decisions?

Since then, we've walked the full path. We've built scenarios from vague worries, gathered data from messy systems, talked to experts, blended numbers, and built models that made uncertainty visible. You've learned to separate evidence from instinct, to explain probability in plain language, and to treat uncertainty as something to be managed rather than feared.

I had a personal epiphany and career inflection point when I read a book published in 2008: *The New School of Information Security* by Adam Shostack and Andrew Stewart. Shostack and Stewart asked a simple question that still echoes today: Why do huge security failures keep happening, even after all the investment and attention? Their answer was that our problem wasn't a lack of tools. It was that we too often rely on anecdotes, fear, and secrecy instead of evidence, rational thought, and transparency. We weren't thinking clearly about security problems. We weren't learning from the disciplines that had already tamed uncertainty: economics, actuarial science, engineering, and many others (Shostack & Stewart, 2008). Reading that book flipped a switch for me.

T. Martin-Vegue, *From Heatmaps to Histograms*, https://doi.org/10.1007/979-8-8688-2300-8_20

Long before I ever heard the term "quantitative risk," that book helped me understand that the real gap in security wasn't technical. It was intellectual. We didn't need better dashboards; we needed better thinking.

Nearly two decades later, Shostack and Stewart's ideas still stand. What's different is that the world around us has changed. We now live in an age where data and automation are everywhere, yet clarity often feels scarcer than ever. The dashboards got brighter, the numbers got bigger, but the reasoning didn't always keep up. That's why this book was written: to give us a way to think, decide, and communicate differently.

And now, as our journey together comes to an end, a new one begins. Artificial intelligence is transforming how we work, learn, and reason. It is dissolving barriers that once slowed risk analysis and amplifying both our reach and our responsibility.

CRQ was the bridge from gut feel to good data. AI is the bridge from data to insight at scale.

This final chapter is about what comes next: for you, for the profession, and for the practice of rational decision-making itself.

The AI Revolution and Why This Is Our Moment

Earlier in this book, in Chapter 3, we talked about how to use AI responsibly in our work. We explored how it's changing the face of risk management and the ethical guardrails we need to build around it. But there's one thing we didn't talk about. It's the one topic that still keeps me up at night.

It isn't accuracy, privacy, or hallucination. It's job loss.

Across technology and cyber risk management, AI is transforming roles faster than most people realize. Some of my colleagues have already started sounding alarms, warning that AI will destroy our field. I'm not as pessimistic as they are, but I do believe a major shift is underway. The risk analyst profession is about to experience a seismic realignment, and it's already happening right now.

If the Industrial Revolution began around 1760, think about what it must have been like to be a farmer in 1761. Those farmers didn't know what was coming. The world was changing right under their feet, but they were too close to see it. Most revolutions feel invisible when you're living through them. That's us. If we don't open up our eyes, we're no better off than the farmers of 1761.

But this time, we can see what's coming, and that gives us a choice. We can adapt now instead of waiting to be surprised later.

I don't believe AI will destroy our field, but it will absolutely change it. The next ten years will redefine what it means to be a risk analyst. Some tasks will disappear. Others will evolve. And entirely new ones will appear that don't exist yet.

The analysts who thrive will be those who take charge of their own development instead of waiting for others to do it for them. Don't wait for your employer, your university, your manager, or the next framework to tell you what to learn. Don't wait for a new book to tell you how to adapt. You need to start now.

Job security will come to the analysts who are deliberate about their growth, who double down on the skills that machines cannot replace.

The Skill Shift

AI is drawing a line between what it can do and what only humans can do. It separates automation from differentiation, as illustrated in Figure 20-1. Skills that are uniquely human differentiators are rising in value, while skills that AI excels at are being automated.

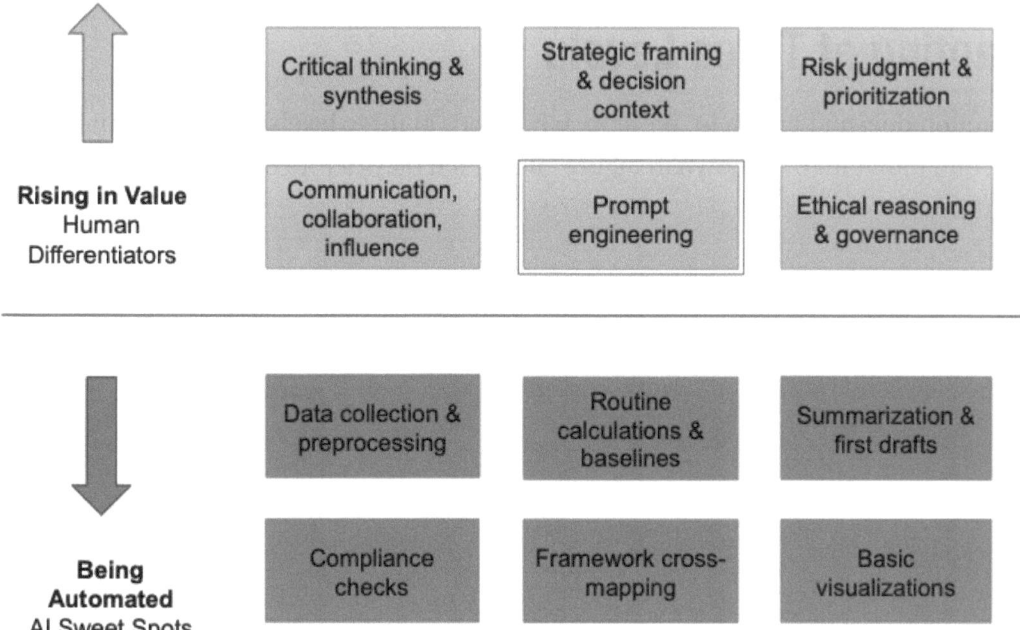

Figure 20-1. *Risk analyst skills that are rising in value vs. those being automated*

In the automated zone, AI already excels at repetitive, mechanical, and low-stakes tasks. These include data collection and preprocessing, routine calculations and baselines, compliance checks, framework cross-mapping, summarization, and basic visualizations.

In the human zone, the green zone, live the differentiators that AI cannot replace: critical thinking, strategic framing and decision context, risk judgment and prioritization, communication and influence, and ethical reasoning and governance.

There's also one transitional skill sitting between the two: prompt engineering.

Right now, prompt engineering is a valuable differentiator. People who know how to structure effective prompts, constrain models, and interpret results responsibly are ahead of the curve. But that advantage will not last long. AI can already create its own prompts, and when AI becomes better than a human prompt engineer, the advantage will shift to those who can ask good questions.

If most of your work sits in the red boxes, you need to start shifting toward the green ones. That's where your long-term value will live. This is the *only* time I'll ever tell you to turn reds into greens.

Adapting at Three Levels

Adaptation doesn't happen in one step. It happens at three levels: organizational, team, and individual, as shown in Figure 20-2. Each plays a role in how we prepare for the future.

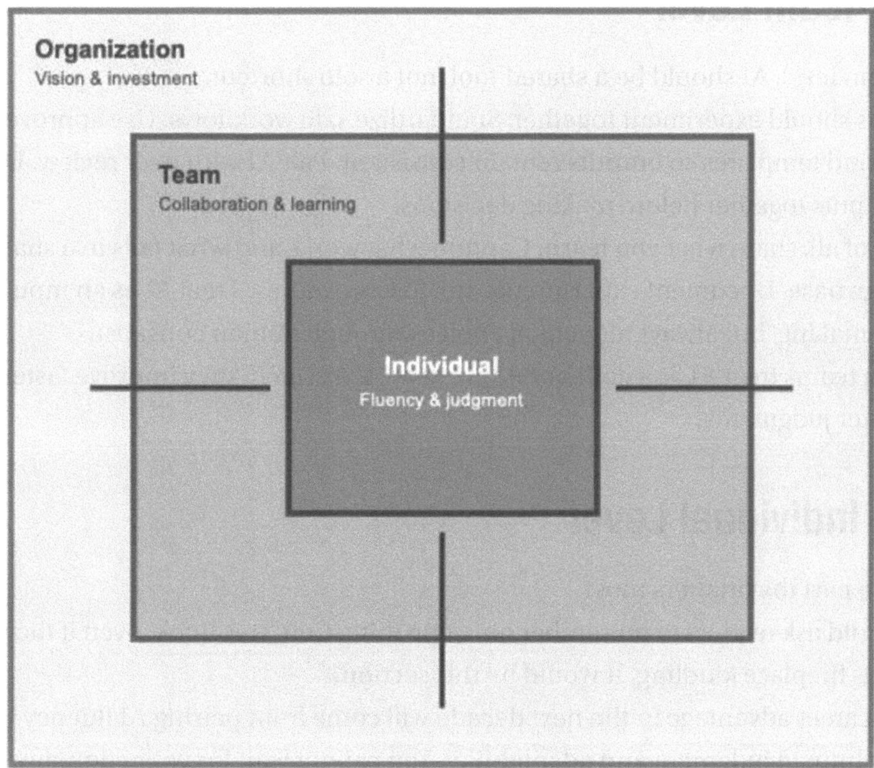

Figure 20-2. *Every level of adaptation grows the others*

1. The Organizational Level

Leaders have to set the vision. Boards and executives should be clear about how AI supports strategy, mission, and values. They need to build guardrails for safe, ethical adoption and create policies that enable experimentation without risking confidentiality.

But most importantly, they must invest in people.

AI will not make analysts obsolete, but companies that fail to retrain and upskill their people will make themselves obsolete. The organizations that thrive will lead by example. They will model curiosity, transparency, and sound judgment.

It would be foolish to think that we can opt out of AI. Any company that ignores it will simply be replaced by one that doesn't.

2. The Team Level

At the team level, AI should be a shared tool, not a solo shortcut.

Teams should experiment together. Standardize safe workflows. Use approved prompts and templates so outputs remain consistent. Pair AI with peer review. Double-check outputs together before making decisions.

Most of all, share what you learn. Capture what works and what fails in a shared knowledge base. Document experiments, not just outcomes. Treat AI as an input to decision-making, but always align final choices through human consensus.

When teams treat AI as a collaborator instead of a crutch, they improve faster and make better judgments.

3. The Individual Level

This is the part that matters most.

If I could ask readers to remember only one thing from this book, even if the rest of it ends up as fireplace kindling, it would be this section.

Your career advantage in the next decade will come from pairing AI fluency with distinctly human judgment and adaptability. You cannot wait for your company or your manager to do this for you. You have to own your growth.

When I started out in information security, I didn't know what I wanted to focus on. I built a home lab to figure it out. I ran multiple computers and virtual machines. I simulated a small company, complete with web servers, mail servers, and an Active Directory domain. That's how I learned pen testing, vulnerability management, and architecture.

You can do the same thing for quantitative risk.

Set up a home CRQ lab. Build a fictitious company—a regional bank, a SaaS provider, a hospital—and simulate its environment. Use generative AI to create synthetic incidents, audits, and tabletop reports. Generate telemetry, ticket data, and continuity tests. Then practice quantifying those risks.

I still do this. My current "home lab" models a midsize US financial institution. It includes synthetic audit findings, incident data, and simulated business impacts. I even run a local large language model on an air-gapped Mac Mini so I can test ideas safely without risking data leakage.

This is how you build muscle memory for the future.

When your employer can't move fast enough, your home lab becomes your accelerator.

BUILDING A HOME CRQ LAB

A personal CRQ lab is your sandbox for the future. It is where you can experiment safely, practice new methods, and sharpen your analytical instincts without waiting for permission or access to sensitive data.

1. **Create a Fictitious Organization**

   Start with something from real life, like a regional bank, a SaaS provider, or a hospital. Give it size, revenue, and business functions.

2. **Define the Business Context**

   Map what matters most to this organization: customer trust, uptime, intellectual property, or compliance. Identify the systems and processes that keep it running.

3. **Generate Synthetic Data**

   Use AI to create incidents, audit findings, and response reports. Add variety such as ransomware, insider threats, and cloud outages. Include after-action reports to enrich the dataset.

4. **Analyze and Model**

   Use AI to summarize and visualize patterns. Then apply the methods from this book to estimate frequency and loss.

5. **Reflect and Refine**

   Keep notes on what you learn and what assumptions you made. Update your fictitious company as new technologies and threats emerge.

Practicing CRQ at home is where theory becomes skill.

Or better yet...

GENAI PROMPT: BUILD A HOME CRQ LAB

You are an experienced cyber risk quantification (CRQ) analyst and teacher.

Help me design and practice in a *personal CRQ home lab* using entirely synthetic, fictitious data. Be structured, detailed, and realistic.

Step 1. Create the organization.

- Invent a realistic fictional company. Suggest 3-4 options across sectors such as finance, SaaS, manufacturing, or healthcare.
- Once I choose one, describe its size, business model, major assets, and critical processes.
- Summarize what matters most to its executives (for example, uptime, customer trust, or compliance).

Step 2. Generate synthetic data.

- Create a set of realistic, fictional security incidents for the company (ransomware, insider misuse, vendor compromise, cloud outage, etc.).
- Include short summaries or bullet points for each: what happened, how it was discovered, what controls failed or succeeded, and rough qualitative impacts (productivity, response cost, fines, or reputation).
- Add a few audit findings or tabletop results to enrich the dataset.

Step 3. Summarize the dataset.

- Present the incidents in a table or numbered list with key fields (category, cause, affected system, business impact, and recovery).
- Write a short narrative summarizing what this synthetic data suggests about the company's risk posture.

Step 4. Stop here.

- Do not estimate frequency or loss. I will perform all modeling, quantification, and visualization exercises using techniques from the book, *From Heatmaps to Histograms.*

- Instead, recommend 3-4 exercises I can do with this data, referencing ideas from *From Heatmaps to Histograms* (for example, "turn one scenario into a frequency model using ranges" or "build a simple loss exceedance curve").

Constraints:

- Use only synthetic, fully fictional data.
- Do not use or request any real company information.
- Keep examples realistic but safe for open experimentation.

Present your response in clear sections and use plain, instructional language, as if you were mentoring a new risk analyst setting up their first CRQ practice environment.

This isn't homework. It's a way to stay sharp. The more you experiment, the more natural this kind of thinking becomes. Once you have your synthetic dataset, use it to practice the exercises in earlier chapters: scenario scoping, frequency modeling, loss analysis, and Monte Carlo simulation.

You can even blend the datasets you create here with external data from Chapter 11 or SME ranges from Chapter 13 to simulate real-world uncertainty.

What This Means

If you've built your home lab or even just planned it out, you've already taken the first step toward the future. You are no longer just reading about risk quantification; you're practicing it. You're learning to think like the next generation of analyst, one who blends data, judgment, and automation responsibly.

AI has already erased much of the friction that used to slow our work. Collecting data, cleaning it, and building models once took weeks. Now it takes hours. The value of a risk analyst no longer lies in producing charts or running calculations. It lies in interpretation, synthesis, and judgment in turning information into understanding and action.

That is what progress looks like. Less time proving that risk can be quantified, more time using quantification to improve decisions.

The field is shifting from explanation to execution, from defending methods to driving outcomes.

The Long View

When I look back at how far the field has come, it's remarkable. Fifteen years ago, we were still arguing about whether risk could even be quantified. Today, we are teaching machines to help us do it faster.

But the real progress is not technological. It's cultural.

Some organizations are beginning to think probabilistically. A few leaders are asking for ranges instead of colors. It is uneven and slow, but the shift is real wherever people care more about decisions than dashboards.

This movement will not end with this book or this decade. It will keep evolving because rational decision-making never goes out of style. It only becomes more necessary.

The work ahead is not to protect data, but to protect reasoning.

Passing the Torch

If you've reached this point in the book, you already have what you need. You know how to define a scenario, collect data, run simulations, and tell a story with numbers. What comes next is harder and more important. You have to use those tools to make the world around you a little clearer.

Teach others. Mentor the next analyst who wants to understand but is afraid to ask. Share your models. Publish your findings. Speak at a conference. Start a blog, newsletter, or podcast. Challenge bad assumptions gently, but *do* challenge them. The field will grow in proportion to how generously we share what we know.

No single framework, model, or solution will write the future of CRQ. It will be written by people who choose to think carefully, speak plainly, and act transparently.

If you do that, you are already part of the next generation.

You will face tools and threats I cannot imagine. Good. That means you are exactly where you should be: at the edge of experience, where data ends and analysis begins.

The Final Word

I wrote this book because I wanted to help you think clearly about risk while keeping the human part of the work intact.

If it has done that, then my job is finished.

The rest is yours.

The world does not need another security risk framework. It needs people who can reason about uncertainty, communicate it clearly, and make choices that stand up to daylight.

That is you now. *You* are the analyst of the future.

Welcome to the rebellion—the rational one.

Reference

Shostack, A., & Stewart, A. (2008). *The new school of information security.* Addison-Wesley Professional.

Appendix A: Jargon-less Risk Glossary

Quant Basics

Confidence Interval: A range showing where the true value probably lies. Prediction and credible intervals are similar concepts for future and Bayesian estimates. (Chapter 4)

Annualized Loss Exposure: A range of financial loss an organization could experience over a year, based on both how often an event might happen and how large the losses could be. It is expressed as a distribution, not a single number. (Chapter 6)

Frequency: How often a loss event is expected to occur within a year, expressed as a range rather than a single number. (Chapter 4)

Law of Large Numbers: The more trials you run, the closer the results get to their long-term average. (Chapter 5)

Magnitude: The size of a loss; the total financial impact of an event. (Chapter 8)

Mode/Median/Mean: Most common, middle, and average values of a distribution. They drift apart when outcomes are skewed. (Chapter 6)

Monte Carlo Simulation: A modeling method that runs thousands of random "what-if" trials to reveal the range of possible outcomes. (Chapter 5)

Percentile (P5/P50/P95): Markers showing how results spread across possibilities. For example, P50 = typical, median case, P95 = worse-than-most case. (Chapter 4)

Range: Upper and lower bounds that describe uncertainty, a clearer and more honest alternative to single-point estimates. (Chapter 4)

Six Forms of Loss: The six channels through which incidents cause harm: productivity, response, replacement, fines and judgments, reputation, and competitive advantage. (Chapter 8)

T. Martin-Vegue, *From Heatmaps to Histograms*, https://doi.org/10.1007/979-8-8688-2300-8

Data and Sources

Base Rate: A population-level anchor for how often an event happens before local adjustments. (Chapter 14)

Data Blending (Bayesian Updating): Merging external, internal, and SME evidence so each new input refines rather than replaces the last. (Chapter 14)

External Data: Industry or public datasets that provide base rates for frequency and magnitude. (Chapter 11)

Internal Data: Logs, incidents, and records showing what actually happens inside your organization. (Chapter 12)

Loss Exposure: Combined view of how often losses happen and how large they are. (Chapter 6)

Subject Matter Experts (SMEs): People who fill data gaps with calibrated judgment and lived context. (Chapter 13)

Decision and Modeling Concepts

Confidence vs. Precision ("Less Wrong"): Progress through iteration matters more than perfect accuracy. (Chapter 4)

Decision Quality/Decision Science: A sound decision requires choices, preferences, and information. CRQ supplies the last piece. (Chapter 19)

ROI (Return on Investment): Compares a control's cost to the loss reduction it delivers, turning risk data into business trade-offs. (Chapter 15)

Risk Appetite: How much risk an organization is willing to take on, given an initiative or decision, balancing the potential loss if it fails against the benefit if it succeeds. (Chapter 19)

Scenario: A structured description of how a loss could occur, defining asset, threat, and potential impact. (Chapter 7)

Value of Information (VOI): The worth of collecting better data before deciding, which helps avoid endless analysis. (Chapter 19)

FAIR Terms

FAIR (Factor Analysis of Information Risk): A framework that measures frequency and magnitude to quantify cyber risk consistently. (Chapter 16)

Loss Event Frequency (LEF): How often loss events occur, combining threat activity and susceptibility. (Chapter 16)

Loss Magnitude (LM): Expected financial impact when a single loss occurs. (Chapter 16)

Susceptibility/Vulnerability: Likelihood that a threat action succeeds once it occurs. (Chapter 16)

Threat Event Frequency (TEF): How often threats act on an asset, such as phishing or scanning attempts. (Chapter 16)

Analysis and Visualization

Coverage Rate: How completely your data or controls observe the environment being measured. (Chapter 10)

Five-Number Summary: Quick snapshot of results: minimum, P25, median, P75, maximum. (Chapter 6)

Histogram: A chart displaying the distribution of simulated results within each loss range. (Chapter 5)

Loss Exceedance Curve (LEC): Graph showing the probability that losses exceed specific amounts, the clearest view of severity. (Chapter 6)

Shape of Risk/Distribution: Shows whether outcomes are stable or dominated by rare, extreme events. (Chapter 6)

Approaches and Mindsets

Bayesian Reasoning: A method of updating beliefs as new evidence appears. Today's conclusion becomes tomorrow's starting point. (Chapter 14)

Heatmap: A color-coded grid of likelihood and impact. Simple to view but often misleading about uncertainty. (Chapter 19)

Qualitative Risk Analysis: Uses categories like high, medium, and low for quick judgment but lacks measurable precision. (Chapter 4)

Quantitative Risk Analysis: Uses numbers, ranges, and probability to express uncertainty and compare options. (Chapter 4)

Appendix B: Six Forms of Loss—Detailed Reference Guide

This appendix provides comprehensive measurement frameworks, calculation methods, and guidance on data sources for each of the six FAIR loss forms. Use this as a reference when building detailed risk assessments or creating magnitude estimates for specific scenarios.

Important Note on Cost Estimates: This appendix teaches you *how* to measure each loss form, not *what* the answer should be. No dollar ranges are provided because costs vary significantly by organization size, industry, geography, and time. Instead, you'll learn the calculation frameworks and where to find current, validated data for your specific context.

1. Productivity Loss

Core Calculation Framework

Basic Formula: Average fully loaded hourly labor cost * estimated hours of disruption * number of affected employees

Specific Measurement Proxies

Idle Labor Cost

- **Base calculation**: Hourly wage * number of affected employees * hours of inactivity

T. Martin-Vegue, *From Heatmaps to Histograms*, https://doi.org/10.1007/979-8-8688-2300-8

- Apply benefits loading factor (typically 1.3–1.5× base wage to account for benefits, overhead, facilities)
- Account for different pay grades across affected teams
- **Data sources:** HR compensation data, cost-benefit analysis, departmental budgets

Missed Labor Output (Revenue-Generating Roles)

- **Sales team**: Average deal size ÷ sales cycle length ÷ working hours per period
- **Customer service**: Revenue per customer interaction * missed interactions
- **Manufacturing**: Production line value per hour (based on output value, not just cost)
- **Data sources:** Sales operations data, production metrics, revenue attribution models

Delay Cost for Time-Sensitive Projects

- Project value * percentage completion delay
- Opportunity cost of delayed market entry (compare to competitive launch windows)
- Contractual penalty clauses for missed deliverables
- **Data sources:** Project management systems, contract terms, market analysis

Specialized Role Calculations

- **Idle contractor time:** Contracted hourly rate * affected hours (from contract terms)
- **Idle executive time:** Total compensation ÷ annual working hours * affected hours
- **Manufacturing operations:** Production line value per hour * downtime hours
- **Data sources:** Vendor contracts, executive compensation filings, production dashboards

Advanced Considerations

Cascading Effects

- Map downstream impacts on dependent teams or processes using workflow diagrams.
- Assess supplier/partner productivity impacts through relationship mapping.
- Measure customer-facing service degradation via SLA metrics.
- **Analysis method:** Process dependency mapping, critical path analysis

Recovery Productivity Loss

- Reduced efficiency during system restoration (typically 40–70% of normal productivity)
- Training time required for new processes or workarounds
- Catch-up work requiring overtime premium (typically 1.5–2× normal hourly rate)
- **Data sources:** Historical incident recovery data, training time estimates from HR, overtime policies

2. Response Cost

Internal Labor Costs

Incident Response Team

- Calculate IR team hours * fully loaded hourly rate.
- Include on-call premiums and overtime multipliers per company policy.
- Account for different skill levels (junior analyst vs. senior engineer vs. architect).

- **Data sources:** HR compensation data, incident response runbooks (time estimates), historical incident logs

Cross-Functional Response Time

- **Executive crisis meetings**: Executive hourly rate * meeting duration and frequency
- **Legal coordination**: In-house counsel time * rate
- **Communications team**: Hours spent on internal/external messaging
- **Data sources:** Calendar analysis from past incidents, legal department time tracking, communications workload estimates

External Service Costs

Forensics and Investigation

- **Digital forensics firms**: Research current hourly rates, adjusting for incident complexity and specialization
- **Legal discovery support**: Specialized e-discovery and legal technology services
- **Expert witness fees**: Varies significantly by expertise and jurisdiction
- **Data sources:** Vendor RFPs, recent public breach disclosures, legal fee surveys, Gartner/Forrester analyst reports

Emergency Support

- **Security consultant rates**: Vary by specialization (malware analysis, cloud forensics, OT/ICS security)
- **Emergency system restoration**: Premium rates for 24/7 rapid response
- **Crisis communications/PR**: Retainer costs plus hourly engagement fees
- **Data sources:** Vendor proposals, industry rate surveys, professional services benchmarks

Notification and Communication Costs

Regulatory Notifications

- **Legal fees for filing preparation**: Research current rates for cybersecurity-specialized counsel
- **Regulatory liaison costs**: Ongoing coordination with oversight bodies
- Translation services for multi-jurisdictional notifications
- **Data sources:** Legal rate surveys (AmLaw, Chambers), regulatory guidance on notification requirements

Customer/Stakeholder Notifications

- **Per-record notification costs**: Varies by delivery method (email vs. postal mail vs. call center)
- **Call center surge capacity**: Temporary staffing and training costs
- Website/portal modifications for breach disclosure
- **Data sources:** Breach notification service providers, call center staffing agencies, web development rates

Ongoing Response Activities

Credit Monitoring Services

- **Per-user annual cost**: Varies by service level (basic monitoring vs. comprehensive identity protection)
- **Identity theft insurance**: Additional coverage options
- Fraud monitoring setup and administration overhead
- **Data sources:** Credit bureau pricing (Experian, Equifax, TransUnion), identity protection service RFPs

3. Replacement Cost

Physical Asset Replacement

Hardware Costs

- **Server replacement**: Research current pricing for equivalent or upgraded capacity
- **Endpoint replacement**: Account for device type (desktop vs. laptop vs. specialized equipment)
- **Network equipment**: Varies significantly by scale and capability
- **Data sources:** Vendor price lists, existing procurement contracts, hardware refresh budgets

Software and Licensing

- **Operating system re-licensing**: Per-seat or per-core costs
- **Application software**: Variable based on vendor pricing models (perpetual vs. subscription)
- **Security tool re-deployment**: Per-endpoint or network-based licensing
- **Data sources:** Software asset management system, vendor licensing agreements, procurement history

Data and System Restoration

Backup Restoration

- **Cloud storage retrieval fees**: Review provider pricing for data egress and API calls.
- **Restoration validation time**: Hours required per critical system for integrity verification.

- **Data integrity verification**: Specialized testing and validation procedures.
- **Data sources:** Cloud provider pricing calculators, RTO/RPO testing results, IT operations time estimates

System Rebuild Costs

- **Server rebuild time**: Hours per system * technician hourly rate (varies by system complexity)
- **Application reconfiguration**: Time required per application for settings, integrations, and customizations
- **Integration testing**: Enterprise environment validation across multiple systems
- **Data sources:** IT operations standard work estimates, configuration management documentation, past rebuild projects

Credential and Access Management

Credential Reissuance

- **Digital certificates**: Varies by certificate authority and certificate type
- **Hardware tokens**: Per-unit cost plus provisioning time
- **Smart cards**: Card cost plus issuance infrastructure and labor
- **Data sources:** PKI vendor pricing, identity access management (IAM) system data, procurement records

4. Fines and Judgments

Regulatory Penalty Frameworks

GDPR Penalties

- **Tier 1 violations**: Up to €10M or 2% of annual global turnover (whichever is higher)
- **Tier 2 violations**: Up to €20M or 4% of annual global turnover (whichever is higher)

- **Mitigating factors**: Intent, mitigation efforts, cooperation with authorities, breach notification timeliness
- **Data sources:** GDPR enforcement tracker databases, legal analysis of precedent cases, regulatory guidance

HIPAA Penalties

- Tier-based penalty structure with annual maximums.
- **Factors affecting penalty severity**: Knowledge level, correction timeline, and violation scope.
- Recent enforcement trends show increased scrutiny.
- **Data sources:** HHS Office for Civil Rights enforcement actions, healthcare compliance legal analyses

SEC Cybersecurity Penalties

- Corporate penalties for inadequate disclosure or material misstatements
- Individual penalties for executives who knew or should have known
- Disgorgement of avoided losses or ill-gotten gains
- **Data sources:** SEC enforcement actions database, securities litigation reports

Civil Litigation Costs

Class Action Settlements

- **Per-record settlements**: Highly variable based on data type, harm severity, and jurisdiction
- **Statutory damages**: Range defined by applicable privacy statutes
- Actual damages plus attorney fees when plaintiffs prevail
- **Data sources:** Securities class action clearinghouse, privacy litigation databases, legal settlement reports

Defense Costs

- **Securities litigation defense**: Varies by case complexity and duration
- **Privacy class action defense**: Depends on scope and number of plaintiffs
- **Regulatory enforcement defense**: Investigation response and hearing costs
- **Data sources:** Legal fee surveys, D&O insurance actuarial data, corporate legal budgets

Contractual Penalties

SLA Violations

- **Service credit percentages**: Review contracts for specific penalty structures.
- **Liquidated damages**: Pre-negotiated fixed amounts for specific breach types.
- Customer termination rights and associated revenue loss projections.
- **Data sources:** Contract management system, customer agreements, revenue forecasting models

5. Reputation Damage

Customer Impact Metrics

Customer Churn Analysis

- Compare baseline churn rate vs. projected post-incident churn rate.
- Calculate customer lifetime value * incremental churn count.
- Model churn acceleration (customers leaving sooner than historical patterns predict).
- **Data sources:** Customer relationship management (CRM) data, historical churn analysis, industry benchmarks for similar incidents

Acquisition Impact

- Increased customer acquisition cost (CAC) due to diminished trust and brand concerns
- Conversion rate decline on marketing campaigns (monitor key funnels)
- Sales cycle extension for new prospects who cite security concerns during evaluation
- **Data sources:** Marketing analytics, sales pipeline analysis, win/loss interview data

Market Valuation Impact

Public Company Metrics

- Stock price movement analysis in days/weeks following disclosure
- Market capitalization reduction (isolate incident impact from market trends)
- Credit rating impacts and resulting increased borrowing costs
- **Data sources:** Stock market data, analyst reports, credit rating agency assessments, peer company comparisons

Private Company Metrics

- Valuation impact in subsequent funding rounds (compare to pre-incident projections)
- Deal flow reduction for M&A opportunities
- Partnership renegotiations or terminations
- **Data sources:** Venture capital/private equity market analysis, term sheet comparisons, partnership contract reviews

Employee and Talent Impact

Retention Costs

- Increased turnover rate * replacement costs per role (recruitment, training, productivity ramp)
- Retention bonuses required to prevent talent flight
- Increased recruiting costs due to employer brand damage
- **Data sources:** HR metrics, exit interview data, recruiting cost analysis, employer brand surveys

Brand Repair Investments

Marketing and Communications

- Increased advertising and PR spend to rebuild trust (campaign-level budgets)
- Crisis communications retainer and ongoing PR counsel
- Customer loyalty programs, service credits, and goodwill gestures
- **Data sources:** Marketing budget analysis, PR agency proposals, customer retention program costs

6. Competitive Advantage Loss

Intellectual Property Valuation

Development Cost Method

- Calculate total R&D investment in compromised assets.
- Sum employee time invested in development * loaded hourly rates.
- Add third-party development costs and licensing fees.
- **Data sources:** R&D budget allocation, project accounting systems, patent/IP development records

Revenue-Based Method

- Project revenue from products/services dependent on compromised IP.
- Calculate market advantage duration * competitive margin.
- Estimate licensing revenue potential if IP is monetizable.
- **Data sources:** Product revenue forecasts, competitive analysis, IP licensing market data

Market Position Impact

Competitive Timing Loss

- Quantify first-mover advantage value in targeted markets.
- Calculate revenue impact of delayed product launches (compare to launch window analysis).
- Estimate market share loss to competitors who gained advance intelligence.
- **Data sources:** Market research reports, competitive intelligence, product launch analysis

Strategic Information Value

M&A Impact

- Assess negotiation position weakening due to leaked strategies (scenario analysis).
- Estimate deal value reduction from information asymmetry.
- Calculate lost acquisition opportunities due to premature disclosure.
- **Data sources:** M&A advisor assessments, deal valuation models, transaction history

Customer Relationship Value

- **Calculate customer list value**: customer acquisition cost * customer count.
- Model competitive poaching risk using stolen customer intelligence.
- Assess partnership renegotiations based on leaked terms and conditions.
- **Data sources:** Sales and marketing data, customer acquisition analytics, partnership agreements

Appendix C: Data Types Quick Reference

A risk scenario tells you what to measure, but you may not be sure what form that data will take. As you review industry reports, internal documents, incident reports, logs, or interview SMEs, you will be searching for and recording data types, then categorizing them as data values. H are the most common types you'll encounter:

Data Type	Unit Examples	Example Data Value	Example Unit
Binary Indicator	0/1, true/false, yes/no	Yes	MFA enabled=yes
Counts	events, incidents, findings, tickets, vulnerabilities	4	incidents
Data Volume	bytes, KB, MB, GB, TB, PB	50	GB of exfiltrated data
Frequency (Over Time)	events/year, incidents/month, breaches/decade, once every three years	0.33	events/year
Monetary	USD, EUR, GBP, JPY, etc. (specify currency symbol or code)	\$250K–\$600K	USD (loss)
Probability/ Proportion	unitless (0–1), % (0–100%)	0.18 (= 18%)	probability
Rate (Normalized Frequency)	events/1,000 users, incidents/10,000 emails	7	phishing emails per 1,000 users

(*continued*)

T. Martin-Vegue, *From Heatmaps to Histograms*, https://doi.org/10.1007/979-8-8688-2300-8

Data Type	Unit Examples	Example Data Value	Example Unit
Ratio or Index	failures:hours, breaches:assets	0.18055556	compromise-to-account ratio
Record/Asset Quantity	records, rows, customers, endpoints, VMs, containers	5,000	records
Time	seconds, minutes, hours, days, weeks	3–5	hours of downtime

Appendix D: Data Source Evaluation Framework

Important: This framework provides guidance, not rigid rules. Use your professional judgment to adapt these range adjustments based on your specific organizational context and stakeholder requirements.

Quality Factor	Question	Evaluation Guidance	Range Adjustment
Averaged	Does this single average hide the real distribution?	Check if ranges, quartiles, or percentiles are shown and if data is broken down by severity/type. **Red flags:** Only global means reported, "average breach cost is $4.5M" with no range, different incident types lumped together.	Convert to range
Biased	Who benefits if I believe this number?	Assess funding sources and potential conflicts of interest. **Red flags:** Vendor-sponsored studies promoting their solutions, consultants measuring their own effectiveness, teams self-reporting performance.	×2

(*continued*)

T. Martin-Vegue, *From Heatmaps to Histograms*, https://doi.org/10.1007/979-8-8688-2300-8

Quality Factor	Question	Evaluation Guidance	Range Adjustment
Close Substitute	Are you using adjacent data because you don't have exact data?	Evaluate how directly the data measures what you're modeling. **Red flags:** Using phishing clicks to estimate breach costs, Twitter/X sentiment for financial impact, desktop uptime for server availability.	x2–x3
Context Stripped	Were important limitations removed when cited? *Note: Often fixable by returning to original source*	Check if original caveats, limitations, and scope are preserved. **Red flags:** Headline numbers used without context, "conditions apply" details omitted, nuanced findings oversimplified.	×2
Correlation As Causation	Does this claim definitive cause-and-effect without proof? *Note: When presented as definitive proof rather than acknowledged correlation*	Look for controlled experimental design and careful language about correlation vs. causation. **Red flags:** Blanket statement like "MFA prevents all breaches" based on correlation, post hoc analysis claiming definitive causation, single correlations presented as absolute proof.	Do not use
Definitional Drift	Have key terms changed meaning since this was collected?	Look for consistent definitions and acknowledgment of any changes. **Red flags:** "Breach" definitions that changed post-GDPR, "incident" scope that expanded since collection, shifted regulatory definitions.	×2

(*continued*)

Quality Factor	Question	Evaluation Guidance	Range Adjustment
Ethical Violations	Was this research conducted unethically?	Check for proper consent, privacy protections, and adherence to research ethics. **Red flags:** No consent for sensitive data use, subjects harmed by research, violation of research ethics standards.	Do not use
Exercise Based	Is this from a simulation rather than real incidents?	Evaluate realism and validation against actual events. **Red flags:** Single tabletop exercise results, unrealistic assumptions, no validation against actual events.	×2
Extraction Quality	How reliable was the data extraction process?	Look for validation and quality control in data extraction. **Red flags:** High OCR/parsing error rates, no validation of automated extraction, single-person manual copying.	×2
Fabricated	Is this data completely made up?	Verify chain of evidence to original sources. **Red flags:** Cannot trace to real source, claims seem impossible, numbers change when challenged.	Do not use
Fraudulent Source	Is this from a known bad actor?	Research organization's track record and reputation. **Red flags:** Organizations caught falsifying research, previous fraud/misconduct, deliberately misleading track record.	Do not use

(continued)

Quality Factor	Question	Evaluation Guidance	Range Adjustment
Geographic Mismatch	Does the legal/ regulatory context match yours?	Assess similarity of legal systems and regulatory environments. **Red flags:** EU GDPR penalties for US models, Asian costs for European orgs, different legal liability frameworks. **Consider:** How fundamental are the regulatory differences?	First, seek comparable data from similar jurisdictions. If unavoidable. consider SME adjustment
Old Data	Is this outdated but still widely cited?	Consider how quickly the threat landscape changes and whether fundamental patterns remain stable. **Red flags:** Data over three years old, outdates technology, legacy system metrics for modern environments.	×2
Methodological Transparency	Can I understand and verify how this analysis was done?	Look for sufficient detail to evaluate and potentially replicate the work. **Red flags:** "Proprietary analysis methods," missing key analytical steps, no definition of critical terms, vendors who won't explain scoring methods, results that vary on refresh, manual analysis without documentation.	Completely opaque methods: consider exclusion. Incomplete but partially documented: ×2. Well-documented: no adjustment

(continued)

Quality Factor	Question	Evaluation Guidance	Range Adjustment
Missing Error Bounds	Is this presented as falsely precise?	Check for confidence intervals, margins of error, or ranges instead of point estimates. **Red flags:** "Exactly 23.7% of organizations," no uncertainty acknowledged, precise percentages from small samples. Consider: How misleading is the false precision in your context?	×2 or SME adjustment for false precision that could mislead decisions, ×1.5 for minor precision issues
Partial Coverage	Does this only cover part of the environment?	Assess what might be missing and whether coverage is documented. **Red flags:** Unknown coverage gaps, "comprehensive" claims without details, cherry-picked high-visibility systems only.	SME adjustment or ×2
Privacy Violation	Was this data obtained through illegal means?	Verify legal collection methods and proper data handling. **Red flags:** Data stolen in breaches, unauthorized system access, privacy law violations.	Do not use
Publication Bias	Were only interesting/dramatic results published? *Note: Affects most research to some degree*	Consider whether boring or negative results might be missing. Green flags: systematic data collection, includes negative results, complete datasets published. **Red flags:** Only "newsworthy" breaches included, success stories only, dramatic incidents over-represented.	×2
Retracted/ Corrected	Has this research been officially withdrawn?	Check for retractions, corrections, or methodological challenges. **Red flags:** Journal retractions due to errors, major corrections invalidating findings, post-publication methodology flaws discovered.	Do not use

(continued)

Quality Factor	Question	Evaluation Guidance	Range Adjustment
Scale Mismatch	Does the organization size actually match yours?	Check if the data comes from organizations similar to yours. **Red flags:** Fortune 500 data applied to startups, small business costs for enterprise analysis, no size breakdown provided.	SME adjustment or ×3
Self-Reported	Did organizations report on their own performance?	Assess potential bias in self-assessment. **Red flags:** Voluntary surveys about security posture, teams self-assessing effectiveness, "How secure do you think you are?" questions.	×2
Survey Quality	Is this survey reliable and unbiased? *Note: Covers methodology, sample size, and promotional bias*	Evaluate survey methodology, sample size, and potential marketing bias. **Red flags:** Hidden/small sample sizes (under 100), self-selected participants (LinkedIn polls), biased samples (conference attendees only, customers only), promotional surveys with gift cards, results that promote sponsor's solutions, customer-only surveys labeled as "industry data," no confidence intervals. Consider the survey's scientific rigor vs. promotional intent.	Clearly promotional with no scientific value: consider exclusion. Poor methodology but some value: ×3. Moderate issues: ×2.
Synthetic	Is this artificial data used for real-world models? *Note: Fundamentally misleading for actual risk assessments*	Distinguish between real incident data and simulated scenarios. **Red flags**: Generated test data used for real analysis, simulated attack scenarios only, no connection to actual events.	Do not use

Index

A

B

T. Martin-Vegue, *From Heatmaps to Histograms*, https://doi.org/10.1007/979-8-8688-2300-8

C

E

F

G

H

I, J, K

L

M

N

O

P

Q

R

S

T

U

V

W, X, Y

Z